TEN BOB AN HOUR

by Steve Phillips

TEN
BOB

AN HOUR

Edited by Chris Newton

MEMOIRS

Cirencester

Published by Memoirs

MEMOIRS

Memoirs Books

25 Market Place, Cirencester, Gloucestershire, GL7 2NX
info@memoirsbooks.co.uk www.memoirsbooks.co.uk

Copyright ©Steve Phillips, August 2011
First published in England, August 2011
Book jacket design Ray Lipscombe

ISBN 978-1-908223-11-1

Printed in England

Dedication

In memory of my Nan and Pop, Gladys and Jack Froud, and my Mom Lilly Froud

Preface

Fifty years ago next month, a 15-year-old Brummie school-leaver called Stephen Phillips walked into the reception area of a big Midland manufacturing company to start an apprenticeship in engineering. That was me. I hadn't a clue what was coming – the dirt and grind, the hard work and the long hours, the legpulls and laughter, the calamities and the comradeship, and the slow graduation from greenhorn to skilled man.

The next five years would prove arduous, difficult and dirty, but at the end of it all, thanks largely to some of the best mates and colleagues I ever had, I managed to emerge a trained and qualified engineer on the holy-grail pay rate of ten bob an hour – that's 50p in today's coinage. It doesn't sound like much, but it was a lot of money in those days.

This book is about those never-to-be-forgotten years.

Steve Phillips

August 2011

Prologue

"You can put that cigarette out for a start, young man. A Guest Keen and Nettlefolds apprentice does not attend his first day at work smoking!"

The speaker was a rotund bloke, probably forty-odd, with a red face and gingery wiry hair. He must be the boss, I thought (I hadn't heard the correct term yet – 'gaffer').

My mate Jim Richmond sheepishly nubbed out his fag and tucked it behind his ear, careful not to disturb his Tony Curtis DA hairstyle (duck's arse, if you're wondering).

Bloody hell, I thought. It's just like school. I hope you don't get the whack for smoking here as well.

It was September 1961 and I was standing in the foyer and reception area of Thomas Haddon and Stokes in Digbeth, Birmingham. I looked around at the 20 or so other young lads. They were all 15 to 16 years old like me and dressed in trousers (not jeans) and jackets, some in ties, some in open-necked shirts spread wide outside the lapel of the coat.

Ginger introduced himself. "I'm Mr Cockcroft, your Apprentice Supervisor. Welcome to the GKN South Birmingham Group of Companies. Today we will outline the history of Mr Guest, Mr Keen and Mr Nettlefold and show you the Apprentice Training School. The Senior Apprentices will take you on a guided tour of the factory.

"Tea break is at 9.30 for 10 minutes and lunch will be served in the canteen from one till two. There will be another tea break at 3.30 pm. Before you leave this evening you will be given a clock card and number and be shown how to clock in and out."

That was my introduction to a working life which would continue for the next 45 years. There would be different jobs, different factories, different industries, but all within the wonderful world of engineering.

The first day was a blur, just like a first day at school. I met a whole new crowd of people, each of whom might turn into anything from a lifelong friend to just a bloke you worked with. By the end of the day I knew how my life was to be mapped out for the next month, the next year and the next five years. By then I would be 21 and ready to emerge into the big wide world as a fully-skilled craftsman. Steve Phillips (formerly known as Froudy), fitter/turner, indentured apprentice, dreaming of earning ten bob an hour. A bloody fortune.

CHAPTER ONE

Davy Crockett might have been born on a mountain-top in Tennessee, but I made my debut in a council house in Chilton Road, Yardley Wood, when the dust was still settling from the Second World War. It all happened upstairs in the big bedroom, with the fire grate on the wall and the en-suite outside in the garden. At just after midnight on the February 27 1946 Lilly Froud, just turned 19, gave birth to an eight-pound baby boy - me.

In those days fathers didn't attend the births of their kids, but mine would have had a bit of a problem even if he'd wanted to, as he was back home in America with his wife and three daughters. His days as a fighter pilot battling the Luftwaffe were long over, and so I hope were his days of breaking the hearts of young English girls.

Mom was a great gal and I loved her dearly, but in those days there were no free flats for young single mothers. Families stuck together, so I was brought up by her mum and dad, Jack and Gladys Froud, in Chilton Road.

Nan and Pop thought the world of me. Ten years before my birth they had lost their son Billy, my Uncle Billy as he should have become, when he was seven years old. They thought all the love had gone from their lives. Instead they showered it on me. Jack had toured the UK with Buffalo Bill and his Wild West Show in the early 1900s, but that's another story. Mom married an old schoolmate, Eddie Phillips, who was in the Royal Marines, and he knocked her about before buggering off to do the same to the Communist-backed North Koreans in the Korean War. He was never heard from again - either killed in action or deserted, we never knew. I think it took Mom seven years to divorce him for desertion.

Mom's is another great story - fairground worker, jazz singer, a one-time alibi for the Krays, passing her driving test in London when over 60. A beautiful woman. She went on smoking the funny fags until she had a stroke in her 80s.

CHAPTER ONE

I went to the local schools in School Road and failed the 11-plus. Two
or three of my mates passed and went on to Moseley Grammar. Did I feel
jealous? I don't think so. I hadn't done any homework, because I was too
busy playing football.

When I was about nine or ten years old I became a keen trainspotter. Like
all the lads, I wanted to be either a train driver or an ice-cream man.

About this time I began to help my Great Uncle Norman, my Mom's
uncle, who had his own painting and decorating business with six blokes
working for him- yes, he was on the posh side of the family. He had an Austin
A35 van and a three-bedroom semi in Shirley with an upstairs bathroom.
During the school holidays he taught me to hang wallpaper and paint. Great
Uncle Norman was keen for me to join him when I left school. His own
son was severely disabled and would never be able to work.

One day in August 1958, when I was twelve years old and playing about
in the road, I saw two lads I knew. They were only a couple of years older
than me, but they were in Army uniform.

"We're in the Army Cadets" said one of them. "We march on parade and
go camping. We train with real rifles, it's great!"

I thought, if I can lie about my age to get a paper round, surely I can tell
the Army Cadets I'm 14. By February 1961, still only 15, I was a full corporal,
a cross guns marksman (.303 rifle) and held three shooting cups at Altcar. I
was News of the World 202 Champion and 33rd at Bisley out of a combined
cadet shoot of 5000. But I'm getting ahead of myself.

I might have failed the 11-Plus, but I passed the 13-Plus all right and went
to Handsworth Technical School. Before I left in July 1961 I attended a Junior
Leader Regiment for two weeks. My career choice seemed to be between
soldier, painter and decorator or apprentice in trade. My Nan and Pop told
me, get a trade Steve, it'll always see you through. I decided to take their
advice.

At that time the Birmingham Mail was full of job advertisements placed
by the big local factories - GKN, Renolds Chains, Lucas, BSA, Accles &

2

Pollock, Ward, Wilmot Breeden, the list was endless. They all required a yearly intake of apprentice toolmakers, electricians, fitters, turners, millers, die sinkers, plumbers – and that was just in the Birmingham area. Everything was made in Birmingham in those days.

On advice from the Careers Advice Officer I wrote to Austin and GKN applying to their advertisements in the Mail for apprentices. Both firms offered interviews in the July before I left school. I'm on my way, I thought.

I had two older mates who had been working for a couple of years by then. Robin was "on the milk" and at 18 was earning eight quid a week with overtime as well as driving the milk truck. Mugsy was a welder at BSA, earning about the same, cycling to work and nicking parts for his brother's motorbike. The only snag with being an apprentice at fifteen was the pay – two pounds fifteen shillings and eight pence a week. Even today that would only be about seventy quid a week. I didn't find that out when I signed up, but Nan and Pop reminded me that in a few years' time when all my mates were in dead-end jobs on fifteen quid a week, I would be a skilled tradesman with more pay and better prospects.

GKN's T H Stokes factory was much easier to get to than Austin, on the 13A bus route from Yardley Wood to Bradford Street, so I plumped for this one. How our lives depend on little accidents, just like the events in the film Sliding Doors.

The day before the interview with Mr. Cockcroft, I had to get permission to leave school early. No way was I going to a job interview in my school blazer, so Nan unstitched the school badge and I pinned it to my smart jacket so I could wear it to school, then take the badge off for the interview. My schoolmates noticed, but the teachers didn't.

The badge came off when I caught the number 16 bus from Handsworth back into Brum, still paying child's fare, ("I'm still at school, got me pass to prove it") though I was nearly six feet tall and lit up as soon as the conductor had issued my ticket and buggered off. I was almost a working man.

"Why do you want to join the GKN Apprentice Scheme?" said Mr

Cockcroft. He was sitting at his desk and looking very important. I was sitting the other side, shitting myself. "I see you play football for the school." He was trying to get me to open up. Let's face it, your first go at anything is usually a failure, unless you're very lucky. However, we then got chatting about my Army Cadets. "You've done well, why aren't you joining the Army?"

"You have to get up too early in the morning" I replied. I hadn't realised that an engineering career would mean getting up at half past six for the next 45 years.

I didn't think I'd done very well. I'm not sure if I even remembered to tell him I always came top in technical drawing.

After the interview I was off with Mugsy to stay at his sister Marie's place in Bath. She and her husband had a lovely family and a fine house and they made us both very welcome. Mugsy was an angler, so it was a two-week fishing holiday on the Bristol Avon.

In 1961 there weren't of course any mobiles – in fact my Nan and Pop didn't have a phone of any kind. If there was an emergency they used a neighbour's phone or went to the phone box down the road. My future employment was not deemed an emergency and I don't think Marie was on the phone either, so no news filtered through during my two-week absence.

I arrived back home to find two letters from T H Stokes. The first said, in essence: "Thanks for attending the interview, however on this occasion... good luck in the future". Oh well, that was that then. Then I opened the second. It said: "There has been an administrative error... you Stephen Phillips have been offered an Apprenticeship with Guest, Keen and Nettlefolds and should attend T H Stokes at 8.00 am on."

Bollocks. "Nan, Pop - I'm an apprentice!"

★ ★ ★ ★ ★ ★ ★ ★ ★ ★ ★ ★ ★ ★ ★

Frank Davies, same height as me but much more in weight and build and with a dark shock of curly hair, sat with Jim Richmond (who had smoked his dog end by now) and me drinking our tea and dunking custard creams in the canteen for our first afternoon tea break. Even after 40-odd years a tea break can't be accomplished in ten minutes – it's impossible.

"I'm going to be an electrician," said Frank. He lived in Sarah Road, Small Heath. I think Graham Edge of the Moody Blues lived in the same street with his parents. Les Edge was a foreman in the Wire Mill, but more of that later. Jim, I believe, was of the same thoughts as me - an apprenticeship would suit him.

I don't know why the three of us sat together, perhaps because we were all six footers. I was definitely good looking, I wasn't so sure about the other two. All three of us were eyeing up the girls. I'm going to like it here, I thought.

We were told the first week would be devoted to an induction course in the classroom in Birmingham City Centre, introducing us to the history of engineering, James Watt, William Murdoch, Matthew Boulton and Thomas Telford, taking in the science museums in the city. The next 12 months would be spent at Garretts Green Technical College, where we would be assessed and monitored regarding our achievements and suitability for being offered a contract and indentures as GKN apprentices.

This Mr Cockcroft is a bigger bastard than any sergeant major I'd met in my four years in the Cadets, I thought to myself. I was right, as I found out later. I didn't appreciate that Mr. Cockcroft was motivating us all.

At 5 pm I joined the queue to clock out. Then I waited for the 13A at the bus stop outside Bird's Custard. "Threepenny child's please" I said to the conductor - it was automatic, I'd been saying the same thing for almost ten years. The conductor must have thought I was having a laugh. The ride cost me a tanner (sixpence in old money to you).

Pop cut his 'bacca up with his pen knife and loaded up his pipe. "So how did you get on?" he asked. Nan came out of the kitchen with a tea towel in her one hand and cup of Chinese Puzzle in the other. Pop's tea was always stewed and warmed up two or three times.

"The factory was massive," I said. "Great big machines called cold headers, hundreds of 'em, banging away making nuts and bolts by the million and then they go on the thread rollers and then…"

"What did they give you for your dinner?" Nan wanted to know, more importantly. She was very pleased to hear that a good meal could be had in the canteen for less than a shilling.

I was full of it, telling them about the one-week induction course and then the year at technical college, the green all-in-one overalls with GKN on the pocket. In the second year, if I had done OK, there would be a placement in one of the GKN factories as an indentured apprentice, with a rise in wages.

"Bloody 'ell" said Pop. "It'll be a long time afore yow get yer 'ands dirty."

He had worked with steam engines most of his life, running fairground traction engines, big show engines and boilers at BSA and Wilmot Breeden, until he had retired two years before at 73. He even knew about Boulton, Watt and Murdoch's contribution to the Industrial Revolution during the 18th Century. He continued to work as a gardener and odd job man for a firm of Solicitors until he died in 1972, the day after he held my firstborn son. He was then 86.

"You've a lot to learn Steve, but you'll do it, me and yer Nan always wanted to see yer get started" he said. Nan went back into the kitchen, sniffing and dabbing her eyes with the tea towel.

At this time Mom was singing with the Sonny Rose Band at the West End Ballroom in Birmingham and was married to Dougie Roberts, a trumpet player. They were well pleased that I'd landed a good steady job.

Two pounds 15 shillings and eightpence doesn't go far, especially when you're paying out a quid a week for your keep, but I don't remember being short during those first weeks of working. Maybe I'm looking back through rose-tinted specs. I always seemed to have a bit of fag money and I would down the odd beer with Pop and Uncle Norman in the Haven or the Dog and Partridge. Robin had his own van and Mugsy had the best racing pushbike in Yardley Wood.

Years later, on the eve of my wedding, Nan handed me a hundred quid. She told me she had been saving ten shillings from my pound every week.

I'd always liked to go chasing after the girls and at fifteen and a half I'd had my share of snogging and groping. I think I would class myself as a semi-virgin. There were three girls I'd gone out with for a month or so each and I had brought each of them home to sit on my Nan's leatherette settee. Many years later I found out I had been conceived on it. However, when I started work I was "between girlfriends". With in a couple of weeks of starting at Garretts Green Tech, that would change.

★ ★ ★ ★ ★ ★ ★ ★ ★ ★ ★ ★ ★ ★

"Stephen, smoking under the age of 16 is against the law," said Miss Jones, who was in charge of our induction course. This caused great mirth among the other apprentices sitting round the classroom. She had copped me having a fag outside.

"But I'm fifteen and a half, Miss!"

"Well you can smoke half a cigarette then, but not where I can see you" she replied. It was my turn "in the barrel" (having the piss taken) that morning, and everybody had a good laugh.

She was good looking, as I remember, with a nice figure and lovely brown hair, and I'm sure we all fancied her, even though at 30 or so she was far too old. More to the point, she was good at her job. She didn't lecture at us. Instead she set us tasks and targets to achieve. She pointed us in the right direction. In small groups, almost like a treasure hunt, we set off to the Science Museum and James Watts Museum to discover for ourselves. We would report back every day about midday to pool all the knowledge we had gleaned.

Even though it's now 48 years ago, certain facts have stuck in my mind. In the mid 18th Century the steam engine was extremely inefficient. James

Watt used his skill and ingenuity to turn it into a usable machine. Within a few years he moved from Scotland to Birmingham and became a partner to Matthew Boulton, who owned a factory in Birmingham just north of the city centre. This factory soon became the most important producer of steam pumping engines in the world, supplying engines to tin and copper mines in Cornwall, paper and cotton mills in Lancashire and for work on the fast-expanding canal network – the motorways of their day.

In 1777 a 23-year-old engineer named William Murdoch walked from his home in Scotland to Birmingham for an interview with Boulton. He had heard about the cutting-edge technology of the day and wanted a job. Boulton was impressed. Before offering him a job, he commented on Murdoch's hat.

"It's made of wood, sir and I made it on a turning machine I've invented" he said. Boulton immediately saw the potential in manufacturing of the machine his new recruit had invented, and the lathe was born.

Joe Healy was my chargehand when I finally started to get my hands dirty in the fitting shop at United Non-Ferrous Metals. The characters in that factory were unbelievable and I could write a book about the good times and experiences I had. As you know, because you're reading it.

Joe was a truly skilled craftsman who'd forgotten more than I would ever know. He always said the lathe was the most important machine tool in the shop and a good bloke on a lathe "can mek anything".

All metal turning lathes have a lead screw, which allows a thread to be cut. One of the questions Miss Jones tasked us with was how the first lead screw was made. It was rather like the age-old question of which came first, the chicken or the egg.

We found the answer. A round steel bar about six inches in diameter and 24 inches long was set up on the bench. Two lengths of rope were wound together around it. Then one length was removed, which left you a guide for subsequent cutting by hand tools, hacksaw, hammer and chisel and file. That first lead screw is in Birmingham Science Museum. Miss Jones did us proud.

★ ★ ★ ★ ★ ★ ★ ★ ★ ★ ★ ★ ★ ★ ★

"Yow get three overalls each, one on yer back, one in the wash and a clean 'un in yer locker. The works van will bring the clean 'uns and collect the dirty 'uns from the college every Monday morning. It'll cost you a bob a wick and if Cocky finds anybody with a dirty overall cos they've knackered up the system yow'll be bollocked up hill and down dale and med to wash 'em yourself.

"Now, Blues supporters first. Villa fans can fuckin' wait." (Birmingham City and Aston Villa were the city's two great rival teams – still are.)

Brian was a little bloke with National Health glasses. How he said all that with a fag in his mouth I'll never know, but he loved his job as Head Storeman.

How would I get to the college? I decided it would be the 13A from School Road to the 11 Route at Swanhurst Park, then round the Outer Circle to the stop past the Swan at Yardley, then on to the 16 for Garretts Green. It should take about an hour. Once I was 16 I could buy a motor bike. I couldn't wait for Monday morning to arrive.

The Senior Engineering Lecturer, with Cocky alongside him, welcomed us to the college and outlined the training programme. Each day we would spend approximately four hours in the classroom and four hours in the workshops, studying engineering principles and theory. We would be concentrating on safe practices at all times, with the aim of taking and passing the City & Guilds London Institute Craft Examination Part I. The electrical apprentices would attend different workshops.

My group consisted of about six apprentices from the GKN group, six from

Renolds Chains in Tysley, a couple from Cadburys' and a few each from Wards and Lucas - about 20 in total. Our lockers were just outside the workshop, and down the corridor was a gym with ropes, wall bars and a 5-aside and basketball pitch. The canteen was huge and there was a recreation room with snooker tables, table tennis and a dart board. There was also a large function room with a stage for dances. It really was a fantastic place. As I sat there in the canteen with Jim and Frank dunking custard creams, I wondered – where have all these young birds come from?

★ ★ ★ ★ ★ ★ ★ ★ ★ ★ ★ ★ ★ ★

I would spend most of my weekends on the rifle ranges at Kingsbury, near Tamworth. Wet or fine, I'd be there practising. I would cycle over the bridge by Tritiford Park, up Highfield Road to the Stratford Road, turn left and on to Cateswell House Cadet and T A Centre, opposite Hall Green Railway Station. Lieutenant Croyer would cram at least 4 of us in the back of his Morris Minor van alongside our personally-sighted .303 Lee Enfield rifles with at least 500 rounds of live ammunition. You can't shoot at targets 500 yards away with blanks or pellets from an air rifle.

At the end of the shooting season, if we had ammo left over, we would have a bit of fun with the Bren gun, which fired 400 rounds a minute. Looking back it's difficult to believe all this firepower was kept in the middle of suburban Hall Green, locked up but with no special security. Billy Kilmartin, Frank Blake, Pete Cassidy and yours truly were always there. A few years later, when I bought my first house in Kingsbury after completing my apprenticeship, Billy, who went on to join the TA, would roll up on a Saturday morning with these weapons and modern semi-automatics on top. We would shoot all Saturday, then rather than have to take it all back to the barracks we would leave it in my hallway or garage and go up the Royal Oak. Such innocence. The IRA and the scourge of terrorism were all in the future.

When we passed Tyburn House on the Kingsbury Road, where the Spitfire factory used to be, there were still barrage balloons. Castle Vale was still at the planning stage. Elvis, the Shadows, Helen Shapiro and Petula Clark were in the charts. The Beatles were still the Quarrymen, and Love Me Do was a year in the future.

So I had a steady job with prospects, but I didn't really have a clue what I wanted to do, no goals or targets. Are all young people like that? I believe my Nan and Pop wanted me to better myself and achieve more than they had, but all "parents" want that.

We had a regular weekend camp at Walton Hall, just outside Stratford on Avon (years later Danny La Rue bought it and turned it into a luxury hotel). We'd go on night manoeuvres and initiate the new recruits by applying boot polish to their tender spots.

One Saturday night Billy, Pete Cassidy and 'Corporal Phillips' cadged a lift into Stratford and went to the pictures. I met a young girl there and we went on to have a few dates over the next couple of weeks, nothing serious. Hitching back from Stratford that night, all three of us were picked up by an Army 10-tonner and piled in. Pete disappeared into the back with three adult WRACs, and when we arrived at Walton Hall 20 minutes later his trousers were round his gaiters. Perhaps Billy and I had BO.

The college looked impressive, built on three floors with beautiful red brickwork and an abundance of windows. I couldn't guess how many classrooms there were.

The college canteen was laid out with individual tables, each with four chairs. The lecturers' tables were arranged in a long line down one wall. As you walked in through the double wood-framed, glass-panelled doors, you turned to the right and saw that the whole length of the wall was taken up by a stainless steel servery with the equipment for serving everything from snacks, soft drinks and crisps to three-course meals. There was always a choice of two or three main dishes and a pudding.

As you might imagine, with some two or three hundred students and 30-odd lecturers in at any one time, there was a constant loud, murmuring hum. You could smoke in the canteen, though not in the classrooms or workshops. Something else different from school – we actually wanted to be there.

All the apprentices were employed and earning a wage, even if it was a low one, but many of the other students were not sponsored. Even so everyone knew they were receiving some of the best training available for their future jobs and careers. This wasn't a university and we wouldn't be doctors, bank managers or lawyers, but we did all have the opportunity to be factory supervisors, works managers or company directors. And to get off with girls.

Geoff and Dennis from Renolds Chain knew where all the talent had come from – there was a large secretarial and office training facility within the college. We would be seeing them here every day. "Crumpet on tap, can't go wrong" as Geoff put it.

There was plenty of larking about, but we didn't shirk our studies. In fact we soaked up our training like sponges. It wasn't that it would pay our wages for the next 50 years, just that we enjoyed it.

Most of the apprentices carried their books around in those old-fashioned briefcases that look like doctors' bags, handed down from their dads probably.

A dark blue canvas rucksack with biro graffiti gave you more street cred.

We used to play a prank with people's bags. The classroom windows were pivoted horizontally in the middle, so when you opened them till they were flat the top half of the window stuck out outside the building and the bottom half protruded into the classroom. If you took your eye off your bag for a second, you would turn to find it was being dangled out of the window, ready to plummet three floors to the ground. You just had to shrug your shoulders, mutter curses at the perpetrator and trudge down six flights of stairs. Unfortunately on one occasion the window two floors below was also open and the bag smashed through it. The poor lad sitting next to it was combing bits of glass out of his hair all day.

We had different lecturers for different subjects - maths and geometry, technical drawing, materials, steels and plastics, the steel-making process, machine tools, cutting tools, measuring equipment, manufacturing processes, report writing - it was endless. Two or three nights a week we had homework. At least there wouldn't be any exams for nearly a year.

In the workshop there was only one instructor/lecturer. "I'm Mr. Fisher and I'll tell you when you can call me Harry," he said. "The workshop ain't the playground, mess around in here and you'll end up blind, no fingers on yer 'and or yer 'air ripped out by the roots.

"Now then, all those wearing Slim Jim ties, take 'em off. Put all yer fancy rings and watches in yer pocket, do the buttons up on yer overalls and roll yer sleeves up. During the year I'll give you a glimpse of what it is to be a craftsman. With any luck I'll get yer through Part 1 of the City & Guilds without losing a finger."

He was a great bloke, tall and approaching 60 with a full head of grey hair. He had started work with BSA Machine Tools at 14, just before the end of the First World War. After reaching the position of Machine Shop Superintendent he had decided to move into training.

All us young lads swore in conversation between ourselves, but it was most definitely not on in our world to swear out loud. Apart from the odd 'bloody' or 'daft bugger' I'd never heard my Nan, Pop, Mom or any member of my family swear. Same as in college you wouldn't dream of swearing in front of a lecturer. I mention this because Mr. Fisher had a particular turn of phrase, one I still use nearly 50 years on. "Kin'ell" he would say. If you did a good job or if you dropped a clanger Mr. Fisher would always say "Kin'ell".

So with my watch in my pocket, my overall sleeves rolled up and the buttons done right up to my chin (I didn't like having to do that, most unfashionable), I started work as a craftsman.

To produce a tapped hole with say a half-inch Whitworth thread you had to consult the thread chart to identify the correct diameter twist drill to use. You drilled the hole, using suds as coolant, then tapped it by hand using a wrench. To produce a good tapped hole you smeared the tap with tallow, a greasy, smelly, horrible mixture with the consistency of lumpy rice pudding, and a right bastard to get off your hands.

Geoff and Dennis had been working at Renold for about a month and they knew the difference between tallow and hand protection cream. Geoff said you should put plenty of tallow on your hands at the beginning of the day to protect them and make it easier to wash the dirt off later. Unfortunately I missed the wink he gave Dennis and the rest of the lads.

I duly smothered my hands with tallow, almost up to my elbows. Everybody was pissing themselves – the bloke in the tool stores, a couple of technicians from next door. Even Mr Fisher poked his head out of his office when he heard them laughing. "Kin'ell!" he said. I scrubbed and scrubbed my hands and arms, but hours later I still stank like a dead pig.

I was on my way back to the workshop when one of the lads told me he had just come past the gym and seen a load of girls playing netball. "You want to see 'em – they've only got T shirts and knickers on," he said. We thundered off like a herd of elephants. Even though the windows in the double swing doors were a reasonable size, they could not accommodate a dozen heads peering into the gym. It was true. They were all wearing T shirts and knickers (not the lacy type, big blue ones). They soon noticed the rabble at the window and started giggling and nudging each other, until a large busty woman in shorts with a whistle round her neck came striding towards the door. By the time she got to it the corridor was empty again.

"Did you see the blonde with the big tits jumping up to the net?" said Dennis.

"Couldn't miss her. I've seen her in the canteen, her name's Diane. I bet I go out with her before you do" replied Geoff.

The banter went on until Harry returned from his cup of tea and we all resumed marking out, centre punching, drilling, hacksawing and filing to make our tap wrenches and centre finders.

Learn to use hand tools first, was Harry's motto. Hit your thumb with a hammer to get rid of your inexperience before you work on a machine, where a mistake will cost you your hand or your eye. Looking back, he set us all on the right road.

A couple of days later I was standing in the queue for a cuppa when I recognized three of the girls who had been playing. There was some banter about the knickers, all in good fun. We collected our tea and went back to join our usual crowd. The girls stayed on their tables and the lads on theirs, with only the odd glance at each other.

Little did I know I had just met my future wife.

CHAPTER TWO

A couple of Christmases before, Mom had bought me an acoustic guitar. With the aid of Bert Weedon's Play In A Day and a little practice, I could now strum about five chords. My best was It Takes A Worried Man To Sing A Worried Song. Hank Marvin I was not. But Mugsy had an electric guitar, an amp and a speaker with a microphone, and he was forming a group. Spikey Wayne, the maths and music teacher at Yardley Wood, had discovered I could sing a bit (in fact I had once sung in a choir in Birmingham Town Hall). So with Mugsy's dad out and his mum Nellie wearing earplugs, me, Mugsy and Rollo (he had an electric guitar too) practised in Mugsy's bedroom.

I soon gave up the guitar - it was murdering my fingers, and anyway Cliff didn't have to play, he just sang. But we soon had a formidable line-up. I was occasional lead singer, Mugsy played rhythm guitar, Chris Jones lead guitar and Kenny Bland was on drums. Chris Kefford, on bass guitar, went on to be a star. He formed the Move with Roy Wood and became Ace Kefford.

We practised at youth clubs in Shirley, just down the road from the railway station, upstairs in the Warstock Pub, in a café on the Stratford road and anywhere else where they would put up with the row and not charge us. We were all dead keen, talking of giving up work and going professional. There was talk of giving Germany a shot.

Soon a new singer appeared on the scene, and this bloke was prepared to wear a gold sparkly suit. By then I had my motorbike, a steady girlfriend and exams to swot for, so I was happy to wait for stardom. Billy and I used to watch the group. They were getting better. In fact in an hour's playing they were only repeating three or four songs.

"We've got to start earning some money from this, not just pissing about, if we're going to turn professional" said Mugsy one night after a particularly good practice session upstairs in the Warstock. We were having a pint of mild, one shilling and threepence.

"This room could hold over a hundred people," he said. "If we charged two bob entrance we'd have ten quid to whack out. That's two quid each for us and any over Steve and Billy can share if they run the door." Mugsy was serious.

"How are we gonna get a hundred people to come?" I said.

"Easy, we all tell all our mates."

Two weeks later, with a raffle book of tickets, me and Billy sat on the door upstairs in the Warstock. The group was tuning up and we were waiting for the rush. The tickets were necessary because the toilets were downstairs and Charlie the gaffer was not going to open the bar upstairs. "There will be too many young 'uns and I can't risk me licence" he explained. So anyone leaving the room and wanting to come back in would have to show their ticket. Me and Billy were good at management.

By nine, when the group took a break, we had sold 25 tickets. "They'll all be up in the second half, they're having a drink downstairs. Anyway let's have another beer on the stage, we've only had a couple so far" said Mugsy.

The second half kicked off with Long Tall Sally and by 10 o'clock another five 'fans' had appeared and 10 more pints had been delivered to the stage, plus another four for me and Billy, the hard-working management team.

It was a good night. The 30 fans had a great time, Mugsy and the group were pissed, me and Billy were pissed and there was no trouble. Even Charlie was impressed.

"Where were all our mates?" said Mugsy. "Still, we must have about three quid in the kitty, that's nearly 10 bob each." I was surprised he could talk, let alone add up, but Mugsy could always hold his beer.

As the money was counted I was beginning to feel a bit nervous.

"Thirty bob. One pound 10 shillings. Where the fuck's the rest gone?" "

"Beer for the boys" said Billy.

Charlie was locking up. "That was a good night, lads. What would you to say to making it a regular do? And by the way, who's paying me for the room?"

"How much is it?" we all asked, dreading the answer.

"I normally charge three or four quid, but because it's a Wednesday night you can have it for thirty bob" he said.

★ ★ ★ ★ ★ ★ ★ ★ ★ ★ ★ ★ ★ ★ ★

Five days a week I would leave home to catch the quarter to eight bus opposite the Co-Op, next to the Haven pub in School Road, arriving in Garretts Green just before nine. I don't ever remember being late. After a month or so all our group had settled into the nine-to-five routine, generally with classroom and Engineering Theory in the morning and Workshop Practice in the afternoon.

Everyone had permission to use Harry's Christian name by now, and under his experienced eye we were introduced to all the machine tools in the workshop. In the morning we were taught the correct angles to use on the cutting tools and how they changed depending on the material and its hardness, and just as importantly how to measure the work we produced. We were using micrometers and Verniers which could measure to an unbelievable one thousand of an inch, half the thickness of a human hair. They were very different from the easy-to-read digital read-out equipment we have today – you had to work at these.

You had a little disc about the size of a half crown (a bit bigger than a 50p piece) with your number on it, and when you needed a tool you would take it to the stores, hand it to the storeman and collect whichever tool or piece of equipment you needed. We were repeatedly set up by being sent for such items as a tin of elbow grease, the Gaffer's deckchair, a sky hook, an ear clip, a hard punch or a long weight (and Bert would make sure it was very long).

A year later in the factory the system was similar, except that it was done with paper. Joe Healy would write you out a chitty which you handed in to Bert Roe in the stores and he'd shuffle off to get the tool you wanted, moaning about the bugger who had interrupted him from the Daily Mirror crossword.

We had machine tools as well. The lathes could swing up to about a 12 inch diameter, the millers and grinding machines had beds up to 24 inches and the shaper would stroke up to 18 inches. These were all relatively modest in size, but much bigger than I'd been used to in the metalwork classroom at school. When we went on day trips to factories as Walter Summers in Halesowen, BSA Tools in Mackadown Lane, Jones and Shipman or Taylor and Channon, the lathes, planers and power presses were immense.

"Right then" said Harry Fisher one afternoon. "I'm going to teach you young craftsmen how to screw." A few sniggers rippled around the group as we watched him set up a two-inch diameter mild steel bar in the three-jaw chuck on one of the lathes. Quickly centre-drilling the end and clamping the tailstock with revolving centre in position, he took a quick ten thou off the diameter, all the way down the length.

"Look in your reference charts and tell me the TPI, pitch, angle of thread and depth for a two-inch BSF thread," he said. We all eventually came up with the correct information and Harry proceeded to show us how to grind the high-speed tool bit to the appropriate angles and set the gearbox on the lathe to produce the right TPI and pitch. He put a fresh wad of chewing tobacco in his mouth.

"You all know a cutting tool must be kept cool when machining, and that's why you have a pumped supply of coolant on all machines, otherwise you lose the edge on the tool. Only use a trickle, you're not removing a lot of metal per cut. It's important you can see the cutting action clearly, otherwise you'll have a right smash up. Watch the dial on the leadscrew and engage the travelling nut."

We all watched in amazement as the tool travelled down the length of the revolving bar and cut a perfect shallow V in the metal, producing a screwthread.

Then, a fraction of a second before the tool would have smashed into the revolving chuck, he disengaged the leadscrew with one hand and simultaneously, in the blink of an eye, wound out the cross slide with the other.

I'll never be able to do that, I thought. I'll smash up half the machines in the workshop.

He increased the depth of cut by 10 thou and repeated the procedure. Should I tell him he hasn't put his coolant on, I thought to myself?

My question was answered when on the third cutting pass he coughed and spat out, bang on the cutting tool, a supply of brown, tobacco-flavoured coolant.

★ ★ ★ ★ ★ ★ ★ ★ ★ ★ ★ ★ ★ ★ ★

By November 1961 my 16th birthday was three months away, so it was motorbike countdown. I hadn't saved much, but I did have certain assets – a Dawes 10-speed racing bike, a single-speed track bike with chrome strengtheners on the front forks and a five-foot snooker table with balls and cues. If that wasn't enough there were always the clothes on my back. I really wanted that motorbike.

I used to cycle to the drawbridge just up the road from the Aqueducts in Shirley and every night there would be a gang of lads with BSA Road Rockets and Triumph Bonnevilles. One big bloke, Slobby Combes, even had a 1000 cc Vincent which had a speedo that read to 150 mph.

One Friday lunchtime I was thinking of this as I stood in the queue in the College canteen and realised one of the netball girls was next to me. She was tall, five foot nine, long legs (I had last seen them in navy blue knickers), brown hair tucked behind her ears and a pretty smiling face. We had exchanged the odd word and glance during the last month, so I knew her name was Pauline. Now it was crunch time.

"Hi Pauline" I said. "Would you like to go to the pictures tonight? The Alamo is on at the Kingston. It starts at half past seven." I don't think I took a breath as I said it.

It was done – I'd asked her out. I was sure nobody had overheard, so at least if she turned me down my mates wouldn't know about it.

"I know where it is, it's at the top of Kingston Hill near the Blues ground. I'll get my dad to drop me off." And she was gone.

Blimey, I'd got a date. I'm not telling anybody, I said to myself, not even my Nan and Pop.

Three o'clock arrived and it was tea time. Our group of about eight apprentices all squeezed our chairs together round one of the tables.

"What are you doing tonight Steve?"

"Not sure" I replied. "Out with me mates I suppose."

"Come with us if you like" offered Jim. "Us lot are going to the pictures to see The Alamo, it's all about Davy Crockett, stacks of action."

"Which picture house?" I mumbled.

"The Kingston's got the best seats. If the film's no good you can watch the couples snogging in the back row" Frank replied.

Oh shit, I thought to myself. Pauline's in her class - I can't contact her, and if I did she'd think I'd changed my mind.

Shit!

On Fridays we finished at four and caught the bus to Haden and Stokes to collect our wages before going home. My Nan and Pop didn't have a phone and I didn't have Pauline's number anyway. But there was no way I could sit in the pictures with a new girlfriend with that lot watching. We would have to go somewhere else, but where? The next nearest picture house was halfway down the Coventry road.

Normally at four on a Friday afternoon all the apprentices were off, but this particular day everybody seemed to be hanging about. I began to sense that's something was up.

Harry Fisher was locking up his office. "See you lads on Monday. Steve, let me know how Davy Crockett gets on tonight."

I looked around at the others. "Phil heard you ask your new girlfriend for a date" said Geoff. "You're the first one she has said yes to."

That made me feel pretty good. I walked away feeling on top of the world as the strains of "Davy, Davy Crockett, king of the wild frontier" followed me down the corridor. Half the college knew I was going to the pictures that night, and who with.

"I'm going to the pictures tonight Nan, meeting a mate from college, got to be there before half past seven" I said. "I've had fish and chips for lunch in the canteen (I was now calling it lunch, though to Nan and Pop it was still dinner), so I'm not really hungry." I still ate the tea they had prepared.

I went out in my best tapered trousers, open-necked shirt and my "interview jacket", which was the only one I had at the time. I got off the bus at Camp Hill and walked past the gothic church, down under the railway bridge and over the canal and up the start of the Cov (the Coventry Road).

Pauline was standing on the steps outside the entrance to the Kingston, dressed in a grey mackintosh, hands in her pockets and a scarf around her neck. When she saw me she waved to someone in a big old fashioned Austin with shiny headlamps, running boards and mudguards. I could see her younger brother staring at me through the windscreen. Her father slowly drove away back down the Cov towards Hay Mills.

We paid the four shillings for two tickets and walked into the darkened cinema. Carefully avoiding the back row, we sat about five rows down. I kept nervously looking around for a small gang of sniggering apprentices. They never appeared of course, but it was at least half an hour before I dared to put my arm around Pauline's shoulder.

It was a great film. Afterwards I saw my date on to her bus and walked back to Camp Hill to catch the 13A to Yardley Wood. I had to get up early in the morning to go shooting on the Ranges. We were going back to Altcar the following spring and Lt. Croyer had entered the team for Bisley in the summer, so wet or fine we had to practise.

By now quite a few of the apprentices were going out with someone, so to be seen chatting to a girl was no big deal and Pauline and I started sharing some of our tea breaks. I think it was a Sunday afternoon a week or so after our first date when I was invited to tea to meet her mum and dad. Pauline lived in Kingscliffe Road, Hay Mills, not far from Beddows, the famous fish and chip shop. It took three buses and a five minute walk - I really did need that motor bike.

Mr and Mrs Smith had put on a nice spread with sandwiches and cake. Bobby, her little brother, had been well scrubbed for the occasion. His hair had been well plastered down, but it still insisted on sticking up,

My Nan and Pop reciprocated the following week and then we went to the Haden and Stokes Christmas dance together, so we were now definitely "going out".

One day I heard that Reg Spruce, who lived next door to my Uncle Norman and Aunt Ada in Shirley, was selling his motorbike. It was a Francis Barnett 225 cc Cruiser (in those days you could ride a bike up to 250 cc even without passing a test), and he wanted fifty quid for it. He had had it for three years and had used it to go to work, but now he was buying a car.

Billy came with me and we looked it over. It was dark green (they all were), with a two-stroke engine. It was wonderful, and I wanted it.

The big snag was that I was still four weeks away from my birthday in February and I hadn't yet sold my assets as planned. I asked Reg if he could hold on to the bike for a week while I worked out what to do. "That's ok," said Reg. "I ain't got me car sorted yet and until I do I need the bike for work anyway."

Where was I going to find fifty quid on two pounds 15 shillings and eightpence a week? I had no way of borrowing it.

But I'd always loved a challenge. Nan's friend Lily Smith had a son who bought the snooker table, Billy Waters had the Dawes 10-speed and my mate Custard paid me a fiver for the track bike. I had about twenty quid in the Municipal Bank, an old account my Nan had set up when I was born. Even so I was a good few quid short.

Nan and Pop came to my rescue, as they always had. I repaid them over 10 weeks.

The walk to Reg's house with the money took me three quarters of an hour. The walk back, pushing the best motorbike in the world, took me an hour and a half. It wasn't taxed or insured.

At the bottom of the garden Pop had built two sheds (probably without permission from the council). When I was little they had been used for chickens, to make sure I had a fresh egg every morning, but they were now used as tool sheds. My new bike fitted into the shed a treat. A long cable

23

from the kitchen supplied an electric light, and I spent the next couple of hours polishing every spoke with Brasso chrome cleaner. Reg had looked after the bike well, and they came up a treat.

The week before my birthday I managed to tax and insure my pride and joy and buy a crash helmet – don't ask me where I found the money. Mr Smith gave me a pair of leather gauntlets that reached up to my elbows, along with his old sleeveless leather jerkin with four big buttons up the front. I looked like someone from Dad's Army. With an L plate stuck on the back and my college scarf tight around my neck I pushed the bike up the path, kick-started it with my right foot and set off.

My Pop used to work at Wilmot Breeden in Tysley and when the buses occasionally went on strike he would borrow my push bike to get to work. He told me how to get to the Swan at Yardley without following the bus routes. Once at the Swan, it would be easy.

I left home at the usual time, bought a gallon of petrol for three shillings and sixpence (about 4p a litre) and was in Garretts Green before half past eight. My travelling time had been nearly halved. The wider joys of motorcycling became apparent on the way home, when it pissed down all the way. I didn't mind a bit.

The world was now my oyster. After tea I rode the bike around for hours, ending up at the drawbridge in Shirley where I parked the Francis Barnett alongside the big machines. Everyone knew you had to start learning on a little bike, so there was no piss taking, only congratulations. When I bought a bike 30 years later the biking fraternity was still the same, though the bike I bought in 1992 cost three times as much as my first house.

Terry Huggins lived in Glastonbury Road. He was 18 and a regular at the drawbridge on his Ariel Arrow, a fast 250 cc sports bike, and we often went out together. One summer's evening on the way to the Red Lion at Earlswood we were larking about when he shot past me. Even if my bike had had the power I wouldn't have responded (I was probably chicken). Twenty yards in front of me he lost control and ended up bowling down the road with his bike in the ditch.

I swerved around him, braked and ran back to find him sitting in the road laughing his head off. "That was a fucking good 'un" he said. He jumped back on his bike and by the time I got to the pub he had finished his first pint.

Somebody gave Terry a beating with a bicycle chain at the fairground on Billsley Common once and he went straight back home for his air rifle and went back up to the fair to sort it. The bloke had gone, fortunately for him. That was Terry, a good lad on your side but a bit wild. A month after our Red Lion escapade he was overtaking a coach on the way to Stratford Mop when he hit a car head on. He was killed outright.

The months flew by. I was really enjoying my studying and my confidence with the lathes, millers, grinders and shapers was increasing in leaps and bounds. My fear of wrecking the machines was proving to be unfounded.

The Intermediate Part 1 City & Guilds exams were now approaching. For the practical part we were issued with a drawing of a metal component which would require the use of all the machine tools in the workshop. The other component we had to make was to be mainly crafted by hand with a small amount of drilling, tapping and reaming. We would be allowed 15 hours to complete the practical, together with five three-hour classroom exams in maths and geometry, engineering drawing, metrology, materials and production processes.

The week before the exams, the lecturers took us through papers from previous years highlighting important questions of principles of engineering, while Harry did the same in the workshop. I didn't do much socialising that week - it was all swotting. Pauline was doing the same. We had now been going out for six months. "Our Pauline's courting" her granny would say.

Failure in these intermediate exams would be a disaster. No apprenticeship would be offered, and if you wanted to sit them again it would mean three nights a week for the next year. We were all under pressure, and there was no larking about.

The main hall was being used for the exams. About a hundred students were seated at individual desks arranged three feet apart in long rows. "I could do with a fag," Jim whispered to Frank and me. "Roll on 12 o'clock" I replied.

Armed with my log tables, slide rule (it would be another 10 years before the calculator was invented) and writing materials, I sat looking at the maths paper which was lying face down on my desk.

"Gentlemen, the time is 9.15 and you have three hours to complete the exam paper. There will be no talking or conversing of any sort. If you wish to leave the room please put up your hand and I will attend your desk. If you complete the paper before the allotted time, bring it together with your belongings to my desk and leave the room quietly. Make sure you write your name and course reference number on the top. You may now turn over your paper."

I'd been through all this many times at school, and it always terrified me. Would I blank out? Would I be able to understand all the paper, some of it, or none of it? Well, I would soon know.

I duly filled in the front of the paper with my name and course and looked at the first page. I knew a little of the techniques of sitting exams, and they had been emphasized by the lecturers in the run up to this week. Quickly read all the questions in the paper and decide which you believe you fully understand and will be able to answer comprehensively and correctly. Do these first – leave the difficult ones till last. It's common sense really, but sometimes in all the tension common sense disappears.

I read through the paper. There were a couple of right bastards which I knew I would really struggle with, but you did have a choice of questions. I'm glad I put the work in, I thought to myself. It wasn't too bad. I was reasonably confident that I could do a good job on 75% of the paper, and I'd be OK-ish on the rest. I dug out my slide rule and got stuck in.

After 15 minutes or so one lad, not from our course, got up from his desk looking deathly white. He collected his stuff, walked to the front and put his paper on the desk. He looked as if he was about to be sick.

At the end we all went outside into the yard, everybody talking at once, lighting up and relieved that the first exam was over.

Half an later we were in the workshop for the start of the practical and Harry was issuing all of us with two engineering drawings. One showed a mild steel shaft 12 inches long with eight different diameters ranging from 1-3 inches, two screw threads, four flats on one diameter and a diameter which had to be case-hardened and ground to a tolerance of plus or minus half a thousandth of an inch.

"You've done all this in the last 12 months, so don't worry" Harry assured us. "Before you start cutting metal I want you all to fill in the Method of Manufacture form – this is part of the exam. Before you do, we'll have an open forum to make sure we follow the correct sequence of operations. If you don't start off correctly you'll never be able to finish it to the drawing."

The second drawing wasn't so bad. A half-inch plate had to be hacksawed and filed to a profile, with four dowel holes and four tapped holes, ground flat to 0.475 inches plus or minus two thou. Again a Method of Manufacture had to be completed before work started. I was keen to get started, but it would take most of that afternoon session to finalise how we set about manufacturing the components. Half the class started work on the hand-crafted plate while the others started machining the shaft.

Mild steel contains up to 0.25% carbon plus a very small amount of lead to improve the cutting ability of the steel. In its normal state it cannot be hardened or heat treated. To fully harden steel you need a carbon content of up to 0.5%. Then, after heating it to a glowing red and quenching in oil or water, the steel will be extremely hard. You would then temper it back, just like a medieval sword maker. This shaft, however, needed to be hardened on one diameter only, as a journal to run in bronze bearings, leaving the rest of the metal relatively soft. This would be achieved by inducing carbon into the appropriate surface.

I faced both ends to the required overall length, drilled the ends with a centre drill and mounted it between centres on the lathe. Because you were machining on one machine, removing it to the miller for subsequent operations and then the universal grinder for finishing, you could not use either a 3–jaw or 4–jaw chuck. Machining between centres would ensure the accuracy, and more importantly the concentricity, of the shaft. It would run true, not "wobble" or "run out".

The bell rang. It was 5 o'clock and I had only just made a start. Looking around, so had everyone else.

"There's no rush" Harry assured us. "It's achievable in the time, and you don't want to scrap it when you're only half way through. If I think you need a little extra time later in the week you can stay over at night, I'm teaching the night school anyway, and no–one will know." With a bloke like that on your side we all stood a chance.

Because it was exam week I was setting off to college really early just to make sure I wasn't late. But as I approached the Swan on the second morning my faithful Francis Barnett stuttered, coughed a few times and conked out. I kicked it over a few times, then shook the tank – no petrol! What a prat. It was 8.30. On the bike it would have took me 10 minutes, but now I had two buses to catch to get to Garretts Green before 9.15.

I pushed the bike on to the car park of the undertakers', explained my predicament and was told to wheel it round the back out of sight and make sure I collected it before 6 pm.

To cut a long story short I got there at 9.16, just in time.

"Steve, someone's nicked your bike" Frank said.

"That's why I was late. I ran out of petrol at the Swan" I replied.

Travel problems soon disappeared and my thoughts were channelled into the next stages of machining my workpiece. During tea break one of the older Apprentices offered to give me a lift back to my bike, and he had a petrol can in the boot.

My shaft was going to plan, with all dimensions correct (or so I thought) to the drawing. All the surfaces except the one to be case hardened had been coated with a sulphate that would not absorb the carbon. The process to induce the carbon to a depth of 40 thou would be done Wednesday morning. My workpiece would then ready for final polishing, removing the sulphate and grinding the hardened surface. The tolerance of plus or minus 0.0005 was quite achievable on a universal grinding machine.

Mounting my piece between the centres on the grinder I measured the diameter. Bollocks – I had not left enough metal on from the turning stage. You would normally allow 15–20 thou to grind off, but I had left only about 5 thou. Would it be enough to "clean up"? The drawing specified 2.500 inches plus or minus 0.0005. This meant it must measure between 2.4995 and 2.5005.

Harry saw me looking at bit worried and came over. "Take it very steady," he said. "You only need to lick the surface with the wheel without taking too much off."

I was sweating. All the other features were bang to drawing and my screwcutting and milling were perfect.

Harry could have done it for me with his eyes shut, but he had to walk away. The grinding wheel was spinning at 3000 RPM and I had to just touch the revolving work piece without removing any metal. It was vital that the dark carbonized surface cleaned up and I still had five thou to work with. A gnat's cock, in engineering jargon.

I had almost a full diameter of shiny ground finish when I stopped the work piece and measured it. 2.4995 – bottom limit. I couldn't remove any more metal. I decided that the tolerance was the important part and removed the shaft from the grinder.

"You made the right decision," Harry said later. "You'll lose a mark or two, but it's rare for a student to make a part 100% correct. Everyone will have a couple of features not to drawing."

The hand-crafted component was not too bad – coating the steel plate with engineers' blue, marking out the profile and hole centres with the vernier height gauge, dotting the scribed lines, centre-punching the hole centres and then hacksawing, filing, drilling, tapping and reaming the holes. Then taking off the sharp corners and grind flat to the tolerances on the drawing.

Job done. By about three o'clock on the Friday afternoon everyone had finished.

The City & Guilds Examiners would be there on Monday to go through all the papers and we would get our results about two weeks later.

"We can't wait that long!" we all cried. "We'll be on our holidays!"

"Then you'll all have something to think about then when you're eating your ice creams at Blackpool. Seriously, I've been involved in some of the marking and

you ain't done too bad. I'll make skilled men of you yet."

My holidays in July 1962 were almost a week at Bisley, followed by the annual Army Cadet Camp on Salisbury Plain. It would be the middle of August before I would know if I had passed.

CHAPTER THREE

"Last two days of practice before our first National Shooting Event" Lt. Croyer announced as we piled into his Morris Minor van, together with four Lee Enfield .303 rifles and 500 rounds of ammunition. There were no seats in the back and a rifle was uncomfortable to sit on for the hour it would take to get to the ranges at Kingsbury.

We're now back in the early spring of 1961. I was just 15 and still at school, but I'd been an Army Cadet for three years (I lied about my age - at over six feet tall I could get away with it). I had been shooting competitively for almost two years and wore the cross guns of a Marksman on the left forearm of my uniform, just below my Lance Corporal stripe. We would practise all day and return on the Sunday to do it all again. It was school holidays the following week, and we were going to compete in our first major event, the North Western Command Weapon Meeting at Altcar Ranges near Formby in Lancashire.

On arriving at Kingsbury we checked in with the Range Warden and Molly the red setter jumped all over us as usual. Driving down the narrow tarmac road that separated the two 500-yard ranges, we parked up behind the butts outside the Target Shed. Each target was five feet square on a strong timber frame with two four foot support legs. We hoisted two of them on to one of the trolleys which ran on the railway lines from the shed, and pushed them along the rails round to the back of the butts. There were 50 firing points, so there were 50 target stations and the rails ran the full length of some 100 yards of track. In competition all firing points would be in use, but today was practising for just the four of us. Other teams might arrive during the day, but they would get their own targets.

Billy and I stayed in the butts and Lt. Croyer, Frankie Blake and Pete Cassidy drove back up to the 200-yard firing point. The butts were a mound of earth 15 feet tall and 20 feet thick and the inside where we worked was lined with two feet of reinforced concrete. A .303 bullet traveling at 1800 feet per second will penetrate six inches of solid oak at 200 yards, so we needed to be safe.

Crack - the first warmer came down, raising a puff of dirt in the huge bank of earth directly behind the targets. Rifles need to be warmed up for accuracy and following the next crack we hoisted up one of the targets - the other lowered automatically on a counterbalance. Another crack, a sighter and a small hole appeared in the target.

There are four rings on long-range targets, the bull, inner, magpie and outer. Using a long pole with a large white triangle on the top we pointed to the top right hand corner of the target, indicating that an inner had been scored, then pointed to the exact position of the bullet hole. The pointer was then dropped from view and the target pulled down out of sight, automatically raising the other target.

The bullet hole was patched with a pasted square the same colour as the inner - all the rings were different colours. Armed with our paste pot, brush and hundreds of perforated patches on a roll, we would be there for an hour, after which the roles would be reversed.

The first thing you always did on picking up your rifle was to point it skyward, open the bolt to ensure the magazine and breech were empty, close the bolt and pull the trigger to hear the comforting click. Then you can start shooting.

Occasionally I would put my warmer into the very top of the butts, showering the lads underneath with a pile of earth, but they always got me back. A couple of rifles firing every 10 seconds or so didn't make too much noise, but it took me quite a time to learn to ignore the noise of 50 in a competition and concentrate on my breathing and squeezing the trigger.

We took a break to eat our pre-packed sandwiches in the green wooden sheds which we shared with private shooting clubs as well as the TA and other cadet teams. A bottle of pop and we were back shooting. Then targets away, back to Cateswell House Barracks and home on my 10-speed for my tea.

Then we did it all again the next day. The four of us were averaging 90 to 95 out of 100 regarding points for the different disciplines, so Lt. Croyer was pleased.

We fired at 200 yards, 300, 400 and 500. You had to make adjustments for the strength of the wind and the distance, especially at 500 yards. If the wind was strong the allowance was so much that you were aiming at the target next to yours, four feet away.

That first year at Altcar, competing in our first Major, our team came second out of over 100. The team received a big silver cup, and more importantly we each received an individual 10-inch version. Mine was engraved L/Corporal S. Phillips, 2nd Place North Western Command Weapon Meeting 1961.

Lt. Croyer told us we would win it next year.

★ ★ ★ ★ ★ ★ ★ ★ ★ ★ ★ ★ ★ ★ ★

Now the time had come for us to find out if he was right. As soon as we broke up from college on the Friday I would be off to Bisley. The only fly in the ointment was that it meant waiting three weeks to hear my exam results. If I passed I would be offered a five-year apprenticeship and a placement at United Non Ferrous Metals Ltd (in those days part of the GKN Group). If I failed... who knows?

While I had enjoyed my time with the cadets, my priorities were changing. I loved motor bikes, and couldn't wait to pass my test and get a bigger one. I'd been going out with Pauline for almost a year now, and my Nan and Pop still thought learning a trade was better than joining the Army. Don't forget that it was only 17 years since the Second World War had finished.

I parked my bike up in the yard and joined the others having a smoke and discussing last week's exams. Most of us thought we'd done all right, but nobody was boasting.

"Come on you lot, we've got work to do" Harry called, sticking his head out of the door. "All the machines need a bloody good clean, oil and grease, and my office and the inspection department next door need painting."

We all looked at each other in dismay. We had expected a cushy week.

"By the way, you're all going on a couple of factory visits. There'll be a day at BSA Machine Tools down the road and another at Wickmans' in Coventry. And on Friday I've organized a basketball competition. Two of the teams are girls – the ones you randy lot have been chasing for the last 12 months."

There was only one possible response. "'Kin'ell!" came the chorus.

We put on overalls and got stuck in brushing and removing all the swarf and pieces of metal from every machine in the shop, underneath the benches and between the tool cupboards. Every time we had used a machine in the last 12 months we had cleaned it - "Harry's Rules" - but now he wanted a proper job doing.

"We'll leave the final oiling and greasing till Thursday," he said. "It's important all the machine slideways and beds have a good coating of oil because they're not being used again till September, and by then they'll have a film of rust all over them if we don't. Right, now who out of you lot can paint? It's only the walls, I don't want you lot up ladders."

"My uncle is a painter and decorator and I've worked with him during the school holidays" I said, before I had time to think. I should have kept my trap shut.

One of the lab technicians employed by the college was going to supervise and help me make a start in the Inspection Room. Brian was about 20 and dressed as a teddy boy with drainpipe trousers, brothel creepers, a proper Tony Curtis, DA and side burns. He also wore glasses.

All the measuring equipment was put away and the metal cupboards, benches and walls were brushed down. "We can make a proper start in the morning" Brian said, looking at his watch. I was seeing Pauline that night, so I didn't want to hang about.

The following morning as I put on my overalls I couldn't see any dust sheets in the room. Uncle Norman always laid one immediately under where

34

he was working, "Just in case you drop a spot of paint".

Setting the first five-gallon tin of white Dulux on the bench, Brian prised the lid off with a screw driver, picked up a length of wood and tried to stir the mixture. It seemed very thick.

"This is no good, we'll be here all day stirring this," he said.

He looked around and saw the bench drilling machine in the middle of the room. "That'll stir it up great" he said. "All we want now is some sort of paddle to put in the drill chuck." He wandered off and came back with what looked like a small propeller attached to a spindle, which he clamped into the chuck.

All machine tools have a variety of spindle speeds, which you select with a gearbox, as in a car. The slowest speed on this particular driller was about 100 revs per minute, while the fastest was close to 1000 rpm. I backed away. As far away as I could.

Brian admitted later he should have checked which speed the machine was set on. He switched on, and the home-made stirrer immediately got entangled with the wire handle of the paint tin. The tin proceeded to revolve around at the full 1000 rpm. Within a matter of seconds, Brian was covered from head to foot in white paint. He stepped back in horror with the driller still running, and the whole room was splattered, including all the cupboards, benches, doors and windows. At last the tin came free and rolled on to the floor, spilling the final gallon.

The rest of the apprentices heard the racket and came running in to see what had happened. We were all falling about laughing, but Brian was crying.

When you're a kid you don't see danger. In those days eye protection was only used for the grinders, while lathes, millers and drillers were all operated without safety glasses. In later years everyone in the machine shop I managed was issued with safety specs, with prescription lenses for those who normally wore glasses, all at the expense of the company. But that didn't happen till 1977.

Brian could have been blinded if he hadn't been wearing his normal glasses. It was the first works accident I had witnessed, if not, sadly, the last. Needless to say all painting ceased.

The visits to BSA Machine Tools and Wickmans were an eye opener to a young apprentice. The machines were enormous. The workshops were twice the size of a football pitch, with massive overhead cranes carrying huge slabs of steel to be machined, bored and turned. There were two foot long measuring micrometers (the largest I'd seen till then were no more than three inches). There were supervisors and foremen striding about. It was a different world.

In both factories we were showed around in small groups by senior apprentices, 19 and 20 year olds who seemed to know most of the workforce by name, exchanging banter and jokes. "Still shagging young Mary in wages?" an elderly man operating a large vertical boring machine asked our guide. He blushed and smiled to himself, so I guess he was.

Sandwiches were laid out for us and afterwards we watched a film about the history of the company, its products and how they were made.

One shop in Wickmans particularly impressed me. The jig boring department was a clean air room, and we could only look at it through large windows. We gazed in wonder at the six craftsmen, who according to our guide were on eleven shillings and sixpence an hour – a fortune. Remember that average earnings have gone up by a factor of 36 since then, so that would be like twenty quid an hour in today's money.

Our workshop was now spotless, with new white lines painted on the floor. All the machines were cleaned up, with the slideways well oiled ready for the next term and the arrival of another influx of first-year apprentices.

Then it came to the basketball match. Although we were a pretty tall side, with Frank, Jim and me all over six feet, the first few games were against teams of lads who were older than us and we got knocked all over the gym. Still, we were warming up for the main event.

"Where are the girls?" I said to the others. As I turned round the doors opened and in they trotted. We all knew each other by now, but we still whistled at the shorts and pleated netball skirts (no big navy blue knickers this time).

The same big busty lady who had been in charge last time blew her whistle and addressed the teams. "Right, before we start I want you young gentlemen to listen to the rules of netball."

"Netball?" I said. "What's netball?" My team-mates were scratching their heads.

Mrs Busty heard my question. "Netball, young man, is a non-contact sport. You cannot run with the ball. Upon receiving the ball you remain still and pass it, hopefully, to your team mate."

This definitely ain't basketball, I thought. Ah well, it'll be a bit of fun.

On dates with Pauline the rules of netball had not been high on our priorities for discussion, so I didn't know she had been captain of her grammar school team. Another small point which we all quickly realized was that all the girls were extremely good players and Diane, the blonde with the big tits, had even represented Warwickshire.

We kicked off, or whatever you do in netball. The girls passed the ball effortlessly, skipping nimbly around us. Every time we made contact, Mrs Busty blew up for a foul. We never got a look in. We hardly touched the ball, never mind the girls' bottoms. Naturally we lost by several hundred.

Harry watched the game with a big smile on his face.

★ ★ ★ ★ ★ ★ ★ ★ ★ ★ ★ ★ ★ ★

We made the trip to Altcar in a Morris Minor van, me sitting on a cushion on the floor at the back. As we drove into the Mersey Tunnel I thought about Lt. Croyer's promise that we would win it this year.

For three years we had practised and played in all weathers, even in pouring rain and high winds. Like most people, I hated shooting in the rain. Even lying on a ground sheet with your poncho over your back you got soaked. The rain would blur the target 500 yards away and drops would sit on the blade of the front sight. My Nan used to go mad when I arrived home dripping wet, threatening to come up to Cateswell House Barracks to tell this Croyer bloke a thing or two. But as Lt. Croyer said, "Any bugger can shoot in the sunshine".

We arrived at the Ranges about tea time (no M6 in those days) and got settled in. Most of the teams were in long wooden billets, with the spill-over teams in large Army issue tents all supplied with sleeping bags. Our rifles were kept locked in Lt. Croyer's van.

The first two days of the competition took place in lovely warm spring weather. After the 200 and 300 yard disciplines of "grouping" (all five rounds within a three-inch diameter circle, measured by a wire ring) "snap" (a small target the size of a soldiers body appearing for five seconds, then withdrawn) and the usual scoring of bulls, inners, magpies and outers, we were in third place. As we went into the final day, any of the top five teams could have won.

After tea and a game of ping pong, the four of us lads sat in our tent. "I tell you what I've noticed," I said to Billy. "All the cadets in the other teams talk a lot posher than us."

"I've noticed that too" Billy replied. "Ain't got the foggiest idea why."

"I'll tell you why," said Lt. Croyer, ducking into the tent and stretching his lanky legs. "There are nearly 200 cadet teams from all over Great Britain shooting here. Apart from us and two other teams, they all come from public schools." We didn't even know what a public school was.

On the morning of the final day I awoke to the sound of steady rain falling on the tent. "That's all we want, a good soaking," I said to myself. "Come on lads, breakfast's at seven and we're on butt duty at eight."

The two teams ahead of us had not performed well at 500 yards in these conditions and you could see their discomfort – they looked like drowned rats. Now it was our turn. If we shot as well as we knew we could we would overtake them and win, but it would be quite a challenge in this weather. Unless we really cocked up we couldn't be caught by the teams below us.

Croyer took us to one side. "You see how them soft public school lot have bottled out because of a drop of rain. They only shoot when the sun shines.

Do you want to come second again? Now get on that 500 yard firing point and show this posh lot that the three years I've been training you ain't all been a fucking waste of time."

None of us had ever heard him swear like that before.

So we went out in the rain and with 50 other cadets firing at targets we could hardly see, me, Billy, Frank and Pete dug into the experience we had gained from all the times we had shot in similar conditions.

By three o'clock the rain had stopped and hundreds of cadets and their officers were gathered in groups looking at the long table with all the medals and cups.

"In third place, the cadets of Rochester School, attached to the Royal Staffordshire Regiment" the Major announced. Four lads marched up with their officer to receive the medals and cups.

"In second place, the cadets of Swanbourne School, Royal Welsh Fusiliers."

We must have been either first or fourth, I thought.

"In first place, and winners of the 1962 Western Command Weapons Meeting, are the cadets from the 4/5th. Battalion, Royal Warwickshire Regiment, Cateswell House Detachment."

Croyer was dancing – literally dancing. "We're the first non-public-school cadets to do it!" he roared.

I don't remember the drive home, but I do remember putting the large silver cup on Nan and Pop's upright piano, with 'Corporal S. Phillips' engraved on it.

★ ★ ★ ★ ★ ★ ★ ★ ★ ★ ★ ★ ★ ★

The netball game was over, the college had broken up for the summer and I was riding to Bisley with Frank Blake and Billy for our first international shooting competition. Lt. Croyer was driving down with the other members and the rifles. Although we were now National Western Command champions, this was a different ball game as we would be competing against the best cadet shots from all over the world. There were nearly 500 teams from the Army and Royal Air Force, Canada, India, Australia and the rest of the Commonwealth.

We did well. We won a couple of the smaller competitions and I was placed 33rd individual shot out of thousands.

"We'll win the lot next year" said Lt. Croyer. The team returned to Bisley in 1963 and did just that, but Corporal S. Phillips did not. I left the cadets late in 1962. Motorbikes, my apprenticeship, exams and courting were taking over.

It was only when I rode back from Bisley that I remembered that my exam results would be waiting at home. Pass and I'd got an apprenticeship for the next five years. If I failed – God knows.

I parked the Frannie Barnett in the shed and walked into the kitchen carrying a big bag of dirty washing - I'd been away almost two weeks. Pauline was in the front room.

The letter from City & Guilds London Institute was sitting on the table in the bay window. Nan and Pop hadn't touched it.

I had passed - second-class, but I'd passed. In six months' time I'd be 17 years old and earning nearly six quid a week (I hadn't heard of overtime yet).

During that first year, only two of the 20–odd apprentices had decided to leave and seek employment elsewhere. All those who had sat the exams had passed. Mr. Cockcroft was pleased, although he was disappointed that none of us had achieved a first-class pass.

"You'll all have to do it next year," he told us. "Phillips, Richmond and Davis will report to United Non-Ferrous Metals, just across Digbeth in Adderley Street. Mr Hall will be waiting for you. Enrolment for the second year City & Guilds course takes place the first week in September at Garretts Green. I'll see you at your factories once a week for an update on your progress and the college will send me a regular report. Your indentures and papers will be prepared for signing in the next few weeks. Well done lads!" He does have a heart, I thought to myself.

Arthur Hall was the Safety Officer and general dogsbody, affectionately known throughout the factory as Brother Hall. A little man with a mass of bushy, wiry white hair, he always dressed in the same shabby suit. But he was a nice old bloke.

"I've got your clock cards and numbers sorted and I'll go through your hours of work and safety in the factory. Then Dave Wilmer, the Senior Apprentice, will give you a tour of the site. You clock in at 7.30 am. Four minutes late and you're deducted 15 minutes' pay. Tea breaks are 10 minutes – one at 9 am and one at 3.30 pm. Lunch is 1 to 1.30. You clock out at 5 pm. From next week the hours of work have been reduced nationally by the Unions, so you'll be clocking out at 4.30 pm." He paused for breath. "It's not compulsory, but there is an apprentice section in the AEU.

"Frank, you will be introduced to Alf Foe, who is the Foreman in the Electricians Shop, and you Steve and Jim to Tommy Carter, Foreman in the Fitting Shop. If you require any help or advice please come to see me. We've got to look after you young lads."

As Brother Hall finished, Dave Wilmer knocked on his office door. Dave was 18, green overalls, a couple of pens and a six-inch steel rule sticking out of the top pocket, which had 'GKN' in yellow letters embroidered on it. His hair was smart and fashionable and his tie was tucked into his shirt.

"How did you get on last year?" he asked.

"We all passed" I replied.

"So did I."

The factory covered a huge area, with four bridges spanning the Birmingham canal system. There were production shops on both sides of Adderley Street and the first floor offices ran from Liverpool Street to Glover Street. After nearly an hour I was completely lost.

Both Casting Shops had massive furnaces, each holding up to two tonnes of molten brass bubbling away at 1000 degrees and waiting to be poured into enormous billets. These would be carried by crane over the canal to the Britannia Extrusion Mill, where they would be cut into three-foot lengths, reheated to 750 degrees and extruded into rod or wire. Dave was explaining all the processes, and we were taking in barely 10 per cent of it.

"You all need to get a pair of 'toe 'tectors', Dave told us. "They are boots or shoes with steel toecaps. Apart from the safety aspect, they'll last longer. Normal everyday shoes will be ruined in the factory. Brother Hall will sort you out."

Frank went off to meet his foreman in the electricians' shop and Jim and I were taken to meet Tommy Carter in the fitting shop. Tommy was a sour-faced man in his early sixties, brown cowgown, collar and tie and a flat cap. In the five years until he retired, none of us ever saw him without his cap or without a Woodbine between his lips. Neither did we ever see him smile.

So in the second week of August 1962, aged 16, I started proper work. Looking around the Fitting Shop, my first reaction was how old all the blokes looked. Micky Plant was in his early 20s and John Waller, another apprentice, was 17, but everyone else was either bald or grey-haired and looking totally worn out.

One exception was Joe Healy, a small sprightly man who wore a bib and brace, which included attached trousers and a separate jacket. I hadn't seen this type of overall before. Joe was the chargehand, and from day one he appeared to take me under his wing. Although he too was in his early 60s, he had a permanent twinkle in his eye and a spring in his step. I soon found that what he didn't know about machining metal was not worth knowing.

"Get Dave Wilmer to take you across to the Bar Mill" he said. "Old Bonehead is falling behind with turning die blanks." Then he went back to his pride and joy, the Dean, Smith and Grace lathe, reputed to be the Rolls Royce of centre lathes.

"You're OK on the lathe, Steve?"

"Yes Mr. Healy" I replied. He turned and smiled. "Joe's the name, son."

The Bar Mill was the other side of Adderley Street from the main works behind the canteen and snooker room, and you approached the entrance across the car park. "You can park your bike there, Steve," said Dave. "That's my A40, the grey one in the corner. Don't call him Bonehead by the way, he don't like it. And don't mess with his pigeons." I wondered why people called him Bonehead and where the pigeons came into it.

The die shop where I was working was a small area enclosed off from the main Bar Mill and extrusion press. Out of the window I could see an enormous horizontal press being fed with red-hot billets of brass which were literally being squashed into long lengths of brass rod. It was just like squeezing toothpaste from a tube, but at 1500 tons per square inch. The tools to produce the rod were called dies, and I was going to make one.

Bonehead was finishing off a die by polishing it with diamond paste. I lifted the 9-inch diameter steel blank and tightened the 3-jaw chuck. I watched the high-speed tool bit traverse along the blank, removing about 100 thou off the surface, and listened to the noise of 1500 tons of extrusion press the other side of the window. I was doing a job.

CHAPTER 4

"Right young man, before you take the riding test I want you read the number plate on that dark green Vauxhall parked 25 yards away."

It was a fine morning early in September and I was about to take my motor-cycle test at the test centre near Wake Green Road. There were no written papers, no pre-training on car parks with instructors watching you slowly weave around cones. This was 1962.

I read out the number on the Vauxhall, answered a couple of questions on the Highway Code, traffic light sequence and stopping distance, and that was it.

The examiner held a clipboard with a Biro attached. "I will stand on this corner. I want you to ride down the road and keep turning left around the block. You will ride past me a number of times. The first time I require you to ride at walking pace, controlling your bike without putting a foot to the floor. The next time you must slow down, brake correctly and bring your bike safely to a complete stop, putting both feet to the ground."

Billy and I had been taken around the route a few times by Alan who had passed a month ago, but it's always different on the day. I badly wanted to pass because I wanted a bigger bike.

Mr Clipboard continued "On the third circuit I want you to turn right at the traffic lights into the road opposite to where I'm standing and again keep turning right until you are back here. During the test you will be required to make an emergency stop." Alan had told us the examiner puts his foot out into the road and claps his hands and you have to slam on the brakes.

"Before any turning you must observe to the rear (motor bikes had no mirrors in those days, unless you fitted them yourself), signal correctly with your arm (no indicators) and keep to the speed limit at all times."

It was 11 o'clock and there was very little traffic. I put on my crash helmet and set off. I rode around the test route, going through all the manoeuvres and waited waiting to slam on my brakes. After three circuits I realised that the examiner had disappeared. Then, just as the lights went green, a bloke walked out in front of me without warning. He was holding a clipboard. Oops. I stamped on the brakes.

"I'm afraid you have failed," he said. "Not enough rear observation before hand signals, and lack of overall observation on the road. A little more experience is required."

Fair enough. Next time I would make sure I passed.

★ ★ ★ ★ ★ ★ ★ ★ ★ ★ ★ ★ ★ ★ ★

The Bar Mill was 200 yards long and 75 yards wide, with iron and steel girder work 50 feet high holding up the metal, corrugated and glass-panelled roof. A 25-ton crane ran on tracks the full length of the shop. At the far end was an extrusion press. The cold bar-drawing benches, the next manufacturing process, were laid out in front.

In the cellar underneath was a rotary furnace which heated the brass billets to 750 degrees. By the time it got round to be lifted to the press above, the billet was white hot and ready to be extruded into one-inch or half-inch diameter rod or bar.

As the hot metal, driven by 1500 tons per square inch of pressure, snaked out of the die it was collected by a man who grabbed the glowing bar with steel tongs and run 25 yards with it, stripped to the waist because of the heat. As he ran he would shake the rod to keep it as straight as possible. The rod would be sheared. As the man walked back he would pass his mate, rushing past him to do exactly the same thing with the next length. Then the first man would take his turn to grab the next rod, and back he'd dash to the shearer. It was hard, hot work.

You couldn't slow down the furnace, so these blokes worked as a team and took their tea breaks and sandwiches together. The process never stopped, as long as the mill was running. There were three daily shifts, 6 am to 2 pm,

2 pm to 10 pm and 10 to 6. The new 2500-ton extrusion press in the Britannia Mill was operated by push buttons, but not this old bugger. Every operation was actioned by huge three-foot levers, just like an old-fashioned railway signal box. Harry would work his bollocks off, pulling and pushing the levers all day.

The press driver was a man called Harry Harcourt. He had the same haircut as all the other men - like a 1950s football star, short back and sides, middle parting, scraped flat to the head. Harry stood there in his blue overalls for eight hours at a stretch, eyes looking everywhere. He needed his men to help him earn his piecework bonus. They would get their share as well, as long as he pushed them. During my first few days in the Bar Mill die shop I would have a fag break from turning die blanks and marvel at how hard this gang of men was working.

Down below there was Clubby the furnace man, loading the billets of brass in the cellar underneath to keep production rolling. As long as he did his job and the red-hot billet was delivered on time, nobody thought of old Clubby.

One of Harcourt's gang poked his head inside the door and yelled "Arthur, get the new lad to nip down below and get the sandwiches from Clubby." Then he disappeared quickly back to the press.

Arthur told me that at the back of the press I'd find a steel staircase down into the cellar. It was 8 am and I'd only been at work since 7.30, but the production blokes on the press had started at 6 and it was now their breakfast time.

I descended into the semi-darkness, where I found a huge circular machine slowly revolving. It was warm without being stifling hot. The furnace had to be well insulated for efficiency and the gas-fired burners weren't too noisy.

Something dark and furry moved in the corner, shooting across the floor. A rat, I presumed. I hated rats. They had said there were hundreds of them down here because we were right next door to the canal. Then I heard a shout. "Yow'd berra hurry up and get Harcourt's gang their breakfast. I ain't gor all day meself!"

A small man limped towards me, carrying two cardboard boxes filled with parcels of white paper bags. In the gloom I could see he was dressed in a striped collarless shirt, a dark waistcoat, trousers and gaitered boots. I grabbed hold of the boxes and rushed back upstairs.

"Nobby usually brings 'em up. but he reckons he's got the shits this morning" said Harry Harcourt. He proceeded to dish out the parcels. His second-in-command was pulling the levers, keeping production going while breakfast was being served.

Each parcel was marked in Biro - S and T (sausage and tomato), B and E (bacon and egg). It got complicated when someone had ordered sausage, bacon and egg

with brown sauce. They didn't teach you this at Garretts Green.

In less than five minutes Harcourt had eaten his breakfast and was back driving. All his gang were either eating or covering for someone who was. Officially they were all entitled to the 10 minutes break, but they took only five. They were on piecework, so the more they produced, the more money they earned. The gang might have cursed Harcourt for making them graft, but they knew he was helping them to earn their bonuses at the end of the week.

Bonehead was a craftsmen who could make a steel punch by hand. A round one was easy, but the squares and hexagons took skill. You hand-filed them with French files, then hardened and tempered the polished punch. Then you punched out the steel die plate to the correct size before hardening and tempering it. The plate would be used to draw the annealed brass wire through - round wire for bolts and screws, hexagonal for nuts. For the last few years this type of toolmaking had been used only for odd shapes and 'specials'.

All the extrusion and cold drawing was done using the magic of tungsten carbide. This material was much harder than the best tool steel and could only be cut or polished by a diamond. A new technique called spark erosion enabled you to machine the material electronically and then polish up the surface with diamond paste. This did not require the traditional skill of the toolmaker.

Bonehead, like all other employees of the time, had no company pension to look forward to. He just hoped that his skill would see him through.

"Bloody hell Steve, slow down a bit!"

I'd been there almost a week, and Bonehead had suddenly realized how many die blanks I had turned. "Go and have a walk about" he said. "Ill show you how to drill them out later on."

The cellar underneath the press fascinated me, despite the rats. It was like another world down there. I walked down the stairs and around the rotary furnace to a small metal table with a couple of wooden boxes as seats. There was Clubby.

"Gimme a minute to load this billet and I'll be with yer" he said, and limped off. When he came back he explained. "Me name's Eric, but I've always been called Clubby on account of me short leg." I looked down and saw that his right boot was built up by some six inches. "Old Bonehead'll drive you barmy, tek no notice of him. Have a cup of tea. I've got a minute or two before the next billet guz in."

That was my introduction to Eric 'Clubby' Barnsfield. Disabled from birth, yet he never lost a day from work in his life, apart from when the BSA was bombed during the War.

For a 10-minute tea break it was too far to walk back to the main fitting shop and I didn't want to sit with Bonehead, so I'd have my breakfast (sandwiches from Nan) in the cellar with Eric.

"That big black rat you thought you saw last week was our cat. Tommy Rushton, Tommy for short, the senior cat in United Non Ferrous" he said. Bang on cue a large, almost black cat stirred beneath the steel table. That's funny, I thought to myself, the Works Manager has the same name. Back then Rentokil hadn't been invented and large factories had no reason to discourage cats. They kept themselves out of the way during the day, sleeping in cellars and corners . At night they hunted the rats and mice. Eric looked after a large family of cats.

"Hi up" he cried "Here comes Horace." I didn't know it at the time, but the original Horace Burton was our Works Director. His namesake, a great big ginger cat with a striped tail, swaggered into view.

"They even cross the road from the main works to visit me when I'm on my shifts. Don't ask me how they know."

Most mornings between 8 am and 9 am a dozen or so cats from full-grown adults to little kittens would attend breakfast in the warmth of Eric's muffle. They were all named after, in Eric's words, "the gaffers upstairs".

Eric lived in a terrace house just round the corner in Watery Lane and looked after his widowed mother. "The two to ten shift suits me the best," he said. "I've got the morning to get me mother sorted, do a bit of shopping and make sure she has a bit of dinner with me before I come to work. I always pop in to see her when I've finished my shift. She says she can't settle till I'm done in the factory. Then I call in the Barrel for a couple of pints."

"The pub would be closed by then," I said.

"The back room's always kept open till midnight to give the shift workers a chance for a drink. The gaffer's all right and there's never any trouble. Anyway, Charlie the copper from Digbeth is in most of the time when he's working the night shift, so everybody behaves themselves."

Eric's favourite stories were about the bombs during the war.

"The Germans must have known we made the raw material for shell cases, same as they knew the BSA made armaments. The nearest they got to hitting our factory was a couple of bombs that landed in the canal. The factory wall and the front of the Barrel were covered in shit, slime, old bikes, even dead rats. Nobody was hurt apart from one old bugger who slipped on the pavement, and he was pissed."

Eric could tell a great tale, but it was now 9.45 and my tea break was over.

"The next operation on these blanks is the drilling," said Bonehead. I had turned about 10 die blanks and he was showing me how to set up the vertical drilling machine.

"I've set up and operated drillers at the college, Arthur," I said, picking up a 1-inch twist drill.

"Yow can't learn fuck all at them places" he replied. "I'll show you the way I've done it for 30 years."

I was beginning to understand why he was called Bonehead.

Each 8-inch diameter blank was drilled in the centre and counterbored on the front face. Then a tapered hole was produced on the rear face, all with coolant running on the tools. Subsequent operations were carried out in the main fitting shop across the road and every day or so (it had been once a week before I started) a battery-operated flatbed truck would arrive and I'd help load all my work on to the back and watch it disappear down to the Bar Mill.

Bonehead kept pigeons. They were his pride and joy.

"'I've won some good money with 'em" he said. "I keep 'em in the garden and me and our kid race 'em. Most Saturdays and Sundays we tek 'em all over in his van." Now I knew why he wouldn't work weekends.

Bonehead seemed a different person when he was talking about his birds. He became less gruff in his speech and manner, almost kindly.

"Come on, I'll show yer" he said. At the back of the shop I'd already noticed a large cage with pigeons in it, but I'd taken Dave's advice and left them alone.

Bonehead's hands were rough from 40 years of hard work, but he tenderly lifted out one of the birds, gently stroking it and cooing. This wasn't the Bonehead I knew. "I had to bring her in on the bus so I could look after her, she ain't bin well" he said. "Nor the other two. I hope they ain't got anything serious."

"Don't the gaffers mind?"

"They can fuck theirselves" he replied, carefully putting the pigeon back. "I'll know they're all right when I let 'em fly round the big shop outside."

This I had to see. I normally took my own sandwiches to work. I couldn't afford the bacon and sausage delights at 9.30 am or a cooked meal every day in the canteen, and anyway I always had a hot meal at night at home. Even in October 1962 you weren't a millionaire on four quid a week.

To have a chat and see Jim and Frank, sometimes I would eat my sandwiches in the "dining room" in the fitting shop. This was an area tucked away in the corner where all the lockers stood. Everyone had a locker allocated to them to keep their clothes and personal belongings in. When you changed to go home you hung your overalls in your locker. About 30 lockers lined the wall and Brother Hall had got my name on one of them. Frank had his own in the electricians' shop and Jim was working in the main die shop in the Wire Mill.

The "dining table" was two steel Morrison air raid tables welded together, extending to almost 15 feet. The variety of "dining chairs" around the table beggared belief. Pride of place went to a rejected and repaired Tommy Rushton high-back leather swivel chair. Current owner: Norman. A battered, oil-stained cottage style-armchair. Current owner: Black Bat. An old leather seat from the front of a Rover 90, nailed to an orangebox, to lift it off the floor. Current owner: Pat Dowelling (Paddy).

There were plastic chairs pinched from the canteen and long wooden planks supported by anything to lift them off the floor. The tablecloth was newspapers, changed on a weekly basis by the new lad in the shop – me. No Page Three in those days, otherwise there would have been a tit for every place mat. Billy Wiggins always sat on the wooden planks, smoking Senior Service.

During the next seven years I was to spend many hours around this table listening to the lives and the stories of men who had worked such long, hard hours over the years, up to 40 years in some cases. They had not contributed to a pension, but they hadn't been given the chance. Would they have done so if they had?

These men came from all backgrounds. There were Irish Catholics, Irish Protestants, Brummies, White Russians, Poles, Arabs. Around this table I began to understand what "them and us" meant.

Walking in off Adderley Street you passed the Security Office, always manned by at least one uniformed guard, descended a small flight of stairs, clocked in, turned right and walked down the dark passageway. The old electricians' shop was on the right, and opposite the lift you turned left into the fitting shop. Immediately on the right was the blacksmith shop. Here, set on a sawn-off tree trunk two feet in diameter and 18 inches high, an enormous anvil was held in position by four steel pegs hammered into the wood.

Alongside a roaring furnace driven by bellows, John the Blacksmith would be crashing his hammer down on to a glowing red hot piece of steel to flatten it against the anvil to the required thickness, or bending it around the pointed pommel. When the metal cooled and didn't flow, John would push it back into the hot coke to be reheated.

He was a small wiry man dressed in a collarless shirt rolled up to his elbows, with a large leather apron that reached down to his shins. Both his arms were muscular, but his right arm, the one that wielded the hammer, was almost twice the size of his left. The original colour of his flat cap was hidden by years of coke dust and grime, but the white silk scarf around his neck was spotless every morning.

He was well into his sixties, and in all the years I knew him I never knew his surname. Later in my training I would spend a month working alongside this friendly Irishman, and it would be the hardest job I ever did.

Years later John made a proper horseshoe, and on our wedding day he handed it to Pauline as we walked down the aisle. She thought it was another cardboard replica and nearly fell over when she felt its weight.

Tommy Carter's office was on the left, with Joe Healy's next door. To the right the wall was lined with workbenches with vices bolted on and tool cupboards underneath. These were the fitters' benches, including the one used by Mack the Welder. The rest of the shop was laid out with lathes, milling machines, radial drillers, surface grinders, universal cylindrical grinders. Same as the college really, but much bigger. The largest lathe was 30 feet long and used for turning the massive steel rolls used for rolling the brass rod.

Walking past Joe's office would lead you to the dining room. While all the men clocked on at 7.30 am, at least a dozen of them would start the day by sitting round the table in their personal chairs, drinking tea, smoking and reading the paper. Not till 7.50 would Joe swagger out and shout at the top of his voice "Come on, you horrible shower. You know what time Caggy gets in". Caggy (Tommy Carter) always arrived bang on 8 o'clock.

★ ★ ★ ★ ★ ★ ★ ★ ★ ★ ★ ★ ★ ★ ★

"I'm telling yer, Bonehead, if them fucking pigeons ain't in their cage by the morning I'm bringing my nipper's air rifle in."

Harcourt was mad. Two days before, Arthur had bought in another two birds because he was concerned about their health. Very early that morning, as they all appeared to be improving, he had let them out to stretch their wings.

"There's five of 'em now, flying and shitting all over the place. This is a production shop, not a fuckin' aviary!" Harcourt shouted above the noise of the Extrusion Press. I'd noticed that he was wearing an old blue canvas cap which I hadn't seen before.

Arthur stood there looking up and shaking his tin of grain to try to coax the pigeons down. They were loving it, swooping down from the steel girders 40-odd feet up in the roof of the Bar Mill and skimming the gang of men running the massive machine below before returning to sit on the crane and peering down.

"I've kept 'em in the cage too long, probably overfed 'em as well," said Arthur to me. All the blokes in the shop were having a good laugh, but old Arthur looked worried to death. He loved his pigeons and was concerned for their safety, flying around in a factory environment.

A couple of other apprentices quickly joined the audience. Frank was in the shop seeing to a breakdown on one of the drawing machines.

"This is a bit of a laugh," Dave Wilmer said. "I just hope none of the gaffers walk in."

When the flock flew down to sit on the rails, Arthur slowly approached them, shaking the tin and quietly talking to them. He reached out to stroke the lead bird, but before he could gently take hold of it all five of them decided to take another spin around the shop. After 30 minutes the show got a bit repetitive, and the audience returned to their work. But as the afternoon went on different blokes kept coming into the mill to watch poor old Bonehead trying to catch his pigeons. I went back into the Die Shop and carried on working.

Arthur never worked overtime, normally clocking out at 4.30 pm every day. But when I clocked in the following morning, I looked at his card. He had clocked out at 7.45 pm.

"They were hungry by then. Anyway I was still at work so I don't see why the fucking gaffers shouldn't pay me" he said.

CHAPTER 5

It was December 1962. I'd finished my three months in the die shop in the Bar Mill and would now be working in the Fitting Shop under the guidance of Joe Healy.

Two months before I'd enrolled back at Garretts Green Technical College for the second year of my apprenticeship. I was attending one day a week and studying for the next stage of the City & Guilds course.

Harry Fisher, the workshop lecturer, was well pleased with all of us and we all thanked him for his help in getting us through last year's exams. "It gets harder every year so don't think you know it all just yet" he told us.

Every evening at 4.30 as I clocked out of the factory, I noticed there were only a couple of other people doing the same. Where were all the rest? There had to be nearly 100 other workers who were not on shifts. The next day Jim Richmond let me into the secret.

"Everybody works overtime. Clock out at 5.30 pm and that hour earns you time and a third. Saturday morning is time and a half. Sunday is double time."

I did some calculations in my head. I wanted to work some overtime.

The following week, by working an extra hour at night and a Saturday morning, I put myself on more than five pounds ten shillings, with a good rise due on my 17th birthday in a little over two months' time.

"You coming to the works Christmas party in the canteen, Steve? It's free beer and they've got a band."

Dave and John, the Senior Apprentices, were talking at the same time. It was 1.15 pm and we were all eating our sandwiches round the metal table in the Fitting Shop. Some of the younger ones were nodding and saying they would be there, but the old blokes were taking no interest.

"We flog our bollocks off for that lot upstairs and all they give us is a fucking party at Christmas" spat Alf George, universally known as Black Bat. "They can stick their free beer up their arse as far I'm concerned."

55

Alf was a highly-skilled universal cylindrical grinder, working to tenths of thousands of an inch, and I was now working under his supervision. He was a staunch supporter of the Conservative Party.

"With the Tories in charge the gaffers earn well and there's always a good supply of crumbs for the likes of us. The Labour lot will ruin the fucking lot of us." Clearly Alf wouldn't be going.

In the four months I'd been working in the factory I had been introduced to all the different production shops and met the foreman, together with the various managers. During the next five years I would be spending up to six months in each department as part of my apprenticeship.

"You want to see the Christmas trimmings they've put up in the offices upstairs" I told my mates. "They're everywhere."

The youngest in the shop was also the "gofer", so as long as I was seen to be carrying something I could go virtually anywhere in the works. I had just returned from the drawing office, and as I walked down the long corridor I had looked into all the different departments - the laboratory, production control, engineering, wages and accounts.

"Why can't we have some trimmings here?" I said, waving my arm around the assorted chairs and tables in the corner of the Fitting Shop. The younger element all agreed, but some of the old men were muttering under their breath "fucking kids."

We took no notice of them. The following day I and another lad hung some streamers we had brought from home across the walls and ceiling above the place where everybody sat to eat their sandwiches. I replaced the newspapers that served as the table cloth and bleached all the filthy tea mugs until they were sparkling. While Joe was out of the shop we hung a balloon with Merry Christmas on it above his office door. Even the old 'uns were impressed. The following day Black Bat bought in a battered old Christmas tree and Billy Wiggins gave me a packet of balloons and six hanging lanterns. Billy Law, one of the fitters, who was over 70 and the longest serving employee – he had started in the factory just after the First World War – said he had seen "fuck all like it in 50 years".

The canteen works party was on the Friday night before the factory broke up on the following Monday, which was Christmas Eve. We had Christmas Day and Boxing Day off, returning to work on the Thursday.

"Worked out bad this year" remarked Dave. "It's crap when you just have the two days."

Pauline and I had missed the college dance because she had been ill with the flu, and as Dave said, you don't bring your girlfriend to the works party, there would be stacks of birds there anyway.

My Francis Barnett was running fine and I had another riding test in January, but this last few weeks approaching Christmas, especially at seven in the morning, I hadn't realized how bloody cold it was riding a motorbike. I ended up covered in frost, my fingers and toes were numb and my knees were locked solid. I didn't know the next two months were going to be the coldest on record.

After jumping off the 13A, the walk to United Non Ferrous Metals took about 10 minutes. I arrived at the door to the canteen just after eight o'clock. On the ground floor underneath were the toilets and snooker room. There was one full-size table and one three-quarter. I'd always enjoyed snooker (in 1962 it wasn't on the telly) and planned to have a game before going upstairs. I was expecting Jim Richmond in five minutes. Jim was a better player than me. We had been practising two or three nights a week after we had finished work.

The double swing doors were locked and the room was in darkness. The main windows on Adderley Street were frosted and you couldn't see through them.

I was sure I had heard something, or someone. It sounded as if one of the cats might have been locked in. I walked through the arch, but instead of going towards the Bar Mill I turned right towards the gaffers' petrol pump, where there was a small window that looked into the snooker room. Peering through with my hands cupped around my face I soon realized what had made the small noise. It was certainly not one of Clubby's cats.

Lying on her back on the snooker table with her dress up around her waist and her toes pointing at the ceiling was one of the senior clerks from the offices.

CHAPTER FIVE

Graham Morris was the pipe fitter and welder, 30 years old and good looking with blond hair and a matching moustache. He was also the best snooker player I had ever seen. Men from the snooker halls in and around Birmingham would appear on occasion, and word would quickly spread round that Graham had a challenger. A skilled man's wages in 1962 was about twenty quid a week, say thirty quid with overtime. At almost 17 I earned about six pounds a week. One night the previous month twenty-odd blokes had watched Graham play best of five frames against someone who arrived with a big reputation. He won the final frame with a 75 break and pocketed 100 Pounds. Graham also drove a top of the range Ford Zodiac.

All these thoughts were going through my mind as I watched Graham practising his very special skills on the snooker table. He didn't even need the overhead light.

Upstairs the band was playing, a few couples were dancing and a large crowd stood at the serving counter drinking. All the younger lads and apprentices were grouped together. I joined them with my beer and looked around the room.

"Should have had a pop group, not this old-fashioned lot," I said to the rest of them.

Tommy Rushton was well over six feet tall, mid 50s, distinguished grey hair with a pencil moustache. Immaculately dressed in a dark blue three-piece suit, he looked every inch the works manager. That's what I want to be, I thought to myself. Because of a bad back Tommy always wore a support which made him stand dead straight with not the slightest stoop. He was going around the room briefly having a word with everyone - production workers, engineers, foremen and all the wives. George Macdonald, the works engineer, was with him.

"They don't have to do that you, know" Mick said. Dave replied, "Them two gaffers are all right. I've known em for over two years and they'll always talk to you."

The two managers approached our small group and spoke to all of us by name, even us new lads, before moving on to another group.

"Who's that lot over there?" I asked Dave, indicating three couples who were very smartly dressed – one woman was wearing a fur stole round her shoulders.

"Three directors and their wives. They'll be pissing off soon, they always do" said Dave.

Graham Morris had completed his "snooker practice" and was drinking with Johnny Price, assistant foreman in the Casting Shop. Pricey was 26 years old and tall with jet black hair. I thought he was a really good-looking bloke. Put a guitar round his neck and he'd be Elvis Presley's double. These two were big mates and a right couple of Jack the Lads. I think Graham was telling him how he had potted the pink earlier, because Pricey was having a right laugh.

We new apprentices went up to the bar together and returned with a fresh pint each.

"You young wire pullers shouldn't be drinking at your age" Pricey said as we walked past them. "Still – get stuck in lads!"

I was enjoying the night. The buffet disappeared almost as fast as the canteen manager served it up. We had pork pie and egg sandwiches, washed down with plenty of free beer, and I was feeling on top of the world. Jim was chatting up Pat, a young girl who worked in the wages office, when out of the blue Joe Doyle tried to punch Tommy Rushton on the nose.

Pricey and Graham were there in a flash. They grabbed hold of Doyle and got him out. "You're pissed Joe. Now fuck off before you lose yer job," Pricey told him.

Me, I managed to get home on the bus – just. The other passengers on the top deck didn't appear to notice a daft young bugger at the back throwing his buffet supper up.

I arrived at work on the Monday, Christmas Eve, at 7.15 am, absolutely frozen as usual. The creases in my second hand Belstaff were filled with frost. I'd been taking it steady because it looked a bit slippy and I parked up under the Bar Mill where it was dry and warm – the car park was open to the elements. I had my rucksack on my back with my old tape recorder in it to play a few pop songs in the afternoon.

All the factory worked as normal until 1 pm, though most of the blokes had a drop of whisky in their tea at breakfast time. At lunchtime everybody stopped work.

"All the foremen have fucked off home, yow won't see Caggy again and them upstairs are having a piss up" said Black Bat. He knew the score. "Healy's all right, he's one of us. But don't you young 'uns fuck about, you'll spoil it."

I was going to a Christmas Eve Dance with Pauline that night and had to meet her at 7.30, so while all the young blokes went down the Waggon and Horses I entertained the old 'uns with my tape recorder. By half past two most of the blokes had returned and were sitting around the table drinking beer or whisky-flavoured tea. All the machines were turned off. Nobody was doing any work this afternoon.

Jim, Frank and Dave said "You coming up to the offices Steve? They're having a party." I took off my overalls and followed my friends upstairs. Every office had music playing and people dancing. Couples were snogging in corners. Beer and bottles of wine were everywhere.

"You're the new apprentice with the motor bike." A very good-looking woman in her late twenties or early thirties approached me, staggering slightly. "I want you to give me a ride." She looked at her colleagues and smiled, then took my arm and escorted me downstairs. Outside the main factory entrance she lifted up her skirt to her waist, showing her stockings, suspenders and panties, cocked a shapely leg over the saddle, gripped me tightly and said "Come on then". Half the office staff must have been looking out of the windows as we rode off down Adderley Street.

We did a couple of trips around the block, with more people gathered outside on the pavement and hanging out of the windows every trip, until we finally pulled up and my lovely pillion passenger gracefully swung her leg off my bike, kissed me and modestly adjusted her skirt.

Where had I seen those lovely legs before? It took me a second to remember. I've been a big fan of snooker ever since.

★ ★ ★ ★ ★ ★ ★ ★ ★ ★ ★ ★ ★

Nan and Pop were going to spend Christmas Day with her brother, my Great Uncle Norman, and Aunt Ada. Mom was working and singing in London and I was spending the day with Pauline and her family. It was a good day. Albert and Ivy put on the usual spread, and although they were all were teetotallers there were a couple of bottles of beer for me.

Apparently it was traditional for them to finish the meal before the Queen's Speech and then have a good walk. I could have done without the stroll across Heybarnes Rec with the wind whistling around my ears, but I enjoyed it.

I stayed the night, sleeping on the settee downstairs with Albert telling me about his experiences in the war until he was sure his daughter upstairs was fast asleep. No courting that night, and not much bloody sleep either.

Albert loved clocks. He had a large wall-mounted Westminster chiming bugger right above the settee, and it kept me awake all bloody night ding-donging every 15 minutes.

The next day, with work the following morning, I thanked Pauline's parents and set off home to Yardley Wood about five o'clock. At the top of Kings Road as I rode across Tysley Bridge, it started to snow. By the time I got home it was a blizzard. I rode at walking pace, with both feet touching the ground. I turned into Chilton Road, down the entry and tucked my bike into the shed.

"I've been worried to death, Steve." Nan was at the kitchen door waiting for me. "You're on the bus in the morning."

This was the start of the freezing winter weather of early 1963, and there would be quite a few mornings on the bus during January and February, together with lots of skidding practice, a few tumbles and always the bone-chilling cold.

In January the weather got extremely bad. The snow that had fallen had frozen solid, and even on the main bus routes there were deep ruts – not too bad for a bus or car, but on a motor bike it was nearly impossible. I spent most of the time trundling along swinging my legs and just touching the road surface. Each morning, by the time I arrived at work I was a block of ice. Then, with a steaming mug of tea in one hand and a fag in the other, I was ready to start up the big Jones and Shipman surface grinder, under the very watchful eye of Alf George.

The die blanks I had been turning, drilling and counter boring in the shop across the road had only one hole in the middle to house the tungsten carbide insert. These dies were for the two small 1500 ton presses, one in the Bar Mill and another at the back of the Wire Mill.

The new Britannia Press was 2500 tons and the dies had two holes. The press, which was so powerful that it could extrude two at a time from a much larger red-hot billet, was in a brand-new purpose built shop called the Britannia Mill.

Every extrusion die had to be finished by being turned on a lathe equipped with a taper turning attachment. It would be heat treated, when the one or two carbide dies would be inserted, and after being allowed to cool it would be ready for final finishing by grinding.

"Before starting the machine you must bleed the hydraulics, Steve" Alf explained. For all his hatred of the working system and the gaffers, Alf cared passionately for his grinders, keeping them well serviced and clean and not allowing anyone to go near them, let alone work them. Dave and John, the older apprentices, together with yours truly, were the only ones for a very long time.

A number of the old craftsmen seemed to welcome the new young lads, happily showing them the tricks of the trade you didn't learn from books and eagerly passing on their knowledge. Others, however, thought we were a bloody nuisance. There were one or two who saw us as a threat to their livelihood and would hardly tell or show us anything.

Alf thought we were in the bloody nuisance category, but while he would never admit it he enjoyed showing us his skills. Within a few hours he realised I knew a little about the horizontal grinder and went off to work heat-treating the dies.

"Steve, slow down. You'll fuck the job up." Alf was concerned. The pile of surface ground dies awaiting the next operation was mounting. "Cut a bit of wind."

Cutting a bit of wind meant leaving the machine running with the grinding wheel revolving at 3000 revs, the coolant splashing and the 36-inch table going backwards and forwards, but without removing any metal. The grinding wheel had been lifted 10 thou off the surface.

"Alf, you could put two die blanks on the bed and grind two at a time."

"Yow've got a lot to learn, young 'un. Just tek it steady for a bit."

I followed his advice and took it steady. I wasn't 17 yet – who was I to show these blokes how to make tools they had been producing for the past 20 years or so? One day I myself would introduce a method that would halve the number of dies that needed to be made – but that was far in the future.

With both the horizontal and universal grinders cutting wind, Alf turned to me.

"I see yow've got a motor bike. I was known as Young George of Smethwick in me scrambling days and I won a couple of races out near Stratford on an old Greaves."

He wore wire frame glasses. His grey hair was scraped back and there were blackheads on his nose and cheeks. With his pipe never out of his mouth, he was not the most handsome of 60-year-olds.

Peter Phipps was an engineer in the Production Office, and he was walking through the Fitting Shop as Alf was telling me of his prowess on a motor bike. "Look at that prat" Alf said. "Left university a year ago, he's on bloody good money, paid if he has a day off and knows as much about engineering as a dead rabbit. It makes me fucking spit. I'll tell yer another thing as well Steve, even a young lass of 16 working upstairs on the staff gets more holiday than me, gets paid if she has a day off and starts at half eight in the morning. I've been here 25 years and I've come to work when I've been fucking dying cos I couldn't afford to lose a week's pay."

I was beginning to understand Black Bat's anger.

Outside, the big freeze continued. My test had been cancelled because of the weather, and I had another date in February. That would probably be better, because by then I'd be 17 and the insurance would be cheaper.

The roads that particular morning didn't look too bad. The snow plough and gritter must have been out early, because a two-foot pile of melting slush was lying in the gutter as I approached the traffic lights on Wake Green Road.

I was doing about 25 mph when the lights changed. No problem, I thought, plenty of stopping distance. But the rear wheel suddenly snaked away. I was surprised that natural instinct made me steer into the skid, but I over-compensated and the wheel swung savagely the other way. The bike went sliding down the road and I ended up head first in a bloody great pile of freezing cold slush. It was all down my neck, inside my helmet, my gloves, my boots, everywhere. I was drenched. And my left ankle was hurting.

"You all right, mate?" A bloke who had been standing at the bus stop on the other side of road was shouting as he ran towards me. Halfway across he went into an ice-skating routine, with his left leg parallel to the road and both his arms flailing about like a windmill. He tried switching legs, but it failed to stop him from hitting the ground hard and ending up sitting alongside me with his arse soaking wet.

"Fucking slippy, ain't it?" he said. "Must be black ice."

My ankle hurt, but I could stand on it. My intended saviour helped me to pick my bike up and get it started. He was rubbing his right knee, and when he

pulled up his trouser leg a nasty blue-black bruise was forming.

"Yow want to stick to the bus in this weather, much safer" he called over his shoulder as staggered back to the bus stop.

I arrived at work on time but I walked into the Fitting Shop looking like a drowned rat. I got my boots off to dry my feet and saw that my ankle had swollen quite a bit. A few of the blokes had a look.

"Definitely busted, six months off work." Pat Dowelling liked a joke. "Ask Joe if you can see Sister Susie when she comes in. Seriously, it only looks like a sprain."

After Joe had shouted at everybody up to start work, I limped into his office.

"Come off me bike this morning on the ice" I told him. "I think I've sprained my ankle."

"Hairy Arse will be in at nine o'clock. She'll sort you out, providing she ain't making Caggy a cup of tea." He finished off his brew before issuing a stores chitty to one of the fitters.

Both grinding machines were busy cutting wind and I was sitting on a large toolbox alongside the Jones and Shipman, nursing my ankle as Alf continued with my factory education. "Sister Susie is a retired SRN and she runs the surgery. Yow know where it is." I nodded. "She makes Caggy more tea in a day than his missus. Silly old sod's over there most of the time. But don't call her Hairy Arse, for Christ's sake."

"No Alf" I replied.

Sister, as she liked to be called, the Nursing Sister of United Non-Ferrous Metals, was Hattie Jacques' double. Big and busty, she stretched her blue nurse's uniform to the limit and beyond. Starched cap on her head, jowled face heavily made up, bright red lipstick. Black stocking legs with sensible shoes. Compared to some of the accidents she had handled in the past (and there had been quite a few), mine was trivial.

Tommy Carter was sitting in the surgery drinking a cup of tea and lighting up a Woodbine as I knocked and limped in. After examining my foot she assured me it was only a sprain, nothing broken.

"Try to keep off it for a couple of days" she said, looking at Tommy. "Ill see to it" he replied.

When I got home I told my Nan I'd tripped in the factory and the nurse had sorted it. I ate my tea and looked at the frost and snow outside. No way was I going out again.

Riding to college at Garretts Green once a week wasn't too bad. It was later in the morning and by now the roads had been salted and it was a bit less cold. The emphasis this year was in the classroom, with less time in the workshop. Harry was pushing the first years as he had pushed us, and was introducing us second year apprentices to the complicated cutting of gears, spiral milling, square and multi-start threads and the dividing head. Even I was now saying "Kin 'ell."

My second riding test was the following week, and the weather in the middle of February 1963 was still cold. However after six weeks of practice I was getting used to handling a bike in these conditions, and the council was getting better at clearing the ice and snow.

Saturday morning overtime was important to me. Setting off from home one morning at 6.45 down School Road, I turned left at the bottom into Priory Road and up into Tritterford Road.

This time there was no twitching of the rear wheel – no warning at all. I totally lost it.

I sat there watching my bike spinning around in the middle of the road. Shit, I've hurt my leg. No-one to help me this time.

After five minutes or so I managed to get to my feet. This hurt. I'd better try and get back home.

I left the bike outside and knocked on the front door. Nan was down in a second.

"Jack!" she shouted. Pop was in the back. "Quick, Steve's hurt himself!"

"I'm all right," I said, as they struggled to get me on to the settee.

Nan returned 10 minutes later, just ahead of the ambulance. She had been to a neighbour to use the phone.

"Can you stand on the leg, mate?" the ambulance man asked. "Now try walking around the chair." I duly obliged, feeling daft.

"You ain't broke it" he said. "If I was you I'd use the bus this weather."

I had my favorite breakfast of fried bread and tomato juice on the settee, but I'd still lost five and a half hours at time and a half.

$\star$ $\star$ $\star$ $\star$ $\star$ $\star$ $\star$ $\star$ $\star$ $\star$ $\star$ $\star$ $\star$

I felt really pleased with myself as I removed the two L plates from my bike outside the test centre before riding back to work. I was already thinking about a bigger machine. Billy and Frank Blake favoured the single-cylinder models from BSA and Velocette, but I fancied the twin-engined Triumphs.

Quite a few of the younger men in the factory rode motorbikes. Terry, an electrician, had a superb Norton Dominator 600 cc twin. Phil had a 500 cc Speed Twin and Bob Scott (who was over 40) had a beautiful Triumph Thunderbird. Unfortunately, for a 17-year-old the insurance premiums for these machines plus the cost of buying one were out of my range for the time being. Sensibility and affordability said a 350 cc.

One Saturday afternoon I paid visits to the two branches of Grays on the Hagley Road and Coventry Road and Vale Onslows on the Stratford Road, accompanied by my team of experts. I think there were five of us.

"The 350 BSA Gold Star is faster than the Triumph 21" Frank said, looking at the two machines side by side in the showroom on the Cov. "Close-ratio box, clip ons and rear-set foot rests. It'll just do the ton."

I preferred the apparent comfort of the 350 cc Triumph, and the fact that it was 105 guineas. The Gold Star was 145 guineas, plus a lot more insurance. The salesman allowed me £35 part-exchange on the Francis Barnett, and the rest would be £75 on HP over 12 months, with Pauline's dad acting as guarantor on the loan. I was as pleased as Punch coming out of the showroom on a gleaming, light metallic blue Triumph with twin polished chrome exhaust pipes, its twin-cylinder four-stroke engine purring like the proverbial cat.

$\star$ $\star$ $\star$ $\star$ $\star$ $\star$ $\star$ $\star$ $\star$ $\star$ $\star$ $\star$ $\star$

CHAPTER FIVE

I'd been working with Alf George for about four months now, covering all aspects of finishing the extrusion dies, heat-treating the steel and pressing in the tungsten carbide inserts, together with a great deal more work that needed grinding in the factory.

After the brass rod had been extruded into straight lengths it was usually reduced in diameter by cold drawing through tungsten carbide. This process imparted an extremely bright shiny finish to the surface of the metal, and most importantly sized it to within two thousands of an inch (0.002").

Some brass rods were sized by rolling through extremely hard steel rolls, and after a while these rolls became worn and had to be ground out to the next size. This was not easy, and even I appreciated that you could not rush this type of job. Different types of grinding wheels were used and stringent procedures had to be followed. I'd learned at college how to ring and balance the wheels, but the ones used on Alf's grinders were bigger, up to two feet in diameter.

"I've kept me eye on yer and yow seem to know what you're doing" he said. "All yow young uns are in a rush, but when you're doing this type of work yow must slow down." He was gently tapping the grinding wheel with a small ball pein hammer before balancing it. "If it sounds dull it means it's cracked, so fucking chuck it. It's got to ring like a bell."

Mounting the wheel on its flanges and inserting the spindle, he placed it on two knife edges that had been levelled on the surface table using the bubbles in the spirit level attached. The wheel slowly rolled up and down the knife edges until it found its natural balance, with Alf adjusting the balance weights in the flanges. Exactly the same as the machine they use when you have a new tyre fitted.

"The grinding wheels are much better these days, but you must be careful" he went on, lighting his pipe. "If one shatters at 3000 revs it's like a fucking bomb. There's still a mark in the wall above the fitting benches 30 yards away from when the last 'un went. If anyone had been in the way it would have killed 'em.

"Another tip, always turn off the cooling suds a good minute before you

68

stop the wheel. If you don't, the bottom of the wheel will hold the suds like a sponge and when you start it again it'll be out of balance. To achieve real close tolerance work you can't stop the wheel anyway, even when you're measuring the workpiece."

Quite a few had told me that Alf was a nasty old bastard, but as we set up the universal grinder together I knew I was getting a wealth of wisdom from the bloke who was better known as Black Bat.

Having a game of snooker with Jim after work, I suddenly noticed he was starting to fill a pipe. "I'm buggered if I'm paying half a crown (12p) for 20 fags anymore" he said. "I can save 10 bob a week smoking this." He tapped the tobacco down and lit it with a Swan Vesta.

He was using one of the modern pipes, with an aluminium stem and a bowl that could be replaced by unscrewing and swapping it for a different size or shape. Within minutes the snooker room was filling up with the sweet aroma of Nutty Flake. Before he took his shot he had a couple of puffs, placing the pipe on the window ledge and returning to pick it up, vigorously sucking and blowing.

This looks a bit like hard work, I thought to myself, taking a leisurely drag on my cigarette. Still, 10 shillings a week is a good saving. I might give it a go.

A couple a days later I sat on the toolbox watching the surface grinder traveling backwards and forwards as I lit my new pipe. It took about five minutes for the machine to grind off the 10 thou from the die blank, so I had time to enjoy my smoke. Alf was on the next machine, puffing away with his pipe in his mouth. It looked right for an elderly man. For a 17-year-old I wasn't so sure. I was also beginning to realise how much equipment you had to carry around in your pockets - a pouch, a tool to pack the tobacco down, the pipe and the matches. I could see some of the other blokes in the shop looking and smiling to each other, but I didn't care - I was saving money.

I wasn't really enjoying the pipe. There was too much messing about, so with Alf the other side of the shop and out of earshot I approached the table in the corner to a chorus of "Here comes Young Black Bat".

When I arrived home that night, Pop was surprised at the gift of a new pipe, hardly used.

Apart from pipes and snooker, Jim Richmond and I loved to dress smart. Both of us being tall – I was six foot five by now - a suit looked good on us, and Jim was an immaculate dresser. So the one day a week we attended Garretts Green Tech, Jim wore a suit. We still had a locker near the workshop and I was putting my helmet and jacket away and putting on my GKN overalls when I heard a gasp from a couple of the apprentices. I turned to see Jim walking down the corridor dressed in a superb three-quarter-length shorty overcoat. It was light grey and flecked with black. His collar was up, he had his hands in the pockets and he was smoking his pipe. He had got the hang of gripping it in his teeth by now.

"Morning all" he said.

"Bloody hell, that's a smart coat. Where did you get it from?" I asked.

"Austin Reed, 12 quid" Jim replied.

"I tell you what mate, I wouldn't mind one of them myself," I answered. I was truly impressed. We all were.

That particular morning we were in the workshop until lunchtime and we were getting to know the new first years who were there full time. I noticed what a difference there was between a fairly confident 17-and-a-half year old and an inexperienced 16 year old. Our year had not only had 12 months under the watchful eye of Harry, but another eight months working much larger machines in the factory. We approached the lathe, millers and grinders with no qualms, whereas the new lads appeared slightly nervous.

"You lot was the same last year you know" Harry said to me. "But they'll come on."

"They ain't got a bad teacher" I replied, nudging his arm.

It was just before tea when someone came into the workshop to report that smoke was coming out of one of the lockers in the corridor.

"Take your time, no rushing about." Harry ordered and led the way out. He made sure it was only a small amount of smoke and it was restricted to the one cupboard.

"Whose locker is it?" he asked us.

"It's mine," said Jim. He took the key out of his pocket and opened it up. He had put his new overcoat in there, carefully folded, an hour earlier.

A large circle of smouldering material surrounded the pocket where he had tucked his pipe away.

Everybody commiserated with him. It had cost over a week's wages, and now it was ruined. Jim hardly said a word the rest of the day.

Out of respect I waited a month before I visited Austin Reed myself.

CHAPTER 6

The freezing weather of early 1963 was now a memory. Spring was here and I was enjoying riding my new Triumph to work arriving at 7.15, having a cup of tea with everyone before getting my hands dirty. I was working an hour's overtime every night, every Saturday morning and regular Sundays.

At 17 my basic pay was over six quid a week, but it was boosted to almost a tenner with the overtime. It weren't too bad being an apprentice.

"Steve, nip into Tommy's office, he wants to see yer" said Joe one morning. I wondered what I had done wrong.

"You're doing all right young Steve, and I've told that prat Cockcroft the same," said Tommy. "He's a right fucking idiot. All the paperwork to fill in on your progress. I told him I ain't got time. If he wants to do it himself he can. You'll have a good report from me and Joe.

"By the way, you're in the Casting Shop with Bob Brown for the next couple of months."

He really was a miserable bugger, but at least I'd got a good report.

Bob Brown was a softly-spoken Irishman, 50 odd, slightly portly with a round friendly face. He was a regular around the dining table in the Fitting Shop, so I knew him. All fitters had a mate to help with the heavy mauling and slogging, carrying or wheeling the toolbox, footing the ladders and generally helping the skilled man in his work. All these blokes, fitters and electricians and their mates, worked as a team, sometimes in a dangerous environment.

Big Harry was Bob's mate. A Brummie, he was as tall as me but at least five stone heavier, with greying hair scraped back and a big face. His great love was his Vauxhall Cresta, five years old, polished to bits and only ever driven from Washwood Heath and back. Woe betide anyone who parked too close to it in the car park.

If it was a fine morning, Bob and Harry would walk down Adderley

Street, turn into Glover Street and into the Casting Shop main gate. If it was raining they walked through the factory.

"I'll introduce you to Jim Cooper, the senior Casting Shop foreman, first" he said. "He insists on talking to anyone new who comes into his shop."

I'd seen Jim Cooper in the snooker room many times, whacking the balls around the table and shouting "That was a fucking good shot!" or "Gerrout o' that yer bastard!" when he had snookered his opponent. He was larger than life in more ways than one - 25 stone and six foot four with a shaven bullet head, open-necked shirt showing half his belly and a white cowgown always hanging open. He was Big Daddy's double.

"Sit down lad. The caff's fucked up this morning, but there's a bacon sandwich going if yow want it." He welcomed me into his office, chucking the Daily Mirror on to Johnny Price's desk. "Watching you in the snooker room, you might be following in Graham Morris's footsteps."

Pricey looked up. "He'll need more than a cue in his hand if he does that."

Jim smiled knowingly at Pricey's comment and spoke more seriously to me.

"I don't have to tell you that this is a dangerous shop with molten metal being poured. If I hear of you running or fooling about I'll kick your arse into Glover Street and you won't be allowed back in while I'm foreman. Do you understand?"

I nodded nervously. "When you've finished your breakfast Johnny will show you round the two shops and you can go back to Bob Brown. Now where's me paper, I'm gooin' to the bog." He was off.

The old Casting Shop looked a dark, forbidding place with walls that needed cleaning and the windows in the roof too dirty to allow any sunlight through. The six furnaces were on ground level in a straight line down the shop, with each pouring nozzle pointing down into the concrete pit below.

The steel, water-cooled moulds were on rails at the bottom of this pit, and when the ton of molten brass was ready to pour the caster, by operating the control panel, would position the mould directly under the lip of the furnace. Then, using a hydraulic toggle, he would very slowly tilt the furnace to allow the liquid metal to pour, just like a cup of tea. It was fascinating. Johnny Price was explaining the mix of copper and zinc to give the correct type of brass, 60/40 or 70/30, and other metal traces that had to be added.

"How does the caster know if it's the right mix?" I asked.

"All the pure zinc and copper is weighed on the big Salter scales over there. When we think it's correct, the caster takes a sample of molten metal from the furnace with this steel ladle and pours it into a small mould. Within five or 10 minutes the lab upstairs gives us the OK either to pour or to add some more zinc or copper. We make up most of the mix from huge deliveries of scrap brass, swarf, cartridge cases from all over the country."

"Bloody hell" I said.

I watched as the liquid slowly filled the mould, the caster easing back the furnace to allow the last few drops to splash over. Peering into the furnace you could see there was still a considerable amount of metal bubbling in the bottom.

"You must always leave some ready to start melting the next load, otherwise you'll damage the furnace" said Johnny. He had answered my question before I'd asked it. "With the help of the water jacket it'll be cool enough to remove in about 15 minutes."

Out of nowhere appeared fork-lift trucks loaded with brass scrap, ingots of copper and zinc. Tommy Best (I knew his name now) was loading his furnace ready for the next pour.

The new Casting Shop was much bigger, lighter and better laid out, with two furnaces each capable of holding 2.5 tons of molten brass. The procedure of casting was the same, but these larger furnaces poured into three moulds instead of one, with each billet weighing 700 kilos.

Bob Brown and Harry had a small area down in the pit near one of these 2.5 tonners, where they had a couple of chairs, a table-cum-workbench and a large tool chest containing all manner of spanners, wrenches, tommy bars and hammers.

"We're out of the way down here and every half an hour me and Harry have a bit of a patrol checking things out," said Bob in his soft Irish lilt. "Anyway, they'll soon come shouting if there's a breakdown. Sort a brew out Harry, and then we'll show Steve the jobs that have to be done on a daily basis."

You could hear the men and fork-lifts moving about on the steel floor above our heads, along with the occasional bang when someone dropped a ladle or one of the long steel tools used for stirring the molten metal. Every time it happened I jumped. "You get used to it," said Harry, handing me a cup.

All the moulds in both shops were cooled by a flow of water. If for some reason the mould got too hot, the billet would get stuck and the usual production method of pushing it out wouldn't work.

All this water was circulated through two centrifugal filter pumps which filtered it clean. Scraping out the gunge and washing the filters was a shitty job, but it had to be done daily. V belts, shear pins, driving keys, shafts and flanges would shear regularly and if the broken part could fall off it would, usually in the most inaccessible, dark and dirty corner of the shop. At least if all the machinery was working you had nothing to do. As Jim Cooper would say, "If the fitters are sat on their arses, my production is running." A sentiment supported by Tommy Rushton. But any breakdown meant getting stuck in, if necessary until midnight.

With my trusty spanner in one hand and a big hammer in the other, I could wander anywhere.

Most casters wore a vest with a leather apron, a cloth cap and light towel around their neck to soak up the sweat, along with leather gaitered boots. Leaning on the rail to stop myself falling into the pit I would watch Danny Williams working his row out (an old Brummie term meaning working exceptionally hard).

Danny was a massive Welshman covered in tattoos, who worked stripped to the waist. After loading his furnace he would sit and have a smoke. Forty years old and strong as an ox, he would pick up the heavy steel bar, 6ft long and 6ins x 2ins with a curved end. When the metal was liquid he would stir it for a minute or so, have a couple of seconds rest and repeat the process for up to 10 minutes to ensure no solids remained. The impurities and scum would be skimmed off the top, revealing the golden colour of bubbling brass at 1000 degrees. The sweat would be pouring from him. No-one had eye or face protection.

One day he handed me his huge heat-resisting gloves and invited me to have a go. I managed about four stirs. Within 20 seconds I was knackered.

"It ain't all brute strength, Steve. Most of it is knack, technique and years of practice." Jim Cooper had come up behind me. "Here, give us the gloves." he proceeded to stir the molten brass as though it was a cup of tea.

The other casters stopped for a minute. "Fuck me, Cooper's doing a bit!" shouted one of the blokes. "Jim, come and do a bit for me, I'm tired," yelled another.

Everybody was enjoying this bit of fun and a break from the non-stop graft. Big Jim was smiling his head off and loving every minute.

"Show's over, yow lazy bastards" he roared. "Get back to work!"

Tommy Best was in the Barrel having a quick pint, but when he returned to his furnace and heard about Jim "doing a bit" he had a good laugh as well.

Health and safety as it's known today didn't really exist in 1963. Very little of this type of engineering takes place in the UK today anyway. It may sound daft, but most of the blokes in the factory above the age of 40 had gone through the horrors of World War Two, so eye, face and ear protection was a low priority.

Anyone working in such a hot environment must take on regular liquid to replace the sweat they lose from their bodies, and Tommy Best was a strong advocate of this principle. Tommy's intake of liquid was a pint in the Barrel while his furnace melted two tons of metal. On a good shift, if he worked hard, Tommy could shift 12 tons of brass and half a dozen pints of Ansells' Mild.

Once he had charged his furnace he would have about 15 minutes before the hard work of stirring and sweating would begin. He was a small wiry Irish bloke, old for a caster in his late 40s, and he always wore a three-button vest with long sleeves. He probably wore long johns to match under his corduroy trousers. He also owned a talking parrot.

★ ★ ★ ★ ★ ★ ★ ★ ★ ★ ★ ★ ★

It was a warm evening in the spring of 1963. Any seriously keen biker would be parked in the car park of Alex's eating a piping hot steak and kidney or chicken and mushroom pie and balancing his tea on the saddle of his machine. There were 40-odd motor bikes of all types there, BSA and Triumph being the most common makes, but there were also plenty of Velocettes, Matchless and Nortons. There wasn't one Japanese make. Though Honda was importing the 250 cc Super Dream with electric start, capable of a comparable speed to a British 500 cc, they hadn't yet really caught on.

Everybody wanted a Road Rocket, a Bonnie or a Norton. Was it because we all loved to keep a drip tray under the engine to catch the oil leaks? Probably.

Alex's was a magnet every night. It stood on a corner opposite where the Apollo Hotel now stands in Smallbrook Queensway. I was in a group strolling around admiring the bikes there when I saw my first pair of cowhorn handlebars. Sweeping up to over a foot high before turning back down and with strips of leather dangling from both grips, they looked amazing. Attached to the front of the bike were chrome crash bars with two spot lights. I'd fallen in love.

"Where did you get 'em from, mate?" I enquired.

"Vale Onslow's on the Stratford Road" the owner replied. I didn't ask the price – it was irrelevant. I had to have some.

Billy's Dad had a garage attached to the maisonette where they lived in Shaftsmore Lane, and all the work on our bikes was done in its warmth, with his father sat watching and his Mom supplying us with tea. Special long control cables for the clutch, front brake and twistgrip had to be made to reach the high bars, but by teatime on the Saturday my cowhorns and crash bars with two spotlights had been fitted.

"Let's go down Smokie Joe's tonight" I suggested.

"You only want to flash yer bike" Frank replied.

"I'm going anyway. I rang that bird we met last week and she'll be there about half seven" said Billy, rubbing his hands together.

"See you later then."

When I got home I deliberately parked on the pavement outside and went in to have my tea. I wanted the world to see my bike.

Smokie Joe's was a famous transport café in Northfield, on the Bristol Road. This was the A38, one of the main trunk roads to the South West and the new M5, which at the time had only two lanes and stopped at Worcester.

Riding out of the city centre, we stopped at the traffic lights at Priory Road. The 30 mph dual carriageway of the A38 lured us on. Three abreast, we accelerated from the lights glancing at each other, the Triumph, BSA and Velocette together. We weren't racing, just having a bit of fun. With no traffic in front of us I glanced at my speedo. It was hovering around 60 mph.

As we approached Selly Oak I started thinking about slowing down. But even with my helmet on I thought I could hear bells ringing. Probably the wind, I thought.

The black Wolseley police car with its roof-mounted bell overtook us just before the road narrowed into the single lane of Selly Oak shopping centre. We parked our bikes at the side of the road behind the police car. As the officer walked towards us, taking out his notebook, I noticed a crowd had gathered watching. They probably thought we were bank robbers being apprehended following a police chase.

We eventually arrived at Smokie Joe's just before eight o'clock and parked up well away from the big lorries and car transporters. The giant Austin works was just down the road.

We walked into the café. Billy's date was sat at a table talking to another girl drinking a cup of coffee

"Lets go up the Lickey Hills" Billy suggested. I didn't want to sit in a café

with my cowhorns and spotlights waiting outside, so off we went. Billy's girl jumped on his bike and her friend sat behind Frank on his BSA. It was almost dark by this time, and my new spotlights, together with the bike's headlight, were brilliant. You could almost see the Lickeys from Northfield.

Standing in the amusement arcade, smoking and looking at my bike, I could hear Billy going through his chat-up lines. "We're going for a bit of a walk," he said after a few minutes. Right next to the arcade was a dirt track that led up into the Lickey Hills and woods. She opened up her handbag and took out a pair of flat shoes. "Don't want to ruin my best high heels," she said. Billy always was a charmer.

Riding back from the Lickeys with all my new lights blazing away I swung into Chilton Road. about 10 o'clock. I just about squeezed the bike through the front gate without scratching my new accessories. That was tight, I thought to myself. Even the path down to the back gate seemed narrower than usual.

It took Pop nearly a week to widen both gates, remove a course of bricks in the shed and fit a new door. Until then, most of Yardley Wood could admire my bike parked in the front garden.

Now that the light nights had arrived my snooker practice suffered because I'd sooner be out on my bike. With two or three others we would regularly have a run to Stratford on Avon, stopping at the cafés in Shirley, or jump on the new M5 down to Worcester, where there was no chance of being caught for speeding because there was no limit on the motorways, yet.

* * * * * * * * * * * * *

One morning before walking round to the Casting Shop with Bob and Harry, I was having a cup of tea in the fitting-shop dining room when Dave asked me if I would be going to the sports day the next Saturday.

"I always go with all me family" Norman the turner said. "It's a great day out. Races for the kids, prizes an' all."

"With all your kids Norman, one of 'em at least has to win summat," said George.

"It's not just our factory Steve. All the group including Haddon and Stokes go. I bet there was five hundred there last year," Dave added.

"And there's a beer tent" said Pat Dowling. Pat liked a drink. He also worked part time in the Rainbow pub at the end of the street.

Strolling down Adderley Street, Bob told me more. "It's a good day out and a bit of fun. The first races in the afternoon are for the children, egg and spoon, sack race, you know the sort of thing, as well as normal sprint races. Old Brother Hall works hard and there's stacks of sweets and prizes. But the best laugh is when the dads and other adults have their races. Specially when they've been in the beer tent for a couple of hours."

In the early 60s all large engineering groups had sports fields, football teams and cricket teams, and all the match results and leagues were printed in the Mail and the Argus on Saturday night.

GKN had a beautiful ground in Bills Lane in Shirley, just off the Stratford Road, with two football pitches, a cricket pitch and a lovely old green-painted pavilion. I'd been a few times to watch the "Wire Works" (that was us) play other factories in Division 6 of the Works League, bearing in mind in those days there were 15 Divisions.

Bro. Hall had a programme of events printed for all the GKN group. After all the races, the Tug of War and the Yard of Ale, there was to be an exhibition football match between United Non Ferrous Metals (the Wire Works) and a Birmingham City 11.

As we walked into the Casting Shop, Danny shouted, "I've a billet stuck in the mould. The seal bust at half six this morning and water's been pissing out for over an hour. The billet's cool but the ram won't shift it."

The looks on the faces of Bob and Harry meant we had at least an hour of bloody hard graft, manually pumping the hydraulic jack to slowly push the billet out of the mould.

The mould was tipped horizontally and moved down the rail track to the end of the pit underneath the furnaces, close to the area where we had our workbench. A 50-ton jack was positioned against the wall, its ram just touching the offending billet, and a four-foot tommy bar was inserted into the jacking slot. With Bob Brown supervising, Harry grabbed hold of the huge bar and started the jacking process. It would be my turn next.

It took almost five minutes just to put the pressure on. Then Harry took a break. "This is a right bastard," he muttered before swinging the bar a couple more times. Together Harry and I manhandled the tommy bar. The billet had moved about 10 inches. Only another six feet to go.

If the mould isn't cooled by the water jacket and overheats, then the cooling molten brass literally welds itself to the surface of the steel mould. After half an hour of all three of us pulling and pushing the handle, the billet was halfway out of the mould. You could see the scar of brass being dragged out where it had stuck to the steel of the mould.

"Time for a brew." Bob said walking to the work bench. Harry and I looked at each other. "Your turn" he said, gratefully sitting in his chair.

A cup of tea and a bacon sandwich cures all. Ten minutes later we were ready for another go. After another half an hour of us all taking turns jacking the billet was almost free. There was only 18 inches to push out, but in the last minute it had stuck solid.

With Bob watching the front of the billet, Harry pulled the four-foot bar backwards and forwards, his whole body straining. Even with my weight on the handle it would not budge.

Then, with a loud tearing screech, the billet shot out like a bullet from a gun. It hit the wall, bounced back and slammed straight into Bob Brown. Three quarters of a ton of solid brass was now lying across Bob's right leg just below his knee, trapping him on the floor.

Harry clambered over the jack. "Steve! See if we can lift it off him!" he shouted. But it was impossible. The billet was too heavy. Bob was deathly white and cursing loudly. "Get up the top and tell Jim Cooper, I'll look after me mate down here" ordered Harry. I scrambled up the iron ladder to ground level.

By this time a couple of casters who had heard the crash were peering over the rails into the pit below. "Fucking good job it weren't hot, it would have killed him, but I reckon it's bust his leg" said Danny.

The door to the office was open. Jim was eating his breakfast. Johnny Price looked up from the paper as I burst in.

"There's been an accident underneath number one furnace and Bob's been hurt," I blurted out.

Both Supervisors were on their feet immediately and running towards Danny's furnace, dreading the worst. Accidents in this working environment were usually serious. For a man his size, Jim Cooper amazed me. He literally slid down the vertical steel ladder into the pit and was beside Bob in seconds.

"How yer doing Brownie?" He said taking hold of Bob's hand.

Watching from above, I realized that Jim was assessing the situation.

"Pricey, get up into the crane and wait. Steve, use the phone in my office and tell Sister Susie we've got a busted leg in the Casting Shop. For fucks sake don't call her 'Airy Arse.'" He looked up at the growing audience and shouted "And you fuckers can get back to work!" Even poor old Bob underneath 700 kilos of billet with a broken leg managed a smile.

Sister Susie came into the shop with her medical bag in her hand. She was quickly followed by two gate security guards carrying a stretcher and leg splints.

Sister Susie very carefully inched down the ladder into the pit where Bob was lying and made him as comfortable as possible with a rolled up blanket supporting his head. "The ambulance will be here in 10 minutes, but we need to lift the billet off his leg before we do anything else" she said to Jim. "I can then put splints on his leg. But how are we going to get him up out of the pit?"

Jim called up his two best slingers. "Don't use the chains, they'll slip," he told them. "Use the new webbing straps." Then he looked up into the roof of the factory and roared instructions to Pricey, sitting 40 feet up in the cab of the 20-ton crane.

Sister Susie was examining Bob arms, neck and leg. "I'm in dreadful pain with my leg" he managed to say between gritted teeth. "That's probably a good sign" she said. "You haven't injured your back. "We'll soon get you to the hospital."

As she comforted her patient, Jim was helping the slingers to wrap the six-inch wide webbing straps around the ends of the billet, trying to avoid bumping Bob. Then with the straps in position he signalled Pricey to lower the huge hook of the crane to within four inches of the loop attached to the webbing. There was no need for verbal orders - the slinger instructs the crane driver by hand signals. By deft movements, Jim was telling Pricey what he wanted him to do.

Very slowly, with everyone holding their breath, the crane lifted the billet. If it slipped it would fall back on to Bob. It was hanging totally out of balance, but it could not be lowered again, because that would have caused more pain. Skilfully Pricey and Jim made sure it was clear of Bob's body before they slowly moved it well away. The straps were removed and the crane was re positioned awaiting the next delicate manoeuvre.

Sister Susie expertly applied splints to the broken leg. "Now, you men carefully lift him so we can get the stretcher underneath" she said.

By this time most of the Casting Shop were hanging over the railings watching as the slings were attached to the stretcher. Bob, assured that he had "only" broken his leg, was almost smiling through the pain. He was lifted out of the pit and up to ground level, where the ambulance was waiting.

"He'll win the three-legged race on sports day, that's a cert" said one of the casters as he returned to his furnace

When the offending billet was lifted out of the pit, it stayed in the shop for over two months, until Bob returned to work. By then someone had painted in large black letters "BROWNIE'S BILLET". Factory humour.

Workers on the clock, as opposed to staff, did not receive wages if they were absent due to sickness or an accident, and sick pay from the state and employer was extremely low, so if anyone was genuinely off work for a week or more a collection was organized. The normal contribution from an adult was about 10 shillings (50p), and the collection was only made in the department were you worked. But Bob was lucky. The Fitting Shop contributed as well, as did all the blokes in the Casting Shop. I collected over 50 quid, swelled by the fiver Pricey and Jim chucked in. Foremen were on the staff.

Joe Healy was the only one not to contribute. "I never do," he said. I thought this strange, because in my opinion Joe was a great fella. He was giving me all the help and advice I wanted when I had to use any of the machine tools to repair or replace broken equipment from the Casting Shop. But I respected his view and didn't ask why.

When I was married the factory had a collection, and there was another on my 21st birthday. On neither occasion did Joe contribute, but he did give me presents that were personal to him and his craftsmanship.

CHAPTER 7

It was late June 1963 and exams were two weeks away. Harry had been right – it wasn't getting any easier. New subjects had been introduced during the term with more in-depth detail and knowledge to absorb, but after going through the previous papers we felt confident.

We were taking Part 2 of the City & Guilds of the London Institute in Mechanical Engineering Craft Practice, and the emphasis was on the theory behind the practice. We still had to produce a machined component to much more exacting accuracy. However, riding to work on Saturday morning, exams was the last thing on my mind, because this was Sports Day. I needed the overtime, so I'd planned to finish at 12 noon, pick up Pauline from Hay Mills and go straight to the Bills Lane Sports Ground.

Bro. Hall had produced a printed programme of events starting at 1.00 pm, listing all the races and age groups with the Moms' and Dads' competitions, including the Tug of War and the Yard of Ale, which started about 4 o'clock. The presentation of prizes was around 5 pm, with the football match kicking off at 5.30. The rumour in the factory all the week was that some of the players from the Birmingham City side who had lost the Cup Final against Manchester City in 1957 would be playing. Bro. Hall knew one of the players, Gil Merrick.

The Wire Works had a good football team, and while I had always played at school level I had not yet got involved in works football.

Johnny Price had been the goalkeeper for over five years. He was a great big strapping bloke who would smack you in the face if you scored a goal against him. Dave Wilmer, the Senior Apprentice, was a skilful inside forward, together with Micky Hassett, whose dad worked in the Wire Mill and was Senior Shop Steward. Jim Richmond played at right half, and at centre forward was a new young lad who had just started in the Wire Mill as a trainee and had scored four goals in six games. At 17 Micky Madden was six foot three. He wasn't fast but at 14 stone he could knock down a brick shithouse if it was in the way. Billy Little, a wire drawer, who had been injured and captured at Dunkirk, had last played for the works as centre half seven years before, but insisted on coming out of football retirement to play against the Blues. He was a big Villa fan. This would be our best side.

As I clocked out and climbed the stairs to Adderley Street I saw there were four coaches parked outside the canteen, with mums, dads and kids milling about and Bro. Hall organizing the crowd. There were blokes in the factory who would not get involved in the social side – the "them and us" syndrome. But most of us appreciated the fact that the gaffers were putting on a day out for all the family, including transport to and from the sports field with entertainment and prizes.

I arrived at the sports ground just after 1 o'clock and in beautiful sunshine I parked up my bike behind the pavilion. Pauline and I went for a stroll about.

The races involving the younger children were just getting under way, and Norman from the Fitting Shop was trying to sort out his five kids in their different competitions.

As skinny as a rake, with a face like a rat and bald apart from a Friar Tuck hairdo, Norman was dashing about like a fart in a bottle. He was just the same at work. He would always try to remove as much metal as possible in one cut on his lathe and make the machine groan and shudder, as other machinists nearby told him to slow down.

Norman had five kids in the races during the afternoon. On top of this his youngest, who was 11 months old, was in the Beautiful Baby Competition which was to be judged by Sister Susie, so he had a bit to do. His wife couldn't do much to help as she was seven months pregnant.

As employees from five GKN factories were present there must have been about 700 people there. The races were well organized, with plenty of eggs and spoons and sacks provided. The beer tent was rocking. By 4 pm everyone was ready for the adult competitions.

United Non Ferrous was favourite for the Tug of War, Tommy Best for the Yard of Ale and Jim Cooper and Charlie Colley for the Three-Legged Race. Charlie Colley was senior Foreman in the new Britannia Mill where the 2500 ton extrusion press was located, together with four large draw benches which could cold-draw brass rod up to two inches in diameter. Located at the end of the shop was a state-of-the-art automatic rod storage racking system. It was one of the largest shops in United Non Ferrous, equivalent to the size of five or six football pitches.

Charlie was a little bloke, only five foot six, slim with thinning white hair and a round happy-looking face with, unusual for a man approaching 65 years of age, bright eyes. But he ran his gang of men with a rod of iron. He would fuck them up hill and down dale for the slightest misdemeanour. Someone had written on the inside of one of the toilet cubicle doors "I don't sit here to count my lolly, I sit in here to hide from Colley". Charlie was also a member of the Magic Circle and always entertained the children with magic tricks on Sports Day, before taking part in the famous annual three-legged race with the six foot four, 24-stone Jim Cooper.

All the children's races were completed and Bro. Hall handed out prizes and sweets to everyone. Every child got something.

Jim Cooper had been in the beer tent for two hours by the time the announcement over the PA system called for the adult competitors. I would guess that a lot of people had witnessed this race before, because a large crowd had gathered around the 100 yard track. Ten couples were tying their legs together, but someone had to provide a chair for Jim to sit on while Charlie lashed their legs with rope. The difference in size between the two men caused a smile while Jim was sitting down, but when he staggered to his feet it was hilarious. The top of Charlie's head was tucked underneath Jim's armpit. His time in the beer tent had left Jim a little unsteady, but Charlie was doing his best to support his partner.

Bro. Hall blew the whistle and nine three-legged racers started hobbling down the track. They fell, got up again, fell down again, bumped into each other, even pushed each other over in their attempt to win the race.

"Right then Charlie, it's time we got cracking," said Jim. He picked up Charlie with one huge arm and strode for the finishing line, swinging his partner along on his hip as a mother would a baby. The other competitors were shoved unceremoniously aside or got a swipe from Charlie's swinging leg. With the crowd roaring with laughter and encouragement, the favourites won by a mile. Just as they did every year.

"I think I deserve a pint before the Tug of War, I'm fucking knackered," Jim whispered to Charlie as he untied their legs. I was slowly beginning to realize the power these foremen wielded in the factory and (in most cases) the respect their men gave them. The managers were seldom seen on the factory floor, and they certainly weren't in evidence on a day like today, getting stuck in and having a laugh with their blokes. Everybody knew that come Monday morning Jim and Charlie would be chasing the arses of these same men and bollocking them if they dropped a clanger.

The Casting Shop won the Tug of War against all comers and two of Norman's kids won a couple of races, but when Gil Merrick, Trevor Smith and Noel Kinsey, three international players, led the Birmingham City 11 out on to the field, we didn't exactly feel confident of winning the football match. Billy Little and Pricey had been in the beer tent for a few, but now they proudly trotted out with the rest of the Wire Works team and proceeded to warm up, passing the ball about and whacking a few shots to Pricey in the goal mouth. The Blues 11 were made up from a couple of current players, three retired professionals and the rest from the youth team.

The kick-off was delayed by five minutes so that a couple of our players who'd had a couple of pints could have a quick pee. They returned to enormous applause from an expectant crowd of almost 1000. Word had got round.

The elderly pros put a foot on the ball, slowing the game down, and looked up with all the time in the world before making 30 yard passes to one of the City's young lads, who skipped round our elderly defence before blasting the ball past Johnny Price. To be fair he produced some magnificent saves and kept the score to a respectable 7-nil at half time.

During most of the first half all the famous Blues players were organizing the queues of spectators waiting for autographs, occasionally excusing themselves so that they could slip back into the action and, in Gil's case, pull off a save before thumping the ball back up the field. Bro. Hall was well pleased, because everyone was enjoying themselves. With five minutes to go the Blues were 11 goals to nil in the lead.

Following one of his saves Pricey booted the ball up field and it was picked up by Dave Wilmer, who with a mighty kick crossed the ball into the direction of the Blues penalty area where Micky Madden should have been waiting. He wasn't.

After the game Micky told us he was worried that he would miss out on getting autographs from Gil Merrick and Trevor Smith, which was why he was standing in the queue with his autograph book and pen in his hand.

It was a beautiful flighted cross from Dave, struck with pinpoint accuracy. Micky was standing there thanking Gil for signing. The ball hit him on the back of his head and spun into the roof of the net.

The crowd erupted. Once Micky realised he had scored, he went dancing around the pitch milking the applause. It's not every day you score against a goalie with 23 England caps.

For weeks after Sports Day young Micky was as famous as the man who had shot Billy the Kid. It was nearly as long before Billy Little could walk again, thanks to his aches and pains.

★ ★ ★ ★ ★ ★ ★ ★ ★ ★ ★ ★ ★

This second year of exams took place two weeks before the College broke up for the summer holidays. All the apprentices in our year spent virtually the full week at Garretts Green Tech sitting three-hour papers in a variety of subjects. In the workshop we had to produce two components, similar to last year but to much closer tolerances and accuracy. The turned part consisted of a shaft that included a machined gear, fully hardened and tempered with two ground diameters, a keyway and two screw threads. Once the shaft had been completed on the lathe it was transferred to the horizontal miller and set up between centres using the dividing head. This piece of equipment would, with the correct gear tooth milling cutter, produce the 30-tooth gear as specified by the drawing. The other part was a 6 inch square plate, 1 inch thick with five holes.

The diameters of the holes were tied to plus or minus 0.001 inches, easily achieved with careful drilling and then reaming. The problem was the geometric tolerance, ie the distance between each hole was tied to plus or minus 0.002 inches – four thousandths of an inch or just twice the thickness of a human hair.

"Need a jig borer for that, Harry" I said during the discussion to determine the sequence of operations.

"Any silly bugger can make it with one of them. You've got to use a toolmaker's button, slip gauges and a face plate."

The one-inch plate was ground flat on both surfaces and then ground on all four edges so that it was perfectly square. Painted in engineers' blue, the hole centres were marked out, drilled and tapped half inch BSF. The distances between the holes would be accurate to within say plus or minus 10 thou.

A toolmaker's button was a cylindrical hardened steel tube, one inch in diameter, very accurately sized and half an inch long. Using a half-inch cap head screw, the button was lightly bolted to the plate, not too tight because its position had to be altered by gentle taps.

A surface table was an extremely flat surface that was used as a datum (reference) for all measurements and marking out. The plate was placed on the surface table on one of its edges and the dimension from the surface table to the top edge of the button was calculated to ensure the button was on the dead centre of the hole that was required. This was checked by a dial indicator reading from a carefully arranged stack of slip gauges. It was repeatedly checked in both planes and axis, tapping the button until it was bang on centre before the screw was finally tightened.

Slip gauges are one of the most accurate pieces of measuring equipment in the workshop. They were kept in their own felt-lined compartments, secure in a wooden box with each one marked as to its thickness. A standard set would contain about 100 pieces from 0.005 inches thick up to 3 inches. Using combinations in the set, virtually any dimension could be set up. Each slip was so accurate that by sliding them carefully together they would "stick" or ring together.

Now one hole was correctly positioned, the plate was mounted on a face plate on the lathe and slowly revolved, ensuring by using the dial indicator that the toolmaker's button was running perfectly true.

The button was removed, a drill inserted in the tailstock and the hole drilled. Again to ensure the hole was concentric (a drill can wander), two cuts using a boring tool were made, leaving 10 thou of metal to be removed using a reamer. These procedures would ensure the hole diameter was accurate and the position of the hole relative to the other holes would be to the tolerances specified on the drawing. I hoped! Only another four holes to produce.

As in the previous year, Harry was on hand to help and advise if necessary and at the end of exam week all our group were confident.

"You bloody should be, you've been at it for two years now" he told us. Looking at some of the first-year apprentices' faces, they looked worried to death. Just like me 12 months before.

United Non Ferrous would be breaking up for the annual shutdown on the coming Friday. The Tech was shut until September and because I worked in the toolroom/Fitting Shop (ie not production) I could have my holidays outside these main two weeks. It suited the factory, because it gave the maintenance crew, fitters and electricians the chance to get the major jobs done while production was halted. It certainly suited me, because Bob Brown was still off work and Harry his mate had told me there would be stacks of overtime during the shutdown.

"I practically doubled me wages them two weeks last year" he said, walking down to the Casting Shop. "Mind you, it's fucking hard work. All the moulds have to be wire-brushed out. New seals have to go on the water jackets and nearly every nut and bolt has to be checked. But Cooper lets us have a couple of labourers for the really shitty jobs, so it ain't too bad.

"The week before you break up really bang in the overtime, that's pudding week, and you'll get them wages just before you go on your holidays."

Double wages would suit me a treat, I thought. Immediately after the shut down in the second week of August, Pauline and I were riding down on my bike to stay with her Auntie Margaret in Weston Super Mare for a week's holiday and the extra money would be more than useful.

While I was officially attached to the Casting Shop for the next few months, Joe Healy was regularly pulling me back into the machine shop.

"You'll learn more up here than you will down in that mucky hole," he explained. "Plus the fact that you're beginning to know what you're doing and we'll need extra machinists during the shutdown. You don't mind a bit of overtime, do you Steve?"

"No Joe" I replied.

I had told Nan and Pop that for the next two weeks I'd be getting home late from work and also I'd be going to Pauline's for my tea on some nights. How did we manage without phones?

Big Harry was right, it was "effing hard work". Starting at 7.30. every morning, clocking out at the earliest at 6, the latest 10 (which included a free pie and chips) I worked through the shutdown. I was seventeen and a half, young and strong and loved it. There were no showers at home, but there were some in the Casting Shop, so every night I'd have a shower, get changed into fresh clothes and then if I wasn't going to see Pauline I'd pop into the Wagon and Horses for a pint. The usual gang from the factory would be there, playing crib or dominoes. There'd be Graham, if he wasn't practising snooker, Mack the welder, Pricey and a couple of others.

I enjoyed a pint. Even though I was under age, at my height I could get away with walking into a pub and ordering a beer. But because I'd already come off my bike a few times and knew from experience how hard the ground was, I would only have one.

During these stop-offs on the way home I began to realise that some of these blokes were in the pub for at least two hours every night before going home, and in the half hour it would take me to drink my pint they would have at least two. One man would regularly drink eight pints and then drive home to Alcester 20 miles away and have a quick one in his local before settling down for his evening meal. To my knowledge he never had an accident in the time I knew him. The breathalyser was still almost 10 years in the future.

Quite a number of employees on the clock, be they production or maintenance, did not take their full holiday entitlement. A few of the old fellas, particularly if they lived on their own or with an aged parent, would sooner earn an extra two weeks' money. OK, they received holiday pay, which was a legal requirement, but they were not interested in going away. They all moaned about the income tax they paid during this period, regularly going up to the wages office and complaining to the supervisor.

Arthur Twamley was of this persuasion. He was a really great old bloke, a big friend of Joe Healy, wore the same bib-and-brace overalls and operated the shaping machine. He was tall and slim, again with thinning white hair, and while he suffered from a slight stoop due to a bit of a humped back his major problem was gout, in his thumb joint.

"It's like toothache in yer 'and" he would tell me. "I'm lucky really I only get it the one hand. If it was both I'd have to pack it in and goo on the sick." He was quietly spoken and rarely swore and in all the years I knew him he never went on the sick. But because of his service Tommy and Joe would allow him "special holidays". Up until about four years earlier Joe was the only bloke in the shop who could operate the shaper and he would cover for Arthur. The arrival of us apprentices eased the situation because all us young lads knew the basics of this particular machine and could help out.

He had never married, and since the deaths of his parents he had lived in a council flat 30 minutes walk from the factory. His local pub was the White Tower on the corner of Landor Street. He enjoyed his Woodbines and mild ale, but his passion was the horses.

"I can only afford a couple of bob a day, but I do splash out a bit on me holidays" he confided to me as he was showing me the next job. By studying the papers he would know which race meetings were going to be televised during the factory shutdown and would book these days off as holidays.

Arthur's days on holiday all started with a lie-in till about nine o'clock and a bit of breakfast in the local café studying the Sporting Life and any other information he could gather before he returned home for a wash and shave. He would put on his suit, collar and tie and with the papers tucked under his arm stroll along to the White Tower, arriving half an hour before the first race so he could have a pint with his pals before placing his bets.

Listening to Arthur explain all this, I began to realize that all these old blokes were different in their outlook on life and what they enjoyed away from the daily grind of working seven days a week. I also became aware that a lot of pubs totally ignored the hours of opening. In 1963 the pubs closed at 2.30 in the afternoon, but at most meetings the last race was usually 5.30.

"Never a problem" Arthur used to say. "The bookies' runner was there all afternoon and nobody missed out on a bet, but you must get your bet on 10 minutes before the off to give him a chance to nip round the corner."

So with the windows open in the smoke room, the television showing the horses parading in the ring prior to the off, a Woodbine and a pint of mild on the table, Arthur was on his holidays.

I was never a betting man, apart from the National or the Derby, but over the years Arthur gave me two horses, both with the same advice: "The odds are low but put the fucking lot on. All you can afford." He never swore, usually. Sea Bird the Second and Nijinski didn't swear either, but they could run. They were two of the best Derby winners ever.

Nearly every gambler I've met, then or 45 years later, would tell you how much they'd won but never how much they'd lost. If there wasn't a televised race meeting, Arthur would be working. If I asked him how he had got on the previous day he would reply "not too bad" or "did all right." I soon began to realize that "not too bad" meant he had lost a couple of bob and "did all right," meant he had won. I deduced this because he used to give a couple of his mates in the shop tips, and old Joe used to tell me when Arthur had a winner or two because he would have a bet following his friends' advice.

Over the two-week shutdown, Arthur would probably have five or six "days at the races" as he called them. According to Joe Healy there were more days of "did all right" than "not too bad".

Most of the time Arthur's stake was shillings, but he must have splashed out a bit one particular Wednesday because Joe whispered to me that his mate had given him four horses that stood a decent chance. He advised a rollover, where any winnings from the first horse goes on to the next and so on.

"Keep it to yourself Steve, you know Arthur don't like blokes knowing, but I won over 50 quid yesterday and me stake was only five shillings" whispered Joe as we walked to the lathe. I would like to have won 50 quid, but I'd never been really interested in gambling. However, in the lunch break after I'd eaten my sandwiches I went over to the shaping machine and sat alongside Arthur for a smoke.

"I'm going to Weston for a week's holiday on Saturday" I told Arthur, accepting one of his Woodbines.

"I'll be back at work then, but I've enjoyed me break" he replied. "I don't give you young 'uns tips because it's a fools game, specially at your age. It's all right for us old buggers, but you listen to me – there's only one winner, and that's the bookie. Any road, I did all right yesterday and yow ain't a bad lad, so when you're in Weston with your girlfriend have some fish and chips on me." He quietly slipped a pound note into my hand. "And don't tell no bugger!"

He really was a great old bloke.

"I know you only have a couple of bob a day on the horses in the year" I said. "But you mentioned you splashed out on your holidays?"

Carefully looking around the Fitting Shop, he dropped his voice to a whisper.

"When I'm on me holidays I bet a minimum of a quid. Even Joe don't know that" he said.

I calculated his winnings at £200, but I didn't say a word.

In later years Arthur and I would become pals, having a drink after work on Saturday and Sunday mornings. I would drop him off at the White Tower, or when the council rehoused him out at Bromford Bridge, on the site of the old Birmingham Racecourse, I'd leave him in his local, the Finishing Post. I had a car by then – Arthur would not have made a good pillion passenger.

I also had a house, in Kingsbury. For years I would pick up Arthur at seven every morning outside the Winning Post on the way to work. He really was a great old bloke.

The factory would start back on full production on the Monday. I broke up the previous Friday ready for the off to Weston the next day. My Triumph 350 cc "21" had a chrome rack behind the saddle which held a holdall strapped down with bungee cords. Most importantly, I had some serious wages in my pocket. Two weeks' holiday pay (basic) was only £13, but the hours I'd worked the week before (Pudding Week) gave me another £11 - £24 for my holidays. I'll never spend all that, I thought. Anyway Arthur had treated me to one night out, so I was confident of bringing some money back.

In the summer of 1963 the M5 finished at Tewkesbury, so we continued on the winding road of the A38 through Bristol, down to Weston Super Mare and Aunty Margie's house between Weston and Uphill on Sea. Her husband Revers was a local Jack-the-lad whose family were involved in all the donkey rides, fairgrounds and fish-and-chip shops on the front.

Auntie Margie was the youngest of Pauline's mum's sisters, and at 33 years old she had four children, so the house was always busy and loud. While Auntie Margie welcomed us with open arms, I had to sleep on the floor in the dining room while Pauline shared a bedroom upstairs with one of her cousins. Not much courting this holiday, I thought to myself.

The weather enabled us to spend a couple of days on the beach and in the large swimming pool on Weston Promenade. We also explored the coastal resorts of Brean and Burnham-on-Sea, together with the inland beauty spots of Cheddar Gorge and the Mendip Hills. The bike never missed a beat and I thoroughly enjoyed the freedom it gave us to explore the rolling hills and the narrow single-track lanes deep in the Somerset countryside. We discovered a small village called Sexey, which boasted the Sexey Arms Inn and even a girls' school – the Sexey Girls' School! Perfect.

On a couple of evenings Revers and Margie took us to the local Working Men's clubs in the town and a local pub specializing in "proper cider", as Revers described the cloudy, thick liquid that was served up in a pint glass. I didn't match him pint for pint, but I didn't embarrass myself.

The week flew by, with no thoughts of work or studying until we were on the way back, when I wondered if my exam results would be waiting. I dropped Pauline off, had a quick cup of tea and set off home.

I'd only got a first-class pass - the highest result achievable! I was pleased big time.

"Me and yer Pop are so proud of you, Steve," said Nan, hopping from one foot to the other. "Tell him, Jack!"

Pop took his pipe out of his mouth and cocked his head to one side.

"Sup me gum, yow've done all right. Me and yer Nan always knew yow'd ger on. Well done son." They both had treated me as their own son all of my life.

Pop continued, "After our tea me and your Nan are meeting your Uncle Norman and Aunt Ada in the Dog and Partridge, it's our regular Saturday night out and your uncle would love to hear how you're doing with your exams." So just after 8 pm the three of us strolled down Chilton Road, across the Green of the Haven, down the gulley through to Priory Road and went into the smoke room of the Dog and Partridge.

I saw Nan suddenly stop and whisper something to Pop. "Don't be daft, Glad. 'course he's old enough, he's bin at work two years. The usual, Steve?"

With three pints of mild and two Sam Browns in our hands, my Nan, Pop, Great Uncle Norman and Great Aunt Ada toasted my success.

Uncle Norman was in his late 50s and still running a successful painting and decorating business. He was extremely interested in how I was doing. "I congratulate you on your achievement, young Stephen" he said, putting his pint on the table. He was always the gentleman. He would continue to take an interest in my career for another 40 years, and occasionally we would have a pint together in the Colebrook Bar. He died five months short of his 100th birthday.

Like my Nan and Pop, they were lovely people.

CHAPTER 8

It was August 1963, the holidays were over and I was back at United Non Ferrous Metals to start the third year of my apprenticeship. At the meeting at Haddon and Stokes with Mr Cockcroft, it seemed all our year had done well and he was well pleased.

"You all know you have to enroll for next year at Garretts Green Tech during the first week in September. Keep up the good work" he told us, beaming, thumbs tucked behind his red braces. "Steve, before you go across to the factory can I have a word?" It can't be a bollocking, I thought to myself, I've done bloody well.

"These three young lads have just completed the first year at the college and will be working in your factory. Can you take them to Mr. Hall?"

"Yes, Mr Cockcroft" I replied, suddenly feeling quite superior.

A very tall lad with dark curly hair and an innocent face introduced himself as Doug Smith. "We've seen you in the college" he said. "You're Steve. What's the factory like - is it all right? What's the blokes like? I can't wait to get started."

The old buggers in the factory are going to love this fella, I thought to myself s I strolled down Adderley Street casually smoking. After all, I was nearly a Senior Apprentice.

The other two apprentices were a little quieter. Kevin was a small lad with thin brownish hair and sharp pointed features, who was going to be an electrician. Bryn Jury was not tall either but he had a mischievous face with friendly eyes. His father Arthur worked in the Wire Mill and I knew him as a good bloke. Both Bryn and Kevin were aspiring Mods.

"Come back in about an hour Steve, I want you to show the new lads round" said Bro. Hall. "I've cleared it with Tommy Carter." That's an easy morning, I thought.

All three were full of questions, regarding literally everything from working conditions and wages to how the foremen and the older blokes would treat them. I answered them as best I could, trying to remember if I had asked so many questions a year earlier. Surely not.

For all his open and trusting personality Doug was like a sponge, absorbing every scrap of information as we toured every department on the site. We stopped in the Wire Mill so Bryn could have a few words with his dad, and just before lunch I returned the trio to Bro. Hall's office.

As we passed Tommy's office in the Fitting Shop he called me in. "Steve, have a seat for a minute" he said. He offered me a Woodbine before lighting one of his own.

"Brownies starts back on Monday. You've been in the Casting Shop for six months and everyone says you've done a great job. I've even filled in your report that that silly bastard Cockcroft wants done."

"Thanks Tommy" I replied. He went on: "The next shop you'll be in is the Britannia Mill, working with Harry Hanson and Bill Casey. You know them two fitters, don't you?" I nodded. "But for the next couple of weeks Joe wants you in the Fitting Shop to give him a hand. We've got a couple of new lads started."

Walking round to the steel "dining table" in the shop where all the blokes were eating their sandwiches, I was met with a chorus of "Yes Mr Carter, no Mr Carter, three bags full Mr Carter, ta for the fag Mr Carter!" I tried to explain, but gave up with a shrug. I'd learned a long time ago that you can't stop blokes taking the piss.

I didn't particularly enjoy that week because Joe put me on a really old centre lathe with exposed flat leather driving belts that slapped and rattled together. It was bloody hard work to operate and extremely difficult to achieve accuracy or a good finish.

"Any daft bugger can mek a good job on a new machine. You need to know what you're about on an old 'un" Joe told me. "So stop yer moaning."

Any piece of equipment that broke or was damaged throughout the factory was replaced or repaired in the Fitting Shop. It could be anything from a foot-long drive shaft to a huge roll three feet in diameter and six feet long. The old rattlebox I was on could handle up to a foot in diameter and three feet long, but it had a Coventry die head attachment on the tailstock to produce long threaded tie bars. I hadn't done this before, so I suppose I was learning, but I still didn't like the machine.

Just across the gangway was a vertical milling machine, occasionally operated by Billy Wiggins. I say occasionally, because Billy was a Birmingham City Councillor and Chairman of the City Transport Committee, so he very rarely came to work. When the opportunity did arise I would sit with him during break times and listen to his stories.

Billy was six feet tall and 18 stone, with thinning pure white hair scraped back and the remains of a centre parting. He had a large red face and the biggest ears I'd ever seen. He always wore a collar and tie underneath a brown cowgown, and he was never without a Senior Service between his lips.

Billy Wiggins was a great old bloke and in my opinion was honest in his tales. As opposed to following the "management trail" on completing his apprenticeship at the Austin Motor Works in Longbridge, he had become more and more interested in the Labour Party and Trade Union.

For many years he was the Convener (Senior Shop Steward) of all the Unions at the Austin. "But then I got interested in proper politics and won a seat on the Council" he chuckled.

Billy was an acquaintance of Tommy Rushton and the directors of United Non Ferrous and he joined the factory on the proviso that he did not get involved in any union business but could continue the busy schedule demanded by Birmingham City Council.

Billy was sitting on the bench behind the miller watching the smoke from his fag drift. "I won't attempt to influence your thoughts," he said. "You'll make your own mind up, but don't take a lot of notice of old Black Bat. He's Tory barmy and where's it got him? Bitter and twisted with a terraced house in Smethwick."

Every Friday lunchtime after we had finished our sandwiches Billy would say to John Waller, the Senior Apprentice: "Check the tyre pressures and oil in the car for me please, I can't get down to it these days."

John would walk across to the car park and drive Billy's beautiful Consul 375 into the works garage underneath the canteen, where Bert Phillips, the Managing Director's chauffeur, would help him to make sure the Consul was up to scratch.

On the days Billy was at work he always started the morning sitting on one of the long planks around the "dining table" with his cowgown on and a Senior Service in his hand, usually dozing. It was 7.15 am, but we wouldn't be starting until 7.55 anyway.

We now had, including yours truly, six young apprentices who regularly arrived early to have a smoke, a cup of tea and a cadge over someone's shoulder of the Daily Sketch or Mirror. I guess we made a bit of a noise and ruffled the old 'uns' feathers, especially at half seven in the morning.

Billy Wiggins took a long drag of his fag, looked up and watched the smoke rise. There were 20-odd lads and blokes sitting around the table, pulling on overalls or drinking tea. "I tell you lot, I've got 18 months before I retire. When I've packed up on the Friday night, me and the wife will have a lovely weekend with family and all meals out." Billy was getting into his stride. "I'll tell you another thing. I'll go to bed on the Sunday night and set the alarm clock for the usual time of 5.30 am, same as the last 50 years."

Billy was wide awake now, lighting up another Senior Service. He lowered his voice. "I've got a five-pound lump hammer in the shed and after I've set the alarm I plan to tuck it under the bed."

By now everybody was looking and listening to Councillor Wiggins.

"When the alarm goes off I will slowly reach under the bed, grab hold of the hammer and smash the bloody clock to bits." He looked at his audience and joined their smiles. He lit another fag as Joe shouted us all to make a start. "Caggy'll be here in five minutes."

Unfortunately, as in so many cases, Billy Wiggins never got to smash his alarm lock. He died of lung cancer 12 months later. I helped with his collection.

The two weeks I spent in the Fitting Shop before going to the Britannia

Mill was a bit of a bonus, because I was involved around the "dining table" during breaks when the new apprentices began their initiations. Frank, Jim and I had all been through it last year, but young Doug took the biscuit. It began slowly, so it was not obvious to Doug, and we all appeared serious, pretending not to take too much notice.

Pat Dowling was a fitter specialising in overhead hoists and cranes. A sharp-witted Irishman with twinkling eyes, he had historical connections with Michael Collins and the troubles of the 1920s, but that had been a long time ago and although some of the other Irish blokes had Union Jacks tattooed on their arms I never witnessed a problem. Not in 1963 anyway.

"Doug, can you nip down the stores and ask Mr Roe for the gaffer's deckchair? I'll show you where to put it up on the roof. He likes to sit up there for an hour at lunchtime" said Pat.

Doug took the deckchair up on to the roof and brought it down again every day for a week. Nobody said a word.

"Doug, take the sack truck down to the stores and ask Mr Roe for a long weight."

"Yes Pat" Doug replied, trundling off with his truck looking as pleased as Punch.

"I'll have to look for it son and I'm a bit busy, but have a seat. I shan't be too long." The storeman only had to put up with this daftness for a couple of days, so he entered into the spirit.

After 30 minutes or so he asked Doug if he'd like a cup of tea. "Yes please Mr. Roe."

As Doug was finishing his tea sitting outside the stores, another young lad from the Wire Mill came up pushing another sack truck.

"Me foreman's sent me for a long weight, he told me not to be all day about it" he said to Doug.

The penny finally dropped when the newcomer had also been given a seat and a cup of tea and asked Doug how long he'd been waiting. By this time 40-odd blokes in the Wire Mill, which was in full view of the stores and was famous for the workers' singing, were in full song. "Why are we waiting, oh why are we waiting, oh why are we waiting, oh why, why, why..."

The two young lads looked at each other and sheepishly trundled off with their trucks.

It really was great working in a big factory. Well, that's what I had told Doug Smith two weeks ago, and he'd believed me then.

"Before you have your break Steve, there's a new turner starting on Monday, so you can report to Charlie Colley in the Britannia Mill next week. Thanks for your help" Joe said as I passed his office, tea mug in hand on the way to the Fitting Shop "dining room".

Everyone was sitting in their own particular seats, a varied assortment from chairs to long benches. During my 15 months in the factory I had staked my claim to a discarded typist's swivel chair from the offices. With a bit of welding it was as good as new, even though one castor was totally knackered.

"How the fuck can you have a one-man band?" said Pat Dowling, smiling and looking around the lads and blokes in the Dining Room. "Bejasus, if there ever was such a beast he'd surely be seen in Dublin." He lowered his voice. "I've seen leprechauns playing flutes, Paddys banging drums, but may the Pope strike me dead I've never seen a one-man band."

I'd missed the start of this lunchtime topic, but apparently young Doug Smith had mentioned a one-man band.

"Honestly Pat, he was busking in London. My Mom and Dad have got relations in Putney and we all had a day shopping in the West End where all the posh shops are. This bloke was stood on the corner of Regent Street."

Doug was really serious. So were all the rest of the "diners".

"How d'yer mean Doug? What did he play?" I asked. This could be better than a long weight, I thought.

The old 'uns were nodding off. They had eaten their sandwiches and they had probably heard this one before. But had they actually seen a demonstration, albeit in mime? Perhaps not.

"He plays a guitar, a mouth organ, a kazoo, a trumpet, a big drum and four cymbals." Doug was passionate. "I'll bring the snap me Dad took in tomorrow."

"You know what I think?" Pat had finished his sandwiches and gave his mate a nudge. "The bloke's got a tape recorder round the back."

"No he ain't" said Doug.

Billy Wiggins spoke up. "I saw a busker in London once when I was there for a Labour Party conference. And there was this bloke trying to get out of a locked and chained sack before he was chucked into the River Thames. I tell you what, he was brilliant. But there weren't a one-man band."

"Honestly, me Mom and Dad saw him." Doug was standing up now.

"Well, how did he play all the instruments at the same time?" I asked. Almost 20 blokes looked expectantly on. Doug started to explain about the guitar, the frame holding the mouth organ, the drum operated by the foot etc.

"Stand on this box Doug, we can't see what you mean." Pat encouraged.

Doug went into top gear, strumming air guitar, trumpet, kazoo, lifting his foot to play an imaginary drum on his back and waggling his elbows behind his back to play invisible cymbals. "Toot ta toot ta toot!" he went. "Oh when the saints, oh when the saints, oh when the saints go marching in…"

By now everyone was clapping and singing along, tears rolling down their faces, roaring with laughter. Joe came out of his office and shook his head.

I sneaked a look at Black Bat. The miserable bugger was actually laughing. It was one of the funniest things I had ever seen.

Halfway through Doug had sussed the joke, but as he told me later. "Bollocks. I was having a good laugh anyway. They won't catch me again." He was a great lad.

"I say Billy, that bloke tied up in the sack, did he get out before they chucked him in the river?" enquired Pat.

"No, but as he swam ashore soaking wet I heard him say to his mate "Sod this for a game of soldiers, I'm gonna be a one man band."

Billy smiled as he lit up.

★ ★ ★ ★ ★ ★ ★ ★ ★ ★ ★ ★ ★

"Have you seen the fog Steve? It's really bad. There's talk that the gaffers are going to let us leave early," said Ernie Brown as I sat down for the afternoon tea break. Ernie was a fitter's mate to Harry Hanson. It was November 1963 and I had now been in the Britannia Mill for a couple of months. Having ridden a motorbike all through the previous winter, the worst since 1947, I thought a bit of fog wouldn't bother me.

I'd received a message that there was a phone call for me in the main gatehouse. By the time I got there, Pauline had been hanging on for five minutes.

"Nearly all the buses have stopped running," she said. "I've phoned my Mom and Mr Taylor says I can finish early."

Pauline worked in the Export Department of Wilmot Breeden in Oxford Street, just off Digbeth, opposite the coach station.

"I'll pick you up. See you in a bit" I said, putting the phone down.

Mr. Cadwallander was the Senior Security Officer. "Everybody is going to walk home. Apart from the shift workers, the management have given all the staff permission to bugger off, so you can all clock out." He was a friendly, plumpish man, proud of his uniform, ribbons and cap with a shiny patent leather peak. The three stripes on his arm were from his army days as a sergeant.

The whole of Digbeth was blocked solid with cars and buses, with visibility about five yards, so I took the back streets to Oxford Street. I found it easy on my bike. With Pauline on the back we set off slowly weaving in and around the stationary traffic. The roads were wide enough not to be troubled by oncoming cars until we turned off the Stratford Road towards Yardley Wood

The car drivers had their heads hanging out of their windows and if they were moving at all it was slower than walking pace. Even with my visor up I could hardly see a thing. With both feet touching the road I might as well be walking myself.

At Swanhurst Park I pushed the bike to the top of Tritterford Road and rolled it down to Priory Road. I got home at about 8 o'clock.

We used a public telephone to call Pauline's parents (they were on the phone now) and thawed out with pie and chips, watching the news about the foggiest night in Birmingham's history. It was as bad as a London "pea souper" according to one expert speaking on the telly.

I had difficulty knowing where I was that night, but like billions of other people in the world I knew exactly where I was one week later, November 22 1963. As 3000 miles away the First Lady cradled a dying President Kennedy, I was in the back row of the Adelphi Picture House snogging Pauline.

Dominating the Britannia Mill was the new 2500-ton extrusion press. Viewed from the top of the stairs from the Casting Shop and the Wire Mill, it looked like a huge crouching beast about to pounce on its prey. Massively engineered, it could push a red-hot billet of brass 10 inches in diameter and three feet long into two spinning coils of wire a quarter of an inch in diameter. Tiebars 15 inches in diameter took the strain, their nuts shuddering.

The main body of the machine and casting appeared to tense with the enormous pressure during the extrusion, only relaxing and settling back when the process was completed. The end of the billet was pushed out by the ram and allowed to drop into the chute below with an ear splitting clang of metal on metal. A steel slug was then pushed through the container to clear any brass residue. This slug again dropped into the chute below. The slug and the billet end was lifted by hydraulics and manhandled away by a bloke stripped to the waist.

The monster was fed with ten-foot long billets delivered by overhead crane from the Casting Shop, sawn into lengths on an automatic saw, heated in six individual electric furnaces to a glowing red and automatically transferred on roller tracks to the Press. It was a magnificent piece of equipment. The total investment, as reported in the Birmingham Post early in 1962, was in excess of £1m. Dave Wilmer was in the picture.

Before this massive investment United Non Ferrous had had two old-fashioned extrusion presses, one in the Bar Mill where I had started working 18 months before and one at the back of the Wire Mill. Obviously this new press would replace the old machines, providing the "teething faults" could be ironed out.

When I started in the Britannia Mill in late 1963 these teething faults had only just been recognised, let alone ironed out.

Underneath the press in a purpose-built basement was the hydraulic pump house that provided the pressure for the 2500 tons needed to push the hot brass through the extrusion dies. The noise was excruciating. It screamed. When a seal leaked, Harry Hanson, Ernie and I struggled to cure the problem without shutting down the pumps and stopping the production process. Inevitably we would be covered in a fine mist of pressurized hydraulic oil which soaked into our overalls and hair. Our ears would ring for an hour. If the pumps had to be shut down all the production gang would eff and blind and Charlie Colley would be shouting "How long to sort it?"

"I've got five blokes here sitting on their arses doing fuck all. If it's gonna be over an hour I'll have to start up the old press. The fucking furnace will have to be lit." Charlie the Foreman was a real Tartar.

During the next 40 years I would be involved in the installation, commissioning and ironing out "teething problems" of large plant and machinery costing hundreds of thousands of pounds, and it was never easy. This Loewy Extrusion Press was no exception. As old Black Bat would tell anybody who would listen "Automation today, all to bollocks tomorrow."

There was no doubt about it – when the plant was running it was impressive, with the two gangs working as teams driven by Harry Harcourt on the one shift and Harry Smith on the other.

The main production was in coil. The brass wire was pushed out just like toothpaste, but at 100 mph, and collected in two spinning coiling machines. When the metal had been fully extruded the coils, still red hot, were automatically transferred to a conveyor, which slowly moved 50 yards down the shop, allowing the coils of wire to cool before again automatically being lifted to an overhead conveyor for transfer to the Wire Mill.

The plant could also extrude straight lengths in bar form for subsequent cold drawing on the Schumag draw benches in the same shop.

There were two fitters permanently in Britannia Mill. Harry Hanson was a grey-haired bloke, not tall but extremely slim and fit for someone over 60 years of age, and Bill Casey. Casey was a huge Irishman with massive arms and shoulders, a mass of dark curly hair on top of a big serious face which rarely smiled. He was one mean bastard who didn't like to be upset.

The Loewy 2500-tonner ran on two 10-hour shifts, 6 am to 4 pm and 8 pm to 6 am, allowing four hours for oiling, greasing and essential maintenance, plus Saturdays and Sundays.

Ronnie Hanson was Harry's son, a huge bloke, always smiling and laughing, who was the fitter on the night shift. He occasionally worked Saturdays but always did Sundays. These men earned some serious overtime. Ernie Brown was the Mate, usually known as the invisible man.

When the day shift finished at 4 pm the huge 15-inch diameter tie bars on the press needed, in Casey's words, "tapping up". Each hexagonal nut was the size of a four-seater dining table. The slogging ring spanner had to be lifted by crane and positioned on the nut. My Pop had a 14 lb sledgehammer in his shed, but I'd never seen a 56 pounder before.

Scrambling up into position, Casey looked down. "Hand us up me hammer young 'un!"

"Yes Bill!" I had great difficulty in passing this huge hammer, with its five-foot wooden handle, to a bloke 10 feet above me. Swinging the hammer well above his head, Bill brought it crashing down on the flat anvil part of the spanner. Did it tighten the nut I thought? I took my steel rule out of my pocket and placed it on the tie bar. Ten blows tightened the nut by an eighth of an inch on the length. Casey didn't need a rule to tell him the nut was as tight as it was going to be because after about 20 blows he started to feel the solid shock bounce back through the handle. It was as tight as he could make it.

Stripping off the top of his overalls and tucking it into his waistband, he clambered across to the other tie bar. 'Kin 'ell, I thought to myself.

The fitters' workbench was tucked against the wall. It boasted a vice and not much else, apart from a newspaper tablecloth, dirty tea mugs and assorted seating devices. Anything that needed repairing would be taken up to the main Fitting Shop.

Within a week, under the eye of the saw operator, I was pushing the appropriate buttons to present the 10-foot billet for cutting into three equal lengths and forwarding to the furnaces. Together with Harry Hanson, I was also responsible for changing the three-foot diameter high-speed steel saw blade when it required sharpening. A careful job.

Approaching Christmas 1963, the dining room in the Fitting Shop was again trimmed up with Christmas decorations. We would be breaking up on Tuesday 24th, returning on Monday 30th – five whole days off!

"There's a couple of office parties on Tuesday and I'm invited to the Wages Office in the afternoon" Jim said.

"It's all right for you, you're going out with Pat" I replied. She was one of the clerks. The new apprentices were looking interested. "What's it like? Any birds? It ain't a windup is it?" Doug Smith was getting wise to factory life at last.

"No bullshit Doug, they have some good breaking-up parties upstairs. It was great last year." I wondered if Snooker Legs would be there.

You could work on Saturday 28th and Sunday 29th if you wanted to, but I didn't want to. I decided not to ride my bike to work on Christmas Eve. I was going to the party.

The offices were on the first floor and ran the length of Adderley Street. Starting at the Liverpool Street end were Accounts and Wages, all separate offices and departments with windows overlooking the street. The other side of the corridor overlooked the huge Wire Mill and annealing furnaces. Half way down the long corridor, stairs to the right led down to street level and the Security Office. The Personnel Manager, Jack Insall, had an office on the right. Bro. Hall was next door and then came the bigwigs - Works Manager, Managing Director, Sales Director, Sales Office and Works Engineer.

The corridor now crossed one of the canals. Production Control, the Drawing Office and Work Study were on the left, with the Laboratory and Metal Testing on the right. Now we were at the Glover Street end, where another flight of stairs descended to the Casting Shop. The boardroom and gaffers' canteen was across the road, above Sister Susie's surgery.

"You're going to work smart, Steve" my Nan said as I got ready to leave to catch the bus on the morning of Christmas Eve.

"There's a couple of parties in the office upstairs and I'm going to Pauline's after. I'll be home, but it'll be a bit late." I saw the concern on her face. "I'll be all right Nan."

"At least your bike's in the shed" she said, turning away.

When I eventually sold my bike and bought a car, Nan told me she would never go to sleep until she heard me come down the path and park the bike in the shed. I had often wondered why her bedroom light always seemed to go out just as I arrived home. Must be coincidence, I'd always thought.

As on previous Christmas Eves, not much work was done in the morning. Even the Britannia Press and Mill virtually stopped by mid morning. The plant had to be shut down properly for the five-day holiday and by midday all was quiet, with blokes taking it easy and having a tot in their tea. Even Charlie Colley, same as Jim Cooper, would have a tot with his blokes before, I guess, being invited up to the boardroom. All the foremen had their second in commands, and Charlie's parting shot in front of everyone was "Have a quiet drink here till one o'clock and don't touch a machine. When they chuck you out of the pub don't come back into the factory. Behave and you'll be paid till two. Casey will sort out anybody who fucks up. Merry Christmas." These foremen ran the whole factory, not just the shop floor.

Sitting round the dining table in the Fitting Shop looking at the trimmings, eating a mince pie and drinking my tea with a drop of whisky in it, I was looking forward to walking down to Waggon and Horses. Most people were getting there about one o'clock, but not the old uns.

"I can enjoy meself having a quiet drink here in the shop without all that pushing and shoving, specially that fucking jukebox blaring away" said Black Bat, lying back in his armchair and smoking his pipe. "And don't forget, behave and don't spoil it."

Trying not to be too obvious, we walked down to the Waggon in twos and threes. As I walked into the back room I was met by a wall of sound. The place was heaving with office staff, shop floor staff, Pricey and his mates, nearly all from United Non Ferrous. Tables had been moved to the side and the Dave Clark Five were belting out Glad All Over. Young Doug had a pint in his hand and was rocking. "Ill have a whisky and orange?" I shouted to him.

By two o'clock most of the staff had quietly staggered back, entering the offices by the staircase next to Liverpool Street instead of the main gatehouse. Jim, Frank and I had to help Doug back. We laid him down in the chargehands' office in the Wire Mill, out of the way.

Jim went straight to join Pat in Wages, but I thought I'd pay a visit to all the offices, starting at the far end and working my way back.

"Seems a good idea," said Dave Wilmer. As he was Senior Apprentice I was in good company. "I think I'll stick to Whisky," I said. Dave agreed.

Each office had music, couples dancing and as much booze as the pub down the road. A drink, a dance and a smooch under the mistletoe was the order of the day. By the time Dave and I arrived in the Wages Office we were both well into the Christmas spirit.

In those days all large firms must have had Christmas parties like this. I suppose the arrival of the breathalyzer nine years later and additional employers' responsibilities put a stop to this type of merriment.

This must have been the in place, because Pricey was in here smooching and after five minutes his mate Graham sidled out of a side office with a grin on his face, Miss Snooker Legs behind him smoothing down her party frock.

It was a great afternoon. Doug staggered in just before it was time to go, in time to have the last dance with Snooker Legs.

"I'm going to Yardley Wood to pick up my brother. Do you want a lift, young Steve?" Graham said as we were saying our farewells and kissing everyone in sight. I was holding on to the door, trying to focus my eyes, without much success.

"He's pissed. I'll help you get him in your car. You know where he lives?" Pricey asked Graham. "Yeah, I'll drop him off," said Graham.

I woke up on Nan's settee just after nine o'clock that night. 'Kin 'ell.

CHAPTER 9

My Nan's Christmas-morning breakfast was a slice of pork pie with mustard and a cup of tea with a drop of whisky, a delicacy I have continued to enjoy for over 40 years. Uncle Norman and Aunt Ada would be arriving around noon. The turkey was almost done and all five of us were going to walk up to the Haven pub, five minutes away round the corner.

As we sat in the bar Uncle Norman raised his glass, toasting everyone on our table and those adjoining, and wishing all a Merry Christmas. He then turned to me.

"It appears you had a pleasant Christmas Eve, young Stephen."

"Yes Uncle" I replied.

I spent that night and Boxing Day at Pauline's playing the usual games of Monopoly, cards and chess. The next day, the Friday, the Blues were playing at home, but I was glad I didn't go as they lost 4–1 to Arsenal.

The weather in early 1964 was nowhere near as bad as the previous winter and I rode my Triumph to and from work every day without using the bus at all. We also had the luxury of using Pauline's father's car when we went to a dance, because she had now passed her test, so we could both arrive all poshed up and smartly dressed. I'd be 18 in February, and looking at the apprentice rates of pay that would mean a good rise in wages. I was doing well with my studying towards Part 3 City & Guilds Craft Practice at Garretts Green Tech on day release and enjoying my work in the factory. What would the year bring?

Once I turned 18 I was taking home just over nine pounds 10 shillings a week basic, plus my usual overtime of an hour at night and Saturday and Sunday mornings, which took my gross wages to over £15 a week. Even after stoppages I was picking up well over £12. I would count my wages before unsealing the flap on the little brown packet. The corner of each note was sticking out of the top of the wage packet, allowing the notes to be counted together, and there was a small transparent window so the coins could be checked. If the seal was broken and your wages were wrong - tough shit.

"I've joined the Union" said Jim, flashing his new blue AEU card. You didn't have to join till you were 21, when you got a green skilled man's card, but he had joined early.

A couple of weeks earlier I had been approached by Norman, the Shop Steward in the Fitting Shop, with a suggestion that I join the AEU as soon as I was 18. At that time the factory had three main shop-floor unions, the AEU, Transport and General and the Electrician's Union, and in the Fitting Shop there was a problem because a number of fitters and mates had joined the T & G and this had angered the skilled AEU members.

"A skilled man should be in the AEU, not the fucking Transport and General Workers' Union!" Norman used to get really wound up, almost squaring up to Ted Smart, who was in the T & G. "And we've got sole negotiating rights with management, so you're wasting your time in the T & G" Norman concluded.

During tea break I quietly approached Billy Wiggins. "What do you think, Billy?"

"I can't get involved in their argument, but I can advise you. Norman's a daft bugger in many ways, but he's right. The AEU is the skilled man's union and I've been a member since I was 16 years old. You had to be, working at the Austin. But keep this chat to yourself." He smiled and tapped his nose with his finger.

So the following Friday night I met Norman upstairs in the College Arms on the corner of Shaftmoor Lane and the Stratford Road. I patiently listened to a number of shop stewards from factories throughout South Birmingham discussing problems and disputes, and watched the subs being paid in. Then it came to me being proposed as a member of the AEU. Norman proposed me and another seconded, and that was it. I had my card - I was a union member.

Brother Phillips jumped on to his motorbike and went to meet his girlfriend. It was too late for the pictures.

* * * * * * * * * * * * *

"There's a fire down in the chute!" I don't know who shouted it, but I knew in the first instance it was down to the fitters to try and sort it. The chute was underneath the extrusion press where the red–hot slug end which remained from the extruded billet fell. Graphite grease was used extensively as lubricant in the extrusion process and all the metal surfaces of the chute were covered in this grease, so if any repair work had to be done down there (two blokes could just about work in this confined space) they needed plenty of cleaning rags. Even so you would climb out a right mess.

Two hours before, Mac the welder and his mate had been down in the chute welding a split steel plate. They had left a complete sack full of cleaning rags soaked in grease tucked up in the corner.

Six months before, Bro. Hall had organised a demonstration with fire extinguishers and all of us, fitters as well as apprentices, had had a right laugh spraying the foam about and aiming for each other rather than the small fire that had been started for practice.

Bill Casey was as brave as a lion. He lifted the checker–plated hatch and peered down the 10-rung steel ladder, shouting "Ernie, gerrus a fire extinguisher!" With the big red cylinder tucked under one arm and smoke rising up from the chute, he slowly descended to tackle the sack of rags, which by now was well ablaze.

Production had been halted and Charlie the Foreman was looking down into the chute and assessing the situation. If Casey put the fire out in a minute or two, OK. If not, the fire alarm would have to be set off and the shop and possibly the whole of the factory evacuated. It was only steel and concrete, I thought to myself, but then again, factories do burn down.

"Need another extinguisher, fucking quick!" Casey roared. Ernie and I dashed off to find one.

"What d'yer think Bill, do I set off the alarm?" Charlie was looking worried. It would be a big decision, and he had less than a minute to make it in.

"Where's that fucking extinguisher?" Casey was halfway up the ladder with his head sticking out at floor level.

Ernie came rushing from the corner under the stairs leading to the Casting Shop where the fire extinguishers were hung on the wall, totally forgetting Bro. Hall's training. He was trying to activate the foam by pulling the pin as he ran. The extinguisher erupted three yards from Casey's head. Within seconds it looked as though a snowman was trying to climb up the ladder from the chute. All it needed was a carrot for the nose.

I thought as Casey wiped the foam from his eyes and mouth that he was going to clamber out and give Ernie a smack. Instead he grabbed hold of the extinguisher and pointed the rest of the rushing foam towards the diminishing fire below.

"All right yow fuckin' lot, back to work." Good old Charlie.

We were very close to evacuating almost 700 people. In fact one bloke did evacuate himself. Ernie Brown disappeared for the rest of the day, but he didn't clock out till 7 pm, his usual time.

It was about this time, the spring of 1964, that the management introduced the weekly work sheet. This was a pink A4 card printed with the days of the week, on which everyone had to record the work they did that day or week. Working in Britannia Mill was easy - you filled in the whole week.

"The fucking gaffers want to know how many dies me and Andy are mekking, nosey bastards." Black Bat was relaxing in his armchair, and he wasn't happy. "If they send one of them fucking time and study blokes with their fucking stop watches I'm gooin' to the Union."

Andy Uprichard, the turner who produced the die blanks prior to Black Bat finishing them off, was a laid-back silver-haired Irishman. During my first six months in the factory I roughed out the blanks for Andy to finish-turn. Always helpful to me and all the other apprentices, Andy served his time at Harland and Wolff in Belfast and was introduced to the shipyard by his father Tommy. Named after the designer of the Titanic, Thomas Andrews, Andy had been born the day after she was launched in 1912.

"Before I started work the old fella used to tell me about the great ship that he worked on and supposedly couldn't sink." Andy smoked Capstan Full Strength, and while I loved a free fag I only ever accepted one from him, and that had been a year ago. I had coughed for two days.

"What did your dad do in the Yard?" I asked.

"He was a riveter, along with hundreds more. In later years he used to get his leg pulled about being a riveter on the Titanic. They called him leaky. It's called the craic. You Brummies call it tekkin' the piss."

* * * * * * * * * * * * *

I was still working in the Britannia Mill, and once a week Jim and I would have a game of snooker after work. In fact Bro. Hall was setting up a bit of a mini league with the other factories in the group.

"What's this about a barge trip up the canal, mate?" I asked Jim, just as he was about to take a shot. It was either the sudden question or the dropped ash tray that did it. He miss-cued. I'd got this down to a fine art. We believed it improved our game.

"Bastard!" He looked up from the table, smiling. "It's a great night out. A coach picks us up from the factory at six and takes us down the Stratford Road just past Shirley. The barge seats 50 blokes, all with tables, and there's a bar. On the last trip they booked Len Newbury, who's a dirty comic, he plays the piano and it's a fucking scream." Jim was obviously going.

"Book me a seat," I said, preparing to pot a red. Just before my cue struck the white ball, Jim shouted at the top of his voice "AND IT'S ONLY A QUID!"

On the day of the barge trip I took a change of clothes in on the bus, a nice shirt and pressed jeans. It was spring, so it wouldn't be cold. I'd have a shower in the Casting Shop and be in the Waggon and Horses just before the coach arrived. With luck I wouldn't lose any overtime.

Everyone who was going was in the Waggon. I guess the gaffer had opened up before the official time of 5.30 pm, because there was quite a crowd, all in good spirits and enjoying themselves when I walked in. Even the jukebox was rocking.

We had a beautiful 60-foot-long narrowboat fully fitted out with bench seats, tables, windows the full length and a fully-stocked bar at one end. Len Newbury lived in Ladywood, and someone said he had written a song for Shirley Bassey. He was already tinkling on the piano. After an hour he was warming up with dirty jokes, one-liners and a range of ditties and singsongs. He was as good as Jim said, even to us young lads. On a piss-up on a barge you didn't really want the Beatles.

Somebody suggested that as we were afloat it might be a good idea to have a tot of rum. Why not – I was enjoying myself.

Just after 8 o'clock the barge gently bumped into the bank. "We've arrived at the pub," said a voice. "There's a bit of grub on and we're here for an hour." Who was speaking? It must have been the bloke who had organized the trip. Me, I hadn't got a clue. By now I was an experienced drinker of rum and coke.

The dark water was skimming by 10 inches from my face. It took me a minute to realise where I was, and the fact that I'd stopped being sick.

Someone had hung me out of the door to get some fresh air. Give them their due, the top hatch was lodged on my neck to avoid me from falling into the canal and trying to swim home. A large mug of black coffee later I managed, with help, to find my way on to the coach. Where had the barge gone?

I was dropped off at the top of Highfield Road, which meant a 45-minute walk home. By the time I opened the front gate I was almost sober but tired and cold and it was nearly two in the morning. Nan had just turned her bedroom light out. I was going to work in the morning. No – I was going to work today! We were well into Saturday morning.

"Steve, I want you to hold the spanner on the locking nut at the end of the shaft while me and me Dad try to extract it. It's got to go up to the

Fitting Shop for repair." Ronnie Hanson was explaining the job in hand. "Take an old blanket down with you to lie on." Harry's son was all right, and anyway it was below ground and I was feeling rough. I'd had four hours' sleep, no breakfast and I was knackered. I vowed never to drink rum ever again.

I shifted myself into position. It wasn't easy, especially with a bloody great spanner lying across my chest and six feet below ground. Mind you, the blanket was a comfort.

"Yow all roight down there, Steve?" Ronnie shouted. "Yeah, OK" I replied, thinking about the bacon sandwich I'd be having in about an hour's time.

"We'll be a couple of minutes. I've got to sort a ring spanner."

Unfortunately for the shaft that needed extracting, but fortunately for the young apprentice lying on his blanket, the Hansons were then called to an emergency on the other side of the mill. Oil was pissing out of a seal somewhere.

"Steve, are you all right? Steve? Steve!" A large pair of hands grabbed my shoulders and gently shook me awake.

"Fuck me, the lad had fell asleep," Ronnie said to his dad. Harry smiled. "You all right son?"

"I think so" I replied. "I could do with me breakfast."

Both Ronnie and Harry started to laugh. "Yow don't want yer breakfast, yow'll be wanting your lunch, it's nearly 12 o'clock." I'd been asleep for over three hours, but at least I was on time and a half.

* * * * * * * * * * * *

I'd completed my time in the Britannia Mill. It was the spring of 1964, and while I loved motorbikes and my now shoulder-length hair, I was beginning to be influenced by a number of conflicting ideologies. Bikes were wet, cars were dry. Mods wore dead smart suits, shirts and ties. The Beatles had been going two years and the new music was the Who and the Small Faces. Yep, I had my hair cut. I must have been the only Mod who rode a motorbike, because I would not have been seen dead on a Vespa and my dreams of buying a Bonneville were beginning to fade. I wanted a car.

Pauline and I booked up for a week's holiday with Frank and Jean at a holiday camp at Prestatyn in North Wales. It sounds daft thinking about it now but we booked adjoining chalets, the girls in one and Frank and me in the other, even though I was over 18 and we'd been courting for two years. We travelled by coach and enjoyed the hi-de-hi environment with three meals a day in a huge dining room. The weather was iffy, but it was a week away as adults. The accommodation arrangements were not adhered to. Would we go back? The general consensus was that we would try somewhere else next year.

Arriving back at Chilton Road, I discovered I'd passed my exams, Part 3 City & Guilds Craft Practice. What's next, I thought?

The final year of Craft Practice City & Guilds was a toolmaking supplementary. What would happen if I passed this exam next year? I'd still be only 19, with 18 months of my apprenticeship to go. I had to wait a year to find out.

"You'll be based mainly in the Fitting Shop for the next month or so, but because of your experience you'll be sent on jobs all round the factory, helping a fitter or taking a younger lad with you on the easy jobs."

I was in the office of Mr George McDonald, Works Engineer. He continued: "All reports on your work in the factory and college are good. Keep it up, young man."

He was Scottish, a tall, slim, grey-haired man with a clipped moustache. His office was cramped and full of shelves loaded with engineers' books. At 60 years old, he drove a Morris Oxford estate, a company car. Even at work he wore a three-piece suit with a waistcoat and a hanky in the top pocket.

The previous year he had entertained my Mom when she came into the factory to sign my apprentice indentures and contract. "Please sit down Mrs Phillips, while I organise a cup of coffee. I'll introduce you to Mr Rushton and we'll have a tour of the works." He was a lady's man big time. So was Tommy Rushton. They both loved her.

He might not have had a farm, but Old McDonald was all right. So was Tommy.

I enjoyed it in the Fitting Shop, working closely with Joe Healy and the rest of the old blokes. At eighteen and a half I could set and operate every machine tool in the department – shapers, centre lathes, universal millers, horizontal and vertical millers, large radial drillers and the surface and cylindrical grinders that were Black Bat's babies. Not even Joe Healy would touch these. Having said that, Joe was a magician on the lathe and universal miller.

Without being big-headed, I was proud of the fact that a lot of the older blokes respected my growing skills. These men had started on a lathe, miller or grinder and generally stayed there, not having the extensive, comprehensive training that I and the other apprentices received these days.

"Breakdown on the Britannia Press" said Joe. "Casey's bringing the housing up now and you'll need to take that job out of your lathe Steve, cos it's a rush job." He had just come out of his office after putting the phone down. Bollocks, I thought to myself, I'd just spent 30 minutes setting the bloody job up and I would have to it all over again.

The big tough Irishman walked steadily into the shop with a huge steel fabrication on his shoulder. His blue all-in-one overall was unbuttoned to the waist, showing off a barrel chest covered in black curly hair. Very slowly he crouched down and carefully placed my next job on the floor. Standing up, he stretched and rubbed his shoulder. "That's a tidy weight even for a Paddy" he said. "I need it quick, young Steve, the press is down and I've got Colley on me back."

"Better than that lump of steel" I said with a smile. "How are we going to pick it up, Bill?"

"That's your fucking problem. I'll see you when I've had me breakfast." With that he strode out.

"The bronze bearing needs replacing" Joe said, gently knocking it out.

"But the housing needs skimming. I'll make a new bearing, you skim the housing." What he meant was, he would have the easy job and I'd have the difficult one.

It took me almost to the end of my apprenticeship before I realized Joe was intentionally improving my skills by giving me jobs that would tax my thinking and not the simple tasks. I didn't appreciate it at the time though.

Without an overhead hoist it took three of us to lift the fabrication into the lathe and hold it steady while I gripped it in the four-jaw chuck. Carefully adjusting each jaw independently, guided by the dial indicator, it took me half an hour to set the diameter up prior to machining.

I asked Joe to check my set-up before I started to remove metal from the housing, because if I made a mistake, replacing the fabrication would be extremely expensive - on top of which, the 2500-ton press would be down for days.

Joe strolled over. "Is it set up, Steve?"

"I think so" I replied.

"Is it set up right?" he persisted. What I really wanted was for him to double-check it.

"I think it's near enough, Joe."

"Never mind near enough, is it right?" He wouldn't let go. I thought long and hard, spinning the chuck and looking at the dial indicator, certain it was running true. A deep breath. "It's right, Joe."

"Well that's near enough, then" he replied, turning back to finish off the bronze bearing that a first-year apprentice could have made.

I kissed the bore with the cutting tool, wound on the first 10-thou cut, set the traverse in motion and looked up to the roof, praying.

The new bearing was tightly pressed into the housing I had machined as Casey returned. "Come on you lot, Colley's having a fucking fit."

He crouched down, grabbed hold of the steel fabrication and with an enormous grunt heaved it up on to his shoulder. It was a warm day and Casey obviously had nothing on under his overalls, because as he struggled to position the heavy weight he failed to notice that his penis had flopped out of his fly button. Nobody said a word. There were also no volunteers to gently tuck it back out of sight. Casey was not the sort of bloke to appreciate another bloke's hand on his cock.

"I'll be away," he said, moving slowly under the weight. With his head held high he set off on his journey from the Fitting Shop and through the Wire Mill across the bridge over the canal down back to the Britannia Mill, oblivious to his willy swinging in the breeze.

Two hours later he came back, now suitably dressed and smiling.

"Yow boyos did a good job, workin' perfect now," he said. He had obviously worked bloody hard during the past few hours to get the press running again, because he sat down and welcomed a mug of tea from Pat Dowling.

"I'm fucking knackered," he said, sipping his tea. He turned to Pat. "Yow know that Miss Rigsby, the old maid from upstairs?"

"She's 60 odd, been a secretary for years" Pat replied.

"Well, on the way back to the mill carrying that fucking great weight on me shoulders, she was walking towards me on the bridge when she went all peculiar. I thought she was going to faint. I couldn't help her, I'd got me hands full." Casey looked puzzled at our smiles. Nobody said a word.

I was now regularly having lunch in the canteen and I always had a hot sandwich from one of the local cafés on a Saturday morning, collecting money and orders from most of the blokes in the Fitting Shop. It would take them about 15 minutes to prepare 20-odd sandwiches, all wrapped and suitably labelled. It didn't take me long to realise that rather than eat my sandwich back in the factory I could have a full breakfast sitting down in the café while I waited. It also didn't take me long to find that the owner, pleased that I chose his café to order all these sandwiches, was prepared to treat me to a free breakfast. Even though there were now younger lads than me in the shop I used to say "Don't worry, I'll fetch the sandwiches. I really don't mind."

One morning everybody had a good laugh because old Charlie was eating his bacon-and-egg sandwich when he suddenly gave a huge sneeze, expelling a mouthful of grub. The funny bit was that a full set of dentures, top and bottom, was clamped to it, and it went skidding and chattering along the floor.

"I'm getting engaged," said Mickey Plant. He was 22 years old and a turner. He hadn't served an indentured apprenticeship, but he had been a trainee at Haddon and Stokes and had been transferred to United Non-Ferrous two years before.

"Got yer bird in the club then?" Pat said. "Fucking ain't" Mickey replied, smiling. Everyone had just finished their Saturday morning breakfast and was lighting up. I knew Gwen, Mickey's girlfriend, and she was a lovely girl with short blonde hair, blue eyes and a quick smile. We'd been out as a foursome a couple of times to the Locarno in Birmingham and enjoyed each other's company. Mickey's pride and joy was his beautiful bright red Mini Cooper with four rally spotlights and a wood-rim steering wheel.

"When's the wedding then, Mickey?" I asked.

"Sometime next year, we hope, but we've got to sort it all out. Church, reception, honeymoon, hell of a lot to do" Mickey replied.

"And a hell of a lot of bloody money an' all" Old Black Bat muttered. He was a miserable old bugger.

"Come on shower, yow've had yer breakfast, time to do a bit" Joe shouted down the shop. "Doing a bit" for Joe on a Saturday morning usually entailed repairing or making new parts for Works Manager Tommy Rushton's model railway system. He had a huge layout in his garden, running on 10-inch gauge rails with a steam engine that you could sit on pulling a line of carriages. Tommy would bring in axles, spindles, wheels and all sorts for Joe to turn or machine. He even bought the whole engine in once to demonstrate it working, firing up the boiler and tooting the whistle.

Tommy Carter, the foreman, would occasionally come in on a Saturday morning. He would arrive about half nine, spend an hour or two drinking tea in Sister Susie's surgery, have a stroll around the factory and bugger off by 11.30. That was when the real 'foreigners' would come out. A foreigner was when people bought in parts from home or bits of their car to be repaired, machined or sharpened. Once Caggy had gone, brake drums, exhaust systems, garden shears, cylindrical cutting blades from lawn mowers - you name it, they all appeared.

This particular morning I had a brake drum to skim up on the lathe and a cylindrical blade to sharpen on the universal grinder. That was a packet of 20 fags for each job and getting paid time and a half as well. Mac the welder had two exhausts to repair by welding a plate over the holes. Yep, everybody worked extremely hard the last hour or so on a Saturday morning, and if you couldn't quite finish all the foreigners then you had Sunday morning, and that was double time.

The lawnmower blades were quite an easy job, as long as the grinder was free. The spindle was already centred both ends, so mounting it between centres on the Universal Grinder ensured it ran perfectly true. A quick check to make sure it was parallel, and with the blades slowly rotating it was traversed backwards and forwards past the spinning grinding wheel, just licking the blades and removing about 10 thou. It sharpened them to such a degree they were better than new.

Old Joe the chargehand didn't mind, as long as there were no proper jobs urgently waiting to be done and it only took up the last hour or so.

Most Saturday afternoons during the summer of '64 were spent in my mate Billy's dad's garage tuning motorbikes. Frank Blake had recently bought a Velocette Clubman and Phil a Bonneville, while Billy was building a Venom. The Velocette factory was only 200 yards away, so parts were easily available at low cost. The regular runs were Stratford, Worcester and the bike races at Mallory Park and Oulton Park. Occasionally we'd go to Blackbush for the sprint meetings and a large motorcycle show in Blackpool. Pauline came to the Blackpool show, and because it was such a long journey we would have to stay overnight. Anyway, that's what I told her Dad.

"Carry on up to Gretna Green and take her off our hands" Albert replied, glancing at Ivy, Pauline's Mom. (Back in those days people still used to talk about couples running away to Gretna Green, just over the Scottish border, because you could get married in Scotland without your parents' permission).

Jim was getting engaged to Pat from the Wages office and Frank Davis was getting engaged to Jean, and we'd had Mickey Plant's announcement last week. This is getting to be an epidemic, I thought to myself. I wonder who's going to be next?

CHAPTER 10

One Friday night we had arranged to meet Brian West, one of the regulars, in the lounge in the Haven, so Pauline and I had walked the short distance round the corner from Chilton Road and were enjoying a drink when he walked in. I'd been to school with his daughter Barbara and I'd had a few beers with him during the past 6 months.

"What sort of stone and setting do you want, Pauline?" Brian asked. He was a jeweller.

"Aquamarine as the main stone, in a diamond setting" she replied. I choked on my beer. At least I'd finished paying for my motor bike, I thought to myself, and I was earning fifteen quid a week.

"Come into the workshop in the morning and I'll show you some rings and photographs." Brian worked in the jewellery quarter, which was a large area a mile or so from Birmingham City Centre. It was famous for having around 1000 shops, small one-man jewellers and factories producing gold chains.

"Can we make it after one o'clock Brian, because I have to go to work on Saturday morning" I said, thinking that it was more than important – it was bloody vital.

"No problems, I work myself until about two before having a drink in the Jeweller's Arms. I'll do you a good deal, don't worry. You'll pay half what you would pay in a shop." He dropped his voice. "How much do want to spend?"

"About twenty-five quid" I replied.

"You'll have a fine ring for that, worth over £50. I'll see you about half one tomorrow. Now then, let me congratulate you both. What are you drinking?"

* * * * * * * * * * * *

"Not another silly sod, I don't know what the young 'uns are coming to" said Black Bat. "You think you want to eat it now, but I'm telling yer, in a few years time yow'll wished yow bloody had." He was no romantic.

It was 7.30 on the Saturday and I'd just announced my news. Everybody wished me luck. Separately and quietly, Arthur Twamley said a word and shook my hand.

"S'pose that's another collection. There's one nearly every fucking week these days." Black Bat climbed up out of his cottage-style armchair and walked over to the grinders.

"You don't really mean it, Alf," said Andy.

"Course not" Alf replied, with a very rare smile. "My old woman went off it years ago and these lads are shagging themselves daft. I'm jealous, that's all."

Billy Wiggins looked up from his snooze. "You're lucky Alf. My Missus has to stand on her head and if I'm lucky mine drops in by gravity."

Brian and his partner sat at a wooden bench 20 feet long running the length of one wall directly underneath two large sash windows. Each workplace was scalloped out to allow a craftsman to sit into the bench. A very small vice with special attachments to hold rings was secured to the bench and each man had a kind of leather apron clipped to the bench to catch anything that accidentally dropped from the vice.

As Brian explained: "Gold shavings are too valuable not to collect and a diamond or any precious stone of any size dropped on the floor is impossible to find. It's my bloody money."

Positioned on the bench was a large illuminated magnifying glass, and each craftsman wore special optical glasses that could be raised up from the eyes. A small green safe was tucked under the sink.

An aquamarine in a hopefully inexpensive diamond setting was chosen, and I waited for the price.

"Twenty five pounds it is Steve, and you've got a ring I'll value in writing at sixty quid, but not a receipt, providing you give me cash" Brian said as he very carefully detached the leather apron. I didn't have a cheque book and plastic was several years in the future, so cash was no problem.

"It'll be ready next week, see you then" said Brian as we walked out of his small workshop, down a flight of wooden stairs and into an alley that led to the rear of the Jeweller's Arms. It was drizzling with rain as we rode the Triumph back to Hay Mills. I need a car, I thought.

I was collecting the ring on the Friday. We would have a celebration drink with my Mom, who was coming up from London, Nan and Pop, Uncle Norman, Aunt Ada and Pauline's parents early on the Saturday evening. Nan and Pop were staying the night at Uncle Norman's because we were going to have a party.

"How much do you want for your bike, Steve?" Tommy Waters was Billy's younger brother and I had been at school with Billy. I had also knocked Billy's front tooth out in a fight when we were 14 years old, severely cutting one of my fingers close to the knuckle. The scar is still visible on my finger 50 years on, but Billy's tooth is not.

"Eighty-five quid – it's a good bike, Tommy." I was polishing it on the footpath in Chilton Road on the Sunday afternoon. Tommy, who walked up from Glastonbury Road, had always admired my Triumph 21.

"I know it is. You've had it over a year and you're always on it. I'm interested" Tommy replied.

"I'm getting engaged next week and I'm thinking of buying a Mini."

"No rush. Let me have first refusal" Tommy said, strolling off.

"I'll pick you up just after one o'clock. We can get to Brian's workshop, pick up the ring, drop you off back at Oxford Street and I can still clock back in before 1.30."

It was Thursday night and I was making the arrangements with Pauline for the next day. Engagement ring day! Party Saturday. Not a big do but still a party, even if everybody was bringing their own drinks.

Ring in my pocket, I swung into Oxford Street, dropped Pauline off and rode down the dual carriageway of Digbeth, passing the Old Crown and heading back to work. I had plenty of time and the sun was shining.

The Rainbow, on the corner of Digbeth and Adderley Street, was another local pub that was managed by a gaffer who had no idea of the licensing laws. It was used by employees from Liverpool Bus Garage, who all worked funny hours and shifts and appreciated a couple of pints when they had finished – hopefully not before. But predominantly it was an Irish pub. And while the law in 1964 stated that public houses must shut at 2.30 pm, the Rainbow took a similar attitude to that of the Windmill Theatre during the Second World War: we never close.

If it was wet there would be up to 10 huge Wimpey builders' lorries parked on both sides of Adderley Street down to under the railway bridge. Big Paddy the cellarman would deal with any trouble. If Charlie the copper from Digbeth Police Station was on afternoon duty, he would pop in for a pint. Walking back from the Barrel in Watery Lane, Charlie would have to pass the Rainbow anyway on the way back to the police station. Most blokes appreciated an illegal drink and didn't want to spoil it. If anyone got out of order at least five big Irish fellas would help him out of the door.

I'd just passed the Old Crown and begun to position my motor bike to turn left into Adderley Street. I tapped the box containing the ring in my pocket – still there – and I could see quite a few drinkers on stools outside the Rainbow on the pavement. In front of me I could also see a huge, empty 40-foot flatbed articulated lorry in the centre lane, apparently heading up towards the flyover or on towards the main Coventry road. I'll nip in on the inside, I thought to myself, and turned left into Adderley Street.

I was halfway into the turn when the cab of the artic suddenly and inexplicably swung left, right in front of me. The front wheel of my bike was against the gutter, and there was no way could I lift it up on to the pavement. I was trapped, and the flat bed was following the swing of the cab. I'm in deep shit here, I thought.

The flatbed whacked me on my right shoulder, knocking me straight off the bike and across the pavement. I rolled through the open door of the Rainbow and ended up slamming against the bar. Two tables with at least eight pints of beer had been knocked over and I was lying in a puddle of draught Guinness.

"What the fuck's going on? Has Evil Knievel landed?" Eamonn Ryan wanted to know. I soon realized that I was not seriously injured and my main concern was my bike. I limped outside. I must have hurt something but I couldn't tell what, apart from my pride.

The Triumph was wedged between the rear two pairs of double wheels of the artic trailer. One set of wheels had gone right over the bike.

"Its a good job you were knocked off, Steve" said Eamonn. He had witnessed the accident as he was returning following his lunch break. "You'd have no fucking legs left otherwise." I slowly nodded in agreement, touching the box in my pocket. Still safe.

Bob Scott was Mac the Welder's mate. A happy smiling rogue of an Irishman, he was always out for the craic, provided it was aimed at the Pope. He had a large tattoo of the Union Jack in full colour on his forearm. He was also a keen biker and although he was forty odd he owned a beautiful Triumph Thunderbird. With the permission of Caggy, our foreman, Bob and I managed to push my bike down the road and into the basement under the Bar Mill.

"I'll tell you what Steve, it ain't too badly damaged" Bob said, inspecting my bike. "The wheels are OK, we've just wheeled it down the road. It's a good job the wagon was empty or with 20 tons on board it would have crushed it. It just bounced over yer bike."

It would take three weeks to repair, but it was sold to Tommy Waters fully restored for £85 including my crash helmet. I didn't tell anybody, Nan, Pop or Pauline, the details of the accident. I wasn't hurt, and to tell the truth it didn't really bother me that I could not only have been seriously injured but killed. The invulnerability of youth. Of course I had been very, very lucky.

The engagement weekend went off fine, with the old 'uns disappearing before the young 'uns arrived on the Saturday night. It had been a few years since there had been a party at Chilton Road, and even Mugsy's group arrived just after midnight for a drink. But my main concern was getting a set of wheels – four of them this time.

I very soon got fed up of using the bus. My bike was being repaired in Grays on the Coventry Road and I was now desperately looking for a car. A second-hand Mini was first choice, and the following Saturday afternoon after studying the Birmingham Mail I had three cars to go and see. Albert, Pauline's Dad, was a great help, driving all three of us round Birmingham. He had great experience with cars.

The first one we saw looked ok until Albert pushed his thumb into the offside side front wing and it collapsed, leaving a hole large enough to put your fist in. "Rotten as a pear and poorly repaired" he said to me. The owner had gone into the house to leave us to have a good look at his car. We weren't there when he came back out.

The vehicle in the best overall condition was a light pea-green Mini Van being sold by a small second-hand car pitch in Kings Norton. It was three years old and had done 35,000 miles. After Albert had taken it for a test drive we agreed to pay £245 to include the fitting of a new clutch.

The windows slid backwards and forwards, the doors opened with a length of string and the starter button was on the floor, but I had found my first motor car. The garage arranged hire purchase for £200 over 12 months. It was insured in Pauline's name as she had had a full licence for over 18 months, with me as a named learner driver.

We collected it the following Wednesday evening. I tied the L plates on to the front and rear bumpers and drove home. I'd already had four lessons at a driving school and I'd put in for my test in a month's time.

The first weekend, armed with a sharp knife and a small roll of thick underlay and carpet, I fitted out the back of my Mini Van and tossed in a couple of large cushions, together with a luxurious blanket. I told everybody it was to reduce the road noise. While we were fitting chrome wing mirrors, Albert glanced in the back. "Quite comfy in there" he said.

Two weeks later Tommy paid me for the bike and I bought a made-to-measure Mod suit in a beautiful burgundy colour. I thought I was the dog's bollocks.

Because I couldn't drive unaccompanied, Pauline kept the Mini at her house and I used the bus for work. Roll on my driving test. I had two more lessons at the driving school, together with hours of practice accompanied by Pauline or Albert going through three-point turns, hill starts, reversing and emergency stops. I'd been riding a motorbike for two and a half years, so I was confident on the road, but I was still extremely nervous on my test. My right leg was actually shaking as I drove off with the examiner next to me. It was the same test centre I'd been to for my bike test, in Wake Green Road.

Thirty minutes later I was untying the L plates. I'd passed first time. I dropped Pauline off at work, turned into Adderley Street (very carefully this time) and parked in the street outside the factory. I was well pleased.

At lunchtime all the other apprentices gave my new car the once over. Dave and Johnny already had their own cars, but you could see the younger ones, Doug and Bryn, were thinking to themselves that they couldn't wait. Bryn, following the Mod trend, had his scooter, but even he admitted it was a long journey to and from Tamworth every day.

★ ★ ★ ★ ★ ★ ★ ★ ★ ★ ★ ★ ★

It was the middle of October 1964 and I was four months away from my 19th birthday. I was doing well at college on the toolmaking supplementary and enjoying work at United Non-Ferrous Metals. I had a car and a fiancée. I was doing all right.

Two new apprentices, Ray and Ken, had joined from college a couple of months before and they were treated to all the usual wind-ups that every young lad experiences.

My course was directed at producing a simple pierce and blank tool fitted with sensors to measure the tonnage being used by the power press. Theory involved blank development and tonnage calculations for a great number of different jobs and materials. Harry Fisher was still a great help, and I couldn't help but think that the new apprentices hardly looked old enough to have left school.

On college day Jim, Frank and I would arrive in smart suits, collars and ties, looking very definitely the senior apprentices, while the younger lads would ask our advice about the exams. Harry would nod approvingly.

As November approached I began to appreciate the joys of sitting in a warm vehicle while driving to work at 6.45 am. I felt I must have been mad to have ridden a bike to work all that time, and it wasn't even freezing yet.

I was working an hour over at night and every Saturday and Sunday morning, playing snooker on a Thursday night in the Mini League Bro. Hall had organized within the group, college one day a week. I was seeing Pauline four nights a week and going out the occasional night with Billy for a drink. I was a busy bee.

"You'll be working with Mac the Welder and John the Blacksmith for a month or so starting next week" said Tommy Carter. I was in his office just before he left the factory on a Friday night. "Mine's a bacon and egg in the morning. I'll be in about half nine." He gave me one and a tanner (about 7p) before he stood up and took off his cowgown.

Mac the Welder, Malcolm to his Mom, was a slim bloke who was always on the go. Even when he was eating a sandwich he would be messing about in the huge drawer underneath his workbench sorting out something or other. He was in his early forties and married with four kids, and every night after he clocked out he would play crib or dominoes in the Waggon. The same on Saturday and Sunday afternoons. Mac liked a drink, but he was a bloody good welder.

In a factory that size there were literally hundreds of machines and plant in every production department that needed oiling and greasing on a regular, almost daily basis. Alf Rogers, Frank the Pole and Jan his mate were the three blokes who carried out this work. Alf was a small man, wiry with a pinched face and in his late 30s, who had just become the proud father of his fourth son. He had been born with a withered left arm, but he was always smiling and up for a joke. All these blokes carried huge grease guns two feet long and equally large traditional oil cans. Casey Jones steam-train style. Alf, a Brummie, tended to work in the Britannia Mill, but Frank and Jan toured the whole site with their grease guns and oil cans. Both these men were Polish, forced to fight in the German Army in the Second World War, a number tattooed on their forearms. They had been captured by the Russians and ended up in a prisoner of war camp. They were well into their 60s, grey, stooped and shuffling. They spoke little English but were extremely conscientious in their daily duties. Their respect for authority was obvious in their total subservience to the foreman and chargehands. Their masters had trained them well. But factory life is cruel...

Frank and Jan had an earlier lunch break to the main factory to enable them to oil and grease machines while some of them were not running. After they had drunk their tea and eaten their sandwiches, they would both fall asleep for 20 minutes or so before starting work for the afternoon. They snoozed sitting in two old car seats raised up on blocks of wood around the dining table in the Fitting Shop.

Because it was November 5 in a few days' time, we decided to give Frank and Jan a bit of a wakeup from their slumbers. The plan was to place a bunch of bangers tied to a lighted candle that would take 20 minutes to burn down to the blue touch-papers on the fireworks. This device would be planted under Frank's seat just before they sat down. A couple of trial runs perfected the timing.

So at 12.25 pm, just before Frank and Jan arrived, the candle was lit and placed under the seat. All the young lads were aware of the joke, but most of the old 'uns weren't.

By 12.40 both old soldiers were beginning to nod off. Caggy the foreman had gone home for lunch - he always disappeared at 12.30.

Then Tommy Rushton strolled into the shop with George McDonald. We all looked at each other.

"Oh shit," we said in unison. "We'll all get the sack," I said.

Dave Wilmer took the initiative. He walked briskly towards the two managers and engaged them in chat. We all were very much aware that within seconds a bloody great bang was about to take place. Hurry up for fuck's sake, I said to myself. At last, after what seemed an eternity, Tommy and George strolled out of the shop and into the lift up to the offices.

Dave returned to our little group, hovering round the corner from the snoozing Frank and Jan. "Has the candle gone out?"

"What did you say to the gaffers?" Dave opened his mouth to reply when there came a series of sudden and very loud bangs.

The effect on Frank and Jan was not funny. For a second or two, before they realised where they were, they appeared terrified. Then they were both very angry. We jokers disappeared, the shout of "fucking kids" ringing in our ears.

A few days later I asked Dave what he had said to Rushton and McDonald.

"What you lot didn't know was that Arthur the canteen manager had rung Joe Healy to say that if I saw Mr Rushton on the shop floor I should remind him it was Mr Shakespeare the Managing Director's birthday and pre-lunch drinks were being served in the Boardroom" Dave replied with a huge grin. "Did you think I just told 'em to fuck off?"

Everybody laughed, but no more jokes were played on Frank and Jan. Alf Rogers would be next, but we left it for a couple of weeks.

★ ★ ★ ★ ★ ★ ★ ★ ★ ★ ★ ★

"Never look at the arc without the mask, even from a distance it'll damage your eyes. You won't feel it immediately, but in a hour or so you'll think your eyes are full of grit and they'll be red raw." Mac the Welder was introducing me to arc welding. "It sounds obvious, but don't pick up anything you've just welded, it'll be fucking hot. Mind you, it's like catching your prick in yer zip. You only do it once." He had a way with words.

With my face mask on and peering through a small, extremely dark glass panel I couldn't see a bloody thing, until I touched the workpiece with the

12-inch welding rod. A very bright light now lit up the two pieces of mild steel I was attempting to weld.

"Now slowly move the rod along the joint, keeping it just off the metal." Mac had his own mask on and was closely watching me.

Smoke was rising and there was an electric crackling buzz.

"If the rod gets too close it'll stick, just twist it free. You're doing all right." Mac was a good instructor.

This was something we had not covered at college, so I was a bit nervous, but after a run of about six inches I lifted the rod away, the arc ceased and I lifted my mask, feeling pretty good.

"Not bad for a first time. It's the same as shagging, you get better with practice. Now, I'll explain the settings on the machine and different rods for varying metal thickness." Mac pointed to the dials and levers on the generating set.

He was a good-looking bloke, a full head of dark hair, but with a grey smoker's pallor. Even in his early forties the small broken veins in his face showed that he liked the booze as well. Mac was a drinking mate of Graham the snooker ace and Pricey the Casting Shop foreman.

"See how I've increased the power on the generator, Steve. Your next weld is on much thicker steel." I nodded, causing the face mask to drop down, and off I went again.

The welding area was in a corner of the Fitting Shop, surrounded by heavy green canvas curtains to protect the rest of the shop from the arc flashes. Bottles of oxygen and acetylene were in cradles bolted to the wall with a pair of bottles chained in a mobile cradle which could be wheeled around the factory. Oxy-acetylene produced a high-temperature flame which was used not only for gas welding or brazing but also, with the correct nozzle, for metal cutting. Over the next three months Mac patiently instructed me in all the basic skills.

All the skilled men, welders, fitters, and so on, had mates. The mate would assist them in various ways and carry or wheel the tool box about - in today's terminology, he was a gofer. It quickly became obvious to me that once you were a mate you stayed a mate. Some tradesmen resented passing on their skills to us apprentices, but even the most forthcoming would not dream of training their mate to increase his skills. They were all very protective of their own jobs.

Bob Scott was Mac's mate, and while Mac always took his breaks and ate his sandwiches behind the green screens, Scotty sat at the dining table entertaining all and sundry with his Irish wit and William of Orange drumming on the large metal guard at the back of Andy Uprichards' lathe. Pat Dowling, as a Catholic, never made any comment. He was in his mid forties and chubby with dark, thinning hair, and most people would put up with Scotty.

Bob Brown, the Casting Shop fitter, would bring Scotty to and from work every day in his A35 Austin. For Scotty to ride his beloved Triumph Thunderbird to work the weather forecast had to be for a heatwave with no rain for five years. He was also a big pal of Tommy Best, the caster.

"You've worked in the Casting Shop, Steve, and so have you Doug." Scotty was sitting on an old plastic chair that had been chucked out from the canteen.

"Yes Bob" we both replied.

"Did you know about Tommy Best's talking parrot?"

I didn't. I'd had my lunch in the canteen and didn't fancy a game of snooker, so I was sitting at the dining table with all the other blokes, smoking and waiting for 1.30 pm to start work again. Scotty had the floor.

"Last Saturday I called into Tommy Best's. I knocked the door for five minutes before the bugger opened it, and then he left me standing on the bloody footpath." Scotty paused. Black Bat, Billy Wiggins, Arthur and the other old 'uns began to wake up from their naps. Had they heard this one before? I hadn't.

"I let meself into Tommy's house and closed his front door, thinking yer man's had a few even though it was only just after five in the afternoon."

Scotty was warming to the tale. "The times he'd let me in and staggered back into the front room and fell on the settee, bejasus I couldn't count."

Even the old 'uns round the table were listening now. With his Irish brogue and twinkling eyes, Scotty could tell a story better than one of the little people who lived in his parents' meadow on the shores of Lough Neagh.

"I peeked into the front room and Tommy was sat at the table with a pen in his hand checking his Littlewoods Football Coupon. The radio was on and the announcer was reading out the results of the Fourth Division." The parrot was in his cage next to the radio. Scotty drew a breath before he continued. By this time all the diners were hanging on to his words.

"I tell you what," Scotty said. "Tommy gave me a right bollocking. He said he had five draws on his coupon and opening the door to me he had missed the last 10 results in the First Division. He was livid.

"I sat down looking at Tommy and then I heard "Aston Villa 2, Tottenham Hotspur 1. Manchester United 3, Arsenal nil. I thought it was the radio repeating the scores until I realised Tommy had turned it off."

"That's a hell of a parrot, I told Tommy." Scotty looked round the table. "He said, no he isn't. He'd still only got five draws, fucking bird was useless."

Christmas and the New Year had been and gone, with all the usual parties up in the offices with the second-year apprentices getting drunk. Young Ray Tysall threw up in the waste bin in the wages office, Stan fell asleep in the Chief Wages Clerk's chair and Ken the Tank slipped while dancing with Miss Snooker Legs, resulting in them both rolling around the floor. She preferred the real young lads for flirting. Me, I behaved myself. I couldn't repeat last year's performance of being delivered home to Nan and Pop's drunk as a skunk.

Scotty was helping me to pull the welding generator and gas bottles back to the Fitting Shop and I'd just repaired a large metal chute under the Britannia Press. It might be the middle of January, but where I'd been working it had been red hot. Using the oxy-acetylene to cut away the damaged and worn half-inch steel plate, I welded a two-foot square plate as a patch, all under the watchful eye of Mac, who had nodded approval.

As we approached the welding area we saw a large steel shaft supported on two wooden battens. It was five feet in length with a six-inch diameter thread at each end and six different diameters ranging up to 18 inches. Tommy Rushton and George McDonald, with Caggy the Foreman and Joe the Chargehand, were all examining the two journals on the shaft. They were both badly scored and worn.

"Both bloody bearings seized this morning," George the Works Engineer was telling Tommy. "I'm not bothered about new bearings, they'll be pennies, but the cost of a new shaft would cost thousands of pounds and it'd take weeks to get one."

Tommy looked worried. "Without that shaft I've got half the Casting Shop out of action" he said.

Joe Healy was looking thoughtful. He turned to Mac the Welder.

"If we turn about half an inch off the diameter of them two journals, you can build the shaft back up by arc welding. That should allow enough metal for this young man to clean up and machine back to the original size." I guessed who was going to be the young man. So did the gaffers.

"Make a good job, Steve," said Tommy.

"Yes Mr Rushton" I replied. What else could I have said?

"Well done chaps" said George as he and Tommy strolled off. "That young Steve's coming on well" I just heard Tommy say to George MacDonald as they both disappeared into Caggy's office. Unfortunately Scotty heard it too.

"Right, let's have a drop of tea and then we'll get the shaft in the big lathe" Joe said, walking off to collect his mug.

"Young Steve's coming on well then!" said Scotty mockingly. The rest of them joined in. "Yes Mr Rushton, no Mr Rushton, three bags full Mr Rushton!" Even I had a laugh about it, but I was glad when tea break was over.

The overhead crane could lift five tonnes and the shaft probably weighed half that, but care was needed. Canvas slings were attached at both ends and it was manoeuvred into position between centres with the lower half of a fixed, two-pointed steady helping to support the weight. The steady was capped with bronze tips that would be lubricated when the shaft was revolving.

"Off you go then." Joe sauntered off. I wish I'd joined the bloody army after all, I thought to myself.

Even though the shaft was mounted between centres, I slowly revolved the workpiece, checking for concentricity by running the dial indicator on every diameter over the total length. It ran true. Tightening the solid tungsten carbide-tipped turning tool into the tool box and greasing the centres and steady tips, I carefully wound the cross-slide towards the slowly-revolving shaft. A job of this size could not be rushed, so I selected a speed of 75 rpm. Just kissing the metal with the point of the tool, I wound the saddle back off, zeroed the dial and put a cut of 100 thou, which would reduce the diameter by 200 thou. I engaged a relatively slow feed and watched the tool remove a nice curly spiral of swarf. I'd learned at a very early stage that swarf was razor sharp and bloody hot, so with a hook I guided the snaking metal into the tray below the lathe.

I turned both journals down to 9.550 inches, just under half an inch under the 10 inch diameter that would be the finished size. With the 10 inch micrometer in my hand I told Joe it was ready for welding. He quickly checked the measurement and called Mac over.

Mac clamped the earth connection to the end of the shaft and proceeded to run a heavy deposit of arc weld over the four-inch length of the journal. After three runs he stopped and asked me to revolve the shaft 180 degrees.

"The shaft is big enough not to distort with the heat, but I want to be 100% certain, so we'll do a couple of small runs and then rotate again until we've built it up" he said, handing me the welding equipment. "I'll be on your shoulder watching. Don't look so fucking worried."

Joe and Mac wanted to finish building up both the journal diameters with weld before we clocked out that evening so it would cool down overnight and be ready for finish turning in the morning. With Mac and me taking it in turns, the welding was finished by 7 pm.

"Can you be in for six in the morning, Steve, to finish it off?" said Joe, locking up his office.

"No problem" I replied, calculating the extra overtime I'd earn.

"Come on young 'un, let's have a pint."

He was an hour later than usual leaving for the Waggon and Horses and Pricey and Graham would be wondering where their drinking mate was, but I was sure Mac would more than make up the pints he had missed. I watched the blokes playing dominoes for a penny a spot, slowly supping the pint of mild Mac had treated me to. I finished it by half seven and Mac was just about to start his third when I left. I had an early start in the morning.

It took me 10 minutes to scrape the ice off the windscreen and defrost the Mini before I could set off to work. It was 5.30 in the morning, but the heater was warm and my Christmas present was keeping my hands warm. A nice pair of brown leather driving gloves would have been even better, preferably holding the wheel of an E-type Jag, but not on an apprentice's wages.

I clocked in bang on six. None of the other blokes in the Fitting Shop were in, but all the workers in the Wire Mill were changing shifts, with night blokes clocking out and the 6 am to 2 pm shift clocking in.

"Fuck me, young Steve's shit the bed this morning" Billy Little roared, causing a good laugh among his mates. "He's been out shaggin' all night. Just wait till I tell his missus." Billy was a great bloke. Tall, heavily built, black hair, centre parting plastered with Brylcreem, he had been captured by the Germans at Dunkirk. He was very much a larger-than-life character. He was also the leading wire drawer in the Wire Mill and always led the singing when the mood took him. It was quite moving to hear 40-odd blokes in full voice in a factory.

Walking from the hot water urn with my tea mug, I heard the strains of "Yes Mr Rushton, no Mr Rushton" coming from a dozen wire drawers' voices. Scotty gets everywhere, I thought. I turned into the shop and saw Joe drinking his tea. I'm glad he's here, I thought.

The shaft had cooled and together we again checked the concentricity of all the diameters and made sure no distortion had occurred. It was fine.

The first cut was very rough and intermittent due to the runs of weld, but after a couple of passes the diameter had fully cleaned up, showing a bright smooth turned finish. The micrometer read 10.125 inches.

"That's bang on" Joe smiled. "Just carefully remove the 0.125 and aim for 10 inches max and 9.995 inches min." I'd got 5 thou to play with. Shouldn't be a problem.

I didn't rush, and even if I say so myself both journals were machined to the exact size. I was well chuffed.

"Just polish up the surfaces with a bit of emery cloth and it'll be ready for Brownie and his mate to take down the Casting Shop" said Joe. "We'll make a Turner of you yet, Steve." His eyes twinkled.

I did feel a sense of achievement and a growing confidence in my ability. A year earlier I don't think I would have tackled a job of this size, or more accurately Joe would not have let me. I told Harry Fisher about it at the college later that week. He smiled. "That Joe sounds as though he knows what he's about."

"He does, Harry. Nearly as good as you."

"'Kin 'ell."

CHAPTER 11

With my 19th birthday there would be another good rise in wages. I'd paid off half the loan on my Mini and was working plenty of overtime, and Pauline was now secretary to the Export Manager at Wilmot Breeden and earning more than me. Just as well, as we were getting married in October. There was so much to sort out, but with the confidence of the young and plenty of help we were sure we could organise it all successfully.

We agreed that we wanted to be married in Yardley Wood Parish Church, at the top of School Road next to the canal bridge. However, the vicar would only agree if I was christened and confirmed. The little matter of christening had been overlooked when I was born. Although I was not particularly religious, I didn't mind attending the necessary instruction on half a dozen evenings. What upset me was the fact that the vicar expected me to attend church on a Sunday morning. That was double-time money.

However I went ahead and was duly christened in the church, and then confirmed a week later in Birmingham Cathedral. After the vicar had explained the birds and the bees and given us some advice on contraception, I was welcomed into his flock and he agreed to conduct the service. Well, it was 1965.

I got George McDonald to write a letter to the vicar explaining that I was a member of a maintenance team and my job involved weekend working, so I might have to miss the odd Sunday morning service. It worked a treat. We attended a couple of church services, and then it was back to double time working. Good old George.

★ ★ ★ ★ ★ ★ ★ ★ ★ ★ ★ ★ ★

"First job every morning is to clear out the ash in the forge and lay fresh coke." It was 7.30 on a Monday morning and John the Blacksmith was shovelling the remains of yesterday's ash into the bin. He was less than two years away from retirement, and although he knew his trade and his job in the factory were disappearing, he was still keen to pass on his skills to "you young boyos" as he called us. He was a small wiry Irishman and I towered over him, but he proved over the next few weeks just how strong he was.

When he had no proper work he would help in tidying up the shop. Caggy and Joe were all right. They were looking after the old 'uns. "Rationalisation" and "efficiency" were still a few years away.

One of our regular jobs in the blacksmith shop was making the large heavy pot stirrers the casters used to puddle the molten brass in the Casting Shop. A cold-rolled section six inches by one inch in cross-section and six feet in length was a tidy weight, but John lifted it off the floor and pushed one end into the forge, piling the glowing coals up over the steel. "It's a lot easier these days," he said, tickling the coals. "The compressor forces the air into the forge, otherwise you'd be working yer bollocks off on the bellows before yow even picked up the fucking hammer."

The blacksmith shop had windows opening on to the canal, but the roof was low and it was like an oven. The heat from the forge blasted into my face. I was sweating, but old John didn't look troubled as he began to scrape away the coals to check the steel. It was red hot.

"Grab hold of the end, Steve" John instructed as he positioned the glowing end of the bar on the anvil before he started to hammer the hot steel into a curve around the pommel. Within a minute or so the steel cooled and stopped flowing. "Back in the forge with it, Steve." He was using a 7lb short-handled lump hammer. He never paused while the steel was hot enough to form, lifting the hammer effortlessly and shaping the glowing hot metal. After each blow to the hot bar he tapped the anvil in a regular rhythm. There was a dull thud when he struck the bar and a bright ring when the hammer kissed the anvil.

"The Blacksmith's Opera." He smiled and paused. "We'll have a quick brew and yow can make the next one."

He placed the cooling pot stirrer on the floor and gently touched the anvil again with the hammer before placing it on the bench. It was quite obvious he loved his tools and his work.

The bar had been in the forge for five minutes when John told me to have a look. I scraped away the hot coals and saw that the end was a bright cherry red.

"That's about right Steve, let's have it on the anvil."

I lifted the hammer and brought it down hard on the red-hot bar, tapping the anvil between blows as John had done. I was glad when the steel dulled and John told me to reheat it. My aching arm and back needed a break.

"The anvil's too low for a lanky bugger like you" John said, smiling. "Now you know what your right hand's for." Another chuckle. "Give it another couple of minutes in the heat and it'll be ready again."

Couple of minutes? I could have done with a half-hour sit-down and a fag.

"You look knackered, son" said Billy Wiggins. I had just sat down at the Fitting Shop table after my lunch in the canteen. I needed a rest, and Billy had noticed me slump gratefully into a vacant armchair.

"The young 'un has suddenly realised there's more to work than standing at a machine all day smoking" said Pat Dowling, winking at the rest of the blokes. "Takes a Paddy to show these young Brummies what hard work is all about."

I was too tired to rise to the bait. I had another four hours of hammering red hot metal ahead of me. There'd be no courting that night.

My first week's wages following my 19th birthday were over twenty quid. My basic was £12 10s, plus £8 of overtime. I didn't realize it at the time, but I was now earning £1000 a year. 'Kin 'ell, Harry would say. I said the same when I saw my stoppages, tax and national insurance.

All the girls in the offices upstairs were coming down to the Wire Mill with pictures of the Moody Blues and asking Les Edge, the foreman, to get Graham to sign autographs. Pauline and I had regularly been going to the Whisky a Go-Go above Chetwins at the bottom of Hill Street in

Birmingham. The Moody Blues were on there one Saturday night and the Spencer Davis Group the next. At ten bob entrance fee, those days were well gone. The Moodys had just had a number one hit with Go Now and Spencer Davis had been nudging the charts for the last three months. It would be another 10 months before Stevie Winwood and his group would have their number 1, Keep On Running. I'd missed my own chance of rock star fame a few years before.

College was going well, work in the blacksmith shop was bloody hard and my Mini Van was running a treat and proving a great courting wagon. Our wedding was eight months away and most of the arrangements had been sorted. Nan and Pop had said that to give us a start we could have one of the bedrooms and convert the main bedroom into a living room. My grandparents were very special people. You only realise how special the people who truly love you are after they have gone. It's too bloody late to tell them then.

A fully-kitted-out blacksmith shop together with a smith as skilled and experienced as John was a rarity, even in 1965. We didn't see any of Arthur's racehorses in the shop, or any other horses for that matter, but John said he could shoe them, given the special metal for the plates and shoes, but not with this "fucking old black iron".

"How would we get the horses down into the factory?" I asked him.

"You're the college kid" he replied, with a twinkle in his eye. He spat on to the hot coals and watched it sizzle into steam.

Black cold-rolled steel was a large part of the work of the smithy shop. The factory produced brass wire and rod by the ton. The blacksmith shop produced wrought iron in almost the same volume for ornamental gates, railings and once even a spiral staircase. Electric twisting machines and tight curling equipment were available for the half-inch square bar which was the main material used. These "foreigners" were manufactured during the week as well as at weekends.

"The gaffers have had me making these gates for years" said John, twisting a red-hot bar into an attractive spiral over a three-inch length. "My guess is that all their mates and neighbours look at their gates and want the same. It keeps me in me job, I love the work and I always get a drink off 'em as well, even Caggy, the miserable bastard."

I'd been working with John for two weeks. The hard work of hammering hot metal was becoming easier and my arms and shoulders were not aching so much. I could even go out in the evenings now.

We made stirrers for the Casting Shop, socket spanners for spark plugs, crow bars from a foot in length to huge great lifting fulcrum bars five long, but the bulk of the regular work was the ornamental gates.

"George McDonald wants to see you upstairs after yer tea break, Steve." Tommy Carter, otherwise known as Caggy, had strolled into the blacksmith shop. "Summat about a spiral staircase." He flicked his fag-end into the forge and walked the 10 yards to his office door. 'Kin 'ell, I thought, what's this?

"Sit down, young man." Mr McDonald welcomed me into his office. "You're working with the blacksmith at the moment, Steve?"

"Yes, Mr McDonald." I could address foremen by their first names, but managers were still called Mister.

"Mr Shakespeare, the Managing Director, is converting a barn at his house near Henley-in-Arden and requires a spiral staircase in wrought iron. His architect has produced the plans, and Ted the draughtsman is going to convert them into engineering drawings for manufacturing. I want you to work with Ted to produce these drawings and then help the blacksmith and Mac the welder to make the staircase."

No-one was listening, so I said "Yes, Mr McDonald".

I knew Ted the draughtsman. He was a mild, gently-spoken man with grey thinning hair and rimless glasses. I thought he would be shocked at the language and the antics in the factory. I was also concerned that office hours were nine to five, and the staff weren't paid overtime.

"You're still on the clock Steve, so carry on as normal" Joe reassured me.

"Any road, there's plenty of work you can do first thing in the morning before Ted comes in, and there's still the weekend work."

As it panned out, after the first couple of days there was plenty to do on the drawing board in the office, and I went straight up after my morning cup of tea in the Fitting Shop.

"Desertin' yer workmates and union brothers then, are yer?" Scotty said, looking around for encouragement from his mates. "White collar and tie man now." Pat Dowling joined in the fun.

At school and college, technical drawing was the only subject I had regularly come top in. I had loved it – all the different pencil leads, point sharpening, accurate dimensioning, handwriting and printing the finished drawing. We had portable desk-mounted drawing boards used with a separate wooden T-square and various plastic set squares. Computers were still 20 years away. However, in the drawing office there were three huge free-standing drawing boards, fully equipped with counterbalanced adjustable cross slides, all with measurements and adjustable angles. This made drawing that much easier and quicker. An adjustable seat with backrest and footrest was all part of the setup. Each board was four feet square and again fully adjustable, from totally upright to horizontal. However, even with all this state-of-the-art drawing equipment I soon found out that a spiral staircase was a right bastard to draw.

The drawing office was located on one of the bridges that crossed the canal system, and long windows looked down on a main junction regularly used by brightly-decorated narrowboats painted with flowers in yellows, reds and greens with fancy buckets and watering cans on the roofs and decks.

"The height from the ground floor to the first floor is 10 feet, so the staircase will have to be made in two sections and completed on site". Ted was thinking aloud and studying the architect's plans. "I think the first job is to draw all the actual steps. A lot of them will be common."

This planning and thinking reminded me of Harry Fisher in the college workshop - don't charge off without carefully thinking the job through. It took the best part of a couple of days before Ted was happy with his plan of transferring the architect's design to an engineering drawing to be issued to the shop floor for manufacture.

Gordon Jones was a technical apprentice who was working in the drawing office at this time. He had left school at 18 with a number of O and A Levels and was studying for his Full Technology Certificate CGLI at South Birmingham Polytechnic. He had never worked on the shop floor, and in my opinion seemed a bit superior to me as a 'craft apprentice'. He said he was studying to be an engineer and eventually wanted to be a works engineer.

Ted had left the office and Gordon was at his drawing board working on the design for a new continuous casting process. He was the same age as me, but rightly or wrongly I believed that for all his A levels he did not have as much engineering knowledge and experience as I did.

"What do you want to be?" Gordon asked me.

"A works manager" I replied without even thinking.

"You'll need better qualifications."

I'll fucking well get 'em then, I thought to myself, returning to my drawing.

Within two weeks we had produced the initial drawings for manufacture and I was beginning to issue the lists of material required and lengths and sizes to be cut. The complete fabrication was made up of hundreds of separate components, flat checker plate for the treads, half-inch flat for the banisters, half-inch square for the stair rails and two-inch box sections for the overall support.

John the blacksmith was in his element, twisting, bending and hammering flat red-hot iron into the patterns and shapes that Ted and I had drawn up. Occasionally he would put his hammer down, scratch his head and look at me. "Who the fucking hell designed this?" he would say. I would then have to sheepishly disappear back to the Drawing Office and ask Ted's advice.

Although I was working in the drawing office and the blacksmith shop I had to fill in a daily/weekly worksheet describing the work we had done and the time spent on each job, the same as everyone else in the maintenance, toolroom and electricians' departments. The old blokes were suspicious.

"Fucking time study by the back door. If they want us on piecework, they can pay us extra." Black Bat was talking to Norman the Shop Steward. "Yow tell 'em, Norman." The younger element in the shop didn't bother, it was all bullshit to them anyway.

"Steve?" Joe Healy called me from his office as I was about to go back up to the drawing office. "One of the secretaries upstairs has a problem with a cupboard, it's stuck and she can't get it open. While you're up there can you have a look?"

Miss Rigsby was well past normal retirement age, grey hair in a tight bun, half-moon reading spectacles perched on the end of a small pert nose. Her steel blue eyes told you she was the Managing Director's secretary and had been so for almost 20 years. She was only five feet tall in her sensible shoes, so I towered over her as she let me into her office.

"Very nice of you to arrive so promptly young man, I only rang Mr Healy five minutes ago." Her voice was clipped and precise. "Would you like a cup of tea and a biscuit?"

"Yes please, Miss Rigsby."

Her little office was next to Mr Shakespeare's sumptuous suite, and as she ushered me in I was amazed at the enormous mahogany desk, highly polished with a red leather inlaid top. I hope the problem ain't with this desk, I thought. All the furniture was a deep burgundy leather, brass studded, and the walls were panelled in light oak. I'd only ever seen Mr. Shakespeare before from a distance, getting in or out of his Humber Super Snipe Estate, usually driven by his chauffeur Bert.

"You're young Phillips, one of the apprentices?" He said, looking up from his desk.

"Yes sir" I replied.

"Finish your tea and biscuits in Nell's office and then see if you can sort out her drawers, they appear to be stuck. Probably lack of use."

I caught a slight twinkle before his eyes dropped back to the documents on his expansive desk. Miss Rigsby bustled me back into her small domain with a disdainful tut. A quick adjustment with a screwdriver and a smear of grease cured the problem.

My worksheet for that day stated that I'd spent one hour smoothing, adjusting, greasing and ensuring the easy sliding movement of Miss Rigsby's drawers.

Nearly all the component parts for the staircase were now produced and I was spending time with Mac the welder fabricating and welding the wrought iron together.

And troubleshooting. A lot of troubleshooting. This didn't fit, that didn't fit. Something was too big, too small, the wrong shape. Would it ever be finished?

It certainly wouldn't be finished the next week. It was Easter, and Pauline and I were driving to North Wales for a few days - the first long run in the Mini. It poured down with rain non-stop, the windscreen wipers packed up and on the Sunday we ended up in a dry county, so we couldn't even get a beer.

"I served my time at the Curragh in County Kildare." John the blacksmith was having, in his phrase, a blow – a smoke. I must have looked puzzled.

"The Curragh is a famous racecourse where they run the Irish Derby. I lived in a little village called Ballymany, a two-mile walk from the course."

"Have you always worked as a blacksmith, John?" I asked him, lighting up a fag and leaning back on the bench. I needed a blow myself.

"I started at the Curragh in 1915 when I was 13. I was an apprentice jockey. The pay was virtually nothing. You were lucky to get the chance to work alongside horses, that was the bit I loved – Grooming 'em, riding 'em. I was horse barmy, so I was. I'd have sat in a saddle all bloody day."

His grey eyes misted over, and a sad smile played in the corner of his mouth as he went back fifty years.

"Did you ever ride a winner?" I asked.

He looked thoughtful, tipped his coke-stained cap to the back of his head and wiped his forehead. Then he gobbed into the red-hot coals.

"I had me first shag in the straw at the back of a stable with a young lass who helped the head groom. I'd just turned 17, so I thought that was a right fucking winner." He laughed, coughing. "I groomed 'em, learned to shoe 'em, cleaned out the stables and yard from six in the morning till it got dark at night and rode the buggers on the heath in training. By the time I'd walked back home it was usually past seven o'clock. In the summer it would be nearly nine.

"I should have been skin and bone, but I was still growing. That was the snag, because by the time I was 16 I was over five foot tall and seven stone. The assistant trainer told me not to build up my hopes. 'You're a good lad John' he said. 'You have the ability and the love of horses, and most importantly the determination to win, I've seen it on the heath. But by the time you're 18 you'll be too tall and heavy.'

"Mr O'Riley was a good fella, so he was, and he was right. The gaffer gave me my chance just before I got too heavy. I was almost 17 and he got me a couple of rides in novice races."

I didn't understand. "How do you mean, John? How could you be too tall and heavy?" I towered above him.

"A flat racing jockey has to be less than eight stone. Ain't yow seen 'em on the telly? They're bloody midgets. Anyway I came second in me first race and won the second. I earned a fiver, which was a bloody fortune in those days, the best part of three months' wages. Mr O'Riley said the only way I could make the weight next time was to cut off one of me bloody legs. So I became a blacksmith."

We went back to the hot, heavy work of forging glowing red steel into the forms and shapes I had helped to draw to produce the staircase for Mr Shakespeare's converted barn. All the smithy work was now virtually finished - we were just re-working the odd mistake.

"One day I'll tell yer about the time I earned a proper fortune" John said, his hammer in full swing.

The staircase was beginning to take shape in the corner of the Fitting Shop, with all the welding being done behind the protection of the green hanging curtains. We had decided it would be in three sections, not two. This would help manufacture, transport and erection and welding on site. By this stage I was heavily involved in the welding with Mac and Scotty and well experienced in picking up hot metal and avoiding burns and eye flashes. It does take time for it to sink in before you learn. Most importantly, I was looking forward to seeing the finished product installed. I'd never been in a posh barn before.

"I was in right fucking trouble with my missus yesterday." Mac the welder had sat down to eat his bacon and egg sandwich. It was half nine on a Sunday morning and Scotty, Mac's mate and I were sitting in the corner of the welding shop tucked behind the hanging protective screens and enjoying our breakfast.

Scotty looked up – he was always interested in a bit of fun. Before either of us could ask why Mac was in trouble with his missus, he finished his sandwich, opened the huge drawer underneath the work bench and started rummaging. He was worried about something. Lighting up a fag, he finally found the G clamp he was looking for.

"Went on the piss with Graham and Pricey yesterday afternoon and got home about half four in the afternoon" Mac continued. "I'd promised me missus I'd be back early so she could go shopping with her mother. I'd said I'd look after the kids." He stubbed his fag out and grinned. "I looked after the buggers all right, fuck me so I did."

"What happened?" I asked. Mac had four children ranging from eight to just 20 months.

"I'd had a few when I got home. She was waiting with her mother, all dressed up sitting in the front room. She and her mother stood up and my missus gave me a right fucking look. You look after the kids and get them their tea, she said. She slammed the door and it nearly came off its hinges."

"You ain't heard half of it yet" Scotty said to me out of the corner of his mouth.

"I gave the kids their tea, the missus had got it all ready anyway" Mac went on. "I put the telly on downstairs for the three eldest, put Simon in his cot and then went for a bit of a lie down. It was dark when I woke up and I switched on the bedside light. The clock said half six - morning or night, I wondered, I didn't have a clue. When I came round I realised young Simon was lying next to me playing with my face and gabbling away, "Dada, dada!" I leaned up on one elbow and put my hand into an open nappy. That was then I woke up fucking quick."

I looked at Scotty. "He'd fallen asleep upstairs," Scotty said. "The kids were playing in the garden when they heard Simon crying, so Gail, the eldest, went up to see to him. While she was changing his dirty nappy on the bed next to her Dad, her brothers and sisters decided to help. It wasn't going too bad until Mick, the eldest son, started throwing clothes out of the bedroom window into the front garden. He was playing parachutes with his pals below. "

Mac was shaking his head. "There was shit all over me and the bed, clothes all over the front garden and the missus and her bloody mother coming back in half an hour. 'Kin 'ell!" Old Harry would have seconded that.

Over the previous three years I had passed the City & Guilds Craft Practice Parts 1, 2 and 3 and I was now trying to pass the Toolmaking Supplementary part of the City and Guilds. My simple pierce and blank tool with sensors was almost completed.

Not for the first time, I wondered what I would study for the next 18 months if I passed. Written exams and practical work took over these concerns, and life at Garretts Green Technical College was a regular one-day-a-week attendance.

"What do you think, Harry?" I was sitting in Harry Fisher's office in the workshop at Garretts Green. I really respected this man.

"You'll pass this year, I'm sure" he replied. "They always allow an extra year, just in case an apprentice fails an exam on the way. My advice is carry on studying and learning. Talk to your apprentice supervisor."

They said Mr Cockcroft was in my view a total wanker, but I wasn't going to say this to Harry. However he saw my expression and nodded.

"Wait and see, young man" he said.

All the component parts of my press tool were now made and the punches, dies and stripper plate were at the hardeners. They should be back for next week, when I'd planned to finish-grind all the bits. A previously-used die set was available which would be used to assemble my press tool, and all being well it would then be ready to mount into the 50-ton press in the workshop.

Jim was making a similar set of tooling, and he was confident it would produce to drawing.

"How's everything going?" he asked me. He too was getting married later in the year.

"Hell of a lot to do" I replied. "We've booked the church, the school hall, the cars and caterers and a week's honeymoon in Cornwall. I hope we ain't forgot anything."

"Pat and me are the same," he said. We were standing in the yard behind the workshop having a smoke, sounding like a couple of old blokes. Jim had decided to concentrate on the small punches and dies that Bonehead made in the factory, and he worked alongside the old bugger in a new workshop that had been built close to the Fine Wire Mill in the main factory. Frank was still learning his electrical trade.

"Have you thought what you're going to do after this toolmaking exam?" I asked Jim. He was six months older than me.

"I'll be 20 in September, with another year to go. I might do a more advanced toolmaking course. What about you?"

" I don't know yet. I've just had a word with Harry and there are a couple of courses available, but as he said we've got a month or two to decide." I stubbed out my fag and we both returned into the workshop.

Little did we know that events beyond our control would influence our future training. But that was still two months away.

What I did know was that Pauline and I were going to Margate for the Spring Bank Holiday weekend – totally unaware that thousands of mods and rockers had the same idea. As we drove up the M1 towards London, we noticed hundreds of scooters in groups of up to 20 or so travelling south. Once we came off the North Circular (the M25 hadn't been built yet) there were even more. Strangely enough we didn't see many rockers on motorbikes.

The weather was fine and sunny on the Sunday, with families on the beach enjoying themselves. Then at about midday it all kicked off. There were running battles down the promenade, rockers were getting chucked into the paddling pools (they were well outnumbered by the mods) and police black marias were charging about.

Like everybody else, we watched from a distance. I suppose it was a bit of fun, and I don't believe anyone was seriously hurt.

"It's a fucking wonder he knows where the factory floor is."

Mr Shakespeare had just walked into the Fitting Shop, and Black Bat had noticed him inspecting the spiral staircase.

"It's cost him fuck all, and him nigh on a millionaire." Black Bat looked at Norman the Shop Steward. "Wotcher goin' to do about it?"

Norman shrugged his shoulders and went back to his lathe.

Alf really was a vindictive old bugger, and he hated management. I used to wonder if he hated the entire world, the way he went on.

"It looks good, well done chaps" said Mr Shakespeare to the gang of men standing in the welding area – Ted the draughtsman, Mac and Scotty, John the blacksmith, Caggy, Joe and yours truly. We all looked suitably proud, fidgeting and shuffling our feet.

"Mr Carter, arrange for delivery as soon as possible."

"Yes Mr Shakespeare, I'll arrange it with Miss Rigsby" Caggy replied. I left the welding area and walked across the shop to join the others having their afternoon tea break. All the usual crowd were sitting around the twin welded steel Morrison air raid shelter which was our dining table. Most of the jumbled assortment of chairs had remained the same during the three years I'd worked in the factory, and I still had the swivel chair on castors.

CHAPTER ELEVEN

"That staircase for old Shakey looks good" Billy Wiggins said, finishing
off his tea and lighting up a Senior Service. He gave me a very faint wink,
and only I saw the hardly noticeable lift of his silver head towards Black Bat.
He's winding him up, I thought to myself.

Pat Dowling and Scotty quickly sussed Billy's intention. "You and Scotty
have done a real good job" Pat said, looking at me.

"I did all the technical work, young Steve just held the steel" Scotty
replied. "But I tell you what, it must have saved Mr Shakespeare a bloody
fortune."

As always, Alf bit. He struggled up from his armchair and removed the
pipe from his clenched teeth.

"Yow silly buggers should realise he's worth a bloody fortune and he has
a big posh free car" (Alf had a Hillman Minx) "and fancy suits and a free
dinner every day and a bloke to drive him everywhere, and we all work our
bollocks off so he can sit on his arse all day." Alf stomped off to his grinders.
"I suppose some of yow arse lickers will be putting the fucking thing up in
his barn." Black Bat was well wound up.

We all looked at each other, wondering what to say. The younger
apprentices were looking puzzled. The old blokes were smiling and nodding.

"They say anyone working at his house gets a full breakfast in the morning
and sandwiches for lunch, all free. His missus is all right but the cook and
maid are great," Scotty said, laughing.

Not to miss out on the craic, Pat joined in. "Graham the pipefitter was
there last month repairing a cistern. He reckoned he couldn't drink all the
tea the maid kept bringing him. He had a bottle of beer with his ploughman's
lunch and the butler gave him a bottle of Famous Grouse as he left." Pat
wiped the tears from his eyes with the back of his hand. Everybody was
pissing themselves.

Alf looked back. "Fucking bastards," he said, jamming the pipe back into
his mouth.

"You wouldn't think old Alf was a Tory" Billy Wiggins said.

The day came for Mac, Scotty and me to erect and weld up the staircase in Mr Shakespeare's barn. The lorry was loaded with all the sections and welding equipment and Bert Phillips, the MD's chauffeur, was going to take us to Henley in Arden in Mr McDonald's estate car. I'd hardly ever spoken to the bloke, but for some reason I didn't like Bert Phillips. He seemed smarmy. He was a heavily-built man, not tall, with grey hair cut short with a side parting and cheek jowls. He was always dressed in his blue uniform and only wore his chauffeur's cap when driving. It was his eyes I didn't like - shifty.

When Bert was not driving the MD about or cleaning the huge Humber he could be found in the snooker room playing a game with one of the foremen, or practising on his own. He was on immediate call if the MD wanted him, but he still had an easy job.

"In the snooker competition then are yer, young 'un?" Bert asked me over his shoulder as we pulled out of the car park on the way to Henley. Mac was in the front with me and Scotty in the back. "Yow've all got to beat me to win the 25 quid" he said, with a smug grin.

"I tell yer what Bert, the time you spend wearing yer waistcoat out leaning on that table yow ought to be better than Joe Davis" Scotty replied, before I had time to rise to the bait. Big-headed bugger, I thought to myself.

Bro. Hall had organized a knockout snooker competition spread over four nights the following week, and Jim and I and some of the other competitors had been practising at every opportunity. Even though Graham Morris was not playing (he was too good, but he had agreed to referee the final) there were at least four players who were better than me. Jim and I were on par, but he was leading our last 15 games by a single game.

"Wake up Steve, we're there." I felt a nudge in the ribs and tumbled out of the car into the beautiful courtyard of a red-brick three-storey farmhouse. The top floor windows were small and tucked into the grey slate tiles and the huge ground-floor bow windows were made up of small wooden panes, some of them with bottled glass. To the right was a barn, in matching brickwork. In the centre of the courtyard was a water feature 10 feet in diameter, again in red brick, and a gentle trickle of water cascaded into a two-foot deep pool below, oxygenating the water for the expensive koi carp which were lazily cruising in it. The stables and garages were on the left.

Bert drove off back to the factory. The sharp white gravel crunched under my Toe Tectors. I knew what Harry Fisher would say.

I lived in a council house with my Nan and Pop, Mac and his missus and four kids had a council house and Scotty rented a flat. The three of us looked at each other in amazement. None of us had ever seen anything like this.

The lorry loaded with all the kit was slowly pulling into the courtyard when an attractive, petite, dark-haired woman suddenly appeared, holding a tray with six mugs of tea on it.

"Follow me you young men, and we'll all have a nice cup of tea before you start work" she said. She strutted towards the barn, pushed open the door with her elbow, set down the tray on a long workbench and sat on an upturned orange box. Her brown eyes were very bright, her features were kind and soft and her wellies were green. I'd only ever seen black ones before. I guess she was in her late forties.

"I'll be back in an hour with some bacon sandwiches. I don't suppose Harold's told you, but I'm Elizabeth."

"The maid's all right" said Mac. "Or was she the cook?" He helped Scotty to unload the sections of the staircase off the back of the lorry and carry them into the barn. I was unloading the diesel generator to drive the welding machine.

"Who the bloody hell's Harold?" I asked.

"That's Shakey's first name" Mac replied, grabbing hold of a couple of G clamps. "Come on, we've got work to do and I want to be back at the factory at six. I'm having a drink in the Waggon." Mac was a creature of habit.

The supports holding the structure were drilled and steel Rawlplugged into the new concrete floor. We were just about to offer the first section up for clamping into place when Elizabeth returned with our breakfast.

"There's ketchup and HP sauce on the tray. I'll see you at lunchtime" she said.

My Nan & Pop, Gladys and Jack Froud

Dressed as a Beatle in 1963 or 64

With my Triumph 21 in 1963

With two mates on the seafront at the Blackpool Motor Bike Show.
I'm in the middle - dig the winkle pickers.

Me getting out of my Mini van outside the council house where I was born

I wore my army uniform to blag my way into Villa Park to watch the FA Cup
semi-final between West Bromwich Albion and the Blues in about 1972.

"The sauce is in a dish, not a bottle," I said. We were all scratching our heads. "Too old to be the maid. Too young and good-looking to be the cook." We all agreed on that. "Housekeeper?" I said.

Lunch was cheese sandwiches with onions and pickle and mugs of tea. By four o'clock, when Bert arrived to take us back to the factory, the first section had been welded into place and the second was all positioned and clamped awaiting welding. He dropped us off in Adderley Street and wound down the window.

"I'll see you in the morning. I've been practising all day young 'un, and I've had a break of 28. You've got no chance." He wound up the window.

Two quick games of snooker with Jim and I was driving home by half six. It was Friday night and Pauline and I were going to the Aero Club at Elmdon.

By half past twelve the following day the staircase was erected, fully welded and awaiting painting. It looked a treat, and we'd been on time and a half for the morning's work. Good old Saturday.

The barn had huge oak beams supporting the ceiling above, with crossbeams running from the upright walls. An inglenook and a walk-in fireplace were built into the gable wall. I hadn't seen anything like this before. Mac and I leaned back on the outside wall admiring the courtyard, lighting up.

"This place must be worth a fucking fortune," said Mac, taking a drag. "Pricey told me Shakey owns all the land as far as yow can see."

"To be sure it will look mighty fine when it's finished." Scotty was washing his hands in the temporary sink, in what would presumably be the kitchen. "Ay up, it's yer man himself." He quickly dried his hands.

"You chaps have done an excellent job," said Mr Shakespeare. "I hope my wife has looked after you." He was dressed in fawn flannel trousers, brown brogues and a light brown checked sports coat. A yellow cravat finished off his weekend attire. Elizabeth, in a pale blue dress (no wellies now), leaned on his arm. Bloody hell, I thought to myself, she's his missus.

Mr Shakespeare reached into the inside pocket of his jacket and drew out a leather wallet. "Well done" he said, putting a £10 note into each of our hands.

162

"I'll see to Ted and the blacksmith next week. But keep it to yourselves." He lightly touched his nose with the index finger of his right hand.

Mac, Scotty and I looked at each other in amazement. Three voices said in unison "Yes, Mr Shakespeare".

On the journey back to the factory, I noticed Scotty smiling to himself.

"What yer thinking, Bob?" I asked quietly, not wanting Bert to hear.

"I was wondering what old Black Bat would say."

I looked alarmed. "You ain't gonna tell him about the tenner?"

"No way. I was thinking of telling him we'd met the cook, maid, housekeeper, butler, head gardener, gamekeeper, private secretary and the woman who does the washing" Bob said as he relaxed in the back seat. "But not all at once. This craic will last a month or two." He dropped off to sleep.

CHAPTER 12

Bert dropped us off at the factory just before half one and I played some snooker with a couple of the blokes who were entered in the next week's competition. We all needed the practice. Then I went up the Blues with Les Green.

I had to get home as soon as the game was over. I was picking up Pauline at seven as it was Mickey Plant's wedding reception.

The snooker room had a table tennis table and a dartboard. There were long bench seats down the full length of two walls, providing seating for spectators, and a large manhole cover near the main snooker table gave access to essential pipework underneath.

Sixteen players had entered. The first prize was £25. The second was £15 and there was £10 for the highest break. Graham Morris wasn't playing – he'd have won with his eyes shut.

Les Green was a much better player than me. Jim Richmond was slightly better than me and the likes of Pricey, Joe Doyle, Big Jim Cooper and a few others I could just about hold my own against, if I played well. As always, the draw was important.

My first match was against Fred Brown, an electrician in his early forties, a quiet, unassuming bloke who had only just taken up an interest in snooker. He'd started to play at lunchtimes and occasionally for an hour in the evening. He had recently acquired his own left-handed cue. He was still learning about the game, and while I was a lot younger I had much more experience. I won fairly comfortably.

Who would I be drawn against in the next round? Jim and I had discussed our dream of meeting in the final as the two young champions. We would have to see about that.

There were no surprises in the first games, and at lunchtime in the canteen the following day Bro. Hall made the draw for the quarter finals. At this stage

I didn't want to be drawn against Les or Jim, but I'd take my chance with the others in a one-frame game. The semi-final was over three frames, but I had to get through the quarters first.

Bro. Hall looked down into the bag and drew out a slip of paper.

"That's a coincidence," he said. "Steve Phillips will play... Bert Phillips."

Bert smirked at me. "While you're working yer lathe or swinging yer hammer I'll be practising. See yer about six o'clock tonight. You've no fucking chance."

At about two o'clock that afternoon Bert was beating Bill Baker the warehouse foreman by 20 points, and Bill needed a snooker, when Miss Rigsby nervously peered into the snooker room.

"Mr Phillips, Mr Shakespeare requires you to collect an important customer from New Street Station. Can you go directly?" She looked around the room as if it was a den of vice and iniquity and scurried out.

"It'll only tek me half an hour," Bert told Bill. "I'll be gone by then" was Bill's reply. "I'll practise on me own, then" said Bert.

At 2.30 Mr McDonald had a phone call from Arthur, the canteen manager, complaining that all the sinks in his kitchens were blocked. "The girls can't do the washing up," he moaned. It was just before three when Graham and his mate lifted the three-foot-square inspection cover in the snooker room to gain access to the pipework below. The drop to the pipes was almost six feet, so Graham decided to fetch a ladder. The problem was soon sorted and the girls were able to do the washing up. But Graham somehow forgot to slide the cover back...

The first man to enter the snooker room was, of course, Bert Phillips.

Pricey told the story later in the pub. He had won his game and was enjoying a pint in the Waggon. "When we walked in I heard some moaning. I thought it was a ghost, or a couple shagging. I looked around but couldn't see fuck all. It was Jim Cooper who spotted him. The poor bugger's head was just about sticking out of the manhole cover."

Pricey smiled as he took a pull of his pint. "Should have been his neck, the idle bastard." Everyone nodded.

Bert had badly broken his leg. Funnily enough, no-one appeared to be overly concerned. He was not a popular bloke.

"You're a lucky bastard, young 'un" Pricey said, looking at me. "You're through to the semi-final on a bye."

Jim's name was the first out of the bag the following lunchtime, and everyone in the canteen stopped what they were doing and watched in silence as Bro. Hall carefully unwrapped the next small piece of paper. Please, not my name, I said to myself.

In a loud voice Bro. Hall announced: "Jim Richmond will play Les Green". Everyone then knew who the other semi-finalists were. Me and Pricey looked at each other.

"Chuck that new cue you've just bought and get yerself a magic wand, cause you'll need it young 'un" he said, standing up from the foreman's table and strolling towards the door. "I'll have a few frames to warm up for tonight."

"Hang on a bit, John" I called. "Let me get Graham to lift the manhole cover off, I might get lucky again."

"Cheeky kids" he replied, smiling as he went out towards the snooker room.

Pricey was a big hard bastard, always taking the piss, but he was all right and he could take a joke. I personally liked and admired him.

Les Green worked in the Fitting Shop as a turner and I got on well with him. He was married with a son and daughter and his wife Carol was a schoolteacher. Pauline and I had visited their smart three-bedroom semi in Sutton Coldfield a few times on a Sunday afternoon. In his late thirties, with light ginger hair and a happy grinning face, he was nearly always smiling. He was a keen Blues supporter and we had regularly walked up Kingston Hill together on a Saturday afternoon after work. He was also a good snooker player who had attempted to improve my game. "Never leave your opponent a shot," he would say.

"You've beaten Pricey before Steve, so don't worry" said Les. We were having a mug of tea. "He's beaten me more times though" I replied. Les leaned closer and dropped his voice.

"You know the way he plays – slam bang wallop, shit or bust. Play him safe and he loses his patience. That's the way to beat him over three frames."

Les was right. Everyone had seen Pricey whacking the balls around the table with a loud "gerrin yer bastard!" when the red slammed into a pocket after rebounding off two cushions at 100 miles an hour. He was even more cavalier if he'd had a few pints.

Les and Jim's semi-final was to start at 5.30 that evening and my match was scheduled for seven. The final over five frames was the next night. Les was currently leading the highest break, with 35.

By 5.35 nearly all the seats were taken along the wall nearest to the full-size table as Bro. Hall flicked the coin to see who would break off. "Heads" called Les, and heads it was.

"You can break, then" Les said, chalking the tip as Jim positioned the white ball with his cue.

I sat on the red leatherette seating level with the black ball and watched Jim play a good safety shot, just kissing the outer red of the triangle of balls before gently rebounding the white off two cushions and returning it to the base line. I wonder where Pricey is, I thought to myself, he would normally finish at five, and as a foreman he was on staff and didn't get paid for overtime. Mind you, from what I've heard theses blokes earned nearly 35 quid a week.

By half past six all the seating had been taken up and a dozen chairs had been borrowed from the canteen upstairs to cater for the extra spectators. Jim had played well, not many mistakes, but Les was good. He won in two straight frames.

"And the next semi final is between Steve Phillips and John Price." Bro. Hall checked the paperwork on his clipboard, filling in the score from the previous match. I was already warming up on the three-quarter table and concentrating on short potting, wondering where my opponent was, when Pricey burst through the double swing doors.

"Right then, let's get cracking. I've left me beer on the table in the Waggon and I want to get back before it gets flat." He'd obviously had a drink. Graham, who was his mate, followed him into the room grinning.

No doubt about it, Pricey was a great character. That was why the room was full – people were looking forward to a bit of a laugh. Looking around, I was surprised to see a number of the old 'uns from the Fitting Shop nodding encouragement in my direction. Miss Snooker Legs quietly slipped through the door holding a gin and tonic.

"Yer want to make it interesting, young 'un" said Pricey, lighting up a cigarette. He slipped the smart Ronson lighter back into his waistcoat pocket and smiled as he chalked his cue. He really looked the part - the Hurricane Higgins of the Wire Works.

"A couple of quid?" I suggested, trying to appear nonchalant. I could just about afford to lose two or three pounds.

"A tenner apiece is what I play for when I'm in the mood" he replied. Oh shit, I thought, I couldn't handle that. Graham saw my concern and took me to one side. Pricey took a quick swig from a hip flask.

"Accept the bet and I'll back yer for half of it. Lose and it'll cost yer a fiver. Win the match and you'll be up by a tenner." He chuckled. "I'll have a right laugh taking the mick if you beat him, and you can do it. He's half pissed anyway."

"OK, a tenner each" I said to Pricey. Could he see how nervous I was? He had a quick tot and went to the table.

He broke off with a thunderous shot, smashing the balls all over the table and scattering the reds, the black and the pink ending up half way down with only the low colours still on their spots. The white cue ball cannoned off three cushions and dropped into the middle pocket. I was four in front and I hadn't played a stroke.

It looked impossible to play safe, so I went for a red, potted it and took an easy blue. I was 10 in front.

But my opponent was in his element with the balls all over the table. He was a bloody good potter and enjoyed watching the balls disappearing into the pockets and screwing the white back into position for the next shot. He won the first frame 65 to 33.

Les looked at me and I could read the message in his eyes - slow it down. Graham surreptitiously lowered and raised the flat of his right hand.

My break-off was perfect, hardly disturbing the pack of reds with the cue ball returning to within three inches of the back cushion. This game was very different. I was trying to stop him from scoring and pinching the odd 10 or 15 break. Soon I was leading by five points with all the colours left, and safety play was easier with just six balls on the table. I also sensed that Pricey was getting pissed as well as pissed off. Graham had slipped him a new flask.

After another five minutes of cat-and-mouse, Pricey potted the yellow and green, but I took the frame by potting first the brown, another safety shot and then the blue and pink.

Bro. Hall tossed the coin to decide who would break off the final frame. I won and played the same careful shot as before. This time my opponent adopted a different tactic - he played safe instead of smashing the balls around. How long could he keep this game up?

The scores were low because neither of us had a break of more than 15, but I was hoping that Pricey would lose his patience before I did. I was rewarded after I had made a particularly poor shot and left a possible double. If he doubled the blue into the middle pocket he would be two in front with just the pink and black left on the table. I personally would not have attempted the double but would have gone for a shot to bring the cue ball back to the bottom cushion.

Pricey drew his arm back and made his stroke. The blue slammed into the cushion and rebounded across the middle of the table, heading towards the opposite pocket as intended. But it hit the pocket too hard, juddered in the jaws, shot back across the table and disappeared into the bag. "Ger in yer bastard!" he shouted, his cue held high as he rushed around to sink the pink, the only pot he needed to win. I now needed both the pink and black to win, even if he missed it.

Pricey was on a high. He didn't even take time to chalk his cue before going for another double on the pink to win the match. The spectators all drew in their breath as they saw the pink rattle to a standstill and teeter on the edge.

'Kin 'ell! Just a simple tap in, and I could get on the black. Pot the easy pink and play safe on the black, that's what Les and Graham would do, and that was what I did, leaving the cue ball on the bottom cushion with the black near the centre of the table. I was four in front.

I was determined not to leave Pricey a shot and the next five minutes were not pretty to watch, but then I miss-cued. I'd left the black 18 inches from the top cushion, a fairly easy shot with the cue ball nicely angled near the middle pocket. It only needed a slow, careful shot to finish the match.

Pricey chalked his cue, lit another fag and took a long drag, blowing the smoke high into the air before placing the butt into the ashtray. As I watched my opponent flex his arm I realised he was determined to finish the match in a blaze of glory. Never mind the slow steady pot – he was going to slam the black into the pocket and polish his opponent off with a bang.

Pricey struck the cue ball. The black disappeared into the top left-hand bag with a loud whack, and as it did so, to my delight, the white ball flew straight into the right hand pocket. I was in the final.

"Well done, yer young bugger," Pricey said, slipping me a tenner. "Now yer can buy me a pint down the Waggon."

"You owe me a beer an' all, because I helped to get him pissed" Graham smiled. "But you'll never be any good at snooker, and it's too late now. Too many bad habits."

I'll leave the car in the car park, I thought, it'll be safe there, and I'll only be an hour. I walked down towards the Waggon and Horses tapping my pocket with the tenner in. I was in the final tomorrow night, with another fifteen quid to come even if I lost. That added up to over a week's wages. I was in the money.

"Come on then, gerrem in." Pricey and Graham were leaning on the lounge bar. "Well done young 'un, you stuffed him a treat" Graham said to me, nudging his best mate in the ribs. "Mine's a pint." Give him his due, there were no bad feelings that I had beaten Pricey in the match. He slapped me on the back and pushed a large whisky into my hand.

"Gerrit down yer neck. Yow ain't bad for a kid." Pricey was all right.

Looking through from the lounge, I noticed Arthur Twamley and John the blacksmith having a quiet drink in the corner of the bar. Knowing their favourite tipple, I approached their table with two whiskies.

"You played well, Steve" Arthur said, looking up. John nodded his agreement. "Pricey's a right Jack the lad, to be sure." I guess they'd been talking horses, they always did. While I knew John was not a big drinking man, his usual pale complexion was ruddy and his eyes were bright.

"I'll get yer a pint Steve, same again John?" Arthur stood up and walked to the bar, returning with two pints and a double whisky for the blacksmith. I glanced at my watch. It was 9.15 and I'd had three pints plus a whisky. I was enjoying myself. I could always catch the bus home.

"Did I ever tell you about the time I made some real money?" John dropped his voice and flicked his eyes around the old blokes in the room. "This is a tale an' a half. It would have been about 1933. I was in me early 30s and I'd been second blacksmith at the Curragh for five years. The wages were crap and me and the missus rented a small two bedroom cottage. With three kids it was a tight fit." John gently sipped his Jameson and took a cigarette from me. He nipped off the filter, lit up and continued.

"Mary's sister and her husband Joe had moved to Birmingham five years before with their five kids. Within a month Joe had got a job at the Austin, earning a bloody fortune apparently. She was always writing to my Mary about how much Joe earned, the lovely three-bedroom council house they had, the schools and shops and buses.

"My missus came back after a week's visit there, and she started driving me barmy. John, she said, there's no future here in Ireland. No proper education. No good jobs. Do you think we could move to England?"

John's mouth was set in a grim smile, but his eyes were sad. "Let's have another drink," he said. He stood up, slightly unsteady and ordered a round.

"I loved me job, the horses, the countryside, the yard. I loved Ireland, me Mam and Pa. But I also loved my Mary." He sniffed. "I'm away for a piss." He got up.

I looked at Arthur. "I know the story about the money, but I ain't heard this bit" he said, supping his pint of mild. "We're talking 30 years ago, yer know." He offered me a Woodbine and placed another on the table next to John's glass. I would definitely be catching the bus home.

John came back and sat down again. "It took me months to sort it all out in me own mind" he went on. "One night when the kids were all tucked up in bed, me and my Mary sat down at the kitchen table. "You're right me darling" I said. "Let's get the Derby over and then I'll put me notice in. You write to your Bernadette."

Old John seemed to relax, as though he'd only just made the decision that night. A happy smile creased his lined face. "I'll tell yer what, the fucking bed springs bounced that night."

I ordered the next round and sent two pints through to Pricey and Graham in the lounge. I was still in pocket from the tenner I'd won.

"The Irish Sweepstake Derby had been run since 1866 and in the 1930s it was second only to the English Derby," said Arthur. "Royalty and millionaires from all over the world entered their horses and came to the festival, every year." He was on his favourite subject. "During Derby week, John and the head blacksmith were rushed off their feet, shoeing and replacing plates. Temporary blacksmiths had to be bought in. All the lads, grooms, everybody that worked in the yard used to stand in awe when the Arab owners came, with their huge entourage of bowing and scraping flunkeys, all dressed in flowing white robes. Kings and princes, the lot of em.

"There was one bloke though who wore a normal suit, though it was made of silk, and he seemed to do most of the arse-licking. He was only a little bloke, skinny with jet black hair scraped flat and greased. You could see the brown of his scalp under his centre parting, he had a pencil thin Errol Flynn moustache with a beak of a nose that almost touched his top lip. A right shifty looking bastard, I tell yer."

John drained his glass with a flourish. "My shout" Arthur said.

"Who were they, John?" I asked.

"I have to take that knowledge to my grave. Yer main man is still alive even though he's in his 70s. All his sons are princes, and they're still massive in racing.

"Anyway, little shifty spent a bit of time in the yard during the days before the big race, sometimes with yer main man and his gang but a fair amount on his own talking to every bugger. He even passed the time of day with me once, watching me fit some training plates. I tell yer what, he was a right nosey bastard, asking me about this and that."

"Hang on John, I'm going out the back," I said. The gents was outside in the street. I poked my head into the lounge to see Pricey and his mates laughing and joking. "I ain't kidding, she's got the biggest pair of tits yow've ever seen in yer life." He was on form. I returned to listen to the rest of John's story.

"Ahmed, he called himself, and on the morning of the day before the big race he was in the yard with yer main man looking over the two horses he had running in the Derby. His first horse was 7-4 favorite and his second runner was 8-1. They were magnificent – thoroughbred Arabian stallions. I'd been around horses for nigh on 20 years, but I'd never seen anything like these." John took a sip of his beer and stubbed out his Woodbine.

"Did you get a dead cert tip, John?" I asked, thinking this was how he earned his big money.

Arthur leaned towards me. "At those odds no working man could win a lot of money, we don't have it to put on. Think about it."

Then Pricey pushed open the door of the bar and placed two pints of mild and a large double Jameson on our table. "We're all going round to the Dolls' Club later if you're interested, young 'un" he said to me. He shook hands with Arthur and John. "You two as well." He walked out back to the lounge with a laugh. "A right boyo, that bugger," said John.

The Dolls' Club was a strip joint, just round the corner near the Flyover. I was now definitely catching the bus home.

"I was sat on a bit of a bench round the back of one of the stables having me sandwich looking at the view" John went on. "I looked at the green rolling fields, the training runs, the parade ring and the white rails of the main racecourse of the Curragh. I could just see the hedgerows on the road to my village." John was getting maudlin now. I hoped he would finish the tale before he got too pissed.

John took a taste of his drink. "I'd made me mind up and promised the missus we were off, but I would miss Ireland. I didn't see this Ahmed fella until he sat down alongside me and offered me a Capstan Full Strength. Have you got a moment John, he said?"

Then Arthur took up the story. "John'll never reveal the name of the owner or the horse for obvious reasons" he said. "They paid him a lot of money. That family are still world famous today."

"What the bloody hell happened then?" I was getting impatient.

"The second and third favourites were owned by other rich buggers. Ahmed suggested that I put a loose plate on one of them. You weren't certain which horse you would shoe up because there were four blacksmiths working during the week and 20 runners in the big race, but I reckon the crafty bugger had had a moment with all of us."

"What's a loose plate?" I asked.

"You wouldn't get away with it today, but in those days, well…" John tipped back his old coke-stained cap and scratched his head. "If you fitted a plate with short nails to the horse's hoof, you could be pretty certain that over a mile the horse would lose the shoe. It wouldn't hurt him, but it would upset his rhythm."

"The favourite was a dead cert" John went on. "But the owner obviously wanted a bit of extra insurance. He offered me £50 to fit the loose plate and

£500 if the horse shed it during the race. I was on less than four quid a week and was sailing to a new life in England next week. What would you blokes have done?" We nodded. We understood exactly.

"When me and the missus were cuddled up in bed I asked her what she thought. I always asked Mary about the big decisions in our life, she had more common sense than me. 'Take the money John' she said. She had no hesitation. I reached into my trouser pocket on the floor, pulled out the £50 Ahmed had slipped me and gently handed it to Mary. I'll tell yer what, I thought to meself, it's a good job we're selling up because these fucking bed springs wouldn't last another month."

Old John took a deep breath and relaxed into a whisky grin. "It's about time we buggered off home, Arthur." We both helped him to his feet. "I'll see him home Steve," said Arthur. "It's a 15-minute walk and it'll steady him up."

"What happened then?" I asked Arthur. I wanted to know more.

"The favourite won, the second favourite threw a plate one furlong from home, the owner won just under £250,000 and a year later John, Mary and the three kids bought a three-bedroom house in Smethwick for £400 cash."

I sat in silence for a moment.

"Come on young 'un, Graham's got the car outside and I'm tekkin' yer to see the biggest tits in the world." Pricey grabbed hold of my arm and I fell into the rear leather seats of the Zodiac. The Dolls' Club was literally round the corner and Graham parked his car on the pavement outside just behind a beautiful brand new red E-type Jaguar.

"Johnny's in, then" Pricey said to Graham as he got out. As Malcolm, Graham's brother, was helping me out of the back seats of the Zodiac, a bloke the size of a mountain approached.

"Will it be OK here for an hour, Winston?" Pricey asked. The mountain nodded. "Your friends are upstairs, Mr Price."

The club was packed, and virtually everybody was watching a stripper going through her routine on the stage. A bloke even bigger than the one downstairs moved away from the bar and the audience melted away in respect.

Moses and the Red Sea sprang to mind. "That's big George" Malcolm whispered.

Big George towered over me by six inches, which put him at almost seven feet tall. His black dinner jacket fitted his three-foot wide shoulders like a glove. His hand-made shirt (it must have been hand made, because the largest collar size I'd ever seen was only 20 and a half) was white and crisp, with an inch of cuff showing studded with a gold link. The black bow tie matched his shiny shaved black bullet head. He beamed at us.

"Mr Price, how are you, you old bastard?" he said. They hugged like long lost brothers, slapping each others' backs. Pricey had to reach up.

A couple of pints came over from the bar for Malcolm and me and we stood at the back of the crowd. We could just about see the top half of a naked woman who was frantically shaking her breasts to a disco beat. There were loud roars of "gerrem off" from 50-odd blokes.

"Yer see Pricey and our kid with Big George?" Graham almost yelled above the noise. I nodded. It was impossible to miss Big George.

"The other bloke is Johnny Prescott, the boxer."

"I've seen him on the telly fighting Billy Walker. He's bloody good," I shouted in reply.

"Well next month he's fighting Henry Cooper for the British and Commonwealth Heavyweight Championship. Big George is looking after him."

I was puzzled. "Why does he want looking after?"

Graham shrugged and took a sup of his pint. "Anybody famous, especially a boxer, is open to any drunkard dickhead taking a swing. Johnny's had it before in the clubs, and yes he could flatten 'em but he'd probably lose his licence. The Cooper fight is the biggest of his career and it'll be his biggest earner." I nodded, understanding.

"Come on young 'un, I promised to show you the biggest pair of tits in the world" Pricey yelled, grabbing my arm and propelling us both to the front. "She's on in a minute." Graham and Malcolm were interested as well. They followed in our wake.

When Stardust finally whipped off her bra there was an awed hush, almost like a minute's silence at a football match. "Fuckin' hell" someone said. Then the cheering began. "Gerrem off!" they roared. And she did. She stood totally naked, then squatted down on her haunches and five-inch heels, slowly bringing her knees together. She had a good figure, but her breasts were truly enormous. As she flounced around she picked up a plastic chair, the sort you'd see in a canteen, and placed in the centre of the little stage.

I was leaning forward to get a better view when I felt a nudge in the small of my back. I was sent stumbling on to the stage.

Pricey was beaming. "My handsome young volunteer!" Stardust announced as she sat me down on the chair. I wished I'd gone home hours before.

She straddled me with one long, naked leg and started bumping and wriggling on my lap. I was being suffocated by her breasts. With an effort I managed to extract my nose from the valley between them and look over her right shoulder. The crowd was roaring with laughter. "Goo on, give her one!" they shouted.

Not knowing what to do with my hands, I suddenly realised they had found their way to Stardust's pert, bouncing bottom. Slowly lifting her leg from my lap, she made sure the front row of the audience had a good look at something which was in those days it was totally illegal to show in public. Then she turned to the crowd and jiggled her breasts again. They roared their applause.

My three so-called pals in the front were wiping their eyes, throwing their heads back and doubling over with laughter. They were totally incapable of speech.

"You wait till I see your Pauline" Pricey shouted to me, looking at the rest of the blokes at the bar. Even Big George smiled. The bastards had set me up, but I'd had a laugh and I was certainly enjoying myself.

The fact that I had to go work in the morning, that I was playing in the snooker final in the evening or that I had arranged to go to a new disco at The Navigation in Wootton Wawen was very far from my thoughts. As I made my way back to the bar, I brushed against one of the blokes. I heard a hard voice. "You've just spilt me drink, yer long streak of piss."

"I'm sorry mate" I replied, and looked to see who I'd offended.

He was not as tall as me, probably six foot, but he was heavily built and 10 years older and full of aggression. His short cropped hair receded from a large prominent forehead, above a nose that had been well adjusted by someone. The fingers that gripped his now half-empty glass were tattooed with the letters ACAB. They looked like a bunch of bananas.

"Yow owe me a pint, yer prat," he said into my face, before looking to his grinning mate. "I'll have a drink as well," said the mate. He swigged back his beer and placed his empty glass on the bar.

I reached into my pocket to sort out enough to pay for the two pints. I had no idea how much I'd have to pay at this place. Graham and Pricey had bought the last one.

"Come on, we ain't got all fucking night" said the man I'd offended. He grabbed me by the arm and pushed me towards the bar.

"Leave the lad alone Barry, he's with us." The man turned to see Pricey standing behind him smiling. Pricey obviously knew him. Big George very gently put a hand the size of a shovel on Barry's neck and pressed it down.

"We don't want any trouble tonight, do we my son?" he said, in a voice that sounded like distant thunder.

"Just a misunderstanding, no problem" Barry said, looking at Pricey and me. If he had tried to turn his head to look at Big George he would probably have suffered a serious neck injury.

"My friends are going to enjoy the rest of the evening, and you are welcome to do the same" Big George rumbled. "Don't touch the lad again, the breakfast in Accident & Emergency Department ain't the best in the world even if you've got enough teeth left to eat it." Big George relaxed his grip, smiled and tapped Barry on his shoulder. "Now, you and yer big tough brother behave yerselves."

"Come on Steve, I'll drop you off in Yardley Wood" Graham said. "I'm taking our Malcolm home anyway."

I looked at my watch and saw that it was half past one. It wasn't until I was halfway back that I remembered I had left my Mini in the car park at the factory and would have to catch the bus in the morning.

"Pricey knows a few people" I said, lighting up in the back of the Zodiac and thinking about the blokes I'd met during my evening. Graham half looked over his shoulder and blew smoke out of the window. "He does, but keep it to yourself Steve, OK?" I nodded.

They dropped me off at the top of Tritterford Road, leaving me with a half-hour walk home. I thought it would sober me up, and it did. I turned into Chilton Road and saw that as usual the light was still on in Nan and Pop's bedroom. As I opened the front door I heard a quiet voice from the landing.

"You all right Steve?"

"Yes Nan, I've had a lift home."

I heard her bedroom door close and the light click gently off.

The snooker final was a total anti-climax. Les was two frames up in the first 40 minutes, and as I approached the table to break off in the third frame the doors swung open and Bert Phillips hobbled in on crutches. He glanced at the scoreboard before struggling to sit on the high seats. His broken leg was totally encased in plaster.

Les let me win the third frame. He disguised it well, going in-off while attempting shots and deliberately playing sloppily. Thanks Les, I thought to myself. But I still lost three frames to one.

Les had a break of 43 in the final frame. As Bro. Hall shuffled the paperwork about on the table I heard Graham whisper to Les: "You've had four frames to warm up and I ain't played for a week. Put yer twenty-five quid winnings down and I'll match it in a one-frame game." I could see Les thinking about it. He had never beaten Graham - no bugger in the factory had, even over a single frame.

"Taking the missus out tonight, can't stay," he said. Les was a careful bloke.

"In second place and winner of the runners-up prize of £15 is - Steve Phillips." Bro. Hall was really good at this sort of thing I thought, as he handed

179

me a small white envelope. That makes it twenty-five quid I've won in the competition. I'd forgotten the nine quid I'd spent the previous night, but what the hell.

"In first place and winner of the United Non-Ferrous Metals Snooker Championship is – Les Green!" A small round of applause rippled around the room.

Bro. Hall continued. "The highest break of the competition was also won by Les Green, with a break of 43." He handed Les the envelope with the £10 in. Another, smaller, round of applause as people stood up to leave.

"Before you all go, I would like to say a word," said Les. He had put his cue away and stood by the door. I knew Les was a joker, but I had no idea what he was up to. He was grinning from ear to ear.

"I would like to donate the award of £10 for the highest break of the competition to …" He paused. What the fuck was going on? I looked around. Everybody looked as puzzled as I was.

"…the bloke who had the biggest break - Mr Bert Phillips." It took a minute for it to sink in, then came the smiles and laughter. Bert took the money without a word. He really was a miserably bastard.

"Come on young 'un, yer new girlfriend's on again tonight flashing her tits."

"No thanks John, I'm going out with Pauline."

The disco at the Navigation in Wootten Wawen was pretty good, but I was knackered by midnight. By the time I'd dropped Pauline off it was nearly 2 am on the Saturday and I was going to work in five hours' time.

I quietly closed the door of my Mini, and out went the light in Nan and Pop's bedroom.

CHAPTER 13

Looking back at the end of the summer of 1965, I found it difficult to believe I had been at work for almost four years. I had passed all my exams, held The City & Guilds Craft Practice Parts 1, 2 and 3 and was awaiting my results in that year's course for the Toolmaking Supplementary. My apprenticeship contract (indentures) would be completed when I reached 21. I was wondering what I could study at college while I completed the next 18 months. The question was soon to be answered.

"Wotcher mean, the factory's being sold?" Black Bat jumped out of his armchair. Normally he would lift himself slowly out of it and move sedately from the dining table in the Fitting Shop to the grinders. Now he was too angry for that. He snatched his pipe from his mouth and looked at Norman.

"You're the shop steward - what the fuck's gooin' to happen?"

Everybody stopped what they were doing. It was 7.30 am and the crowd of men and apprentices, all in various stages of getting into their overalls, looked questioningly at Norman.

A slim man stood up. Norman had a bald pate decorated with wisps of Friar Tuck hair in a semi circle above his ears. He was used to pressure - he had six kids.

"The gaffers are arranging meetings in the canteen to inform all employees as to what is happening" he said. "All departments, works and offices will be involved at different times today." He looked as if he would rather be back home looking after his kids, and all the other kids in his road come to that. He looked highly uncomfortable.

"Yow mark me words, we'll all be out of a fucking job" said Black Bat, stamping off. I looked around. The other old blokes were all looking at each other with worried looks on their faces.

"What d'yer think, Billy?"

Arthur Twamley, like everybody else in the shop, respected Billy Wiggins' views and knowledge. Although a shop floor worker, he was an educated man, a councillor and Chairman of Birmingham Transport Committee, and he was also friendly with the directors, although just recently he had not been enjoying the best of health.

"Basically, the Guest Keen and Nettlefold Group is selling United Non-Ferrous Metals to the Delta Group of Companies. Our factory will be called Delta Wire," he said.

Billy Wiggins lit up his favourite Senior Service, let out a small cough, lifted his head and exhaled a long column of smoke. Twenty voices asked the same question together. "What's going to happen?"

I sat down and started to think. I hadn't completed my apprenticeship and I was getting married in four months' time. I might not have a job.

Everyone was looking bemused. More than that, we were all very worried.

Instead of his usual cheerful shout of "Come on you shower", Joe Healy slowly walked out of his office, strolled to his lathe and switched on the motor.

I was now back in the Fitting Shop following my stint in the Drawing Office. Walking through the Wire Mill down to the lavatories, I noticed that nearly all the foremen from all over the factory were gathered together outside the office of Bert Carrington, the Wire Mill foreman.

Billy Little, one of the wire drawers, was talking to Jack Hassett, the shop steward in the Wire Mill. "What's going on, Bill?" I asked.

"All the foremen and managers are going to the first meeting in the canteen. The shop stewards are next, then every other bugger in turn. Won't be much work done today." He fastened the gripping dog to the pointed end of wire before starting up the drawing block.

Walking back, I could see small groups of blokes in worried discussion. Billy was right. Nobody was interested in doing much until they knew what was going to happen to their factory and their jobs.

By the time our department was called up to the canteen it was half past two and we'd heard most of the announcement second-hand from other people, but we all filed in and sat down just the same. Dave Wilmer was only a month away from his 21st birthday, so the question of what would happen to the apprentices didn't really affect him, but we all sat together as a group and looked towards the table set up in front of the serving counter.

Jack Insall, the Personnel Manager, Tommy Rushton, Works Manager, and a youngish bloke who I didn't recognise were sitting at the table quietly shuffling their papers. Jack stood up, looking over his shoulder expectantly. He coughed nervously and Mr Shakespeare appeared, walking briskly to his seat.

"Sorry chaps, couldn't get away from the bloody phone." He sat down and nodded to Jack Insall to start.

"Who's the new bloke?" I whispered to Dave. "Never seen him before" he replied.

"Ladies and gentlemen, thank you for attending" said Jack. "The Delta Group has purchased United Non-Ferrous Metals Ltd from the Guest Keen and Nettlefold Group and with effect from next Monday the company will be called Delta Wire Ltd. The factory has a full order book for the foreseeable future and the management would like to assure everyone that there are no plans to reduce the workforce." He paused, scanning the sea of faces in front of him.

"I believe it's important that we all understand that our jobs are safe." He looked around the room again, sensing that some of the nervous tension had subsided. Blokes were nodding and whispering to each other. A few of them lit up.

"Mr Shakespeare will continue for a short time to help the new managing director settle in before taking a well-deserved retirement." He sat down and old Shakey stood up. I glanced around the room. There was still suspicion on some of the faces. I guess a lot of the old blokes had heard all this before in factory takeovers and still lost their jobs. Black Bat clamped his pipe in his teeth, almost tight enough to snap the stem. His face was purple.

Shakey looked round the room. He seemed tired.

"We have a full order book for the next six months, which is as good as it's been for the last three years" he said. "The company is profitable with a good, skilled workforce and should continue along those lines." He sat down, looking as if he wanted to go home.

"Now, may I introduce Mr Ian Watson, the new Managing Director of Delta Wire?" said Jack, returning to his seat.

The new man stood up. He was tall and good looking, with thinning blond hair, in his early forties, clean shaven with sharp features and a tan. He wore a black polo-neck sweater under a well-cut suit - no collar and tie. I'd never seen a gaffer at work without a tie before.

"I would like to reiterate Mr Shakespeare and Mr Insall's words" he said. "The company is in an excellent financial position and I know we can all move forward towards a prosperous future.

"During the next six months the management structure will be rationalised and working practices throughout every department improved to ensure the overall efficiency of the company. These are exciting times." He sat down.

Jack stood up again. "Any questions?" He sat down faster than a First World War soldier diving into a trench.

The questions began slowly. Blokes were not keen to stand up in front of their workmates, especially under the scrutiny of a load of gaffers, but within five minutes confidence grew. I sat and listened, realising that everyone in the room was seeking the same thing – an assurance that his job were safe and he wasn't "gooin' down the road".

It was the old blokes who looked worried, even though in Birmingham at that time there were plenty of factory jobs to be had. I guess they didn't want the trouble of changing jobs at 50-odd years of age. Jack Insall and Tommy Rushton probably felt the same.

About 12 apprentices were sitting on my table. All the younger lads were looking at me. I could see the question in Frank and Jim's eyes - what about us?

There was a lull for a moment. I jumped up.

"What about the apprentices, Mr Insall?"

Jack looked at me. "All the apprentices will continue with their formal signed indentures and carry on with their courses at the college on day release and their training in the factory. The Delta Group has an excellent training school in Nechells and the apprentice supervisor will be visiting you young men in the next few days." All the lads looked pleased, nudging themselves and smiling.

By the time we all got back to the Fitting Shop it was tea break and the dining table was full of men talking about what had happened.

"That new bloke sounds a bit keen" Pat said, stirring the big brown enamelled teapot. Six of us had formed a tea syndicate, because it tasted better and you only had to make a pot twice a week.

"He's been on Delta's main board of directors for five years, responsible for setting up new companies after they've been taken over" said Billy Wiggins. He's a real whiz kid. Look out for some changes."

"Did you hear him say restructuring the management? That means more fucking gaffers, yow mark my words. Anyway how can yer improve working practices? We've been doing the job for forty years. What the fuck does a kid like him know?" Black Bat was warming up. His wire frame glasses had slipped down to the edge of his nose.

"And I'll tell yer another thing. Who do yer suppose that brand new, free Jaguar in the car park is for? It ain't for Alf fucking George, that's a dead cert."

Everybody laughed. We all imagined Black Bat sitting in the Jag smoking his pipe.

"They'd never allow yer on the Red Cow Car Park in the High Street in that motor, Alf" chuckled Pat. "The domino team would be up in arms."

Scotty, not to be outdone, chimed in. "By the time Alf's team mates had got off their arses to have a look, the Jag would have been pinched. We're talking about Smethwick yer know." We all collapsed with laughter. The worry and tension was fading fast.

Within a few days everything had settled back to normal. We still clocked in at 7.30 am and clocked out at 5.30 pm. What's different, I thought.

With Joe Healy's guidance I was producing a complicated spiral drum cam. It was not a constant spiral – that would have been relatively easy using the dividing head geared to the main lead screw of the universal milling machine. This cam required the angle of spiral to vary from a fast approach to a dwell, a fast decline and then a longer dwell. The cam had come off one of the automatic feeding and shearing machines in the Fine Wire Mill and needed replacing. Even with my four years' experience and study I wouldn't have had a clue how to do it.

A template was marked out, cut and filed by hand. A false sliding table sat upon the main bed of the machine and was controlled by a heavy weight holding the end mill cutting tool in place. Joe could have written a book, because I'd never seen this in all the textbooks I had studied. Even after forty years in engineering, Joe was one of the best craftsmen Id had the privilege to work with.

"Having a go in the sweepstake on the Derby, Steve?" Fred, the shop labourer, had rested his broom against the upright girder supporting the roof and was sitting on the toolbox next to the milling machine. He was a big bloke well into his 60s, with a big red face full of veins. He had to take tablets for something or other, which had the unfortunate side effect of causing extreme flatulence. He had his own little table and chair on the far side of the shop and normally dined there alone.

"How much, Fred?" I asked, stopping the miller and lighting up.

"There's 20 runners and it's five bob a time, five quid for the winner, no second prize. It's shit or bust."

Looking into the bag in Fred's hand I could see about half a dozen rolled up slips of paper. "Ain't many horses left, is there?"

"Ar, but the favourite ain't bin drawn yet." Fred was a mate of Arthur and John the Blacksmith, who knew all about horses.

Five shillings was a fair bit of money for a gamble and the snooker prize cash was long spent. Apart from this sort of thing I didn't normally bet at all. Very occasionally Arthur would give me a tip and I'd bet a couple of bob on his advice. Once I had won over a quid.

Searching in my pocket I found two half crowns.

"Here you are then, Fred," I said, reaching into the bag. I didn't pull out the first crumpled slip, but swirled them around before deciding to choose.

Not wishing to tear the slip, I carefully unwrapped it. Fred was looking over my shoulder inquisitively. He saw the name before I did.

"Fuck me!" I heard him whisper.

"What's the matter, Fred?"

"Yow've only drawn Sea Bird the Second. It's a dead cert."

There were six horses left in the bag and now no-one was keen to have a go, but they all did eventually.

"I've never encouraged you to bet on the horses Steve, apart from a few shillings now and again, but this bugger is different" said Arthur. We were sitting next to his shaping machine alongside the fence to the Electricians' Shop.

"You're bound to win," he said. "Sea Bird is as good as a dead cert as I've ever known." We lit up. I was smoking Embassy Tips in those days and collecting the coupons. A Mini Moke was about 100 Million of them, so I had a long way to go.

"The odds are low. I think he's 7/4 favourite but put on what you can afford. Pat Glennon is a good jockey."

7/4 – the same odds as the horse that had won the race 30 odd years before. A coincidence? An omen? If Arthur was right I'd already got the fiver from the Sweepstake in the bag. I decided to bet a fiver of my own money. Arthur's runner at the White Tower could sort it. I thought about it for a long time, because I wasn't a betting man. But I eventually did it.

I won over twelve quid.

"Number 1 muffle in the Wire Mill will need a new chain next week" said Joe. "I want you to help Billy Law with it."

Billy Law was a fitter who had worked for the company for almost 50 years. He was a little bloke, well over 70, slight of build with thinning pure white hair. He was busy and quick, like a ferret. His angry eyes darted underneath dark-framed spectacles which were permanently perched on the end of his nose. A pipe was always in his mouth and he rarely spoke to anyone -he didn't appear to have many friends in the shop. It was rumoured however that he was keeping the maximum of £5000 in each of two building societies. He didn't have many skills, but those he did he was determined not to share.

His mate Jan was a Polish war veteran. He was a huge man of 18 stone and six foot tall who spoke very little English. Billy treated him like a dog. If Jan was required to wheel the large toolbox out to a job in the factory, Billy would point to it, nod his head and grunt "Come on", and old Jan would trundle along following him.

The Wire Mill was just outside the Fitting Shop and covered an area the size of four or five football pitches. Overhead conveyors carried the coils of wire from the Britannia extrusion press to be stored in racks ready for the next production drawing process. At the end where the old extrusion press had been until it had been dismantled a year before was the fine wire section, drawing brass and copper wire down to diameters of ten thousandths of an inch (0.010"). The other side of the Wire Mill ran parallel to Adderley Street and contained 20 large bull blocks, the rotating drums which gripped the end of the wire and drew it through a tungsten carbide die to reduce its diameter to the required size and give it a smooth shiny surface. It produced a coil of wire some 100 kilos in weight. An electric overhead hoist would lift the coil off the block and lower it on to a low flat truck. Each bull block was operated by a wire drawer and serviced by a team of labourers and fork-lift drivers. In the middle of the shop were three large annealing muffles and two smaller ones for the smaller fine wire coils.

When brass has been worked or drawn (reduced in size) it hardens. Before it can be worked again it needs annealing, a process achieved by heating and subsequent cooling.

All the muffles were gas fired and of the camel back design. A six-foot wide chain with the coils loaded on to the cross bars of the chain would very slowly inch forward, dipping down into a water bath. Inside the muffle the chain would rise out of the water into the actual furnace, to be heated to the correct temperature before dipping down into another water bath for quenching. As the coils rose up from the water at the other end of the muffle they would be removed.

Two men loaded at the front and two at the rear. The five muffles were manned by about 20 Arabs, led by Yafia, who was an albino with a partially white face and pink eyes. He was the only one who could speak English.

"The chain's knackered, it'll just about last the week." Bert Carrington was standing at the loading end with Yafia, showing Bill, Jan and me how the cross bars had been bent and worn and the driving links buckled. Billy nodded briskly, turned and scurried back to the Fitting Shop.

"He's a miserable little fucker, always has bin." Bert offered me a fag. "I've worked here for fifteen years. Even before I was made up to foreman that bugger would hardly wish yer the time of day."

I thanked him for the fag and strolled after Billy and Jan, thinking about the excitement I was in for working with Mr William Law for a week.

The crossbars of the chain were made from one-inch diameter bright drawn mild steel bar, delivered to the factory in six-metre lengths on an articulated lorry. The first job was to cut them into 6' 2" lengths. The bundle of bars was manhandled into the saw and the stop adjusted to the correct length. I switched it on, adjusting the flow of cooling suds so it covered the saw blade. The bundle contained five lengths tightly banded with steel straps. It would take about five minutes to saw through. We were right outside the blacksmith shop, so I went in to join old John for a smoke.

"Got some proper fags today Steve." John said, offering me a Capstan Full Strength. I took a good drag, coughing and spluttering. "Thanks John."

On the large muffle the endless chain probably had over 500 crossbars. I thought, that's 100 sawing operations. I would have to cut down on John's Capstans.

Jan came to my rescue. "I carry on the saw. Billy wants you."

"Thanks Jan."

The outer links that held the crossbars were made from 2" by _" bright flat plate, cut to 10" long, with chamfered corners and a 1" hole in each end to fit over the cross bars. Billy had set up a stack of five links on the table of the radial drilling machine, tightly clamping them together. The holes were marked out on the top plate and centre punched. I wondered if he was going to let me do anything – I didn't want to stand and watch him all day.

"I'll show you the first one and then I'll leave you to it" Billy mumbled, easing the drill down into the splashing suds. "I won't be long." He tapped out his pipe and looked back twice as he walked off. He doesn't trust me, I thought. On reflection it was probably because Billy wanted to do the work himself and not pass it on to anybody else.

I could have done the work with my eyes shut. I engaged the feeding mechanism and watched the curling twist of swarf rise up the flutes of the drill. Lighting up, I began to think. If there were over 500 crossbars to a chain there were over 2000 links, that's 4000 holes to be drilled – and that was just one muffle. And all the links had to be cut to length on the saw. It would take hours and hours of cutting, drilling and chamfering.

When an idea arrives in your brain, it's like a crossword clue. One second you don't know the answer, a millisecond later you do.

The thought that had jumped into my head was a pierce-and-crop press tool. I'd just finished a smaller but similar tool at college. It would knock out these links like shelling peas.

I continued thinking about my idea the rest of the day, with Billy checking up on my work every 20 minutes. He would creep up and stand looking over my shoulder, puffing away on his pipe. Occasionally he'd exchange a few words with old Black Bat before going back to his bench via the sawing machine to check on Jan.

All the crossbars had to be chamfered and a small hole drilled in each end to hold a cotter pin. Thousands of tubes had to be cut to the length that fitted over the crossbars. All these parts then had to be assembled in short sections. It was a massive job – Billy's job. But a press tool to produce the links was, in my opinion a must. Should I mention it to Mr Law?

"How yer getting on with King Billy?" Scotty enquired with an Irish twinkle in his green eyes. "Have yer learned how to use the saw and driller now?" He loved his craic and regularly used to shout "Willie" when Billy Law was about. It used to wind Pat Dowling up as well.

"Not too bad Bob" I replied. "Who was King Billy then?" Pat stubbed out his fag and walked off.

"Can I have a word, Joe?" I stood alongside the Dean Smith and Grace lathe watching the master craftsman at work. He waited until the cutting tool had finished, wound the cross-slide clear and dropped the handle, letting the chuck slowly stop revolving. When Joe wanted you to follow him, say to look at a job the other side of the shop, he would put one hand on his hip and the other arm in a high outstretched downward curve, just like a tea pot. Then he would look over his shoulder and say in a sweet voice: "Walk this way." I followed him as he minced along to his office, smiling to myself.

Joe listened carefully to my idea, nodding thoughtfully and scratching the side of his face.

"I've never bin into press tools meself" he said. "But thinking about it, you're probably right. Have yer mentioned it to Billy?"

"No Joe."

"Don't worry, the miserable old bugger's retiring in six months' time.. He's 75 in December." I felt a bit easier in my mind.

"I'll mention yer idea to him next door" he said, nodding towards Tommy Carter's office. "Put it in the suggestion box an' all. Bro. Hall will get involved then."

I returned to the radial driller. Only another 3,500 holes to drill.

"The Die Shop have organised another barge trip up the cut, and this time we've got a stripper." Jim had come to visit the Dining Room. He usually had his tea break in his own department, but he had felt the need to pass on this momentous news. All the apprentices looked up, grinning. Tickets could be in short supply, I thought.

Jim was older than me by more than six months. He had decided to concentrate on the last year of his apprenticeship by taking the higher toolmaking course. I didn't know what to do for the best.

"The new Apprentice Supervisor from the Delta is here tomorrow," Jim said. "Him and Jack Insall are going to talk to each of us." Jim's foreman, Percy Hollingshead, had told him this an hour before. "I ain't seen Caggy yet this morning" I replied. "I still ain't sure what to do."

I was seeing Pauline that night, so I had a chat with Albert. His advice was to try to continue with my studies and aim for the highest qualifications possible, even if it meant night school. "That's what I did when I came out of the Army after the War" he said. My Nan and Pop had said the same.

I knocked on Jack Insall's door. His office was right at the top of the stairs from the factory floor, opposite the wages office, where he had been Chief Wages Clerk before his promotion to Personnel Manager six months before.

"Come in." I opened the door and walked into the lion's den.

Jack was six feet tall, slim and fiftyish with greying hair and sharp-featured. Not a bad-looking man. He also wasn't a bad bloke either, even though he was a gaffer.

"Sit down, Steve." He offered me a cigarette. "Let me introduce you to Mr Williams, the Delta Group Apprentice Supervisor." We all lit up – everybody did in 1965. I noticed Jack's desk was full of blue cardboard files. One was open. No doubt it had Steve Phillips on the cover.

"You've done extremely well during the last four years, passing all your exams." He glanced down at my file. "The reports from the foremen in the factory are first class. Well done, Steve!"

I was slightly puzzled. "But I'm still waiting for my toolmaking result, Mr Williams?"

"The name's Peter" he replied. "We had your results from Garretts Green yesterday. You passed with credit."

He checked my file again. "You're still only 19?" I nodded. "Have you thought what you want to do for the next two years?" He picked up his phone and ordered three cups of coffee. "Or do you want tea, Steve?"

I was beginning to feel out of my depth. But I had taken Nan and Pop's advice and listened to Albert's views, so I had at least thought about what I would like to do, especially over the last few days.

"I want to continue studying to gain the best qualifications I can. Eventually I want to complete the Institute of Works Managers two-year course. I can do it two nights a week."

Had I said too much? Jack and Peter looked at each, their eyes saying to each other – I told you so.

"You've completed the City & Guilds Craft Qualifications. We'd like to suggest that you study for the Technician's Course. Usually boys join this course at 17 or 18 with O and A levels. If you're successful you will be awarded The Full Technological Certificate in Production Engineering, CGLI. Letters after your name – better than an HNC!"

Peter put his papers down and looked up. "It will mean another four years' study. The company will pay you on a day-release basis for the next four years, provided you continue to pass the exams. It will also involve one night a week of your own time."

I didn't hesitate for a second. "I'll do it!" I almost blurted out.

"You will enroll in September at South Birmingham Polytechnic on the Bristol Road. Well done and good luck."

"Thank you, Mr Insall." I was well aware that not many apprentices were paid for day release after the age of 21.

They were both looking pleased, and I know I was. As I started to get up, Peter added "I almost forgot. I've put you down for three residential senior apprentice courses at the Production Engineering Research Association in Melton Mowbray in Leicestershire. The first starts on November 2. You'll be away for a week, but it's a nice hotel. The company will pay your travel and hotel expenses.

"Have a pint or so, but be sensible" Jack added.

I was half way to the door when I suddenly remembered that I was getting married. I turned round.

"I'm getting married on October 16 and I come back to work off my honeymoon on the 25th. I'll only have a week before I'm off on the course."

The two gaffers looked at each other and smiled.

"After the first two weeks of married life Steve, you might need a bit of a rest for a few nights."

"Yes Jack" I replied. I gently closed the door and was half way down the stairs before I shouted - fucking yes!

My Nan and Pop were so pleased. I had picked Pauline up from work and we had gone straight to Chilton Road for our tea. Nan was fussing around in and out of the kitchen, laying the table in the small bay window, her usual pinny on, tea towel over her shoulder, looking as pleased as Punch. Her little face was a picture.

Did you hear that, Jack? Letters after his name!" she beamed. "Just you wait till yer Mom and Uncle Norman know."

"That's four years away Nan, and a lot of hard work." I sat down on the leatherette settee and stretched my feet towards the gas fire. The old black range had been removed many years before.

Striking a Swan Vesta and putting the flame to a bowl full of Old Holborn, Pop took a contented draw of his pipe. The smoke billowed up towards the dark patch on the ceiling - my grandfather never sat anywhere else.

"You'll do it. Sup me gum yer will," he said, easing himself out of his chair to go out the back to the toilet. We might have a gas fire now, but the lav was still outside.

★ ★ ★ ★ ★ ★ ★ ★ ★ ★ ★ ★ ★ ★

I decided not to make it public knowledge that the company was going to support me through college until I was 23. "Keep it to yourself, Steve" Joe had advised. "There's a lot of jealous buggers about."

He then said something to me that I've remembered for 45 years. We were both at his beloved Dean Smith and Grace. I was now actually allowed to use the machine when a really tricky job needed turning.

"You've done well this last couple of years and yer coming on a treat. I guess you'll want to travel the management journey, I can see it in yer. But when yer on the way up, and even when yer get to the top, never forget where yer came from. Remember, the higher the monkey climbs the tree, the more he shows his arse." I have tried to remember these words throughout my working life. On reflection, I sometimes forgot them.

Billy Law's mate Big Jan didn't sit at the dining table in the Fitting Shop. Instead he sat on top of the work bench alongside the canal, leaning against the wall with the reinforced wire-laced windows above his head.

Cross-legged, he looked like a huge Buddha dozing with his chin upon his chest. He was a quiet, gentle giant, very respectful to supervision. Like Frank the greaser and the other Jan, he had a number tattooed on his arm, courtesy of the Third Reich.

One autumn he mistakenly put his clock forward one hour instead of back and arrived at the factory at 5 am instead of seven. Gate security was 24 hours anyway, and they took no notice. Jan slept on the bench for three hours instead of in his bed at the Polish Club.

During the summer months, after a quick lunch, an impromptu cricket match would occasionally take place in the Fitting Shop. Using a soft tennis ball and a rubbish bin as the wicket, the younger element would have a bit of fun for 15 minutes or so. Most of the old 'uns were tucked up in the corner around the dining table dozing, but there were a few scattered around the shop who took exception to their break being interrupted by "fucking kids". Big Jan didn't mind either way, he was fast asleep on the bench propped against the wall.

Doug Smith was batting one day. He had already whacked a ball that had bounced off the roof and landed in the large tank that held the coolant for Black Bat's grinder. Alf was too busy moaning to notice.

I took a gentle run in to bowl (there wasn't room for a long run), and chucked one down towards the batsman. Doug swung the bat and I watched the ball soar over my head towards the back wall. The workbench ran the full width of the shop and a couple of fitters and mates were sitting on chairs reading the paper, or dozing after eating their sandwiches. Only Jan sat on the bench.

The ball hit him right between the eyes, and he jumped up from his slumber and tumbled off the bench. Billy Law was enjoying his nap and did not appreciate 18 stone of Pole falling into his lap. By the time they had finished rolling around on the floor the cricket team had melted away.

"Yer big stupid bastard! What yer doing falling off the fucking bench?" Billy Law was raging. His pipe was snapped in half and his tea mug was smashed on the floor. If he had a stick he would have hit Jan.

It was the first time in four years I had Jan smile.

There were enough component parts now made to start assembling the muffle chain, and Jan, helped by one of the new apprentices, would continue the monotonous task of sawing and drilling. Assembly was back-breaking work, because the only place it could be done was on the floor – it was much too big for the bench. Billy and I would scrabble about on our knees, sliding tubes over the cross bars, fitting the links and washers and finally inserting the cotter pin in each end of the bar and opening up the pin to hold it all together. For the practical purpose of handling and shifting the chain into the Wire Mill, sections of about five feet in length were produced and stacked up in the shop in front of the long bench.

Bert, the Wire Mill foreman, was sitting in Caggy's office having a smoke and a cup of tea. "They'll be out here looking over our shoulders in a minute, yow mark my words" said Billy Law. He was now beginning to speak to me instead of mumbling. And he was showing me how to assemble this chain, so I had to be doing something right.

"When will yow be ready to replace the new chain, Bill?" Caggy and Bert had strolled over and lit up, leaning against the bench. Billy struggled to his feet, grabbing hold of the bench to help himself up.

"Another three days, I reckon" he replied. Bert and Caggy looked at each other.

"This Saturday then, Tom" Bert said.

When the two foremen had strolled off, Billy turned to me.

"That's a full eight hours' work then, at time and a half." He smiled as he lit up his new pipe.

To replace a chain the muffle had to be shut down, and a Saturday or Sunday was the ideal time to ensure production was least affected. It also ensured plenty of overtime for the maintenance gang of fitters, and I was one of the gang on this particular job. The factory was busy, so the other four muffles were working as normal, annealing coils of wire with Yafia supervising his team of fellow Arabs. They would work all day Saturday and Sunday running the muffles and then cleaning up the whole shop. This was why they had their own restaurant facilities on site.

"Yer workin' all day today then, Steve?" Mick Madden, the young trainee in the Wire Mill, had sat down on the pile of new chains. Mick was the young beefy centre forward who played for the works football team, now Delta Wire. He was just 17 and on Birmingham City's books, regularly playing in the youth team during the past season. The 1965/66 season would start in less than two months and Mick was confident he could break into the reserve team.

"I'll order yer curry," he said. I must have looked puzzled

"Yafia and his gang cook a big pot of chicken and rice all served with their special bread, I think they call it chapati. It's bloody great."

He dropped his fag on the floor and ground it out with his boot. "See yer at one o'clock." He walked back to his bull block, singing Keep Right On To The End Of The Road. Mick was a Bluenose, a City supporter.

With the chain stationary, Billy knocked out the cotter pins each end of the cross bars and withdrew a complete width of link, chucking it on the floor. Jan dutifully moved it aside. A new section of chain was attached to the old one and Yafia pushed the button to start the chain moving. When the five-foot length of new chain had been used up, Yafia pushed the stop button. Jan manhandled the old chain away and Billy and I attached another five foot of new chain. Bloody hell, I thought to myself, this will take all day.

Breakfast had long gone, and the smell of spicy food was beginning to waft around the muffles where we were working. "Dow know how them Arabs can eat that shit" said Billy, hammering in a cotterpin at one end of the crossbar as I did the same at the other. "I've got a meat pipe warming up fer my dinner."

He looked at me. "I s'pose yer gooin' to eat it?"

"Yes Billy" I replied. Jan glanced at me and silently nodded agreement. There really was such a thing as a free lunch. But why had Mick Madden got a fishing rod in his hand?

The Arab restaurant was set up between number 1 and number 2 Muffle. A very low table a foot off the floor held a brown enamelled pot the size of a bucket which was bubbling with a dark aromatic reddish-brown mixture. Small finger-sized pieces of chicken occasionally rose to the surface. A gas ring feeding off the main supply to the Muffle supplied the heat to keep it simmering. Another large bowl overflowed with rice, and there was a pile of chapatis on the table the size of a house. Twenty Arabs, two young Brummies and a Polish bloke were hungry. I was impressed, but where were the knives and forks?

"Yafia is terrified of spiders," Mick Madden whispered to me. "He was bitten once back home in Saudi Arabia. He was only a kid and the nearest doctor with serum was two hours' walk away. The poor bugger almost died. He was in a coma for three days."

"So what's with the fishing rod, mate?" I asked him. I would soon find out.

At just after 1.15 the low table between the muffles was surrounded by a group of blokes dressed in baggy trousers clipped at the ankles and short smock-style shirts. They all squatted on the floor. Jan and I approached the table and sat down. The Arabs tore off pieces of chapati, folded them into a spoon shape and scooped out curry from the simmering pot. Jan was obviously a regular diner, because he tucked in without further ado. Having watched the technique carefully, I followed suit. It was bloody good. Old Billy Law could keep his meat pie.

Yafia was on the floor leaning back against number 2 muffle. He had enjoyed his meal. A cigarette gripped between his two middle fingers, his hand made into a fist, he sucked the smoke through the small hole made by his thumb and forefinger (Moslems were not allowed to let cigarettes touch their lips). He lifted his head and exhaled.

He failed to see the huge black hairy spider two feet above his head. I looked up and realised that it was on the end of a fishing line held by young Mr Madden, who was standing on top of number 2 muffle trying to keep his balance – a difficult job when you're pissing yourself laughing. The spider was the size of Billy's meat pie.

The spider was inched down until it was jiggling up and down just above Yafia's head. His Arab friends sitting opposite him had seen it too, and struggled to keep a straight face.

I knew Mick was a decent footballer, but he must have been an even better fisherman, judging by the way he controlled the black beast and dangled it literally three inches above Yafia's head. He flicked the line gently and the spider just touched Yafia's face before falling into his lap.

The domino players in the Waggon 100 yards away swore they heard the scream. Yafia turned totally white. For a few seconds he froze. When he did move, it was at 100 miles per hour.

Then the sound of laughter made him stop and look back to see that the deadly creature was dancing on the table, skipping over the rice and chapatis before dipping into the big brown pot of chicken curry. Mick had to crouch down. If he hadn't he would have fallen off the roof of the muffle, he was laughing so much.

"What the fuck's gooin' on?" Bert Carrington had called back into the Wire Mill after enjoying a couple of pints and was on his way home. He liked to make sure his blokes had started work after the lunch break on a

Saturday, but the sight of us all messing about and young Mick perched up on top of a muffle with a fishing rod in his hand really tried his patience. He gave everybody a right bollocking.

"Yafia, you tell yer men that I'm fucking angry. If there's any more pissing about you can all clock out and sod off home." He stamped off to his office.

The funny part was listening to Yafia translating the effing and blinding into Arabic while waving his arms about and pointing his finger to mimic the actions of his foreman. It was all gibberish to the rest of us listening, apart from the occasional "very fucking mad". He was still ranting in Arabic when Billy Law returned from his meat pie, wondering what the hell was going on.

Ah well, joke's over, back to replacing the chain. All at time and a half of course.

By the time the whole of the chain had traversed through the muffle and returned to the loading end, it had been totally replaced with new parts in shining blue steel. The old rusty and distorted chain lay scattered in sections around the floor, awaiting removal by the fork lifts.

Martin Riley, one of the drivers, had been steadily working with Jan all afternoon manhandling the heavy lengths of chain on to the long twin forks of his bright yellow Yale 1-ton truck. Martin was a happy-go-lucky Irish fella, not tall, but slim with a big bush of curly black hair. Mid thirties and fully qualified on his fork lift, he was one of the sensible, careful drivers in the factory and always handled his truck safely. Some of the other drivers used their trucks like fairground dodgems. In fact one of them had been officially warned, taken off his truck and put on the broom. He'd skidded on a patch of oil and practically demolished a brick wall protecting one of the Salter weighing machines.

The scrap chain was being piled up across the road on the car park behind the canteen and snooker room, awaiting collection by the scrap man's wagon the next day. It might be Sunday tomorrow, but it had to be cleared so the gaffers could park their cars on Monday morning.

To reach the car park, Martin had to steer his truck loaded with rusty chains carefully through the Wire Mill. past the lavatories, up the slope to the gate next to the bus garage and in to Adderley Street, and turn left and then right under the arch into the car park. After clocking out at half four I just about squeezed my Mini past the pile of scrap, wondering if I should have a pint in the Rainbow. It must have been raining that morning, because there were about five builders' wagons parked underneath the railway bridge. I saw Pat Dowling's car, a Ford Classic. outside. Yeah, I'd worked hard that Saturday, I would enjoy a bit of the craic.

Officially the pub shut at 2.30 and opened again at 5.30, but the magic knock on the green door at just after 4.30 opened up a drinking house full of building workers, bus drivers from Liverpool Street Garage and the odd Brummie who was in the know. The place was heaving. Pat was serving and Charlie the Copper, his helmet carefully tucked away at the back underneath the optics, was leaning on the bar enjoying his pint. He finished his shift at six, but it was only a 10-minute stroll down to Digbeth Police Station, and knowing Charlie he had time for another couple.

The door of the Rainbow opened into a passageway, with the bar on the left, a serving hatch and the smoke room. The toilets were on the right and quite a few drinkers actually stood or sat in the passage. because it was normally a bit quieter than the other two rooms.

A large Jamaican bus driver was sitting on a chair directly opposite the door of the smoke room, quietly reading a newspaper spread on his lap. I had just ordered a pint when the door to the smoke burst open and a red-faced

bloke staggered out. He steadied himself by leaning on the door with one arm, his other hand tightly clamped against his mouth. He almost fell back into the smoke room before taking a step forward and vomiting into the lap of the bus driver.

Nobody said a word, but you could hear everybody's thoughts. Paddy stood there swaying. He wiped his mouth with the back of his hand and sleeve and tried to grope his way to the gents. The bus driver calmly folded the newspaper up (luckily it had caught most of the mess) and asked Pat if he could have a wet cloth to wipe the bottom of his trousers.

"Sorry about that Don, he's pissed and well out of order," said Pat, handing the bus driver a damp cloth and taking the rolled-up newspaper from him. Then Paddy rolled out of the toilet. "Bejasus I'm sorry," he said. "I've had a drop too much." He rummaged through his pockets and handed Don a tenner. "No harm done" said the bus driver, tucking the note into the top pocket of his uniform as Pat and a couple of others helped Paddy out of the door and into the street. Everyone in the passage heaved a sigh of relief.

"Never a problem, anyway" Pat said, smiling. "We've got Charlie next door. He's only had three pints. He would have sorted it if it had got out of hand." Dropping the serving hatch, he disappeared back behind the bar.

I finished my pint. We were going to the Aero Club tonight.

CHAPTER 14

Although Pauline and I were now earning more than £35 a week between us, we hadn't had a holiday because of the expense of the wedding. We had however booked our honeymoon in a hotel on the Lizard Point in Cornwall.

The two bedrooms in my Nan and Pop's house still needed decorating and there were loads of other things to sort out – bridesmaids' dresses, Pauline's dress, my suit. We had a lot of money to find. That was why I was going to work this sunny Sunday morning with the front windows of the Mini slid back (they didn't wind down in those days). It was double time, I thought, driving down the Stratford Road towards Camp Hill. Was it the confidence of youth? I felt as though I didn't have a care in the world.

Billy Law awaited me, and I had to finish off the muffle chain. Ah well, life could never be perfect.

"Come on shower" Joe called across the shop. Everybody slowly got to their feet, finishing off the last drop of tea, stubbing out their fags and gently placing the morning's Sunday Mercurys and News of the Worlds on their chairs ready for the morning breakfast-time read at 9.30. It went well with a bacon and egg sandwich.

The job of fetching the box of sandwiches from the caff had been designated to the youngest apprentice, Ray Tysall. He was a cheery lad of 17 with light brown hair and his green boiler suit overalls always looked too big for him even with the sleeves rolled up. I stole a quick look at the News of the World before jumping up and joining Billy Law, who was scurrying out of the shop towards the Wire Mill to check the new chain. Jan struggled after him, lugging a huge tub of grease.

"Tysall!" Young Ray looked up. "It's about time the bloody tablecloth was changed, it's covered in tea stains. And all the mugs want cleaning." Scotty the impish Irishman was moaning.

"It never got into this shit state when Mr Phillips had the job" he said. He had started calling me Mr Phillips after my stint upstairs in the Drawing Office. Ray was a bit shy, as we all were at 17, unsure of how to handle the piss-taking by the older blokes, especially the craic of the paddys.

The tablecloth was exactly the same as it had been when I had done the job a couple of years before – old newspapers, normally changed once a week, at the same time that all the mugs were given a bloody good scrub. The dining table had remained the same for the last 40 years – two steel Morrison air raid shelters welded together.

"I'll do it straight away" Ray said, putting all the mugs in a cardboard box and clearing the old papers of the table.

The new chain on number 1 muffle had been running for two hours, as Yafia and his team had started at 6 am. He greeted us with a big smile, showing blackened, uneven teeth against his strange white and brown patched face.

"Very good job, Mr Billy" he smiled, his skull cap tight on his head. Turning to his men he jabbered off in Arabic. "Mr Bert very fucking angry" he said. They ran off in all directions.

Yafia looked at me and winked one of his pink albino eyes.

It was a right messy job greasing the new chain, even though you used a flat piece of wood to scrape out the grease from the tub Jan had dragged to the muffle. It got on to your hands and worst of all on to your overalls, where it was impossible to get it off completely. I would have to change them after this morning. Rolling my sleeve up for the umpteenth time, I glanced at my watch and saw that it was twenty past nine. Better wash up, I thought, I've got a sausage and tomato sandwich for breakfast.

As I walked down to the washroom and toilets I could see Martin Riley carefully manoeuvring his fork lift loaded with the old chains towards the slope. Young Ray was walking towards me with the cardboard box full of sandwiches.

"I hope you've sorted the table and mugs," I said to him. "Otherwise they'll be taking the piss big time."

Ray looked chuffed. "It looks perfect. All new newspapers on the table and I've bleached out all the mugs. As good as you used to do." He quickly sped off. He still had lots to do. Each small white paper bag was marked up with 'sos and tom' (Big Harry) 'bacon and egg' (Scotty), or whatever it contained. There were usually about twenty sandwiches, and all had to be ready and laid out on the table in the correct place for each bloke. Sunday breakfast in the Fitting Shop was a special occasion. A Brummie or a Paddy wouldn't know what sacrosanct meant. I certainly didn't.

Ray was laying out the bags containing the sandwiches, each one hopefully in the correct place. I was the first to arrive because I wanted to get out of my greasy overalls, and looking at the new tablecloth I had to admit to myself that he'd done a good job. The newspapers were laid out, double thickness and dead flat, hardly a crease covering the full surface of the table. The mugs were sparkling and the teapot was full and brewing, with steam slowly issuing from the spout. Ray stood there like a celebrity chef, with a smile that said "they can't tek the piss now."

The blokes were just arriving after scrubbing up when I glanced down again at the 'tablecloth'. Oh shit. I looked at my watch, which displayed the date as well as the time. Then I looked back at the dates on the newspapers. No wonder they were pristine. They were today's – they hadn't been read yet.

This could be fun, I thought.

Almost simultaneously the same shout came from nearly 15 blokes. "Where's me fucking paper?"

Ray had disappeared, sandwich in one hand, mug in the other. I was just reading the tablecloth.

A dreadful scream suddenly sounded from outside the shop, a cry of shock and pain that made everybody stop talking and look at each other, immediately forgetting about the new tablecloth.

The three apprentices who were working that morning were first out of the shop. When we arrived in the Wire Mill we could see a crowd of blokes gathered outside the washroom down at the other end of the shop. Bert

Carrington, the foreman, was striding towards the crush, telling people to get out of the way. I could see that the yellow Yale forklift had backed into the washroom wall at the bottom of the slope that led up into Adderley Street. It took me another second or so to realise that crushed between the truck and the wall was Martin Riley. He was still shouting out in pain and panic, his arms struggling to push a ton and a half of forklift off his chest. He didn't seem to be able to move his legs, which were hidden underneath.

"Steve, there's a phone in my office with an outside line. Ring 999 and get an ambulance," Bert said. I dashed off, leaving him organizing a couple of blokes to support Martin while he climbed into the driving seat of the truck. Martin was still screaming as Bert gently moved the truck forward, easing the agonising weight off his body.

No Sister Susie on a Sunday morning. But what could she have done anyway? This was a hospital case. I called the ambulance.

"You and young Madden stand in the Street and wait for the ambulance," said Bert. If it ain't here in five minutes gerron the fucking phone again." Bert looked very worried.

Mick looked at me. We were both frightened. We could still hear Martin groaning at the bottom of the slope.

"What happened, Mick?" I asked, lighting up a fag. My hands were shaking.

"Half way up the slope he parked up and walked back down to have a piss and wash up for his breakfast. He couldn't have put the handbrake on properly, because according to one of the Arabs the truck rolled back down the slope. Martin must have heard the rumble before it hit him because he turned round at the last minute and watched it crush him.

"'Kin 'ell" I whispered. Mick nodded in agreement.

It was over three months before Martin Riley returned to work. His lovely head of dark curly hair had turned totally white, and was gradually falling out. His happy-go-lucky personality had vanished.

My couple of weeks working with old Billy Law and Jan were over and I was now extremely privileged to be working on Joe Healy's pride and joy, the Dean Smith and Grace centre lathe. It was reputed to be the Rolls Royce of lathes, and since Mickey Plant had left (he'd gone to a contract toolroom for a large increase in wages) no other turner had been allowed on the machine.

Even at my tender age I could appreciate the silkiness of all the movements of the slides and the apparent ease of achieving the accuracy required. It just seemed easy. I mentioned this to Joe.

"That's because yer just - and only just - beginning to learn what it's about." His 64-year-old eyes twinkled. "Have you noticed a bit of a tight spot on the cross slide when you wind in? And it's got a bit of backlash."

"No Joe" I replied, wrinkling my brow.

"It needs a new cross-slide nut, and you're just the lad to make it." "Walk this way." He adopted his teapot pose and minced into his office.

Joe was outlining how we would remove the toolbox and strip out the cross slide screw so we could get at the phosphor-bronze nut with the internal square thread when his telephone rang. "Yes Tom" he said. "He's here now." He put the phone down.

"That was Caggy, he's in with old McDonald. They want to see yer upstairs after breakfast. What yer bin up to now, yer young bugger?" He saw my worried face. "It's about that idea of yours for a press tool to mek the chain links."

"I seem to be getting all the difficult jobs," I told Arthur. I was sitting with him finishing my tea. "All the other turners get the easy ones." We were next to his Shaping Machine lighting up one of his Woodbines. "I've now got to make a new bronze nut and it's a square thread, bloody internal and all. Why don't he get Caggy to buy one?"

"Do yer know how to cut a square thread, Steve?" Arthur asked me, easing his old bones up off his chair.

"Done a couple at college, but only external. I ain't done an internal nut" I replied.

"I know you'll keep it to yerself, but apart from Joe and you and the senior apprentices there ain't a turner in the shop who could produce a square thread, external or internal. It's Joes way of bringing yer on."

I washed my mug out and put it on the table. A lot of blokes were still reading the table cloth – it was still only two days old. Ray was no longer in charge of the dining room.

I went up the stairs and knocked on George McDonald's office door.

"Sit down, Steve" he said, putting his hand over the mouthpiece of the large, black Bakelite telephone. "I'll not be a minute."

I'd been in his office a few times. It was small and cramped, with tons of engineering books stacked to the ceiling. Caggy, my foreman, sat there in his brown cowgown silently smoking, his cap tight on his head, not looking particularly interested. He was close to retirement.

George put the phone down just as Tommy Rushton came in with Peter Phipps, one of the production engineers. They stood up.

I didn't really know Phippy – he had never spoken to me in over three years - but I knew he was a university graduate who had worked upstairs in the offices for about five years. Black Bat said he had the engineering knowledge of a dead rabbit. He was 26 and wore rimless glasses perched on a rat-like face and seemed to be looking daggers at me. Why, I thought? I was soon to be introduced to factory politics.

"We've done the costings. Your suggestion of a press tool is a bloody good idea, it'll pay for itself in less than 12 months" said George, looking at Tommy Rushton. Tommy nodded.

"You reckon you can make the tool yourself, Steve?" He looked at me.

"Yes Mr Rushton" I replied. Phippy's jaw was clamped shut.

The penny dropped. It was Phippy's job to come up with ideas like this. He hadn't, and I had.

"Tommy and I have agreed you can make the tooling to produce the links. It'll keep the costs down and give you valuable experience, but we don't really have the equipment on this site" George went on. "We've arranged for you to spend a week or so at A E Harris in the jewellery quarter, using their facilities. The Works Director is a good friend, and he owes me a favour."

Tommy Rushton joined in. "Is that the bloke we made a double wrought-iron gate for?"

"That's him," said George. He looked at me again. "You'll be under the supervision of some of the finest toolmakers in the Midlands, and I've arranged for you to start after the annual shutdown." He glanced at his desk diary. "That's the second week in August."

He looked at Phippy. "Peter, Id like you to manage the project and report to me on progress." Phippy's lips had drawn back, exposing his teeth. He nodded. He didn't seem to be able to speak. Caggy looked as though he was dozing off.

"Oh, I almost forgot." George looked at Tommy Rushton and Tommy nodded. "The company have approved your idea within the official suggestion scheme and awarded you £100. That might pay for your honeymoon, Steve." They smiled indulgently.

Phippy will need a trip to the dentist, I thought, I've just heard his teeth crack.

"Thank you Mr McDonald, thank you Mr Rushton," I said. I couldn't wait to get outside and shout as loud as I could – 'kin 'ell!"

★ ★ ★ ★ ★ ★ ★ ★ ★ ★ ★ ★ ★ ★

"I know about your award, Caggy's just told me," said Joe. He was sitting in his office studying the engineer's manual specifications for the square thread. "It'll get out sooner or later, but don't goo shoutin' it about, especially the hundred quid. And don't get big headed, it won't suit yer, you've still got a lot to learn." I respected this man, even though he was giving me a mild bollocking, and vowed not to say a word.

By the afternoon teabreak I had stripped out the cross-slide screw and had the phosphor bronze nut on the tool cupboard next to the lathe. Overall it was about two inches square and three inches long, with a couple of easily-milled features on the outer surface. The difficult bit was the one inch square internal thread, with a root diameter of half an inch. How the hell was I going to see what the cutting tool was doing when it was up the hole?

I'd produced loads of internal threads on the lathe, which wasn't easy because you were working blind. But I wasn't looking forward to this job at all. Joe placed a lump of dark red bronze on the cupboard.

"Make a fully dimension drawing of the old nut and fit it back on to the lathe. Be careful how you fit the screw, even though it's been heat treated you can chip the thread. Ted the draughtsman says you can use one of the drawing boards upstairs." He strolled off.

"It's the barge trip with the stripper tomorrow night, nearly half the factory will be on board" said Pat Dowling, looking up from the tablecloth. One or two of the blokes who never bought a newspaper thought young Ray's idea of using that morning's papers as the tablecloth was brilliant, and should continue.

"There's only seating for 50 odd," Doug said, looking at the other apprentices drinking their tea. "It'll fucking sink then, 'cause I've been told over 80 tickets have been sold" Pat replied.

Everybody started to laugh. I'd just taken a drag, so I was laughing and coughing at the same time. Black Bat took his pipe out of his mouth.

"It'll be such a fucking crush yow wont see the tart tek her clothes off. I'm glad I ain't a gooin'."

"You'll be missing out on the free beer then Alf." Everybody looked at Pat.

"What free beer, first I've heard of it?" I asked. Pat smiled, his crafty green eyes sweeping the gang sat around the table. I'd seen this expression before. It meant someone was in for a piss take.

He dropped his voice and looked dramatically over his shoulder to make sure no-one else was listening. 20 blokes were now craning forward.

"It's top secret at the moment, but someone who'll be on the barge has suddenly come into a tidy lump of money and if he's the type of bloke we all think he is, then there's every chance we'll all get a drink." Pat looked at me and winked before getting up and strolling off. The bastards! How had anyone find out? I hadn't told a soul, in fact Id only been told myself four hours earlier. Ah well, up to the Drawing Office.

Measuring a component and then drawing it up was relatively easy to me, maybe because I have always enjoyed doing it. Even at school, technical drawing was one of my best subjects. So with the full use of the facilities in the Drawing Office, I produced a drawing of a Dean Smith and Grace cross-slide nut. It may seem obvious, but if you had missed a particular measurement or dimension while you had the component in your hand, it was too bloody late when it wasn't. Double and treble checking my work, I sat back and studied the drawing. It looked all right to me.

Gordon the technical apprentice, who was slightly older than me, had O levels galore and a couple of As. He was also two years ahead of me on the Full Tech Certificate CGLI course. He leaned over my shoulder to look at what I'd produced on the drawing board. You have an instinctive feeling when you think someone is about to take the piss.

"That dimension line is not positioned correctly, and you don't spell phosphor bronze like that" he sniffed, walking back to his drawing board. My old mate Mugsy would have given him a right slap, but he was in Hamburg, rocking around the clock. I shrugged my shoulders, thinking Gordon must be as bad Phippy. A right pair of wankers.

"I'm going to work on the bus in the morning, it's another barge trip up the cut in Earlswood" I said. I had finished my tea at Nan and Pop's and was just about to start stripping the wallpaper off the main bedroom, which was going to be our living room in less than three months' time. Would it all be ready in time?

My Nan, in her usual apron with a tea towel over her shoulder, glanced at my Pop, sitting in his chair smoking his pipe. "It'll be late then?"

"Yes Nan." I knew her bedroom light would go out when she heard my key enter the lock and I was home safe.

The Dean Smith and Grace was fully assembled with the worn nut, and I was studying the drawing I had made to produce the replacement. This wasn't going to be easy. But there was no way I was going to chicken out of the job. While I knew Joe was only 10 yards away, I wanted to sort it out myself, and I knew the old bugger felt exactly the same. I'd studied the drawing for half an hour or so, enjoying a fag while I made sure in my own mind the correct sequence of manufacture. I was confident, so with the bronze block set up in the four-jaw chuck I clamped the tailstock in position and started.

After drilling, I bored the hole to ensure concentricity and then began the tricky job of grinding the small high-speed steel cutting tool which would actually produce the square thread. The finished thread in the nut would have to have a clearance of about two thousands of an inch (0.002) to enable the screw to fit nicely. Too tight and it wouldn't work, too loose and it would be worse than the existing one, inaccurate and with backlash.

The nature of a square thread, particularly in a nut, was that once the tool bit was ground and started cutting you could not adjust the size. If it didn't fit properly it was scrap, and you started again.

With the chuck revolving fairly slowly, at about 50 rpm, I wound on a cut of 10 thou (0.010".) and carefully engaged the lead screw which would carry the tool into the bore at the correct pitch to produce the required thread. It disappeared, and when I saw it emerge at the back of the nut I disengaged the lead screw before the tool crashed into the chuck, wound off the cut and withdrew the boring bar out of the nut.

Breathing a sigh of relief I peered into the hole and was surprised to see, with the aid of the overhead light, the beginning of a spiral square thread, albeit only 10 thou deep. Only another 20 cuts, I thought to myself, engaging the lead screw with another 10 thou wound on. I hoped it would follow the same cut. It did.

I'd started right, so it was now a matter of careful machining to achieve the correct depth of thread. I stopped the lathe. I was going to have a walk down to the lavatory. I didn't need a pee – I just wanted a smoke and to relax a bit.

The talk at lunchtime around the Fitting Shop dining table was the barge trip, especially among the younger lads. The old blokes were dozing. I'd been up to the canteen and enjoyed a plate of fish and chips. It wasn't bad, and I could afford the subsidised half crown it had cost because with overtime I was now earning twenty quid a week.

"What's it like, Steve?" Young Ray and Doug hadn't been on the last trip.

"Can't remember much, I got too pissed" I replied, remembering that drinking rum had not agreed with me. I wasn't getting into that state again.

"I've never seen a stripper" Ray announced, in wide-eyed innocence.

"Nor me" said Doug, looking sheepish.

Pat was listening, and I noticed a crafty smile flicker across on his face. "I'm sure you'll have a whale of a time," he said. He stood up and headed towards the Die Shop where George Cooper worked. George had organized the stripper.

Billy Wiggins struggled up from his nap. He'd been suffering from a bit of a cough and a chest infection.

"'Ow yer gerrin' on with Noddy's nut then?" I must have looked puzzled.

"Yer never noticed the size of Caggy's ears?" he said, lighting up his Senior Service. The penny dropped.

"It's a bloody tricky job Billy" I replied. "You can't see what the tool is doing."

"You'll have a few more tricky jobs in the next 45 years, young Steve." He took on a sad expression and his big, rotund body seemed to shrink slightly as he slowly walked off to his milling machine.

A more experienced turner might have finished the job in half the time, but I had to get it right. Eventually I was satisfied that the thread was correct and as I lit up, Joe strolled out of his office.

"Tickle it up with a bit of emery cloth to tek off the sharp edges and we'll see if it's a good fit," he said. The hour of reckoning was approaching.

It took over an hour to strip out the cross-slide screw and check the fit. By this time it was nearly half past five. I wanted to know if the job was OK before I caught the coach to Earlswood.

I started to thread the new nut on to the cross slide screw. "Hang on, stop rushing" said Joe. "Put a good squirt of oil on and then try it, but slowly."

It felt like slippery silk, clinging with a slight hesitance but moving along the screw with no play or slack at all. "It feels a bit tight, Joe" I said, worried.

He took the nut in his experienced hands and carefully revolved it around the screw, checking for forward or backward movement.

"That's because it's a new nut. It's like a car engine, it needs running in."

I breathed a big sigh of relief. Joe continued, his eyes sparkling.

"It feels even better than the proper spare supplied by Dean Smith and Grace. I've had one in me cupboard for years. Yer comin' on."

I rushed down to the showers and within 10 minutes I was dressed in clean jeans and a new cheesecloth shirt. Climbing the stairs up to Adderley Street, I saw two coaches waiting with their engines ticking over and a long stream of blokes and lads coming from both directions, some from the Barrel and some from the Waggon. The Paddys were coming from the Rainbow. Pat was right. It was a sellout.

"Where's the stripper then?" The coaches were parked up and everyone was strolling towards the barge. The eager ones were already on board with pints in their hands, looking out of the windows which ran the full length of the boat.

"I don't know." George, the organizer, was looking worried. "The agency was told we were setting off bang on seven."

The captain looked at his watch. "We can't hang about, we've got to leave in five minutes." He jumped on to the back and started the diesel engine, and a belch of blue smoke coughed out across the water.

Five minutes later the barge chugged off. Len Newbury banged away on the piano singing his comical ditties, but no-one could hide their disappointment. George Cooper looked furious. He would have to put up with all the piss taking.

As the barge slowly moved around a long curve, fishermen drew in their lines and you could hear the moans. "Fucking pissheads" said one. I couldn't see what the fuss was about from where I stood near the bar at the back, but blokes were leaning out of the windows at the front laughing and shouting.

Then the barge shuddered. The engine had been put into reverse. Slowly it came to rest against the bank.

We all looked up at the bridge. Two blondes in miniskirts and silly heels clattered down the brick slope to the towpath, followed by a little bald bloke dragging a battered suitcase. We would soon find out what was in it.

The girls skipped warily on to the barge, purposely flashing their knickers. The roar of welcome echoed across the water. "Gerrem off, show us yer tits!" Pricey was in fine form.

The barge once again under way, Baldy opened the suitcase and pulled out a blanket, which he hung up at the front of the barge. The two girls disappeared behind the screen, one flicking up what there was of her skirt to demonstrate that only one pair of knickers had come on board. There was a fresh roar of approval.

Old Len Newbury was leaning back having a rest. Baldy had slotted the tape into the sound system and it started to pump out a disco beat. Graham and Pricey were having a right old time and young Ray and Doug were sitting expectantly. I was an experienced stripper watcher – I'd been to the Dolls' Club – so I leaned nonchalantly on the bar. I noticed Pat whispering into George's ear.

The first stripper, dressed in black leather and wielding a long bull whip, went through her routine. The banter of the crowd encouraged her, and soon she was dressed only in her heels, bull whip in her hand and looking for a volunteer.

She got two of them. Pat had cunningly persuaded Ray and Doug to sit

215

near the piano, where he said that there was more room and they would have a better view. They were helpless prey. She pounced on Ray, while her friend jumped on Doug. The other girl was not even wearing a bull whip.

The girls squirmed on the two apprentices' laps, pressing their breasts into the lads' faces and looking at the audience for encouragement. We were all roaring them on. The shaving foam came out, spraying the crotches of the two young men. They looked shocked but they were laughing along with everybody else, obviously enjoying themselves. Pat and George were in fits, slapping each other on the back. Both the girls gave Ray and Doug big open-mouthed kisses and suggestively caressed their foam-soaked trousers before disappearing behind Baldy's curtain. The whole barge erupted in applause and laughter.

CHAPTER 15

It was the end of July 1965 and the main production departments of the factory had broken up for the two-week annual shutdown, giving the fitters and electricians the opportunity to strip out and repair or replace worn shafts, couplings and bearings. Overtime was almost obligatory to ensure the huge list of jobs that had to be completed were done in the time, and most evenings I did not clock out until 6 pm. Saturdays and Sundays I worked till two. You could always have a couple of pints in any of the three pubs in Adderley Street, even though the law said otherwise.

I spent most of the time in the Fitting Shop, welding up worn shafts and turning them back to size and making new shafts and bronze bearings on the lathe, milling machine and grinders. I was working hard, but more importantly I was earning plenty of money. The two weeks flew by and I suddenly realised I'd be reporting to AE Harris the next Monday to start the new press tool for making the chain links. I'd been told to report to the Toolroom Manager, Mr Len Wood, at 7.30, so at a quarter past seven I parked my Mini Van in Northwood Street and walked into reception.

Following a quick phone call (there was a list of names and phone numbers on the wall), Mr Wood collected me.

"Len's the name son, follow me," he said. "You've got a component drawing?"

"Yes Len, and an actual link" I replied, struggling to keep up with him. He was as tall as me, bald with a grey moustache and he could certainly stride out. My Nan would say "He needs a jockey on his back".

"You'll spend the first couple of days in the Drawing Office, sketching up the tooling layout" he said. "We would normally produce a comprehensive drawing for the customer, but this is a favour for George McDonald so a quick sketch will do." He opened the door to the office and introduced me to the Senior Draughtsman. "Look after him, Sid" he said, and strode off.

Sid was a friendly bloke, who made me welcome immediately. "How do yer like yer tea?" he asked, pouring me a mug from an old and battered teapot. "I've been briefed on the job in hand. We'll help you all we can."

I told Sid I had produced only one tooling layout before. He smiled.

"Don't worry, Ill show you how to make a start, it's easy then. We've got tons of similar layouts for you to copy. You'll only have to change the dimensions to suit your link."

I had been a bit worried about coming into a new factory with blokes I didn't know, but it looked all right so far.

When we had drunk our tea Sid took me on guided tour of the factory, showing me the massive power presses in the production shops and the impressive toolroom, which was kitted out with some machines I'd never seen before. It began to dawn on me that while I considered myself a good machinist, I still had a lot to learn about toolmaking.

"That looks OK to me, not bad for a beginner" said Sid, looking over my shoulder and check the layout of the press tool I'd drawn. It was nearly clocking out time on the second day at A E Harris and I was reasonably confident that I had done a half-decent job.

"You did most of the work, Sid," I told him. He smiled.

"When you get downstairs tomorrow the blokes in the toolroom will help, don't worry" he said, pouring us both a mug of tea. I think he could see I was a bit worried, because I was not used to this kind of engineering work. Sid was in his late fifties, but like Joe Healey you could tell he wanted to bring on the young lads who wanted to learn their trade. "I'll have a look at the tool when you've finished it" he said.

Driving to work the following morning I did feel nervous. At Delta Wire, even though I was only 19, I was beginning to be recognized as a good machinist who could do a decent job. At A E Harris I was someone from a different trade with not much experience. Ah well, gerron with it, I told myself. I was there to learn.

Roy Charlton, the toolroom foreman, was a bloke of about 50 dressed in a white coat, his thinning hair combed over his head in an attempt to cover his baldness. He welcomed me, but I soon realised that Roy could have done without an extra job to do in his busy toolroom, specially with a novice to look after as well.

Roy introduced me to one of the toolmakers. "Malcolm, I want you to look after the new lad for a week" he said. Then he buggered off back to his office.

"Tek no notice of that miserable bastard, we all call him Bobby on account of his hairdo" said Malcolm, offering me an Embassy. "I s'pose yer've got the same wankers at yer place?" I said we had.

After I had worked for a few hours under Malcolm's experienced eye, he nodded in approval and left me milling up the die and punch plate.

Tea breaks were the same as at Delta Wire, with groups of toolmakers sitting on an assortment of makeshift chairs tucked away behind machines and in corners. I sat with Malcolm and his mates and listened to their chat, drinking my tea from a borrowed mug.

"Who's the new lad then, Mal?" A tall thin bloke with a droopy grey moustache and bushy overgrown eyebrows had joined our little group. "Hope he's paid his whack in the tea school."

Malcolm gave me a sly wink. "Yow be careful what yer say, Nobby. He's working here for a couple of weeks on a pierce and crop tool he's designed as part of his engineering degree at the university. The gaffers wanted him to be under the guidance of the top toolmaker in the shop." Everybody coughed and spluttered, laughing at Malcolm's little boast.

"Top fucking wanker in the shop, more like" Nobby said, with a huge grin which exposed tobacco-stained teeth. "What's yer name then young 'un? Who d'yer support? It'd berra be the Villa." He jumped up and slapped me on the back. "If yow wanna know anything about proper tool mekking, yow cum and see me, because the tosser yer working with is a fucking Bluenose and knows jack shit."

Watching the milling cutter machine the block of tool steel, I began to realise that every factory had the same characters – the piss takers, the wind-up merchants and funny blokes. It helps the day go by.

By the middle of the second week all the parts had been machined and the punches and dies were away at the hardeners'. I was helping Malcolm with another job. He was a quiet bloke in his late forties who wore his hair long over his collar and had sideburns down to his chin.

He pushed his glasses up his nose. "What's yer music then, Steve?"

"The Who, Small Faces, Otis Redding" I replied. He thought for a minute.

"Yer a bit of a Mod, then." I nodded.

"Me, I've got quite a collection of Buddy Holly. Everything he ever recorded, I think." Listening to him talk about his collection I began to realise he loved his music. Working under his guidance I soon became aware of his skill and his desire to pass it on. A young Joe Healy, I thought to myself.

All the hardened parts came back, and following Malcolm's advice I finished all the components on the grinding machines. I assembled the tool into the die set and swung it, with the help of the electric hoist, on to the bench.

"Is it finished now then?" I looked around to see Phippy standing there with Len Wood and Bobby Charlton. Malcolm came to my rescue. "Ready for production trials, Roy" he said to his foreman. Phippy opened his mouth to say something else but was interrupted.

"Let's gerrit in the press, then" Len grunted as he strode off.

When they had all buggered off Malcolm looked at me. "Who was that little shit from your place then, coming here and tekkin' the piss?"

I shrugged my shoulders. "One of the wankers of the world" I replied, swinging the tool off the bench with the hoist.

The tool had to come out of the press twice for adjustments - Malcolm called it 'tickling up'. Nobby called it the 'okey cokey tool - in out, in out, shake it all about. But at the end of the trials it was knocking out chain links every five seconds.

Sid from the Drawing Office picked up a link as it shot out of the tool, measuring it with a micrometer. He looked at me and nodded.

"Not too bad" he said with a smile.

"Thanks Sid" I said.

Sitting in the Jeweller's Arms, I offered Malcolm an Embassy and we studied our pints. I was back at Delta Wire in the morning and the press tool was about to knock out a run of 10,000.

"I bet yow was a bit worried Steve. It was all your baby" Malcolm said, taking a sup of Ansell's Mild.

"I don't think I was really. I knew it would be a better method of production." I replied, reaching for my pint.

He gently put his glass on the table. "I'm a good toolmaker and I enjoy showing yow young uns, but I've never bin able to stick me neck out like yow've done" he said. I frowned, not quite understanding.

"Yer still young and have no worries. It would have made no real difference to your career at your age if the tool had failed. But one day sticking yer neck out will make a difference. It'll cost yer yer job. But I guess yow won't be on the shop floor all yer life. Good luck to yer." He stood up. "Another pint?"

"Thank you Malcolm" I replied.

Driving home to Chilton Road I was thinking about what Malcolm had said about believing in your judgment and sticking your neck out. I still couldn't see the problem. You don't, when you have the confidence of a 19-year-old who's beginning to think he knows it all.

★ ★ ★ ★ ★ ★ ★ ★ ★ ★ ★ ★ ★

It was early September and time for enrolment at the colleges. Before I started my Production Engineering Technician course at South Birmingham Polytechnic, I wanted to a have a final chat with Harry Fisher at Garretts Green. He had been such a great help to me and all the apprentices since we had first started work as 15 year olds. I wanted to thank him.

The opportunity came when the three youngest lads had to get to Garretts Green for their enrolment, but didn't have a car or motorbike. They would have to catch the bus. "I'll see if I can take you in the Mini" I told them. "Let me have a word with Joe."

"Moaning about catching the bus? Yow young buggers don't know yer bloody born," said Black Bat. It was morning tea break in the Fitting Shop and he was being his usual cheerful and happy self.

"I had to walk to work every fucking morning, rain or shine, pissing down most of the time, two miles there and two miles back because I couldn't afford the bus fare when I started" he went on. All the blokes were sat around the steel table supping tea, reading their papers and smoking.

"Was them the days yer were wearing out a pair of clogs every few months Alf?" Scotty said, smiling. He wouldn't miss out. "They tell me the clogs got so wet once they started to grow little branches with leaves on."

The craic was on. Black Bat sat puffing on his pipe, realising he'd walked into it and trying hard not to smile. Pat continued.

"I'll tell yer what, Alf's family lived in the biggest and best semi-detached cardboard box in Smethwick High Street." The laughter began.

"Yow can laugh, but them were fuckin' hard times I tell yer" said Black Bat. He struggled up out of his armchair and strode off to his grinding machine.

"How long d'yer reckon you'll be then?" said Joe, opening one of the drawers in his desk to get the pass out book.

"We'll leave about twelve and be back about half two. I'll take the other lads in my Mini, it'll save 'em time and I really want to say thanks to Harry" I replied. Joe nodded. He wrote out four pass outs and handed them to me.

"Don't none of you clock out, just hand the slips to the gateman?" he said. "I'll clear it with him next door." He nodded towards Caggy.

"We're off in a bit, so get yerselves washed up and changed. Yow ain't getting in my Mini in dirty overalls." I looked at Doug, Ray and Ken, the youngest, who had only just completed his first 12 months at college and was still finding his feet in the factory.

"Yes Steve" they replied in unison, rushing off down to the washroom. The power of authority, I thought to myself watching them go. Out of the corner of my eye I could see Joe smiling to himself.

I opened up the twin doors at the back of my Mini Van and Ray and Ken tumbled in, making themselves comfortable on the thick carpet. They pushed the woollen blanket up behind the two front seats and adjusted the large cushions so they could lean against the side.

"Bloody hell, it's like a little bed in here," Ken said to Ray as they settled themselves in the back. Doug eased his long legs into the front passenger seat (he was as tall as me and still famous for his one-man band show), but he was 18 now and a good bit more factorywise.

"Not many get out the back of Steve's Mini without being shagged" he said with a smile and a wink to me. "I'd behave yerself if I was you."

"And no smoking" I said over my shoulder, pressing the starter button.

The main Hall at Garretts Green Tech, used for dances and exams, was also used for enrolment. Tables were laid out and the course lecturers stood behind them with a mountain of paperwork and enrolment forms, dishing them out to the queue of eager young apprentices.

I was an old hand at this (I hoped it would be the same at South Birmingham Poly), so with Doug's help we ushered the two young 'uns into the appropriate queue and I started to look for Harry Fisher. I soon saw Bob Skan, the sheet metal lecturer, whose son Peter was a GKN apprentice who had joined the same year as me.

"Your toolbox is still waiting for you to collect from the sheet metal shop, Steve," said Bob, helping a lad fill in his forms.

"I'll pick it up before I go" I replied. I was not going to leave my toolbox. I had spent many hours under Bob's supervision making that tool box. The outer box was 24 inches long, 10 inches wide and 10 inches deep and it had a hinged lid with a carrying handle. It was made from mild steel sheet painted black, and contained a two–inch–deep galvanized tray with a sliding lid to hold small tools like scribers and centre punches. It had all Dutch bends, with no sharp edges. I was bloody proud of that box.

"I'm looking for Mr Fisher" I told Bob.

"He'll be back in 10 minutes, he's a having a cuppa" he replied.

I looked around the hall, crowded with lads and lecturers. I had attended dances here, and more importantly sat nervously through my exams, head down on a lonely desk racking my brain to drag up the knowledge I'd tried to cram into it. I remembered the time my first motorbike had conked out and I had nearly missed the exam, and the poor bugger who had walked out after 30 minutes after realising he couldn't understand the paper. I realised that four years of bloody hard work had come to an end and I was about to start a new era of studying at a new polytechnic the other side of Birmingham. And I was getting married in a month. No problem. I was 19 years old and the world was my oyster.

"Nostalgia is a thing of the past," said a voice. I looked around to see Harry standing next to me. "Me and Bob and a few from your year are having a cheese cob or summat in the Cherry Tree, seeing as most of yer are leaving. I'll see yer there in 10 minutes." He strolled off.

I told the lads I'd meet them in an hour and went down to the sheet metal shop to collect my tool box. After putting it into the back of my van I walked across to the Cherry Tree.

"Yer moving up to the technicians' course then" Harry said, taking a bite from his cheese and onion cob. After taking a quick sup of his pint he looked at me. "Yer realise that's another four years of study?"

"I do Harry, and I'm going for it. Hopefully I'll take the two year Institute of Works Managers course after that as well."

He smiled. "Kin 'ell, yow'll be an old age pensioner by the time yer finished."

"I hope not. I wanted to thank you for your help and guidance these last few years."

He nodded. "Yow ain't the only one who realises that gaining extra qualifications will help you in the future. It'll be a hard slog, but go as far as yer can. I'll tell yer another thing. I've bin in the game for well over forty years and even I'm still learning." I was surprised. This was a bloke who I thought knew all there was to know about being a skilled craftsman.

"By the time yow've finished studying, providing yer pass the exams, you'll be well set. You'll have the craftsmanship and the technical qualifications."

He finished his pint and looked me in the eyes. "I'll give yer a bit of advice. Even if yer know the answer, ask the question."

He saw my slightly puzzled look. "It stops people thinking yer know it all." I nodded. He was a great old bloke. I tried to keep remembering his words during the next forty years, but I didn't always succeed.

We all arrived back at Delta Wire just before half past two, and by the time we had changed back into our overalls and done a bit it was time for the afternoon tea break.

"What the fuck is Job Evaluation?" It wasn't only old Black Bat who was asking this question, but twenty other blokes who were looking at Norman the Shop Steward with quizzical frowns.

"It's all about rationalising the pay structure across the whole of the factory. The new management want to reduce the number of different rates of pay in our factory. They reckon over 20 hourly rates is too many. It's got to be reduced to five or six, same as the other Delta factories." He looked at his notebook. "Work Study and Production Engineering will be talking to us and setting what they call benchmarks."

"They can call 'em what they like," said Black Bat with a scowl. "Just as long as us skilled blokes are on the top rate."

Every man around the table nodded in agreement. Pat looked up from his paper and looked at Norman.

"We'll have to raise this at district level." The Shop Steward looked worried. Mind you, with six kids he always looked worried.

I guessed that rationalisation of pay rates would not affect us apprentices, because our rates were increased annually until we were 21, when we would go on the top skilled rate anyway. However I had more important things on my mind – like getting measured for my wedding suit, taking Pauline and the bridesmaids for a dress fitting to her Aunty Betty's in Bournville and responding to Les Green's invitation to go "up the Blues". I still had to finish decorating our two rooms, and enrolment at South Birmingham was the next day.

The Polytechnic was on the dual carriageway part of the Bristol Road, not far from the Cadbury site. Driving from the city centre you went under the footbridge and U-turned back.

I was on my own and felt very much the new boy as I went in through the glass doors. The building was more modern with more glass than the classic red brickwork of Garretts Green Tech, but I was going to be here for one day and one evening for the next four years so I'd better get used to it.

Following the signs, I found myself standing in a group of lads waiting to enroll for the City & Guilds Production Engineering Technicians Part 1. Attendance would be on a Monday starting at nine, a break for lunch at 12.30, an hour for tea at five and finishing at nine. By the time I got home I'd just be able to squeeze a couple of pints in before the Haven shut. But I had begun to realise that qualifications were paramount and the only way to get them was through bloody hard work. On reflection I'd left school too early, with no A or O levels, but while I had four years' experience of craft practice and qualifications I had a lot to learn and catch up on the academic side.

After enrolment at the Poly I got back to Delta Wire just in time for lunch and went upstairs to join the queue in the canteen. There was a tense atmosphere. The long table nearest the serving counters was the foremen's table, usually occupied by the regulars, but today every foreman and assistant foreman in the factory was crowded around and three extra tables had been pushed together to accommodate them all.

I picked up my plate of food and sat down next to Pat Dowling, who always used the canteen and would know the score.

"What's up Pat?" I asked, nodding towards the foremen's table.

"The new régime has made all the foremen into superintendents and the assistant foremen into foremen" Pat replied, smiling and scratching his chin. "Not even a fucking Paddy could invent that."

Pat's skill was overhead cranes, and during the next few months I would have to work with him. I was not looking forward to this. I was terrified of heights.

Pat finished off his fag and stood up. "The boys in the shop will have something to say about this lot," he said. I followed him down to the Fitting Shop, thinking that most of the 'boys' were 50-60 years of age. This could be fun.

Many people dislike change as they get older, but Mr Watson, the new MD, was obviously in a rush to make his mark just the same.

"I fucking told yer, dain't I. More gaffers and the bastards are trying to cut our money with this Job Evaluation." Old Black Bat was in full cry as Pat and I sat down around the table looking at the other blokes supping their tea and lighting up after eating their sandwiches.

"Meks no difference to us how many gaffers they have" Bob Brown said, shrugging his shoulders. "There's still Cooper and Pricey in the Casting Shop, so what's changed?" Big Harry, his mate, nodded. Black Bat sucked at his pipe and stomped off.

"This job evaluation and rates of pay stuff is more important than new titles for the supervisors, and you need to keep a close eye on that Norman" said Billy Wiggins. He was in the middle of a bad attack of coughing. Norman looked at Pat for advice. Pat seemed to be taking an increasing interest in union business.

"Let's see what the outcome is of this evaluation," he said. "If necessary we'll take it up at district level. We ain't gonna be robbed."

He looked round the group for support. Everyone nodded, including the electricians who were listening through the wire fence separating the two shops. Their Shop Steward was Bob Crockett, and Bob wouldn't stand any messing about with skilled men's wages.

The Mini was still driving a treat, but I needed to change the oil and filter before our honeymoon trip to Cornwall. I decided to do it on the first available Sunday afternoon I could. It couldn't be that weekend because of all the stuff with the suit and the bridesmaids' dresses, and I couldn't afford to miss Saturday and Sunday morning overtime in the factory. These were my thoughts as I drove down the Stratford Road under the railway bridge at Camp Hill and into Deritend past the temporary flyover which had already been up 10 years.

Everyone was either changing into their overalls, reading the paper with a fag and mug of tea in their hands or nodding off. We clocked in at 7.30, but didn't start until Joe shouted us up just before eight.

It was breakfast time and everyone was tucking into a Saturday morning special that young Ken had collected from the caff.

"I ain't seen old Billy Wiggins this morning. Unusual for him, he gets his car checked over on a Saturday" said Big George Powell. Big George was a turner on the largest centre lathe in the shop – it would swing three feet with the gap bed out and was 18 feet between centres. He never sat around the Fitting Shop dining table but preferred to take his breaks alone at the back of his machine. He was 40, over six feet tall with a large frame, dark hair slicked back with Brylcreem. He rarely smiled. Messing about a year or so before, I had taken a liberty with Big George and was rewarded with a more than playful smack round the head.

"He was a bit rough yesterday with his chest and cough" Pat replied to George, who nodded and walked back to his lathe. George and Billy were pals who enjoyed the odd game of chess during lunch breaks and were both keen Labour supporters. Everybody liked and respected Billy and you could see the old blokes round the table scratching their chins and whispering together.

"Bit more than a cough and a cold if yow ask me" Black Bat seemed to voice the thoughts of us all. Billy had been ill for quite a while.

Clocking out at 1 pm, I strolled down to the Waggon to meet Pauline for a cob and a pint before we went up town to Austin Reed to sort out my wedding suit. All the old gang were there – Pricey, Graham, Mack the welder, Arthur, John the Blacksmith. As I sat taking a sip from my pint I suddenly regretted asking Pauline to meet me here. I had a nasty feeling it was going to be leg-pulling time.

Just after 1.15 the door opened and Pauline walked in. She had caught the bus down the Cov from Hay Mills. Pricey turned from the bar, and the whole room started singing Here Comes The Bride. She looked around the room and smiled. Then she walked up to Pricey and gave him a kiss on the cheek.

"Mine's a grapefruit juice and a cheese cob please, John." Like a good 'un, he dug into his pocket and placed five bob on the counter.

The suit fitted perfectly. It was dark blue mohair, a three-button single breasted jacket with modern small lapels, a waistcoat and tapered trousers without turnups. In 1965 it was the dog's bollocks. It bloody well should have been. It was costing me over twenty quid.

"It needs final stitching and pressing but it'll be ready for collection next week" the tailor said. "It suits you." We all laughed. Obviously a standing joke.

Two of Pauline's cousins were going to be bridesmaids, and on the Sunday afternoon we all set off to Aunty Betty's for the second fitting. No problems, another job out of the way.

Decorating our lounge upstairs was now almost finished. A TV had been rented from Rediffusion (everyone rented in those days, tellies cost so much to buy) and Nan and Pop had given us £50 for a three-piece suite. We chose in a nondescript grey with small wooden inserts as armrests. It was very much appreciated and would last us the best part of seven years.

"When are we going up the Blues, then?" Les Green was finishing off his breakfast and looking round the Dining Table, smiling at all the other blokes.

"When you're married you wont be allowed to" he said. "You'll be too busy shopping with yer missus." We had all the usual banter. "He'll be under the thumb in five minutes". "No shopping, no shagging." "Not tonight love, I've got a headache." By now Id been working in the factory for three years and could almost put up with the piss-taking without being wound up, but sometimes it was hard work.

The Blues were six games into the 65/66 season and they weren't doing very well. "When's the next home game, Les?" I asked. "Portsmouth, this Saturday" he replied. "You up for it?" In unison Pat and Scotty said "He'll have to ask his missus first!" Yep, they were taking the piss.

Monday morning at South Birmingham Poly didn't go too badly. New lads a year or two younger than me were trying to settle into a strange environment, but they were in factory groups – there were two or three together from say Wards in Worcester or Cadburys across the road. I was the lad on his own. However by teatime I was sitting down to a plate of grub with Ron Smith, a technical apprentice from Wards.

Ron was tall and slim and had joined Wards Capstans the previous August after leaving school in the July with a couple of O levels and one A level. He would be serving a four-year technical apprenticeship and was working in the Production Engineering Office.

"You've been at work for four years then, bloody hell!" Ron was surprised. "What are you doing on this course then?" I explained that I had successfully completed all the City & Guilds Craft courses and the company were sponsoring me on the Technicians' Course for the next four years.

Washing his chips down with the remains of his tea, Ron said, "You'll be able to teach us a few things in the workshop then".

"And you'll be teaching me a bit on the maths and calculus" I replied. We were both right.

After my first day and evening at South Birmingham Poly I did manage to make it back to the Haven for a pint.

★ ★ ★ ★ ★ ★ ★ ★ ★ ★ ★ ★ ★ ★

I was working on Joe Healy's beloved centre lathe and had just knocked the machine off for breakfast. It was Nan's sandwiches Monday to Friday – I couldn't afford caff fare every day because I was getting married in a month.

"Tommy Carter and the new Apprentice Supervisor want to see you after break, Steve" Joe called out of his office as I walked to the dining table. What had I done now? The wags around the table had already made their mind up. "Steve's in for a bollocking" Pat said smiling. "I've never seen Caggy look so mad. Tommy Rushton just walked into his office." Even Black Bat was joining in the fun.

After four years of factory piss-taking I was well used to this. "The gaffers have had a collection for a wedding present for me and Pauline" I said. "I'm told that when an apprentice gets married he gets an automatic rise of five quid a week. So you can all fuck off and mind yer own business." I walked away to the strains of "Yes Mr Rushton, no Mr Rushton, three bags full Mr Rushton".

"Sit down Steve." Tommy Carter pulled out his Woodbines and lifted his cap slightly to scratch his forehead. Very few had seen Caggy without his cap. The word was that he slept in it.

"Peter Williams, the new Delta Apprentice Supervisor, wants a short monthly meeting with each apprentice and their immediate foreman to see how things are going. I've told him you're doing all right."

"Thank you Tommy," I said.

"I'm told you are doing well, not just all right," said Peter. "How did the first day on the technicians' course go?" He offered his hand. "Keep up the good work, and don't forget you're on the PERA residential course in November." I could see Caggy thinking, we dain't have all this when I were a kid.

As I stood up Caggy said "Oh, by the way, yer working in the Die Shop next week. Report to Percy Hollinshead on Monday."

I had a small worry about this. As I passed Joe's office I put my head inside the door.

"They don't work Sunday mornings in the Die Shop" I said. Joe looked up.

"Don't worry, there's plenty of overtime in our shop for a half decent turner" he said.

"Thanks Joe" I replied with a sigh of relief. Sunday morning was worth nearly four quid to me.

"I'm having a fitting for my wedding dress this Saturday afternoon, and you're not allowed to be there" said Pauline. We were sitting in her parents' house and she had just handed me a wonderful excuse for joining Les Green to see the Blues. Her younger brother Bobby was a Villa Fan. "The Blues are at home" he whispered, I said nothing.

"She's given yer permission to go then?" It was breakfast time on Saturday morning and the diners were having their craic. "It'll be the last game he ever sees." "He'll be shopping Saturday afternoons once he's married." They were all having a go.

The last hour of the morning was doing the usual foreigners, brake drums, lawnmower blades and welding up exhausts, before we all clocked out at one o'clock. Les and I had left our cars on the works car park behind the snooker room and were strolling down to the Waggon and Horses. Working on a Saturday morning so close to St Andrews and with my car parked up safely under the watchful eye of Security, I had regularly gone to see the blues the previous season, but this year I had had too much on, timewise and expense wise, so this would be my first game. Billy, my best man, was in the Waggon with his Dad (I always called him Mr Bill) and a few other mates, supping and cheese cobbing.

At 2.15 we strolled up Kingston Hill and paid our five bob to stand on Spion Cop. Even in the old Second Division the Blues would normally have about a 25,000 gate. Only the rich sat in seats. Most people stood, in a ground that had a capacity in 1965 of over 50,000.

We had all had a pee in the awful corrugated shed at the top of the stand and were gathered in the usual spot halfway down, level with the half way line. At 2.45, 15 minutes before kick-off, a tinny version of I've Got You

Babe by Sonny and Cher came to an abrupt stop and a crackly voice announced: "Would Mr Les Green please report to the main entrance." We all looked at Les. He was going to miss the kick-off.

Les looked worried. "Hope it's not one of the kids or me missus" he mumbled, struggling to make his way down to the touchline. He clambered over the wall and walked around the pitch towards the main stand and the tunnel where the players ran out.

I lit up a fag and looked casually around the ground. I noticed a couple of blokes walking around the pitch towards the main stand. My thoughts were soon interrupted when Spion Kop began singing "Keep right on to the end of the road" as the players ran out of the tunnel.

"Where's yer mate then?" Billy asked. We were midway through the first half and the Blues were not playing well.

"He ain't missing a lot" I replied, thinking the same as another 20,000 silly buggers who had paid five bob to watch a load of rubbish. If you're a fan, you're always a fan. Forty-five years later I still follow the Blues, though these days I live a long way from Birmingham.

Just before half time I spied Les walking back to us around the touchline. "Everything OK mate?" I asked him as he shuffled back into his spot to watch the last minute of the first half. He had a huge grin on his red face.

"You ain't gonner believe this, I've missed the first half of the game, but I've had a fucking scream. There were fifteen Les Greens in the main office and it took the silly bastards all this time to sort it out. I'm going for a pie, who wants one? I'll tell yer the tale after the match. Yer'll piss yerself." Les was off, laughing his way to the Pie Man.

A cup of Oxo and a steak and kidney pie works wonders. and we were all confident the Blues would turn up in the second half and sort out Portsmouth. Alas, it was not to be. The Blues lost 3-1.

"Come on then Greeny, tell us the craic." Pricey had been in the seats in the main stand and had heard the call for Les Green. He was standing at the bar in the lounge of the Waggon as we all walked through the door.

Les joined us and sat down. He took a sup of Ansells' Mild looked around at his audience, smiled and began.

"I was right pissed off, I tell yer, walking round the pitch just as the players were about to come out, but then again I was wondering if everything was OK at home with the wife and kids. Maybe there had been an accident or something. Any road I gets to the main entrance where the directors park their cars and there's this big fat bloke wearing a senior steward's badge, sweating like a pig he was, waving his arms about and shouting to about 10 other blokes.

"I tapped him on the shoulder to gain his attention and told him I was Les Green. 'Fuck me, not another one' he said. 'Yer berra join that fucking lot over there.' So I ambled over. 'I'm Les Green', I said to one. 'I'm Les Green', he replied. 'And I'm Les Green', said another. Within a minute we were all pissing ourselves with laughter, especially when four more Les Greens joined us."

Our own Les Green took a sup of his beer and looked around the pub. A crowd had gathered and were listening with smiles on their faces. Les continued.

"Quite a few Les Greens were moaning about missing the start of the game, but we were all worried that something might be wrong at home. After a couple of minutes a short, rat-faced man with long thinning hair turned up. He had Kevin, the Senior Steward, trailing in his wake. 'I fucking told yer there were fifteen of em' Kevin said, waving his arms about.

'Would you please all follow me' said Ratface. "We'll go to the General Office and try to sort this out. Kevin said he was off to watch the match. The rest of us squashed into the general office. 'We received a phone call asking for a Mr Les Green to telephone home as soon as possible' said Ratface. That's right, isn't Mary?" A mini-skirted young girl nodded in agreement. Two of 'em said it couldn't be them, because they weren't on the phone.

"Then Ratface turned back to the girl in the mini-skirt. 'What exactly did the caller say, Mary?' he asked her. She said a woman had rung and asked if we could announce over the loudspeaker for her husband Mr Les Green to ring home as soon as possible."

"At this point two more Les Greens got up to go. Neither of them had wives.

Ratface asked the girl if she had left a phone number. She hadn't."

Les took another sup of his pint. "By this time I was getting right pissed off" he said. "I asked the girl if the caller had left a name, hoping this would narrow it down and we could all go back to the game. Ratface perked up. If she had, it would solve the problem good and proper."

"Yes, she did," said the girl. We all listened expectantly. "She said her name was Mrs Green."

In the end Ratface set up two phones for us to use, and within five minutes I'd made sure that my missus and kids were OK. It turned out that the Mrs Green who had caused all the trouble had rung to say she was going to Bingo with her mother, and could Les get his own tea after the game!" Greeny was almost crying with laughter.

I stood up and finished my pint, saying goodbye to Billy. We were going to meet at the Wayfarer on the Stratford road and would probably end up at the disco at the Navigation Inn in Wootton Wawen, or the Aero Club at Elmdon. There I was, 19 years old, on £20 a week, dressed in my burgundy mod suit, a good-looking bird in a mini-skirt on my arm and driving a Mini. I thought I was the dog's bollocks.

It was well after midnight when we left the Aero Club and I still got to work by 7.30 the next morning. It was double time on Sunday.

Following a long day at South Birmingham Polytechnic on the Monday I reported to the Die Shop bang on 7.30 on the Tuesday. I'd already told Percy Hollingshead that I attended college on Mondays. He told me to report to Wally the chargehand.

Percy was a gentle, quietly spoken man in his early sixties with a full head of greying, salt and pepper hair. His reserved manner was very different to the normal factory foremen who effed and blinded at their men throughout the working day. He lived in a traditional semi just off the Wolverhampton Road in Warley and was the proud owner of a brand new Renault Dauphine.

The Die Shop was at the back of the main Wire Mill, near the fine wire machines. Through the windows which ran the full length of the shop you had a pleasant view not only of the canal, but a main junction in the city's canal system. Birmingham had more canals than Venice.

I knew all the eight men in the Die Shop. One or two enjoyed a pint at lunchtime, but they were a very tight-knit group who kept their shop and its business very much to themselves. With the dreaded Job Evaluation Scheme in the offing, certain groups considered themselves the most highly-skilled and would argue strongly that they ought to be in the top pay grade. The Die Shop certainly felt this way. Black Bat and a couple of others in the Fitting Shop would disagree, calling them fucking die polishers. Even at the tender age of 19 I had the sense not to get involved in these matters. IN a couple of years' time I would be a skilled man myself. Even though I knew all the blokes, I was still a bit nervous going into a new shop with new skills to learn.

I walked upstairs to the half glass-panelled door – and found myself in a barber shop.

"Gerrin the queue, young 'un. The last haircut is quarter past eight, before the gaffers arrive," said Johnny Williams, the shop joker. He was finishing off Wally the chargehand with an electric trimmer. He whipped off the towel with a flourish and caught Wally's half crown in mid air.

"Next please," said Johnny. Billy Little, one of the wire drawers, lowered himself into the chair. "Give us a Beatle cut," he said, smiling.

"Yow'll have short back and sides same as every other fucker," said Johnny, picking up his comb and scissors. I watched for a minute or so and realised that Mr Williams was indeed a good barber.

Jim Richmond, the snooker pal who had started his apprenticeship the same day as me three years ago, had been permanently attached to the Die

Shop and was involved in the toolmaking aspect of producing the hardened steel die plates used for drawing small sections in the Fine Wire Mill. He worked closely with old Bonehead, who had been moved from the Bar Mill across the road to a small, purpose-built shop just below the main Die Shop.

Obviously after three years Jim was an accepted member of the Die Shop, as I was in the Fitting Shop. But would another lad in the Die Shop be accepted? I would soon find out.

The workbench ran the length of the shop under the long window. At six-foot intervals there were mounted electric motors, each with small three-jaw chucks. The extremely hard tungsten carbide insert was contained inside a 3-inch soft steel casing and the die was gripped in the chuck and revolved at high speed. The polisher would coat a specially-shaped pointed piece of wood with a paste impregnated with extremely finely crushed diamonds. This tool was then inserted into the die and used to polish and open up the diameter of the tungsten carbide to the required size, removing only about 5 thou (0.005ins). All dies were purchased in at the smallest diameter, and after a couple of ton of brass wire had been drawn through them they were returned to the Die Shop for polishing and/or opening up to the next size.

In the cold drawing process, as opposed to the hot extrusion process, the die had to been extremely accurate (plus or minus 1 thou, .001") and highly polished to a mirror finish.

"Morning all" said Percy he walked into the shop and saw six blokes at their work stations busily polishing dies. "Morning, Percy" came the reply in perfect unison. Before opening his office door he slowly bent down and picked up a handful of hair from the floor.

"Had your hair cut this morning then, Wally?" The chargehand grinned.

"Make sure Johnny brushes up better, don't want the gaffers to know do we?" Percy winked at me, hung up his jacket and put on his white foreman's cowgown. "I'll be in a bit earlier in the morning" he said. "Missus reckons I need a haircut."

"Yes, Percy." The reply was again in total unison.

CHAPTER FIFTEEN

In every department I'd worked in during the past three years or so, most blokes had willingly passed on their knowledge and experience to me, but there were one or two who, while not actually keeping information back, did not appear to be over-zealous about imparting their skills. Wally O'Hare, the Die Shop chargehand, was among them.

Each of the workstations was manned by a die polisher, each of them sitting on his high chair carefully polishing a die insert. There didn't appear to be a workstation free.

"Just watch old Fred for a bit and I'll sort out a job for yer," said Wally. He walked into Percy's office and closed the door.

Fred was a nice old fella. He moved the soft wooden stick impregnated with diamond cutting paste backwards and forwards into the die, explaining it to me as he worked. "That just might be enough," he said, removing the die from the chuck. "Let's check the size."

Cleaning the surplus diamond paste from the die with a soft muslin cloth, he mounted the die in a miniature draw bench and inserted a short length of pointed brass wire. Then he attached a gripping dog to the pointed end of the wire and with the help of a foot treadle pulled a two-inch length of wire through the die. He reached into the pocket of his brown cowgown and produced a half-inch micrometer.

"Another two thou and that'll be it" he said, squeezing a minute amount of diamond paste from a small plastic tube on to the polishing stick. "'Ere, have a goo, I'll stretch me back." He handed me the die and stood up.

As I sat there carefully polishing out the last couple of thou, Fred told me a little about himself. Born and bred in the Black Country, he now lived in a lovely posh flat in Kent Road, Halesowen and was the proud owner of an elderly Rover 90 with dark red leather seats.

"A mate of mine in the flats bought it new in 1957, but he dropped down dead six months ago coming out of the Royal Oak. It's only done 32,000 miles."

I had seen it in the car park, and it was a beautiful vehicle. Fred lavished a lot of attention on it. My Mini looked like a miniature car when I parked it alongside.

I didn't want to take too much metal out so I stopped the chuck spinning just as Wally waddled out of Percy's Office. Wally was a short, fat little bloke with a superior air and while I had never really had a conversation with him in three years, I was quickly coming to the conclusion that I was not going to like him.

"I hope he ain't fucked the die up, Fred" said Wally, taking it out of Fred's hand. "They need this urgent in the Wire Mill. I've got Bert Carrington screaming down me neck." He quickly drew a length of brass wire through the die and measured the diameter. Fred and I looked at each other and then looked apprehensively at Wally. "It'll do," snapped Wally, putting the micrometer into his pocket before dashing off to deliver the die to the Wire Mill Production Office.

Old Fred scratched his chin. "Tek no notice, Wally gets a bit agitated. Lord knows how he'll gerron if they mek him Foreman when Percy retires."

Wally would be sorely disappointed in a few years' time when a certain Steve Phillips was appointed Assistant Foreman to Percy Hollingshead – but that was in the future.

"Can you use a spark eroder?" It was a challenge rather than a question. Wally had returned from the Wire Mill and was presumably about to give me a job.

I was aware of the principle of the machine. I had studied it at college and had limited experience at setting and operating one. Don't forget this was 1965 and spark erosion was based on a solid copper electrode very slowly eroding through tungsten carbide, a material which was so hard that it could not be machined or cut in the traditional manner. The process was driven by a weak electric current immersed in paraffin. This was light years away from the computerised wire erosion machines of 30 years later.

"Yes Wally" I replied with slight trepidation, wondering what sort of a job I was about to be given.

"I suppose you can use a lathe?" he said, putting a length of copper into my hand. "Turn it to .480 inches, about three inches long, and bring it back to me."

It was on the tip of my tongue to tell this fat little bastard that even at 19 years of age, thanks to the old blokes in the Fitting Shop, I'd forgotten more about machining on lathes, millers and grinders than he knew. But sensibly, I didn't.

"How yer gerrin' on with the die polishers then?" Black Bat asked, sitting back in his armchair and puffing smoke from his pipe. It was lunchtime and I had gone back to my roots. All the blokes were around the steel table finishing off their sandwiches, reading the papers and smoking.

"They ain't die polishers" I replied. "They reckon they're toolmakers." Ten pairs of eyes suddenly focused on me. Black Bat, Andy Uprichard and the other machinists erupted in anger. "Fucking toolmakers my arse!" roared Black Bat. He looked at Norman and Pat Dowling. "You're our fucking shop stewards, this is a load of bollocks!" he shouted. "We mek the fucking tools! Them bastards are just polishers! Have yer seen that wanker Sandpaper Arse polishing a die and doing the fucking crossword in the Daily Mirror at the same time?"

The gentleman in question was christened Sandpaper Arse because of the meticulous way he polished his rear end following his morning ablutions. Apparently anyone going into the lavatory after him would find no paper to wipe their bum apart from the newspaper they took with them.

I finished my tea and made my way back to the Die Shop, clutching the turned copper bar. It was bang on 0.480". I some how doubted if Wally and the rest of the Die Shop blokes would welcome me with open arms when they found out what I had inadvertently started.

Wally showed me how to set the speed and power of the machine and fill the tank with paraffin which totally submerged the die and copper electrode.

"The electrode will cut 10 thou bigger, so the finished diameter will be 0.490 inches" he said. "That'll leave us 10 thou to polish out to 0.500."

The process started with a bubbling in the paraffin caused by the electronic sparks eroding into the tungsten carbide. The bubbles gently burst upon the surface with a faintly electric smell. "It'll tek about half an hour before it's finished" Wally went on. "While yer waiting yer can watch old Fred." He went back into Percy's office.

I didn't realise it at the time, but this was job protectionism, big time. I was from the Fitting Shop, where the men were vying for the top pay grades in the Job Evaluation Scheme, but I was now working in the Die Shop.

Under Wally's watchful eye I removed the die from the spark eroder and polished it out to the finished size of 0.500 inches. George Cooper, the son of Jim Cooper, the Casting Shop Superintendent, was the Shop Steward. He appeared to be watching me closely. I would be glad when I'd finished my stint in the Die Shop.

During the previous three months under the direction of the new Managing Director, every job and task in the factory had been evaluated. The Production Engineers, Peter Phipps and Gordon Jones, helped by other specialists from the Delta Group, had studied every job in the factory, watching the men at work and recording their findings on clipboards. The Casting Shop, the Extrusion Mill, the Drawing Mill, Wire Mill – every Department in the factory had been investigated. You can imagine the anger and resentment of the workforce. But the new Delta régime was determined that the numerous rates of pay would be reduced to five rates, as in the rest of the Delta Group.

Me, I'd got more important things to think about. I was getting married next week.

CHAPTER 16

Though I was working in the Die Shop, I took all my tea breaks and lunch breaks around the steel tables that formed the dining room of the Fitting Shop, listening to the craic of Scotty, Pat Dowling, Bob Brown, Andy and old Black Bat. I was getting married in five days' time, and they were all taking this piss big time.

"He'll be too fucked to come back to work after a week on the job" Pat announced to the diners. "He'll need to come back for a rest."

"He'll get that in the Die Shop sat on his arse polishing" said Scotty. Everybody was having a good laugh at my expense, but I wasn't too bothered because I knew these blokes and respected them. I also suspected that they were arranging a collection for a wedding present for me and Pauline.

"Billy Wiggins has got lung cancer." Big George Powell stood leaning against Andy's lathe. He had quietly walked across the shop from his large lathe the other side of the Fitting Shop. George was a good friend of Billy, and you could see the sadness in his eyes and the slight stoop of his wide shoulders. Every bloke stopped doing what they were doing, eating their sandwiches, drinking tea, smoking, reading the paper. All went very quiet. The young Apprentices also became hushed. Twenty pairs of eyes looked at George.

The other fitters and mates, including John the Blacksmith and Mac the Welder, had wandered over. Even Joe Healy had come out of his office and stood next to Arthur Twamley. Everybody knew 'summat was up'.

"He'd been in hospital for four days so they could carry out tests, but they sent him home last week. I went to see him last night." Big George took a deep breath. It looked difficult for him. "He looks right fucking poorly. The poor old bugger can hardly breathe."

He turned away, and with his head bowed went back to his machine and started work, even though there were still 10 minutes to go before the lunch break finished. Billy Wiggins was a well-loved and much-respected man. Now he would never be able to fulfil his dream of setting his alarm clock on the eve of his retirement and bashing it with his hammer in the morning when he didn't have to get up for work.

No one waited for Joe Healy to shout us up to start work following the lunch break. We all slowly stood up and went back to work.

Billy died four weeks later. His funeral was the biggest Quinton Cemetery had seen for many a year. It was attended by senior directors from many large factories in Birmingham, along with Mr Shakespeare, the retired MD, and all Billy's fellow Birmingham City Councillors, including the Lord Mayor. There were trade union officials from Austin, as well as Norman and Pat representing Billy's workmates from Delta Wire.

The week raced by, but I'd managed to change the oil and filter on the Mini one lunchtime with help from another apprentice, ready for the journey down to Lizard Point in Cornwall, where Pauline and I were going on honeymoon. Both our rooms upstairs in Nan and Pop's house were decorated. A new three-piece suite and a rented black and white TV stood in the front bedroom where I had been born nineteen and a half years before. All was ready. All we needed was for the wedding to go off OK. Pauline had been on tranquillisers for nearly a week.

My first stag night was on the Thursday night in the Haven Pub in School Road with Great Uncle Norman, Pop and Billy, my Best Man. We all supped M&B Mild in the large bar at the front of the pub. There was no way Pop and Uncle Norman would drink in the lounge at the back, because they charged an extra threepence a pint there. On the occasional Saturday night when the Haven had a sing-song and a 'Free and Easy' in the lounge, they had to pay the extra because Nan and Aunt Ada insisted.

I'd been working in the Die Shop for the past week or so, but my heart belonged to the Fitting Shop and the other departments I had worked in during the last three years. So I wasn't surprised when we all returned from The Waggon and Horses on the Friday lunchtime, where I'd bought a round of drinks for what appeared to be half the bloody factory, to be presented with an envelope.

"Thank you" I said to all the blokes around the table. Even old Black Bat just about managed a smile.

Before I could report back to the Die Shop, Joe Healy called me into the office. "Yer know I don't contribute to all these collections." I nodded. "Yes Joe." The old chargehand stood up and opened the door to a cupboard on the wall. He carefully brought out a brown wooden box.

"I know yow ain't got yer own micrometer over 1 inch." I nodded again. "I've had this for donkeys' years" he said, opening the lid to reveal an adjustable micrometer that would measure from 1 inch up to 6 inches. "Don't tell anybody."

I nodded again. "Thank you Joe."

On the way to the Die Shop I had a quick look in the envelope that Pat Dowling had given me. There was nearly 30 quid!

That night a gang of us met in the Royal George at the top of Digbeth and had a proper piss-up. In those days the bridegroom-to-be wasn't usually chained naked to lamp-posts, subjected to strippergrams or shipped off to Amsterdam or Benidorm - this was 1965, and all that sort of stuff hadn't been invented.

I must admit I lost count of the amount of beer and whisky that was put in front of me. Pricey and his mates had dropped in for an hour before they carried on to the clubs. By closing time I was legless. How Billy and I got back to his Mom and dad's house in Shaftsmoor Lane in the early hours of the morning of Saturday October 16 I have no idea. I also don't remember how I got back to Chilton Road, but I do remember being sick all over Billy's Mom's kitchen table. Again memory is strange, specially when you are totally pissed. I do remember that the sugar bowl took the full brunt.

"We'll have a couple in the Shaftsmoor before we set off" I said to Billy. I'd arrived at his place at about noon and the ceremony was at two. I was dressed in my dark blue three-piece mohair suit, starched paper collar and

Slim Jim blue tie. My buttonhole, a red carnation, was pinned in my lapel. Billy's was on the front seat of my Mini.

My Best Man was still in the bath. I left him to his ablutions and sat down in the lounge. I didn't fancy sitting in the kitchen, for some strange reason. His Mom busied herself and was giving me a bit of a cold shoulder. I looked at Billy's Dad. I'd always called him Mr Bill when we went up the Blues or when we worked on our motorbikes in his garage.

"You lads had a few last night then" Mr Bill said with a smile, lighting his pipe with a Swan Vesta and contentedly blowing a large puff of smoke up towards the ceiling.

"I'm really sorry about being sick," I said. "I don't know what Mrs Bill thought of me." His reply was cut off as she came bustling into the lounge from the kitchen and proceeded to polish the TV. Mr Bill winked at me and took another long draw on his pipe.

My Best Man walked into the lounge with a towel tied around his waist, rubbing Brylcreem into his ginger hair. "How's about a couple of bacon sandwiches for the bridegroom and his Best Man then, Mother?" he said.

"You pair of buggers ought to be ashamed of yourselves, getting in that state," said Mrs Bill said as she huffed off to put the bacon on. I looked at Billy.

Mr Bill took his pipe from his mouth and chuckled. "You should have seen the bloody mess our Billy left in the bathroom after we'd got you into the taxi. The Missus was cleaning up till nearly two o'clock this morning."

He looked towards the kitchen, where pots and pans were being banged and clattered around and the smell of bacon was beginning to float through the air.

"I'd leave it a while before you lads have another bit of drink, especially when the Missus is about" he said. He stood up and poked his head into the kitchen. "Chuck a couple of extra rashers in the pan for me, my love."

He smiled at us both. "Good luck today Steve, and don't get our Billy pissed again for Christ's sake, I can't handle another ear-bashing from his mother."

Mrs Bill came out of the kitchen with three plates of bacon sandwiches, two with red sauce and one with brown. "I know you prefer Daddies' Steve," she said with a sickly grin, before returning to the kitchen. "I think all is forgiven, lads," whispered her husband.

Mrs Bill, a cigarette dangling out of the corner of her mouth, poked her head around the door. "I bloody heard that!" she said. "Don't you get in that state again today!" She looked at Billy. "You'll find the front door locked." The pots and pans clanged around the kitchen as my Best Man finished off his bacon butty and strolled off to get dressed. All three of us were grinning.

"Two pints and two whiskys please Gaffer, this daft bugger's getting married today" Billy announced to all and sundry as we walked into the Gents Only in the Shaftsmoor. It was one o'clock.

"Need to get a move on Bill" I said, checking my watch again. I was feeling nervous. "Here's the rings," I said to Billy, making sure he put them safe in his waistcoat pocket.

The rest of the day flew by. The silver Daimlers supplied by the Co-op were on time. The photographers were there to capture all the arrivals at the beautiful Litchen Gate entrance to Yardley Wood Church, and the sun was shining. The banns had been read weeks before and nobody stood up when the Reverend Stephen Shorthouse asked the congregation if anyone objected to the joining of Steve and Pauline in Holy Matrimony.

As we walked down the aisle, family and friends handed paper horseshoes to the bride. Pat Dowling gave Pauline a huge forged steel horseshoe, suitable for a dray horse. John the Blacksmith had made it. She almost dropped it, it was so heavy.

The reception in Yardley Wood School Hall went well. There was sherry on arrival and Pat ran the free bar. The beer was supplied in seven-pint bumpers and the caterers dished up a decent chicken salad for almost 100 guests, all at 25 bob a head, £1.25. The speeches, the band (made up of Mom's friends in the music business) and the dancing I really can't remember.

At the end of the evening Pauline arrived back in the hall wearing the going-away suit she had bought in Oxford Street on a weekend visit to my Mom in London.

"Can you hear a rattling sound?" she asked as we drove down the Stratford Road towards the Barn Motel in Hockley Heath. We were staying there overnight before setting off for Cornwall the following morning. I'd been aware of the noise since we had left Yardley Wood, and was terrified it might be something serious that would prevent us getting to Cornwall. It was approaching 11 pm, pitch dark and we were still three miles from the Barn, and I certainly didn't fancy pulling over on to the verge. But if I carried on, would the engine blow up? We didn't need this at the start of our honeymoon.

"I'll slow down a bit. It's not far now." I tried to sound more confident than I actually was. The rattling appeared to come from both the front and the rear of the Mini. We drove the last few miles at 30 mph, and booked in. Mr and Mrs Phillips - we were legal at last.

"Shall I see what's wrong with the Mini or shall we go to bed?" I said. I was a bit worried.

"Don't be daft" Pauline replied. "We're on our honeymoon."

The next morning we found that all four chrome hubcaps were full of small steel ball bearings. Some bugger had removed the caps on each wheel before we left the Reception and chucked them in.

We arrived at Lizard Point in the late afternoon of the next day. The hotel was in a superb location. It was set on the edge of a cliff overlooking a beautiful cove, with a steep slope leading down to a rough pebble beach. Two fishing boats had been dragged up the beach out of the draw of the tide. The sea rushed backwards and forwards with a loud shushing sound across the stones, and right next to the hotel was a lighthouse. How romantic.

An elderly lady welcomed us into the hotel. "You're on your honeymoon then?" she said, smiling at us with a knowing look. "I'm Doreen, and my husband is Brian. Dinner is at seven and breakfast is from 8 am to 9.30. We don't do meals at midday at this time of the year, but we can arrange a packed lunch at a small extra charge." I looked at Pauline and we both smiled.

The location was truly spectacular, with views from the windows over the darkening, heaving sea, swept every 60 seconds by an intense white beam of light that appeared to reach out miles. It looked like a probing finger.

"You must be the honeymoon couple then." A rotund man with a large curly RAF moustache approached us. His white, open-necked shirt stretched to the limit and was tightly tucked into his black trousers and held in place by a belt that sheltered under a sagging stomach. "I'm Brian. The welcome drink is on the house."

I must admit that I was beginning to get a bit fed up with the honeymoon couple business, but then again, that's what we were.

"A grapefruit juice and a pint of bitter please" I said as Brian handed over two menus. "I can recommend the home-made cottage pie," he said.

We looked round the empty dining room and chose a table overlooking the cliff, the long finger of light piecing the inky blackness in a lazy, regular sweep. "I think we're the only guests in the hotel," Pauline whispered, looking around the room. Before I could ask her why she was whispering, Brian arrived. Now he was a waiter, dressed in a smart yellow waistcoat and a black bow tie. He proceeded to tell us that the soup of the day was tomato and the pork and lamb chops were off the menu. We tried to suppress our amusement at the performance. "We'll both have the soup and cottage pie please" I said.

Brian the waiter wrote down the order, congratulating us on our choice. He returned to the kitchen, presumably to get Doreen cracking on our order.

"Cheers love" I said, toasting Pauline with my glass. "Do you want another drink?"

The meal was fine. As we looked out of the window drinking our coffee, a fine, rolling mist was beginning to gather miles out to sea. The beam from the lighthouse could just about reach it before it lost its intensity and faded away.

"One more in the bar and I'm ready for bed. How about you?" I said, standing up. It had been a long drive. In 1965 the M5 only went down to Worcester, and while I loved my Mini it was hardly the vehicle for a journey of 200-odd miles. Even though we'd stopped for lunch halfway across Dartmoor, both of us were tired.

Our waiter had shed his yellow waistcoat and bow tie and was now Brian the barman, leaning on his bar in friendly conversation with two elderly, craggy-faced Cornishmen. Both were smoking clay pipes which filled the small bar with clouds of sweet-smelling tobacco. Two damp black Labradors lay under a table, twitching and gently snoring as they chased rabbits in their dreams.

The conversation stopped as Pauline and I walked into the bar. The two locals looked at us and nodded and one of the dogs opened an eye and closed it to return to his dreams.

"This is the young honeymoon couple I was telling you boys about" Brian said. The men were both 70 if they were a day. I didn't know about Pauline, but I was getting fed up with all this honeymoon couple business.

"They call me Old Ted," said one of the regulars. "This is me pal, Young Ted. We've lived on the Lizard all our lives."

Young Ted put down his pint. "'Cept for the Great War."

Old Ted nodded in agreement. "'Cept for that lot, arr" he replied, his eyes going misty as he drained his glass.

"Now then, you boys don't start getting maudlin and upsetting my guests." Brian had come to our rescue. I was thankful he called us guests for once, and not honeymooners. "It'll be a nightcap you'll be wanting then?" he said, looking at Pauline and me. "Yes please" we both replied.

As we sipped our coffees, mine with a drop of whisky in it, we listened to the two Teds reminiscing for a lovely half an hour or so, until I noticed my new wife was almost nodding off.

"Weather's closing in fast" Old Ted said quite abruptly, causing Pauline to shake herself awake. "The fog's rolling in from Bass Point. I dunno about these honeymooners not getting much sleep tonight." He winked at Young Ted and Brian, and they all had mischief twinkling in their elderly, rheumy eyes. "I think it's gonna be a long night for all of us."

I didn't take offence at the innuendo, and neither did Pauline. It was a couple of old locals having a joke, and no doubt every honeymoon couple had to put up with this. I was used to the craic in the factory. Did they have a Cornish word for the craic? I bet they did.

What I didn't realize that Brian and the Teds knew something we didn't. We found out what it was just after we had gone to sleep. URRRRR – URRRRR - URRRRR came the sound. We both jumped upright in bed, wide awake in a second.

I swung out of bed and looked out of the window. Gone was our panoramic view of the cliffs and the majestic rolling sea. All I could see was fog. It seemed to be sticking to the windows and trying to get into the room.

URRRRR – URRRRR - URRRRR came the sound again. It was the lighthouse foghorn.

"Ah think it's gunna be a long noight," I said in my best Cornish accent. We both collapsed in laughter and went back to bed. We had to wait two hours for the horn to stop.

The rest of the week was fine, not sunbathing weather but OK for paddling, sight-seeing and sitting on pebble beaches skimming stones. The Bob Fitzsimmons museum in Helston, Lands End, St Ives and Falmouth Castle all came in for a visit. The time sped by all too quickly, and we were soon driving back up the A38 and our new flat upstairs at no. 2 Chilton Road. We'd fixed the rattling, but the exhaust was beginning to blow.

It was a good job we travelled back on the Friday, because I was able to buy a replacement exhaust system on the Saturday. I fitted it myself with the Mini raised up on a pair of axle stands supplied by my new father-in-law. It involved a lot of scrabbling about on my back on the pavement, together with a fistful of sore knuckles, but by mid afternoon it was done, well in time to go to the in-laws for tea.

On my first day back to work I was attending South Birmingham Poly on the Monday morning. While Ron Smith from Wards' in Worcester knew I was getting married, I hadn't really had time to get to know any of the other lads on the Production Engineering Technicians' Course since we had started about five weeks before.

"How's married life then, Steve?" Ron asked as we sat down in the canteen for our morning tea break with another couple of apprentices who worked at Cadburys across the road. I saw the eyebrows of Neil and Kevin lift in surprise. "I didn't know you were away on your honeymoon mate" Neil said. "Bloody hell!" added Kevin.

Don't forget all these apprentices had just finished school, with half a dozen O levels and maybe one or two A levels. They were 17 or 18 and had only been at work for a little over a month. I was approaching 20 and had been at work for almost four years, completing and passing all the City & Guilds Craft Exams before Delta Wire agreed to sponsor me another for four years to study for my Full Technological Certificate.

All three lads smiled and congratulated me. We didn't know each other well enough for proper piss taking – I'd get that big time in the morning in the factory.

I soon got back into the serious nature of the course, with the emphasis on the technical and production aspect of engineering. The maths were of a much higher standard than I'd been used to during my Craft Course, and while I was familiar with most aspects of trigonometry and geometry (tangents, sines, cosines etc), the additional complications of calculating stresses and loads on tooling and structures were not easy. Simultaneous equations and calculus were just around the corner. 'Kin 'ell.

The new subjects to me on this course were Jig Design and Fixture Design allied to mass production. It also covered large-volume production machining involving single and multi-spindle autos and the programming of these machines, including the design of the control cams and programming computerised milling machines. These early machines were controlled by a strip of paper with a series of holes punched in driven by large reels, just like reel-to-reel tape recorders. It may sound archaic now, but in late 1965 this was cutting-edge stuff. Management Techniques, Factory and Group

Physiology – bloody hell, I thought, I've got a lot to learn – and the first exam was seven months away.

I was more than confident that I could cope with Technical/Engineering Drawing. This had been proved in the first few weeks of the course. Because all these technical apprentices had literally come straight from school and I'd had four years' experience in all aspects of metal cutting and machine tools, I was top dog in the workshop, and the lecturer let me assist him in instructing and helping the other lads. Harry Fisher and Joe Healy would have been right proud as I tried to pass on the skills they had imparted to me.

"How did you get on today then?" I asked Pauline. It was just after 10 pm, and Pauline and I were sitting on our new settee watching our new TV and drinking a cup of tea from our new electric kettle. Our lounge in the front bedroom in Chilton would be our home for the next 18 months until we bought our first house.

"Fine" she replied. "I caught the 13A from opposite the Haven Pub to Rea Street at the bottom of Bradford Street, walked through to Digbeth and into Oxford Street. It took me 35 minutes and I was in plenty of time." She sipped her tea. "Coming back tonight took longer, the bus was packed. I shan't sit upstairs again, you couldn't breathe for people smoking."

"It's only on Monday nights, because I'm at the Poly til nine," I said. "All the rest of the week I can pick you up at night." I was confident we could get into a routine.

We were doing all right. I was earning just over twenty quid a week with overtime and Pauline was Secretary to the Export Manager at Wilmot Breeden and earning more than me. Nan and Pop had refused to take any rent from us.

"We'll only miss it when you've got your own place" she had said, looking at Pop. He had nodded in agreement. "It'll give yer a bit of a start." We reached a compromise – we would pay half the gas and electric. My Nan and Pop were very special.

Even though I'd got another week in the Die Shop, my locker containing my overalls and Toe-tectors remained in the dining room in the Fitting Shop and as I walked around the corner passing Caggy's office the craic began. Cheering and banging of metal lockers greeted me as I took my mug out and helped myself to a brew out of the large tea pot on the table.

Ignoring all the ribald comments and piss taking, I took the bull by the horns and loudly announced to all and sundry that "I'd had a fucking good time."

"He really means he had a good fucking time" someone quipped. Everybody laughed and cheered. I was back at work.

As I entered the Die Shop I noticed a bottle of whisky on the serving hatch where the finished dies, suitably labelled with their size, awaited collection from the wire drawers. A note announced that it was Johnny Williams' birthday, and please help yourself to a tot. In capital letters at the bottom it said AFTER ENJOYING YER TOT, PLEASE KEEP IT TO YERSELF. A small glass stood next to the bottle.

Oliver Danks worked with his father Herbert in the Pickling Shop and Oliver had just had his hair cut. As he lifted himself out of the barber's chair, he thanked Johnny Williams for his haircut and tipped him an extra tanner, wishing him Happy Birthday.

"I'll have me tot on the way out" he said over his shoulder. "Not too much Oliver, there's a load more blokes and I've only got one more bottle" Johnny said as the next customer lowered himself into the chair. Oliver lifted his half-full glass and tossed the whisky into his mouth in one. Spluttering and laughing, he put the glass down. "Fucking wankers," he said, chuckling away back to the pickling vats.

I wondered what this particular craic was about, but didn't ask because I felt that I was the lad from the Fitting Shop and in the half hour I'd been back at work after my honeymoon I'd heard that the Die Shop was not being included in the top rate of pay following publication of the Job Evaluation results. Yet certain blokes in the Fitting Shop and Electricians' Shop who were time-served with indentures and papers were.

Another Wire Drawer collected his die from the serving hatch, poured himself a tot, poked his head through the sliding glass window and called out in a pleasant manner "Happy birthday, you old tart." He drank it in one. Johnny Williams looked up from his comb and scissors just in time to see another recipient of his generosity pulling a face.

It lasted another half hour. Nearly 20 blokes sampled Johnny's birthday drink before the secret got out. It wasn't Famous Grouse, of course. It was cold tea.

"There's a management announcement this afternoon in the canteen with all the shop stewards" Norman announced to all the AEU members in the Fitting Shop. We were sitting round the welded steel tables finishing off our sandwiches. "It's the result of the Job Evaluation Scheme. I've heard the whisper that all those blokes with papers to prove their skills will be in the highest pay grade."

"Fucking good job and all" Black Bat said, looking at Andy and another half-dozen men in the group who had served their time as indentured apprentices. "Them dozy bastards sat on their arses polishing dies for a fucking living have had their comeuppance at last" he spat. Big Bob Crockett and the electricians the other side of the wire mesh fence nodded in agreement. Nearly all them were time-served.

The rest of the afternoon was not particularly pleasant. Old Fred was all right, but Wally the Chargehand and George Cooper the Shop Steward had their heads together before talking in whispers to the rest of the Die Polishers. I would be glad when the week was over.

Pauline finished work at five, and provided the weather was fine the arrangement was that she would walk along Digbeth and wait for me to finish at 5.30 and we'd drive home together. It worked fine. The first evening as she waited outside the factory entrance, old Mr Cadwallander, one of the security officers, invited her into the office and made her a cup of tea. This practice was repeated every time he was on that particular shift.

We soon got into a routine, arriving home from work at about 6 pm. Nan and Pop had finished their tea, leaving the kitchen to Pauline and me to prepare and cook our evening meal, which we ate on the small folding table in the kitchen or upstairs in our lounge with a tray on our laps watching The Man from Uncle or the original Star Trek. The bathroom (no shower) was downstairs and the lavatory was outside next to the kitchen door, just as it had been since I was born. Pauline's parents' house in Kingscliffe Road was just the same, so we were used to these arrangements. Nan had put our names down for a council house but we were determined to be the first in both our families to buy our own.

Our joint gross income was about forty quid a week and in four months' time I would be 20 and Pauline 21, which would give us both good increases in wages. Even though we didn't have any savings to speak of (in any case you couldn't legally buy a house until you were 21), we took Albert's advice and opened a small, regular savings account with the Nationwide Building Society.

"You've got to demonstrate a history of saving to get a mortgage," Albert said. It was sound advice, even though he and Ivy did not buy their own house until some five years later.

I had only two days left working in the Die Shop, and I must admit that apart from the precise toolmaking performed by Jim Richmond, my fellow apprentice, and old Bonehead, who I'd first started work with three years before, die polishing, without being derogatory, did not compare to the work of a fully-skilled craftsman. This was reflected in the results of the Job Evaluation Scheme.

The Die Shop men were not pleased, specially when the company decided to create a toolroom, located in its own shop in the Britannia Mill. All the high-precision grinding machines and Andy's new centre lathe, together with the ancillary equipment to produce the tools, harden and heat treat them etc were moved out of the Fitting Shop and installed in the new department.

Black Bat was on top of the world. With his pipe clamped firmly between his teeth and his steel-rimmed National Health glasses perched on his nose he supervised the moving of all the relevant machines, much to the annoyance of Billy Law and Jan, who were doing the practical work of using huge long crowbars to lift the machines on to the rolling bars. These bars were slid under the machine tools and then literally rolled down the shop and out to a waiting low loader to be transported round the corner into Glover Street.

I wasn't sorry when my time in the Die Shop came to an end. I never felt I was learning real craftsmanship.

CHAPTER 17

On the Friday morning of my first week back following my honeymoon, Joe Healy called me into his office. As I walked in he was putting his phone down. "Peter Williams, the Apprentice Supervisor, is in Jack Insall's office, can you nip up there Steve?" I guessed it was about the arrangements for my Senior Apprentices' course the next week at PERA, Melton Mowbray.

Climbing the stairs up to the first floor, I knocked on the Personnel Manager's door. I looked through the small glass panel and saw Jack beckon me in.

"Sit down Steve" he said, offering me a Senior Service and indicating that one of the three cups of tea was mine. "How did the wedding go?"

"Fine" I said. "Everything went as planned and the sun tried to shine. It was a great day." In truth I had difficulty remembering the day.

He took a brown folder from his briefcase and handed it to me. "This is the syllabus of next week's course, together with the location of the Production Engineering Research Association and the George Hotel in Melton Mowbray. You're booked in from Sunday evening until midday the following Friday. Accommodation, including breakfast and evening meals, will be paid for by the company."

Bloody hell, I thought to myself, wait till Pauline and Nan and Pop hear this.

Jack and Peter glanced at each with a slight smile. The expression on my face must have said it all. Handing me a small envelope Jack said, "Ill get you to sign for these expenses Steve." Signing the sheet Jack handed me, I noticed a figure of £10. 'Kin 'ell, I thought.

Jack took the sheet back. "That'll cover your petrol and out-of-pocket expenses. Have a couple of pints in the evening out of the money, but if you fancy a few more pay for them yourself, OK?"

"Yes Jack, thank you" I said, and meant it. He looked serious for a second.

"The hotel will give you a receipt for your bar bill at the end of your stay. Bring that back to me and any cash left over, and don't mention specific amounts of expenses to anyone. People get jealous."

"No Jack. I mean yes Jack." Peter stood up and shook my hand. "Enjoy the course Steve and I'll expect a full report on what you learned and thought of the week. You're one of the first apprentices to attend this course and I'll need your feedback."

Before reaching the door I made sure the tenner was safely tucked into my pocket.

"Did I mention that this is the first week's course? There will be two more before you're 21." I looked back in amazement. Both of them very slightly inclined their heads. "Careful how you go down the stairs, Steve" Jack said, his smile stretching to a full grin.

'Kin 'ell, I shouted silently.

Joe was on the Dean Smith and Grace. He loved that lathe. Some said that if he could have got it down his entry at the side of his house he wouldn't have bothered coming to work. He stopped the chuck. I could see the twinkle in his eye.

"I know yer a married man now, but are yer OK for working the weekend Steve, we've got a couple of big jobs on?"

"I'll be here, no problems" I replied.

"Walk this way" Joe said, sauntering in his own inimitable way into his small office. He sat down. "Yer away on a course then?"

"Production Engineering Research Association in Melton Mowbray. Senior Apprentice Course. I'll be away all the week." He was quiet for a bit and I noticed his brows draw slightly together. His elderly, experienced head tilted to one side.

"Even when yer come back, yer won't know it all."

I knew what he was telling me. The higher the monkey climbs the tree, the more he shows his arse.

"I hear what you say Joe. Thank you."

"Good lad." He eased his 65-year-old frame out of his chair. "When yer come back from yer fancy college, I want yer here on the Saturday morning, if yer can leave yer new bride on her own that is. I'll have yer wages in me drawer."

"Thank you Joe." A truly great old bloke.

"We got some right lucky fuckers working here." Pat Dowling, barman supreme at my wedding two weeks before, nudged Scotty, his fellow Irishman. Looking totally innocent, Scotty replied "What yer mean Paddy?"

All the regulars had just started their sandwiches and were supping mugs of tea and reading the papers. Black Bat was still in his armchair puffing his pipe. That piece of furniture had not yet been removed to the new toolroom.

Pat looked around to ensure he had everyone's attention. Les Green looked up from his chess game, and I noticed the minutest twitch to the corner of his mouth. The craic's about to start, I thought. I wonder who's in the barrel? It didn't take long to find out.

"What do yer boyos think about a bloke who's just had a week's holiday with all the shagging he could handle?" said Pat. "A week sat on his arse polishing dies and now another FREE week in a 5-star hotel with bacon and eggs every morning and best steak every night. Plus..." He paused to look around. Every bastard in the shop was hanging on his every word. I was right in the barrel.

"As much free beer as he can drink every night."

A couple of blokes started to laugh, and I guess the other apprentices knew about the course, because I certainly hadn't publicised these arrangements. I had only just received the details myself.

"Bejasus, that bloke has the luck of the Irish" Scotty, said winking at me. I'd been in the barrel many times over the last few years, and I knew not to get wound up and let the buggers see they'd got to me.

"According to the menu you can have smoked salmon and scrambled eggs if you don't fancy the bacon and sausage for breakfast, and the hotel has the best wine cellar in Leicestershire, that's if you get fed up with drinking the free beer."

I took the Senior Service that Jack Insall had given me earlier and lit up. "It'll be cigars all next week" I said, blowing a large puff of smoke out.

"Never had all this lot when we were kids, did we?" Black Bat looked at the other old craftsmen sat round the table. They all nodded in agreement. "Yer went to night school in yer own time cuz the fucking gaffers wouldn't give yer a day off. And if yer daint, yer wouldn't get yer papers when yer was 21. These kids today don't know they're fucking born, I tell yer."

Scotty looked up. "Was that when yer was walking five miles every day to work in yer clogs Alf?" Black Bat eased himself out of his armchair with a sigh and tapped his pipe out on the corner of Norman's lathe. "I was born 40 years too fucking early," he said. He looked at me and the other apprentices and young lads, Dave, Johnny, Doug Smith, Bryn, young Ray and Ken.

"Good luck to yer lads, and mek sure yer tek it all in." He stuck his pipe back in his mouth and went off in search of Billy Law, who was moving his beloved universal grinding and horizontal grinding machines.

Young Ray and Ken looked at me in awe. "Are yer really gooin' to a posh hotel with free beer?" They asked.

"Ill let you know when I come back" I replied.

"Are we going up the Blues tomorrow then Steve?" Les said, glancing around. "Or are yer going shopping?"

"Fuck off, Greeny" I replied as I stood up and went to swill my mug out before walking to the Die Shop.

With help from Albert, who worked for BRS, I'd planned my route to Melton Mowbray, estimating that the journey of about 50–odd miles would take me an hour and a half, so I would arrive at the hotel about 5 pm, just in time to unpack, have a beer and enjoy my free steak and chips. I eventually found a petrol station that was open on a Sunday afternoon on the A45 just before Coventry and put in three gallons at a cost of 15 shillings, meticulously putting the receipt in my wallet. That should get me there and back and keep Jack happy. The ring road round Leicester caused me a few problems, but I eventually found the A607 to Melton Mowbray and was soon parking my

Mini directly in front of the George Hotel, right opposite the beautiful Norman Church. Next to it was a gleaming red E-Type Jaguar.

By 6 o'clock there were about 10 of us apprentices in the bar having a beer and introducing ourselves. It appeared there were no other residents on that Sunday evening apart from a few locals having a drink in the bar. I soon discovered that the other lads were from all over the country and that they were not all engineering students - quite a few were commercial apprentices, a term I'd not heard before. Some of these guys were 22 or 23 years old and at university.

I soon got talking to Paul, a production engineering apprentice at Wickmans in Coventry. I realised I was probably the only apprentice in the room who had been working for the last four years and had come up through the craft and shop floor, in my Pop's words, "Gerrin' yer hands dirty."

Pauline and I had been to a couple of steak houses and Berni Inns in Birmingham and I'd seen a T-bone on the menu many times, but I'd never ordered one, probably because it was an extra five shillings. But there it was, the George speciality, a 16oz T-bone.

"Are you going to go for it?" Paul said, looking up from his menu. We had both sat down in the dining room of the hotel at a long table reserved for our group. I found out later in the week that it was to encourage teamwork. Paul was tall like me and had his hair cut in the Mod style, with clothes to match - Ben Sherman shirt with button-down collar, smart trousers and soft, slip-on leather shoes. I was dressed very similarly, so we made a good match.

"I think I will" I replied. "I've never had a T-bone before."

"A good fillet steak is much better than yer T-bone. I should know, I've eaten in some of the best restaurants in London. Mind you, they're all caffs to me you know."

Paul and I looked down the table at the guy who had spoken. The oldest in the group, well over 20 and somewhat overweight, he was wearing wide red braces over a yellow shirt - definitely not a Mod. He flicked the ash off the end of his cigarette into the ashtray on the table.

"My name's St John, pronounced Sinjon, the T is silent." He ran his hand through his long floppy blonde hair and elbowed the small grinning guy sat next to him. "What do you say, my man?"

I glanced at Paul. We were thinking the same thing. Had we got to put up with this prat for the next week?

I thoroughly enjoyed my first T-bone, especially as the 15 shillings and six pence was being paid by Delta Wire. The meal wasn't spoiled by the gobbing off of the plonker at the end. There were even a couple of bottles of wine on the table. I soon discovered Paul was a big Coventry City fan, and our conversation about football continued in the bar afterwards. Conscious of Jack Insall's advice I bought myself a pint and listened to St John telling the bar how much his father earned in the City and how much better the E-Type was compared to the Austin Healey 3000. I'll park my Mini round the corner tomorrow, I thought to myself as I finished off my pint.

Two or three of the older apprentices were nodding and smiling at St John's jokes as they stood at the bar. "Put these drinks on my tab barman, and I'll have another large brandy." He was in full swing. His grinning weasel-faced mate looked around the bar. "Anyone else for a session?" He asked. No-one responded.

The weather was fine but chilly as I stood outside the hotel having a smoke before going in for my breakfast. Crossing the road, I casually looked into the churchyard at the gravestones, taking in the dates, which went back well over 100 years. I smiled to myself to see one memorial with a bronze hand on the top, its forefinger pointing to the heavens. Either someone was religious or they had a good sense of humour. Or both.

Paul and I decided to walk the mile or so through the town to PERA and we arrived at reception at five to nine, just in time to see the red E-Type roar into the main car park. St John and Weaselface had been just in time for breakfast. Listening to them it would appear they'd had a right session, stumbling out of the bar at well after midnight. It showed as they gingerly climbed out of the Jaguar.

"They're still pissed," I whispered to Paul as we all moved into a reception area laid out with table and chairs. Coffee and tea were being served by a young lady in the corner.

The main building was a huge red-bricked construction, similar to Garretts Green, with separate smaller buildings approached by walkways and roads. These contained the different Engineering Research Centres, from Metal Forming and Pressing, Metal Casting, Machining and Cutting to Plastic Moulding.

All this was being explained to our group by a tall, handsome bloke, immaculately dressed in a smart dark blue three-piece suit. He was in his early forties and had a neat, almost Mod-style haircut. His slim, modern tie was sharply knotted. His choice was a starched white collar, but it could have been a button-down Ben Sherman, he would still have been fashionably dressed.

"Dog's bollocks, him. What yer think mate?" I whispered to Paul. "Bee's knees" he mouthed in return. We both silently smiled to ourselves.

Mr James Darcy, Engineering Director of PERA, continued. "All your employers are members of our association and we provide a comprehensive service to help and assist our members when they have an engineering or production project that requires in-depth investigation and research" he explained. "We take on the job with the assistance of your own engineers, our highly experienced staff here at PERA and the largest, comprehensive engineering library in the world. You are all here for the next five days. Use this unique facility in the tasks you will be set by my staff."

Darcy looked at the four other guys sat either side of him at the top table. He smiled. "Work the young buggers hard. They're not here for a holiday" he said. "Thank you gentlemen, and good luck in your endeavours."

"Bee's knees" I said to Paul from the corner of my mouth.

"Dog's bollocks" He replied.

"This course is all about you guys seeking out knowledge and information, using your own initiative and the facilities we have here." Dennis Tibbs, Senior Engineer, paused and slowly looked around the room.

"What I ain't going to do is stand in front of a blackboard and lecture you. You're going to do the work."

"Not if I can help it." A faint whisper came from the direction of Weaselface. St John stifled a cough. Tibbs didn't hear the comment, or if he did he chose to ignore it. He went on: "This morning I will be giving you all individual projects and I will expect a full and detailed report on your findings, in writing. These reports, if done properly, will consist of between five and 10 papers, A4 size with drawings and sketches." I looked at Paul. 'Kin 'ell.

"Your reports will be ready by Thursday morning for, if necessary, typing, and any drawings will be made into slides for the projection machine. You will then individually present your findings on Friday to myself and the rest of the group." James Darcy was well right. This was no holiday.

It was approaching lunchtime, and most of the group of apprentices had been quietly studying their projects.

"Hair of the dog, I reckon. What yer say, Blue?" St John winked at Weaselface. We all heard the squeal of the tyres as the E-type headed towards the nearest pub.

"What's your project then?" I asked Paul. We were sitting in the room which was going to be our classroom for the week, eating a sandwich. We all had been issued with a smart PERA folder containing a PERA A4 lined pad, PERA ballpoint pens and PERA propelling pencils. Many years later I would recognize this as good corporate image, but in November 1965 I was still a Brummie apprentice looking for ten bob an hour.

Dennis Tibbs had issued everyone with a folder (yep, it had PERA on the cover), which contained each delegate's project, and we were all seriously studying our task for the next three days. St John and Weaselface would find theirs when they returned.

"Metal pressings and all its applications. Listing advantages and disadvantages of the process" Paul replied, taking a swig from a can of Pepsi. "I ain't got a clue" he added, a frown on his face. "I was hoping it was going to be something allied to where I work at Wickmans. What's yours?"

"Pressure die casting and all its applications etc. Same as you mate, I've got to do some digging." I looked around the room at the other eight young guys. I couldn't see two of them, because they were in the pub round the corner.

Because I'd been working for the past four years and had studied the basics of engineering, I'd been introduced to the pressure die-casting process. I knew it involved literally pushing molten material, zinc, aluminium or plastic, into a mould with great pressure. I had a lot of technical detail to sort out, but I was in the right place to find it and I felt confident that I would be able to present a good report. Facing a group had never worried me. I had instructed and drilled Army Cadets when I was a full Corporal, even winning a drill competition. The slight concern I had was that these guys were older than me and had achieved a higher general level of education. However, I was determined to find out as much as I could about pressure die casting and show what a Brummie born in a council house who had started work at fifteen and a half was made of.

"I wish I'd got your project," I said, looking at Paul. I had finished my sandwiches and had just lit up.

"Why's that?"

" I ain't boasting or bullshitting, but I hold the City & Guilds Toolmaking Supplementary in Press Tools. I have very limited experience, but I've designed and produced two press tools and worked in one of the best toolrooms in the Midlands. If I can I'll help."

Paul looked at me almost in awe. "'Kin 'ell" he said. He had heard me say it the previous night.

"In addition to your individual research projects there will be other training programmes on this week's course." It was 1.35pm, and Dennis Tibbs had started the afternoon session. "As well as being able to gather and absorb knowledge…" Dennis stopped in mid sentence as the door opened and St John and Weaselface walked in. "Sorry we're late, bit of traffic due to the cattle market" St John said as they both sat down.

Dennis was a man in his early fifties with a good head of curly, light-brown hair greying at the temples. He glanced sharply through his rimless spectacles at the two latecomers. "This is not a college or a university, it's an engineering research centre subscribed to and paid for by your employers. These same employers have sent you here to seek out knowledge. Please respect that."

No one said a word.

He continued: " As well as being able to gather and absorb knowledge, you must be able to impart this knowledge to others in the correct manner. Training and giving instruction to subordinates in a structured and interesting way is vital." He paused and looked around, smiling as he lit up an Embassy tipped. "So one afternoon we will learn how to instruct a trainee. You will need to chose a fairly simple task that you can teach someone to do in say ten or fifteen minutes. It's called Job Instruction."

He sat down. "Ah, I almost forgot." Dennis took a draw on his cigarette. "Please feel free to smoke. I would like you all to stand up one at a time and introduce yourselves to me and the rest of the class. We all want to know who you are and where you work." He paused again for effect.

"We can start with the two gentlemen who were held up by the cows in the market, or was it the glamorous Marilyn behind the bar in the George?"

Everybody smiled and chuckled. Tibbs was no fool.

"My name is St John Temple-Fry and I'm 23. I obtained my degree in engineering and commercial management six months ago and I'm Commercial Manager for Maynard Engineering Ltd, a subsidiary of Temple-Fry Holdings." His smile was supercilious as he glanced down at the ashtray and he stubbed his cigarette out. I stole a glance at Paul, who looked a tad nervous.

"Maynards are in the Aerospace Industry. We're involved in cryogenic engineering." St John's smile turned into a smirk as he sat down.

Bloody hell, I thought to myself, what the fuck is cryo-whatsit engineering?

Mr Tibbs stood up. "That's very interesting, Mr Temple-Fry. I'm sure our Cryogenics Laboratory will appreciate your experienced input while you are here. I'll arrange a meeting with the Head of Department." St John looked as though he couldn't give a shit.

Four other course delegates introduced themselves rather nervously. Weaselface explained that he was Kevin Jones, 21 years old and an Apprentice Production Engineer at Maynards. Paul nervously stood up, said his bit and gratefully sat down.

"A worker from the Industrial Midlands." The mocking whisper was very quiet, but I heard it and I knew where it came from. I looked at the pair of them sitting there smirking. Well here's another fucking worker from the Industrial Midlands, I thought to myself as I stood up.

"My name's Steve Phillips and I'm 19 years old. I work for Delta Wire, in the industrial heart of the West Midlands. We supply brass wire for nuts and bolts. In the last four years I have worked in engineering on the shop floor and hold City & Guilds London Institute Parts 1, 2 and 3 and Toolmaking. My employer has agreed to sponsor me for the next four years to obtain the Full Technological Certificate CGLI in Production Engineering."

I paused for breath and looked around. Quite a few guys had raised eyebrows. I sat down and lit up with a shaking hand.

Mr Tibbs looked up from his desk with an expression of appraisal. He pushed his rimless spectacles to the top of his nose and put down his pen.

"You've got your hands dirty, then" he said. I nodded quietly.

The remaining apprentices introduced themselves, and my initial thoughts were confirmed. They were all older than me, better qualified academically but far less experienced in the nitty-gritty of practical engineering. I also had a better overall picture of engineering processes. I'd be all right.

Mr Tibbs stood up. "We have a wide spread of industries represented here this week and you've presumably guessed that your personal projects have no connection with the manufacturing process in your particular factory. That would have been much too easy. You will gather information every morning and take lunch here at PERA." He paused, looking at the E-Type boys. "We will then spend an hour in a group question and answering forum. It's all about you fellas learning how to gather information on the widest spectrum of engineering processes and sharing that knowledge." He sat down. "Any questions?"

After the usual pause, a couple of lads took turns asking Dennis about this and that and I glanced at St John and Weaselface, who had opened their folder containing their project. They looked at each other, shook their heads and silently mouthed. I knew what they were saying. "Haven't got a fucking clue."

"You have another three hours before you finish at 5 pm. Don't waste it" Dennis said. "I'll be here till you leave tonight, and you all know where the library is."

* * * * * * * * * * *

"You having another T-bone tonight, Steve?" Paul and I were in the bar having a pint. We had walked back from PERA on a dark, dry and chilly evening, had a quick shower in our rooms and were studying the menu. A good-looking blonde woman in a low-cut lace top and pencil skirt was behind the bar serving our group, plus a couple of older guests. Before I could answer Paul a loud voice sounded above the hubbub.

"Marilyn, can I have a gin and tonic, make it a large one I'm gasping." St John was standing at the bar, his big round face beaming, his bright red braces stretched over a dark purple shirt, the white buttons struggling to keep his belly in.

Marilyn stretched up to the optics at the back of the bar, ensuring her tight black skirt rode up enough to give a glimpse of her stocking tops. Then she leaned over the bar to reach the ice bucket, which gave her an opportunity to show off her ample bosom. With a flick of her hair she placed the G & T on the bar. "That'll be four shillings, please sir" she said, pouting her bright red lips.

St John tucked a ten-bob note into her cleavage, then looked around and winked. "Have one yourself, and make it a large one" he said. As she turned to the till she looked over her shoulder and replied, "I'm quite partial to a large one." Those close to the bar chuckled. Marilyn was at least five years older than St John, but she was going for him big time.

Listening to the banter in the bar after dinner, it would appear that a carload of apprentices were going into Nottingham that night for a bit of a jolly.

"I'm telling you mates, the women outnumber the blokes by five to one. You can't go wrong. I know the best clubs because one of my old man's factories is in Nottingham and I worked there for a month." St John was in full swing.

He looked at the rest of us. "Anyone else for the Skylark?"

"Make it Wednesday or Thursday night and I'm with you," I said, thinking that I wanted to get my project well sorted before going out on the piss.

"See you lot in the morning then" St John said before whispering something to his mate Weaselface.

Fifteen minutes later I looked out of the bay window of the hotel bar to see Weaselface and three other guys climbing into an Austin 1100. One minute later a blonde wearing a pelmet of a skirt and spikey heels trotted out, looked quickly up and down the road and dived into the passenger seat of the E-Type. Marilyn must finish at ten then, I thought, glancing at my watch.

"I'm having another couple of pints and then I'm off to bed," I said. Paul nodded in agreement.

The next two days were taken up with the study of pressure die casting, the materials used (zinc, aluminium and plastic) and the applications and components produced for a huge variety of industries from automotive, construction and building to children's toys. It was an immense subject.

"Don't get too bogged down in the big picture" said Dennis Tibbs. I'd asked if I could have a word with him, because I was unsure about how much I could do in the time. He took a sip of his tea and sat back in his chair.

"Concentrate on the principles of the process, heat and pressure and a couple of the immediately, easy-recognizable products that are produced in this manner and why" he said. I nodded. Lighting up a cigarette he continued.

"Don't be overawed by the others on the course. It's my job to know the background and qualifications of all you young guys so I can assess the level of difficulty regarding the projects to set you." He paused to take a pull of his fag. "In the last four years you have accumulated hard practical experience. Together with your City & Guilds qualifications, that puts you way in front of these other fellows in general engineering knowledge. I started work at fifteen and a half as well."

Paul didn't require much help from me, because the library was, as PERA said, the most comprehensive in the world. We both presented our projects, complete with drawings and sketches, on the Thursday morning for the typist to produce our reports. The Job Instruction session on the Thursday was, as far as I was concerned, a real eye-opener. Dennis was a brilliant teacher. He explained how to instruct, highlighting the key points and structured stages of training and how to impart knowledge and watch the trainee respond. I was impressed.

"Right you lot, are we all going clubbing on our last night or what?"

We had finished our dinner and I'd eaten my last free T-bone and was sitting in the bar of the George. St John was on form as he looked around the room.

"I'm on for a night out, what about you?" I asked Paul. He smiled. "Yeah, let's go for it."

I glanced at my watch in the semi-darkness - the flashing disco lights were making it difficult to see it. "Had enough?" I shouted into Paul's ear. "It's half one."

We had been in the club for two hours and had had a real laugh messing about and enjoying ourselves. I for one had worked bloody hard this last four days and felt I needed to relax a bit. However I was conscious that I'd had quite a few beers and had a drive of almost 20 miles ahead of me.

Paul leaned close and cupped his hands around his mouth, shouting agreement. Most of the others in our group were beginning to make their way out. We all waved to St John and Marilyn, who were inventing the Dirty Dancing routine in the middle of the floor.

"Can I cadge a lift back with you guys?" said Weaselface. "The bloke I came with has pulled a bird."

"Yeah, no probs" I replied, opening up the rear doors of my Mini Van. Kevin peered into the carpeted and cushioned interior, noting the fluffy blanket rolled against the two front seats.

"Fuck me" he exclaimed. "You could have more fun in here than in St John's E-Type."

"Its been christened a few times, but I'm a married man" I replied, inserting the key and depressing the starter button with my left thumb.

Quietly inserting the key into the front door of the George Hotel, we tiptoed up the stairs to our individual rooms. We'd all been told that the bar closed at midnight and the front door would be locked at 12.30 am. I soon went to sleep. Big presentation in the morning.

What made me wake up I don't know - it might have been the tinkling sound on the window overlooking the churchyard, or perhaps I felt the need to visit the loo. I know it was dark and cold. I looked at my watch and saw that it was half three in the morning. There was a rattling sound at the window, and I realised it wasn't the first time

I had heard it. Some silly bugger was chucking stones at the window.

I peered out to see a bloke who seemed to be searching for something on the ground. He was barefoot and bare chested, dressed only in a pair of trousers.

In the light of the street lamps I could see, dangling from his waist, a pair of red braces.

A gentle tap sounded on my door. I opened it to see Kevin standing there, shivering, wrapped in a blanket. "St John's locked out," he said.

★ ★ ★ ★ ★ ★ ★ ★ ★ ★ ★

"I knew the silly cow was married." St John was trying to warm himself up with a large whisky. The three of us were sitting in his room, enjoying his gratitude in the shape of a bottle of Famous Grouse.

"Just my luck her husband sprained his ankle during his night shift down the local pit. He rolled up in a Coal Board ambulance just as I was on the short strokes." He lit a cigarette with shivering fingers. Kevin and I looked at each other, grinning from ear to ear. I had woken up now all right.

"What happened then?" I asked, helping myself to another tot. I felt I deserved a drink for being woken at this hour in the morning.

"I've had to walk for 30 minutes in my bare feet and I'm fucking freezing." St John drained his glass and poured another.

"Where's the Jag?" Kevin asked, looking concerned. "Where are your clothes?"

St John took a long, satisfying drag, pulling the blanket closer around his shoulders.

"Great big bastard he was. Good job for me he couldn't run."

I started to laugh. Kevin looked at St John, and in seconds we were all pissing ourselves. He was warming to his tale. "We left the club 20 minutes after you lot and I parked the Jag at the back of a pub just round the corner from where she lived. Got nosey neighbours, she said. Anyway, we were stripped off and getting down to the nitty gritty on the settee when a sweep of headlights lit up the sitting room and a vehicle pulled up." He paused and topped up our glasses.

"In mid-stroke I was. Very nearly broke my cock." He could tell a tale, and I guessed this one would be told again. We were in tucks.

"She rolls off the settee and peeps out of the front window. 'Oh my God, it's Mark!' All her clothes and underwear were scattered around the room, draped over the telly and the table lamp. She only had her stockings and high heels on." 'Kin 'ell I said.

"My clothes were all over the floor. 'Quick!' she said. 'Out the back!'

Dashing about like a blue-arsed fly I gathered up my clothes, trying to put on my trousers. 'You ain't got time for that' she said. 'Quick, he'll murder us!'"

He poured a tot in all our glasses and I glanced at my watch. 4.15 am.

St John had warmed up by now. He'd had twice as much Famous Grouse as Kevin and me.

"I managed to grab my clothes and get out of the back door. I was starkers and it was pitch dark. I chucked the clothes over the garden fence and followed 'em sharpish." We were all laughing again. "I'd got my trousers on and was trying to sort my socks when her husband came out of his kitchen door on his crutches. 'Yer fucking bastard, I'll kill yer' he shouted. I took one look and ran down his neighbour's garden. As I scrambled over the back fence I could see him swinging his crutches down the garden. I ran for a couple of minutes before I realised I had nothing on my feet, the rest of my clothes were in somebody's back garden and the keys to the Jag were in my leather jacket, also in somebody's back garden."

Kevin and I were shaking our heads in laughter, but St John was suddenly serious.

"I'm not bothered about my clothes, but the old man will have a fucking fit if anything happens to the Jag." He looked worried, big time.

"Any spare keys?" I asked. He shook his head, dejected.

I finished off my whisky and stood up. "It's just after half four, come on, we'll go back and find your stuff before it gets light. I've got a torch in the Mini."

After checking the E-Type was still OK, we finally found the correct back garden and Kevin and I watched St John creeping about with the torch nervously looking at the house next door. I crept back into bed at 5.30, mission accomplished.

"Will you be on the next course Steve?" St John looked up from his eggs and bacon. "Cos if you are, I owe you a good night out."

"Hope so" I replied with a smile. He was from a very different background to me, boastful and loud, but I was beginning to move away from my first impressions. St John was all right.

The presentations went well. Each delegate had obviously researched their particular subject and I for one had been introduced to at least five or six production processes that previously I had not been aware of. That was the point of the course. The E–Type boys struggled a bit, but they just about did enough.

After dropping Paul off in Coventry, I drove back home, receipts safe in my wallet and two quid to be returned to Jack Insall. I had a lot on my mind. All the other lads on the course had been older than me and much better qualified, and they were all presumably destined for management. The course had opened my eyes.

Thanking Joe for my wages, I walked into the dining room of the Fitting Shop and sat down with a cup of tea in one hand and a fag in the other, peering over Greeny's shoulder at his Daily Mirror. It was Saturday morning.

"How did you get on?" young Ray asked. "Was it really free beer all the week?"

"It was bloody hard work I tell yer, but it was a good course and I learned a lot" I replied.

"Never learned to buy a fucking paper though," Greeny said.

"Had 'em delivered to my room every morning, just before I went down to breakfast" Everybody chuckled. I was one-nil up in the craic.

"Whatcher doing this afternoon Steve?" Dave Wilmer had just turned 21 and was now a fully-skilled craftsman. He was also a very good inside forward for the works football team. "Johnny Price is going to a wedding today and we need a goalie. You've been away all week and we couldn't contact you, but you've played with us before and trained with the team." Yes, I thought to myself, but only half a dozen times in the last six months.

Even getting changed in the dressing room at the Delta's Holly Lane Sports ground in Erdington it felt cold, and when we ran out on to the pitch the blast of wind hit you in the face. I knew some of the team, Mickey Madden, Mick Hassett, Dave Wilmer and Jim Richmond, but there was a very young lad I'd not seen before.

"Who's the lad?" I asked Dave as we warmed up.

"Johnny Pearce, he's 16. He's at Garretts Green full time in his first year before he comes to Delta Wire. If he gets there. He's been on Villa's books since he was 12, but they won't offer anything definite. A couple of big clubs are sniffing."

Dave hit a ball into my body. I caught it and tapped it back. "He's pretty good" Dave said, as he ran to the centre circle to join the ref and the opposing captain.

Young Pearce was like a thoroughbred racehorse in a team of donkeys. He scored three goals and laid another one on for Mickey Madden. His natural speed, vision, distribution – I'd never seen anything like it at this level. We beat one of the top teams 4–3. I did all right, but Pearce was brilliant.

Ron and the other lads at South Birmingham Poly were impressed with my course at PERA, and over the next few evenings I produced my report for Peter Williams. Pauline typed it up for me during one of her lunch breaks.

"You did well Steve. You've had a good report from Mr Tibbs at PERA. Well done." I was in Jack Insall's office. "The next one will be in six months' time," said Peter. I hope it doesn't clash with the World Cup, I thought to myself as I walked back down the stairs.

Caggy was standing outside Joe's office smoking his Woodbine. "Joe wants you in the shop for the rest of this week, but next week can you report to Sam Larkham in the Strip Mill" he said. He flicked his nub end into the tray underneath the Dean Smith and Grace. Joe flinched. Caggy was an ignorant bastard.

The Strip Mill was part of Delta Wire, and the old United Non Ferrous Metals factory was in Upper Trinity Street, off Adderley Street, just round the corner from the Waggon and Horses. From the outside it didn't look like a factory, more like a row of terraced houses. In fact either side of the arch which led into the factory there were houses, which years ago had been converted into offices. Apparently one of the houses had once been lived in by the old factory caretaker, but he and his wife had been found hanging from the top of the stairs just after the war. The premises dated back to the late 1890s and the houses had been left empty for the past 10 years after the administration of the factory had been transferred to the offices in the main works.

I'd been in the factory a number of times during the previous four years, helping to strip down worn parts to be repaired in the main Fitting Shop, but I had never worked there full time. Two state-of-the-art strip rolling machines had been installed about two years before, but apart from that the production facilities were at least 50 years out of date. Because of the layout a fork-lift truck or flat bed could not operate, and apart from overhead Demag lifting devices everything was manhandled on hand-operated trolleys.

In the centre of the factory, surrounded by a green-painted fence, was a huge open gearbox, 50 feet by 40 and containing 20-odd gears up to 10 feet in diameter, all slowly rotating and driving two rolling mills, circa 1920. The bottom of the gearbox was a foot deep in black thick grease. A massive electric motor provided the power.

I was looking forward to something very different. Quite a few people would not enter the factory, let alone work there, especially on the night shift.

"Pat's mate is off sick Steve, can you help him this morning?" Joe said as I struggled into my overalls. I'd been dreading this, because Pat Dowling worked on the overhead cranes and I was frightened of heights. Plus the fact that he was chief piss taker.

Walking down to the Casting Shop, I told Pat I was working in the old Strip Mill next week.

"Sooner you than me" he replied with a grin and an Irish twinkle. "They say it's haunted."

"I'll let you know," I said, looking up the vertical steel ladder that led up to the 10 tonne crane that ran the full length of the Casting Shop.

I followed him up the ladder, thankful of the steel hoops at my back. The crane spanned the full width of the shop, and while we were 50 feet up in the roof, the wooden catwalk was enclosed with safety rails, so I felt quite safe.

Back down after replacing a broken drive chain, Pricey, the shop foreman, was having a smoke and a chat with the security officer on the gate in Glover Street.

"Let three goals in last Saturday then. Fucking plonker," he said. He winked at Pat. "Are yer coming to see a proper goalkeeper this Saturday?"

I knew Delta Wire were playing the top of the league, so I replied "Yep, me and Greeny are going up the Blues."

"Cheeky kids" he replied, walking back into the shop.

CHAPTER 18

It was December 1965. My studies on the Technicians' Course were going well and Pauline and I had settled into a happy routine at Chilton Road. I would be 20 years old in three months' time, with another rise in wages. Another year and I'd be on ten bob an hour.

"What d'yer think Les, shall we go and watch the works team tomorrow?" I asked Greeny. It was Friday lunchtime. "We're going" a couple of the young apprentices piped up. Dave Wilmer looked expectantly at me. "That's settled then," I said. " A couple of pints and a cheese cob after we clock out, and off to Holly Lane."

The Delta sports ground in Erdington was, in its day, a wonderful facility with three football pitches, a cricket pitch, squash and badminton courts and saunas. In six months' time the Spanish national squad, who were playing their games at Villa Park in the World Cup, would be using it as their HQ. But on a freezing cold Saturday afternoon two weeks before Christmas, with a slight flurry of snow in the air, it was not very pleasant.

Even in these conditions Johnny Pearce was head and shoulders above anyone on the pitch, and with 10 minutes to go we were 2:1 up. Then Pricey came off his line to challenge their charging centre-forward. He wasn't quick enough, and took a right smack on his knee. In those days there were no subs, so Mickey Madden, who was the biggest lad in our team, had to pull on the goalie's green jumper. They got one back and we drew the match 2:2. As the team trooped off, Dave said, "You'll probably be playing next match Steve."

I played in goal for the works the next couple of games because of Pricey's knee. He suffered more from the piss taking than from the knee.

"What yer on about, I'm too fucking old? The Russian goalie is over 40."

"But you ain't the Russian goalie." Graham was having a pint with Pricey in the Waggon, and I'd dropped in from the Strip Mill round the corner. I was meeting Pauline at six.

Graham looked at me as I walked through the door. "This bloke's the new young generation." He took a sup and nudged Pricey in the ribs. "Fucking kids," his mate replied.

Graham dropped his voice to low whisper. "Have you seen the ghost of the hanging man yet?" he asked me, hunching his shoulders and looking furtively around the bar. The domino players smiled. Just then I noticed Pauline looking around the door. "I'll let you know," I said, finishing off my pint.

"What's the history of this factory then?" I was sitting upstairs in the maintenance shop of the Strip Mill in Upper Trinity Street. The shop was made up from the bedrooms of three terrace houses that had been knocked into one long room. All the machines were truly antique - an old lathe, pedestal driller, saw and milling machine, all belt-driven by a common, overhead shaft in the ceiling supported in bearings in the rafters. To use any of the machines you had to throw a huge lever on a large electric motor, hold it there for 30 seconds while it built up momentum and then throw it into the running position. All the machines would then be running. It was quite unbelievable.

The workbench ran the length of the room, with windows looking out over Upper Trinity Street straight at the blue brick wall that supported the railway line. Leo sat in a very old and worn leather armchair, his feet up on an old box staring into a warm coal fire, its flames dancing up the chimney. In the late 19th century all bedrooms had a fire grate.

"I've only been here since 1945. The old gaffer took me on when Albert and his missus passed away." Leo's accent was heavily Polish. He was a big man, 65, six feet tall and big-boned, with thinning grey hair scraped back. His sleeves were rolled back to his elbows and you could see six-digit numbers tattooed on his forearm.

"How you like to make a cup of tea? Boss don't come till nine." He re-crossed his legs and settled back into his chair. Scotty had told me a bit about Leo - how he had been in the German Army, had fought on the Russian front and escaped.

"Once we've had a drink I'll show you round the factory" said Leo, pouring a small amount of a clear liquid into his mug. He smiled. "Very good for the chest." I'd met Leo a few times during the last four years and now, sat down in front of a blazing fire, both my hands clasped around a steaming mug of tea, I was warming to this large Polish man with the saddest eyes I'd ever seen. Very gradually, over the next two months, I would find out why they were so sad.

"Mr Larkham be here in next five minutes, we start work," he said, easing himself out of his armchair. I followed his large frame across the bare wooden floorboards, taking in the workbench with a large vice and old hand tools scattered all over the place. Apart from the long window, all the walls were covered with what looked like spare parts for the machines in the factory. Rubber V belts, roller bearings, clutch plates, lengths of chain, large nuts and bolts and a whole range of gears were all hanging from nails hammered into the crumbling plaster. Some areas were still covered with flower-patterned wallpaper. I'd never seen anything like it.

Descending from the workshop by a wooden staircase, I glanced up to see if I could see any evidence of a hook or beam that could support a rope someone might have hung from. I was disappointed.

Leo stepped off the last of the stairs on to a large metal sheet laid out on the floor, which made a loud rattling sound. I followed with the same result, my heavy-duty Toetectors echoing the sound. I wondered why it was there.

We strolled into the main part of the Strip Mill. The main arched entrance into the factory was shut off from Upper Trinity Street by a large pair of green wooden gates, probably painted at the same time as the wooden fence surrounding the antique open gearbox in the middle of the factory. The gates were heavily barred and bolted, inside and out. This factory contained large amounts of brass and copper, a metal that was extremely expensive and much sought after by the scrap men and their unofficial suppliers.

"These two machines are brand new," said Sam Larkham, the factory manager. "They can roll brass sheet up to two feet wide and down to 15 thousands of an inch." He lit up his pipe. "You must be young Steve the apprentice."

Like most people in the factory, Sam Larkham was past his prime and grey-haired. He was dressed in a scruffy suit whose original colour would have been somewhere between brown and black. But he was keen about his job and his responsibility, particularly considering he was approaching retirement.

"They have flying micrometers that automatically measure the thickness of the metal," he said, proudly showing me the equipment. "I'll leave you to Leo, I've got work to do." He rushed off in the direction of the glass-panelled office built alongside the rear wall.

"These new machines I don't know" Leo said. "Any problems, they get outside men in."

We walked around the rest of the factory, Leo proudly pointing out the old plant, explaining its function and describing the repairs he'd performed over the years. "The bronze bearing in that rolling mill has lasted over five years. I hand-scraped it to fit," he said. I could tell he loved this factory.

"Time for breakfast" Leo said, as we passed the large brown clocking-in clock on the wall next to the factory entrance. Approaching the rickety wooden staircase we both stood on the metal sheet, causing another loud rattling sound, before we climbed up to the Maintenance Shop in the converted bedrooms.

"You want toast?" Leo asked, cutting a slice of bread an inch thick. He stuck it on a toasting fork and held it close to the fire in the grate. "Yes please" I replied, lighting the gas on the ring under the kettle. A large white enamelled sink stood on the back wall. In a bowl of water on the shelf above floated a battered butter-dish. Tucked under the sink was a disused paint tin contained Swarfega mixed with a little sand, for scrubbing your hands.

Wiping a dribble of butter off my chin, I asked him what the sheet of metal was for. As I spoke it clanged again. He winked. "Nobody finds Leo asleep" he said. They don't teach you this at College or PERA, I thought.

A bald head poked round the door – Stanley's. "A shear pin has busted on the coupling to the big mill," he said. "It's a rush job."

I jumped up and went to swill my mug out in the sink. "I'll have a piece of toast, if any's going" said Stanley, looking at the toasting fork. "It ain't that much of a rush, and in any case Sammy's gone round the main works." He spread the butter on his toast. "You must be the new apprentice, then?" I nodded. "I'm the foreman, bin here since I left school."

He shovelled the toast into his mouth. "Come on then, we've got a breakdown." He charged downstairs, and a rattle from the steel sheet announced that he had left the building.

Replacing the shear pin was a dirty job. Your hands got covered in heavy grease and oil and your overalls were the same, so when we climbed up the stairs the first thing I did was take off my boiler suit off and have a good scrub-up with the Swarfega and sand.

"Be OK now. Time for rest" said Leo. He stoked up the fire and settled into his armchair. I found an old newspaper and did the same.

An hour later the rattling sounded again. Leo was wide awake when Stanley shouted "Sammy's back!"

★ ★ ★ ★ ★ ★ ★ ★ ★ ★ ★

I continued to clock in at the main works in Adderley, park my Mini in the secure car park and walk round to Upper Trinity Street, arriving about eight o'clock. Leo would usually be dozing in front of the fire. It was soon late January and still bloody cold. Using the antiquated machinery, I'd now machined enough shear pins to last a month and made sure the stock of V belts was adequate and the tea caddy was full. There was not a lot to do now, so I started to bring in my homework from college.

"Some bastard been stealing our Swarfega" Leo said angrily one day as we took off our overalls and prepared to scrub our hands and arms in the sink. "Was full this morning."

I was too knackered to reply. We had just changed a huge roll from one of the old mills, which had involved a lot of mauling and pulling on chain blocks. It was a hell of a job to get it on a bogie and manhandle it into the street. Even Billy Law and Jan from the Fitting Shop had had to help. Jan refused to enter the factory, even though Billy called him for everything.

Leo was on his third cup of vodka fortified tea. It was two o'clock in the afternoon, and unless we were unlucky there would be no more rush jobs that day.

"You young men very lucky" said Leo, savouring his tea. "I left school when I was 13 years old, worked in factory, then joined Polish Army for five years. In 1939 I was railway worker in charge of four men at my village station. I say goodbye to my wife and children one morning and walk to the station. The Germans arrive and say we all have to go to headquarters to register. We were taken in lorry for many hours. After a time we were allowed to get out of lorry to piss in field. My friend Franz asked, when we go home? The officer asked how old he was. Franz said, I am 55. The officer pulled out his Luger. Shot him in the head.

"No-one asked more questions. I never saw my family again."

I sat in shock for a moment. I couldn't think of anything to say, so I made another cup of tea. I lit the gas ring and Leo chucked a few lumps of coal on the fire.

"What happened then?" I asked.

Leo rubbed his stubbly chin and shrugged his wide shoulders. "Another time I tell you" he replied. A few minutes later he was dozing.

Making sure I didn't tread on the metal sheet, I took a quick walk around the factory to show the flag and then climbed the other narrow staircase which was the other side of the arched entrance to the factory. This led into the bedroom of the old terraced house underneath.

Again there was a black fire-grate on the far wall and two sash windows looked across the street to the railway. It was late afternoon and getting dark. In the gloom I could see a row of desks, high and old-fashioned with a multitude of drawers, all covered in dust and cobwebs.

I carefully opened one of the drawers and pulled out a hard, leather-bound book. It had 'Purchase Ledger 1936–1937' on the cover. Other desks produced sales ledgers, all in copperplate handwriting. There were also cheques dating back 30–odd years. I was fascinated.

My Mom, God bless her, had a sixth sense – she could feel things. Very occasionally I'd experienced the same thing. The Castle at Falmouth, on my honeymoon. Granny Andrews, who had died in the room I was born in at Chilton Road, the one that became our temporary living room. I never mentioned this to Pauline, but I felt her presence – always had, since childhood. Just as my Mom did. For years I wouldn't go up to bed unless the lights were on. The feeling would start at the top of the stairs.

I carefully put the ledgers back in their drawers. I could feel the hairs on the back of my neck starting to tingle. I realised that there was somebody in the gloom behind me, but I was too frightened to turn round.

Finally, after what seemed like an age, I heard two blokes talking at the bottom of the stairs. The spell was broken, and I turned. There was no-one there.

"I tell you what, it's a right spooky place." I was having a cup of tea in the Fitting Shop of the main works in Adderley Street. A driveshaft needed repairing and I'd carried it on my shoulder from the Strip Mills. I had done the job many times before – skim a bit off, build it up with weld and re-turn it back to the original diameter. The shaft was now cooling.

"Have yer seen the ghost yet?" young Ray asked, his face eager in anticipation.

"No, but I reckon the place is haunted. You can feel it everywhere" I replied. "There's certain corners in the factory where you get the shivers, even in the day. But as it gets a bit dark in the afternoon that old office upstairs is frightening."

"What yer mean?" Ray asked, his mouth agape. Ken, his mate and fellow apprentice, looked at me with wide eyes. Glancing at Pat and Scotty, the chief piss takers, I lowered my voice and started to tell them that I had been up to the old office upstairs.

"That was where the old caretaker murdered his missus and then hanged himself," Scotty whispered. Ray and Ken jumped.

"For a minute I couldn't move" I said. "I was convinced someone was right behind me." Everyone was looking at me, unsure whether I was telling the truth or having a laugh. I even caught a puzzled glance from Pat Dowling. Doug Smith of One Man Band fame spoke up.

"Load of bollocks. No such things as ghosts, it's all in yer mind."

"Don't be too sure, young Doug" said one of the old fitters. "There's many who won't go in the factory, let alone up the stairs." Several elderly heads nodded in agreement.

Walking back to the Strip Mill with the repaired shaft on my shoulder, I thought to myself that I knew what I had felt in that old bedroom - fear.

Replacing the repaired shaft took an hour, and by mid-afternoon we were scrubbed up and relaxing in front of the fire.

"Some bastard is still stealing my washing soap" Leo said, topping up his tea with a good shot of vodka. He winked and put his forefinger to his lips. I nodded. He trusted me. "I'll sort them out." Then he resumed his story.

"The following day we line up in railway yard with German officer asking who had served in the Army. The officer said ex-soldiers would receive better conditions." He shrugged. "All conditions same fighting Russians." He topped up his tea and settled more comfortably into the armchair.

"They put their number on my arm. Now I was a German soldier. For three years I wore German Army uniform and guarded Jews in camps. I saw things that no man should see. Then in winter we go to Leningrad." He shook his head. "Thousands of people died. Hundred thousand."

He wiped his eyes and nose on the back of his huge fist. "My wife's parents were Jews." His head dropped, his chin slowly subsiding on to his chest. I didn't know what to say. I stood up and took a deep breath.

"I'll have a walk round the factory." I said. I left Leo to his memories.

Anyone playing football in early February, even in the World Cup year of 1966, had to be mad. It was bloody freezing. Pricey was still suffering from his knee, and I was his replacement in goal. At this level in the Works League we were doing reasonably well, winning or drawing our last 5 games, mainly due to the young new apprentice. The opposition couldn't handle Johnny Pearce. He was just too quick.

"He won't be playing for us much longer" Mickey Madden said, supping his pint. We'd just beaten Delta Rods, one of the top teams in our division, and I was having a drink with our centre-forward. "Did you notice them blokes on the touchline today?" I shook my head. "Well, they weren't watching you and me, that's a fucking cert." Mickey had been on schoolboy terms at Birmingham City and he knew some of the local scouts. "He's got a trial at Manchester United next week. They're putting him up for three days."

"You sure they weren't watching us?" I asked with a grin.

"Fuck off and gerrus a pint." Mickey was a proper Blue Nose.

★ ★ ★ ★ ★ ★ ★ ★ ★ ★ ★

Stanley the Strip Mill Foreman was sitting in a battered old upholstered chair with wooden armrests, warming his feet in front of the roaring coal fire, his hands cupped around a steaming mug of tea. It was early February and there was an inch of snow lying in the street below, but we were in the warmth of the old Fitting Shop upstairs.

"I were forty-odd at the time and chargehand in the Rolling Mill" he said. "Because the factory produced brass sheet for mekkin' shell cases, we were on War Effort. Any road, most of us were too fucking old for the army." He scratched his bald head and pushed his wire frame spectacles back to the bridge of his nose. There was a long pause as he cut a couple of slices of tobacco off and thoughtfully rolled them in the palm of his hand before filling his pipe.

"We left school at 14 in them days and I started here just after the Great War. By gum, it were a different world." He paused to light his pipe and smiled. "Edward Larkham was the gaffer, and he had a fucking big car an' all.

286

His son Sammy had just left University and was working in the factory, if yer could call it work. He was never here and when he was he just pissed about."

He paused, a frown creasing his brow. "I remember exactly when Albert Jones was med up to foreman. It were 1935, the week me and me missus got married. A year or two later they med him caretaker as well and Mr Edward let him live in the house next door. Gas and electric paid an all.

"Albert's missus Lizzie were a lovely woman. She would do bacon and egg sandwiches for them as wanted 'em and a bit a stew at dinnertime. She charged, mind, but it were a lot cheaper than any caff."

"But why did she hang herself?" I asked.

"She didn't" Stanley replied. "It were a different woman hanging next to Albert. I know. I found 'em."

The factory bell shrilled loudly. "Ah well, back to work." He groaned and stood up. "I'll tell yer the rest tomorra."

Walking round to the main works to collect my wages, I pondered on the story Stanley had begun to tell me. It had taken place only 20 years ago. I couldn't wait to hear the rest. I tucked my hands into the pocket of my free-issue donkey jacket and trudged through the snow. I would be 20 in two week's time, with a big rise in wages, and a new car was on the horizon.

"It's no bullshit. Something horrible happened in that old factory. I've felt it, and now I'm getting the true story." All the blokes were sitting round the dining table in the main Fitting Shop in Adderley Street - Black Bat and Andy, Norman, Pat, Scotty, George, Les, Browny and Big Harry. The other young apprentices looked at me.

"They found two bodies hanging. One was the old caretaker, but the other wasn't his wife." I looked round. Even Black Bat looked surprised, and he was a right old cynic.

"How do yer know all this?" Doug asked.

"Stanley, the old foreman, told me. It was him who found them." Pat and Scotty, for once, were silent.

"It still don't prove there's ghosts," said Doug defiantly as he stood up.

He was working in the Casting Shop with Bob and Big Harry. Pat and Scotty waited until Doug had disappeared. Then Pat whispered to me. "Shall we try and change his mind?" The craic was on.

★ ★ ★ ★ ★ ★ ★ ★ ★ ★ ★

"Don't use this soap tin," Leo said. "Use the little one on the floor under the sink."

"OK" I replied. I gave him a puzzled look. We had worked hard that morning replacing two shear pins in a coupling and then, wearing wellington boots, we had stood in ankle-deep grease to replace a driving key on one of the shafts and gears in the large open gearbox. Leo looked knackered as we slowly climbed up the wooden stairs to the old Fitting Shop. I put the kettle on and he stoked up the fire. On his third cup of laced tea, he started to look relaxed. He went on with his story.

"In retreat from Russian front I managed to escape from my German masters. After months of walking, hiding in trucks on railways, eating cattle food and berries, I was starving, ready to die." He topped up his tea with vodka. "You no tell gaffers about my drink?"

"No Leo."

"I was found by farmer lying in his barn, freezing and almost dead. He and his wife fed me, kept me warm." He paused and took off his right boot. All the small toes on his foot were missing. Only the big toe was left.

"Other foot is better," he said. "Only two toes gone." He smiled and wriggled his one big toe in the heat of the fire.

"A week later, men from Polish Resistance interrogated me. I told them all I knew about my time in German Army. Guns, training, German officers' names, my wife's name and her Jewish family, everything. I told them I'd witnessed terrible things. A week later the Resistance man returned, with another man, a British Intelligence Officer. They asked me if I would help them identify war criminals. I said yes. They brought me to England."

Bloody hell, I thought. I lit up a fag.

"The British found me lodgings in a Polish club in Handsworth and got me my job here after the war."

"You weren't here then when Albert and his missus died?" I asked. He shook his head. Ten minutes later he was dozing again.

"Sammy's fucked off round to the main works and the factory's working OK," said Stanley. "Put the kettle on, young 'un." He had settled himself into his usual chair and was rubbing his bacca between his palms. He chucked a large lump of coal on the fire. "Fucking cold down there in the works." He struck a Swan Vesta and drew contently on his pipe.

"I helped the coppers cut old Albert down," he said. "He was stone cold, like a slab. Him and Lizzie were married just before he went off to France in 1914, but he was one of the lucky ones. He came back from the Somme with a steel plate in his head, and Mr Edward took him on." He scratched his chin. "It must have been a couple of years afore I started."

"What happened then?" I asked.

"You young buggers are always in a rush" he replied, puffing at his pipe. "They had three children, but two died in infancy, they daint have the injections and hospital care for kids in them days and only Jack survived to manhood. It might have been better if he daint. Albert and Lizzie adored him. He was their life. He could have had a job in the factory working on munitions for the war effort but he was headstrong, like his dad. All me mates are joining up, he said, I ain't working in your factory. Albert and Lizzie were upset. But they were heartbroken when they got the telegram telling them their only child had been killed in action on the beaches of Dunkirk.

"It's a fucking hard life, and then yer die."

Leo had woken up, and I put a mug of steaming black tea on the box next to his chair. I left plenty of room for the vodka.

"The doctors said it was consumption, but I reckon it were a broken heart" Stanley continued. "Lizzie died, God bless her, 18 months later."

He took a long pause, as though he was travelling back to 1942.

"Albert was totally demented. Mr Edward gave him a week off to sort things out. He told him his job was secure. But Albert went on the piss."

The old foreman re-lit his pipe. "It took Albert a good three years to get over losing the two of them. But he ran the factory with an iron hand, nobody fucked about and the gaffers were happy enough. Mr Edward had a new Rolls Royce and young Mr Sammy had one of them new sports cars, I think it was an MG or summat. They had plenty of petrol coupons - war effort. Then Albert fell in love."

He slowly shook his head, tapped his pipe out and refilled it.

"Everybody told him he was being a fool. His mates in the pub, blokes at work. I was one of his chargehands and I tried to tell him. But he wouldn't have it.

"Gloria Day had been chucked out of her lodgings for the umpteenth time and was literally on the street. Some said that's where she earned her living anyway. I knew her and her family because I grew up in the same street, and she didn't have the best upbringing. Her parents didn't give a shit about their kids and the house and their bit of a yard was a tip."

He paused and lowered his voice. "Her two elder brothers had been teaching her the practical side of the facts of life since she was 13 years old." Stanley sighed. "She didn't charge in those days." I could begin to guess how this story was going.

"They met on the night of VE day. All the local pubs had a do, people drank till the beer ran out. That's when Gloria moved in with Albert. A free roof over her head and grub on the table. She was just turned 30, and Albert was 55.

"For the first few months everything was hunky dory. Albert was charging round the factory with a big smile on his face and the work was being belted out of the factory. Mr Edward even gave us all a pound bonus at the end of one month. That was a day's wages." He suddenly looked sad. "It went downhill very fast after that."

He looked over his shoulder. "Fuck me, it's nearly dark. Best get back down to the factory." He sighed, got up out of his chair and disappeared down the staircase. The steel sheet rattled, and Leo woke up.

I'll have another look up into the old office next door, I thought to myself, flicking my nub end into the fire. I was feeling brave.

In the office it was more than gloomy, but you could just make out the wooden stairs rising up into the darkness of the old bedroom. Standing at the bottom of the stairs looking up, you could see the heavy wooden beams that supported the ceiling, but I felt nothing strange, so far. I lit up and started to climb the staircase. Soon I was standing in the old bedroom with its dusty office furniture alongside the outside wall. I soon started to feel the shivers, and it wasn't because there was an inch of snow outside either. Call it imagination if you like, but I knew this room had seen something nasty.

The following morning I spent with Mr Larkham, or young Mr Sammy, as the old blokes called him. He wasn't a bad old bloke. Grey, thinning hair and dark frame spectacles the size of small windows. Only John Lennon and his fans wore small gold frames then.

"My grandfather started the business in 1880, collecting scrap metal in a horse and cart" he said. "Ten years later he and my father had a small amount of capital and they managed to persuade the bank to give them a loan. The business expanded." The phone rang, and Sammy picked up the large black Bakelite handset. After saying 'yes' and 'no' a few times he replaced the phone.

"Where were we?" He scratched the side of his face. The phone rang again. "Don't go into business, it's a bloody nuisance" he said, picking up the phone again.

"When my father acquired these premises in 1912 he was Managing Director and my grandfather was semi-retired. Our main production was rolled brass sheet. By 1914 we couldn't make enough of it. The Ministry of Defence took 95% of our production for shell cases, and my father bought half the street and trebled the size of the factory." He paused. "Let's have a cup of tea."

During the rest of the morning Sammy explained the process of rolling sheet brass, annealing and pickling as we strolled around the works. He wished everyone good morning, and made a point of talking to all the old fellas.

As we sat down in his office he sighed out loud. "You know, there are over 20 blokes out there who were already here when I started work in 1920" he said. He shook his head in disbelief. "Mind you, me and my father always paid 'em well. His motto was, if we made an extra pound, we'd give the lads an extra farthing. I can't do that now."

"How'd yer gerron with Mr Sammy?" Stanley the Foreman asked as we sat down for a cuppa. It was afternoon tea break, and hopefully there would be no breakdowns. Provided the factory was running and Mr Sammy was round at the main works, Stanley was happy to warm his feet in front of the fire.

"It took me a week or so to notice the change in Albert," he said. "His smile had disappeared and he was angry with the blokes, fucking em up hill and down dale for no reason at all." He took a sup of his tea. "And he was spending more time in the Waggon." He shook his head sadly. "Albert was a pal as well as me Foreman, but I couldn't tell him. When Albert sat down in the pub with his pint and started playing dominoes, certain people would sup up and walk out. An hour later they'd come back in again. Every bugger knew where they'd been and who they'd been shagging.

"Afterwards some blokes said it was the steel plate in his head that made him do it. Me, I dunno." Stanley re-filled his pipe and continued.

"That last night a bloke come in the Waggon, he was half pissed and loud. 'Give us a pint gaffer, I've just had a right good fuck and it was just round the corner' he said. I only happened to be in the pub that night cos it was a big domino match. I told the coppers the same." Stanley stoked up his pipe and Leo chucked a lump of coal on the fire. The old foreman continued.

"Albert stood up, his face a mask of anger and rage. 'Don't rush mate, there's another waiting after me' said the loudmouth. He roared with laughter. Albert dashed outside.

"The next morning we all found ourselves stood in the street waiting for the gates to open. It was half seven and they should have been opened half an hour before. A couple of the blokes had been chucking stones up at the top floor windows, shouting for Albert – 'come on, yer lazy bugger'."

Stanley dropped his voice. I was mesmerized.

"I knew something was wrong. Mr Sammy arrived just after eight and got out of his MG. 'What's going on, Stanley?' he said. I was Senior Chargehand. "The factory's locked, we can't get in," I said.

"Where's Albert? He was searching for the factory keys. He unlocked the doors and we all walked into the gloom.

"We saw the two bodies hanging motionless at the top of the stairs. There was a single old chair on its side at the bottom. Twenty minutes later the place was full of coppers."

Stanley sat back in the old chair. "It was a right old fucking do." He looked at Leo. "Can I have a drop of yer cough mixture?" He poured a drop of Vodka into his mug, wiped his hand over his head and looked closely at his pipe as he slowly shook his head.

"The Coroner's Report said Gloria Day had been strangled. There were finger marks on her neck to support this, and the bedroom had evidence of a violent struggle, with items of furniture disturbed. It was concluded that some unknown person had then hung her by a rope. Albert Jones had hung himself while the balance of his mind was disturbed. There was only one chair found at the bottom of the stairs. No-one else was suspected of being involved."

My eyes were agog. I looked at Stanley. He shrugged. "Old Albert weren't a bad bloke."

Over the next few days I never said a word about what Stanley had told me, nor did I venture into the old house next door.

The next day I joined the crowd in the main Fitting Shop for the afternoon tea break. As Joe shouted us up, he called me over.

"Tek a couple of the young 'uns with yer Steve, Sammy Larkham's got a load of paperwork he wants shifting back here." The three young apprentices and I walked slowly down Adderley Street, passing the Waggon and Horses before turning into Upper Trinity Street. It was cold and getting dark. As we entered the arched entrance, I saw Pat Dowling walking down the road, his toolbox in his hand. Scotty was just behind him.

"Where's the staircase and bedroom, Steve?" Young Ray asked. Instead of going straight ahead across the well-lit factory towards Sammy's Office, I led the other three apprentices towards the old terraced house next door, and as we all turned left into the dark corridor that led to the stairs I stopped dead in my tracks.

Two bodies were hanging from the beam at the top of the stairs.

I was frightened to death. What I was looking at was not possible.

The others all shouted out in shock. The next day Doug said he hadn't shouted, but I can tell you he did. Young Ray couldn't speak.

The as we stared at the bodies hanging there, we noticed something odd about them – they had no feet. They were dressed in boiler suits and the legs had been tied up. No doubt to stop the rolled-up newspapers from falling out...

We all started to laugh with relief.

"Fucking Pat and Scotty have done this," I said.

"Told you there was no such thing as ghosts" said Doug, but with much less confidence than before.

When I asked Sammy for the files of paperwork he wanted taking round to Adderley Street, he looked puzzled. "Someone's pulling your leg son," he said. "I never asked for any paperwork to be taken."

"We're in for some serious piss taking in the morning," I said to the others. As we walked past the security guard he let out a low 'hooooo!' and rattled his keys. "Old Albert and his missus get yer, then? Hooooo!"

"They were all shit scared I'm telling yer" said Pat. He and Scotty were in their element, and every bugger in the shop was pissing themselves with laughing.

In four years I'd never seen old Billy Law crack a smile, but he was enjoying a right old chuckle as he struggled out of his boiler suit. He paused and took his pipe out of his mouth.

"That old factory worn't part of our place in them days, but the murder of the woman and Albert hanging himself was in all the papers" he said.

The ghostly wails followed all four of us through the main works, but not in the Strip Mill. A lot of the old 'uns had known Albert, and as one of them said, it hadn't been that long ago.

Caggy had told me to report back to the main Fitting Shop the next week, so this would be my last few days working full time in the Strip Mill. I'd learned a lot about the process of rolling sheet brass, and under the watchful eye of the experienced operators I had helped to set up and run the two high-tech machines, as well as the massive old Rolling Mills. In principle it was just like helping my Nan pass wet washing through her mangle outside the back kitchen, only instead of towels and sheets it was brass sheet.

I also learned a great deal about people. Leo, like a lot of other old blokes who helped to train me, was a character I would never forget. While he never mentioned the horrors he said he had seen, he would occasionally, after a few strong teas, talk about the lighter side of his war - chasing and stealing chickens in an attempt to feed himself, or helping himself to milk from the churn, even from the cow. "If you starving, it don't matter," he would say.

We had been working in the open gearbox wearing our wellingtons for over an hour, and after we had changed into normal workboots we climbed up the stairs into the old Fitting Shop. I chucked a few lumps of coal on the fire and lit the gas ring under the kettle. Before we left the shop I'd remarked to Leo that the Swarfega tin was full up. "You not touch!" he told me sharply.

As I approached the sink my nose twitched. When I looked into the paint tin, I realized why. While we had been out, someone had put their hands into half an inch of Swarfega - and four inches of shit.

"Fuckers won't steal my soap again," said Leo said with pride.

I sat there in the darkening shadows, the old desks and fire grate barely visible in the gloom, wondering about the layout of the furniture when this had been a bedroom. No, when this had been a scene of unimaginable violence and murder. The bed would have been there, opposite the two sash windows. A wardrobe there, a dressing table against that wall – who knows? I sat there in silence, not even lighting up.

You don't have to look to see some things. You just know, as though you can see through the back of your head. My Mom was the same.

I never went back to Albert's bedroom.

CHAPTER 19

It was the second payday in March 1966, the first after my 20th birthday. I was studying my wage slip - seven and six an hour! Nearly there, I thought to myself, thinking what I'd do with all my money when I was on ten bob an hour.

I'd worked my normal overtime of an hour a night for four nights (Mondays I was at college) plus Saturday and Sunday mornings, and my wages were nearly twenty-six quid. Even after stoppages I was well chuffed with my pay.

"Did you see that car back there?" I asked Pauline. "The 1100?" she replied, glancing at me with a knowing smile. I nodded. We had been discussing changing our faithful Mini Van for a proper car for the last week or so, confident we could afford it now we had both received pay rises.

The little showroom was on the traffic lights on the Warwick Road right next to Tyseley Railway Station. The cream Austin 1100 with red leatherette upholstery was sitting on the forecourt with £425 in large white numerals on the windscreen.

The salesman, whose name was Alan Mead, wore the obligatory light tan, three-quarter length sheepskin coat, its white wool collar tucked up around his ears against the weather.

"Lovely motor, just two years old and only one previous owner" He was warming to his spiel. "I've been using it myself this last two days. It won't be here tomorrow." Yeah, right.

We opened the doors, bonnet and boot and gently kicked the tyres. It was a nice car, and it had five seats.

"How much will you allow me on the Mini?" I asked. Mr Mead stroked his salesman's moustache. "Let's have a cup of coffee in the office, I'm sure we can do a deal" he said.

"Don't touch your savings Steve, that's towards the deposit for your house" said Nan. We were sat in their front room downstairs. Pop had gone up the

Haven for his couple of pints. "You can pay me back every week." Three days later I was the proud owner of AOE 713B. It didn't have the romantic comforts of the rear of the Mini Van, but it was a proper car.

★ ★ ★ ★ ★ ★ ★ ★ ★ ★ ★ ★ ★

I'd been working in the main Fitting Shop for a month on Joe's beloved Dean, Smith and Grace centre lathe, producing everything from simple shear pins and bronze bearings to long shafts with square threads requiring fixed and running steadies. In his own way Joe was bringing me on.

A lot of the machining jobs in the shop were regular jobs which were given to the other blokes who had done them before or the younger apprentices. In a factory the size of Delta Wire there were plenty of breakdowns and broken bits which needed replacing. All the manufacture of tooling and dies had been transferred to the new Toolroom.

I was enjoying the Production Engineering Technicians' course and didn't feel out of my depth. It was based on the principles of large volume production, as opposed to the skills of the craftsman. Yes, I had a lot to learn.

"Yer too fucking old, yer daft sod" said Graham as Johnny Price eased himself on to the bench seat in the lounge of the Waggon and Horses. I'd just clocked out after working a Sunday morning, and was enjoying a pint with Arthur Twamley.

Pricey had played in goal the previous afternoon and had aggravated his old knee injury again. Delta Wire had won 2:1 and we were now in a cup final for the lower divisions of the Works League.

"Leave it to the young 'uns." Looking at his mate, Pricey agreed. "My missus is saying the same" he replied. "Can't even get me leg over for a shag with this fucking knee." Everybody chuckled as they shuffled the dominoes. The final was two weeks away, but I doubted if Pricey would be playing, the way he was hobbling around the pub. He was also over 30, as practically every bloke in the pub kept reminding him. He could take the piss big time, but he could take it as well. Pricey was all right.

"You'll be working with Bert Thompson and his mate Ted Smart for the next week, Steve. All the rolls in the Waterberry Farrell Rolling Mill need changing." Joe was showing me my next job and Caggy had poked his head into the chargehand's little office.

"OK Tommy" I replied. When Caggy had buggered off I saw a slight frown cross Joe's face. "You'll learn more with me than them pair of prats" he said quietly. "Still, it's all experience for yer." He really was a great old bloke. I guessed he would have to do a bit while I was away, but that was not a problem with a craftsman of Joe's skill, especially as he'd be on his beloved lathe.

"Working with Atlas and Penis then are yer?" said Scotty as I sat down. It wasn't a question but a statement. I wondered how on earth he knew, when I'd only been told myself five minutes before. The factory telegraph, I supposed.

Bert Thompson was the skilled fitter and Ted Smart was his mate/assistant, who helped him to carry out his work, fetching and carrying tools, footing ladders and taking the lion's share of any hard slogging with hammers and jacks. Bert was a fairly small bloke, five foot eight or so, and well into his fifties, with light wispy hair and a perpetual worried look on his face. He had a huge barrel chest and a pair of shoulders to match. He was very proud that his lack of height coupled with his upper body strength enabled him to easily pick up weights most blokes couldn't handle and effortlessly swing them up on to his wide shoulders. Everybody called him Atlas, but not to his face. After four years in the factory I knew all the fitters, and Bert was not a bad bloke.

Ted Smart was a very different character. He was Shop Steward for the Transport and General Workers' Union in the Fitting Shop, and a lot of men didn't like him. "Nothing more than a fucking labourer" said Norman and Pat, Shop Stewards and members of the skilled AEU. "The Transport and General shouldn't be in our shop poaching." Ted was not a popular chap. His wife was Chief Wages Clerk upstairs, and while not openly admitting it, he knew everybody's wages and would drop out sly innuendos.

Ted was 50 and tall with grey hair. He was very proud of the fact that he had the biggest cock in the factory. In fact he was so proud of it that he would flash it about to any new employees, usually to the young lads in the lavatory. He lived in a detached house in Sheldon - paid for by his missus, his enemies said - and according to the blokes in his local pub he was factory engineer.

The Waterberry Farrell Mill was a 10-stand tandem rod rolling mill, behind the old Casting Shop and next to the new one in Glover Street. Up to one-inch diameter brass rod, supplied in 500-kilo coils from the Continuous Casting Plant, would be reduced to a finished size by passing through 10 pairs of hardened steel rolls. Each individual roll would have an accurate half-circle profile in its circumference, and when the mating pair of rolls were forced together they would make an exact diameter.

Each set of rolls reduced the diameter of the rod by about 0.020". and after many hundreds of tons of rod had been rolled they needed regrinding and polishing up to the next size. I'd reground many of these rolls myself when I worked on the universal grinder with old Black Bat over two years before. There was always a complete set of fully ground-up rolls ready for production, or there was supposed to be.

All the main tools and equipment necessary to carry out a complete change of the rolls were locked in a huge free-standing tool box. It was more of a tool shed than a box, and it contained all the different sets of rolls for the various diameters, all ready for production.

The supervisor's office for the Casting Shops was between the two, with one window looking out into the old shop and the opposite one looking into the new. Pricey and big Jim Cooper were sitting eating their breakfast as I walked past, and Bert and Ted were heading towards the Waterberry Farrell Mill. Production of this rolling mill was the responsibility of Jim and Pricey as it was in their department.

Tommy Best, one of the casters, was standing outside the office. As he spotted me he shouted, "Ay up boys, it's the new works goalie." I could see Pricey look up from his Daily Mirror. "They say he's better than Gordon Banks" Tommy went on. Pricey mouthed through the window "Tommy, fuck off back to work." Big Jim Cooper smiled.

Each set of rolls was totally encased in a large sheet-metal guard, bolted in position by six cap head set pins. Under the instruction of Bert Thompson I unscrewed each one and we carefully lifted the guard away and placed it against the wall.

"I won't be long. I've got a bit of union business with the steward in the Casting Shop" Ted said as he sidled off. Bert didn't say anything as we proceeded to unscrew the one-inch locking nut holding number 1 roll in place. Using the special three-armed extractor we slowly drew the roll off the shaft. Close inspection of the half diameter profile showed marks in the hardened steel surface which had started to cause score marks in the rod. It would only get worse.

After about an hour, Ted returned. "I'll go back up the shop and mek our tea, Bert," he said before disappearing again. He's an idle bastard, I thought.

Bert and Ted took their tea breaks and sandwiches at lunchtime, sitting next to their workbench on the long back wall of the main Fitting Shop. They rarely, if ever, visiting the steel-tabled dining room. The lockers containing their overalls were against the side wall adjacent to the bench. Though Andy and Black Bat had their own toolroom they both occasionally lunched with the gang, mainly to catch up on the factory gossip and to quiz Norman and Pat on union business.

"How yer doing with Atlas and Penis then?" Scotty asked as he stood up and stretched. "Has he flashed yer 'is cock yet?"

I felt a bit embarrassed. "Bert's all right" I replied.

"Fucking has to be, don't he" Black Bat muttered. Most of the old blokes around the table silently nodded. The young apprentices looked at me, puzzled.

I shrugged my shoulders. "I ain't seen much of Ted this morning because he was on union business," I said.

"Union business my fucking arse!" Black Bat spat out. "He's the idlest, craftiest, biggest-headed bastard that ever drew breath. And we all know how a bloke of his fucking age managed to ger out of being called up in the War. Fucking bastard!" He stormed off.

301

What had I started now, I thought to myself.

"Got a minute, Steve?" Arthur Twamley said. I had just washed my mug out and was putting it back on the table, noticing that the tablecloth was up to date – Ray and Ken must be doing a good job.

"Don't tell Ted Smart anything," Arthur whispered. "Black Bat's right, he's a right bastard and he tells Caggy everything. Every Friday night he buys him all his beer in the Ivy Leaf Club in Sheldon." He touched the side of his nose and looked at me closely. "I ain't told yer that!"

"But why does Bert put up with him?" I asked. "He's done nothing but walk about this morning." Arthur stroked his chin. "We'll have a quiet drink and I'll put yer in the picture. But don't tell the bastard anything."

"How's married life then young Steve, gerrin plenty?" I looked up from fitting a reground roll back on to the spindle of the Waterberry Farrell. Ted Smart was casually leaning against the machine, a smirk on his face. "Three times a night, Ted. How about yerself?" I replied.

Bert smothered a cough. "Doing well at college an' all ain't yer, I'm told."

The bastard was trying to wind me up. "Nearly as good as you did Mr Smart" I replied. I knew from the look on his face that I had made an enemy.

I had rung Pauline to tell her I'd be working until six that night, so she would be catching the bus to her parents' place and I was meeting her there later. That would give me a chance to have a pint with Arthur.

"Keep yer distance from that Smarty" he said. We had just sat down in the bar in the Waggon and lit up. Arthur took a sup of his mild and wiped his lips with the back of his hand.

"I think I've upset him anyway. He was trying to wind me up and take the piss, so I gave him some back. He didn't like it."

"That's Smarty all right, he likes to get on people's backs. A lot of blokes hate his guts. I'll tell yer a bit about him." He took a long pull from his pint.

"I know Black Bat's a miserable old bugger, but he's dead right about Smarty being a two-faced bastard. He might be a Shop Steward for the T and G, but he tells Caggy everything that goes on in the shop. Caggy don't tell the Gaffers upstairs, he couldn't care less about union business, but he keeps Smarty up his arse for the free Friday nights on the beer."

I thought for a bit. "So that's why Bert can't complain about Ted's idleness?"

Arthur smiled and took a drag. "That's one of the reasons." I must have looked puzzled.

"The other is that Bert owes Smarty a lot of money." Arthur put his empty glass on the table. "Got time for another?"

By the next day nearly all the rolls had been changed in the Waterberry Farrell Mill, but the final pair of finishing rolls still needed grinding and sizing. Bert and I had worked well together. He had instructed me on what to do and had then carefully watched me at work, giving advice and help when necessary. He was a good fitter and millwright. His so-called Mate, having realised I would be assisting Bert, spent most of the time on union business.

"These finishing rolls need grinding and apparently Alf George ain't in today," said Jim Cooper, the Superintendent. "This mill has got to be running, otherwise I've got the gaffers on me back."

Bert and I were having a bit of a rest, and I had just lit up. Smarty appeared from nowhere.

"Let's see if Clever Dick can do it then." Mugsy would have smacked him.

It may have been a long time since Joe Healy had used the Universal Grinding Machine, but there was no doubt that he was a skilled enough craftsman to form-grind these rolls. Other apprentices who had worked with Black Bat over the years could have done it, but two of them were at college today.

"By the time I've set up the machine, mounted the special wheel, trimmed it with the diamond, put the rolls on the mandrel and ground them, it'll take me less than two hours" I said, stubbing my fag out under my Toetectors. "Now if my labourer can carry the rolls down to the toolroom, I'll get cracking." Big Jim and Bert burst out laughing. Smarty's face turned purple.

Everybody around the dining table was laughing. Black Bat had been to a family funeral the day before, but someone had told him what had happened and he was having an early morning cuppa to hear it first hand. He was chuckling big time.

"Fuck me, I wished I'd been there to see that" he said. "He lit his pipe and shook his head. "Hope yer left my machine clean and tidy, Steve."

"Yes Alf" I replied. He stood up, still shaking his head, and paused.

"Yer know, we needed some new young blood in this factory." He shuffled off down to the Toolroom. Arthur offered me a Woodbine and we both lit up.

"Years ago Smarty boasted about how he dodged being called up in 1940. He'd just got married and his missus got him a job in a munitions factory on war work. Her father was Works Manager. After the war she got him the job here too, as a fitter's mate.

"You know Billy Little, the wire drawer? You know he was wounded and captured at Dunkirk?" I nodded and leaned forward. "Smarty started here well after the war, 1950 or so. He'd been gobbing off in the Wire Mill about the new detached house he'd just bought and how hard him and his missus had worked in the Spitfire factory.

"Billy went for him. According to the blokes in the Wire Mill, he would have killed him if they hadn't stopped him. It took four of 'em to pull him off.""

"Come on shower, time to start work" Joe announced. It was 1.30 pm. Though the Waterberry Farrell Mill was now up and running, I continued the rest of the week with Bert and Ted, mainly repairing the wheeled boogies used to move the coils of wire around the Wire Mill. A couple of wire drawing blocks had to be replaced. The worn ones were built up with weld, like a worn shaft, and re-turned. Ted was still making sly digs at me, but I was not responding.

"Steve, Black Bat's got a couple of rush jobs on in the Toolroom. Can you go down and help him out today?" Joe had collared me as I walked into the shop. "Yes Joe" I replied, thinking it would make a change from repairing trolleys.

The Toolroom was a small shop, and by the time all the machines and equipment had been shoehorned in there was no room for the luxury of a dining table. Instead we had a couple of wooden planks, supported at each end by boxes tucked against the wall behind the Jones and Shipman surface grinder, while another box served as a table. To act as a fire escape, a small half-door had been installed in one wall. This opened out on to the towpath of the canal outside.

Rather than walk back to the Fitting Shop, I was sitting outside eating my sandwiches watching the occasional brightly-painted barge slowly chug past. Most were decorated with roses and castles and rows of similarly-painted buckets. It was an enjoyable way to spend your lunchtime, specially in the warm spring sunshine.

"Bet yer glad to ger away from that prat Smarty." Black Bat and Andy had struggled out of the low door and joined me on the towpath.

"He's not a nice bloke, Alf" I replied. Black Bat then told me a similar story to the one Arthur had told me. I didn't say anything – I just nodded at the appropriate times.

"He's up Caggy's arse and he's got Bert by the short and curlies" said Alf.

I put my tea down. "How d'yer mean Alf?"

Scratching the stubble on his chin (it wasn't called designer stubble in 1966), he continued.

"Bert left his missus a couple of years ago and set up house with another woman. Last year he was desperate for money. His ex was threatening court action and bailiffs were knocking on his door. Smarty lent him five hundred quid."

"That weren't bad of him," I said.

Alf snorted. "Bert's gorra pay the bastard back a fiver a week for three years."

I did a quick mental sum in my head. "'Kin 'ell" I said.

"I know what I'd do," said Andy Uprichard, the ex-apprentice from Harland and Wolff. "I'd pay him the 500 quid back and tell him to fuck off."

Alf took his pipe from his mouth. "It ain't that simple" he said. "Smarty's a big-mouthed bully and Bert's frightened of him. The bastards even told blokes he'll be made a fitter soon." He tapped his pipe out and struggled to his feet.

"If that ever happens the fucking factory will come out on strike." He clambered through the half door back into the toolroom.

CHAPTER 20

Having arranged to meet Pauline at her Mom and Dad's later that day, I chucked my football gear into the boot of my new car and set off to work. It was the first Saturday in May, and Delta Wire was playing in a cup final that afternoon. It might only have been for the lower divisions of the Works League, but it was still a cup final. We would be playing on the Delta Sports Ground in Holly Lane, Erdington, where in just over a month's time the Spanish national side would be training for their World Cup games at Villa Park.

Bro. Hall had arranged a team meet in the Wire Mill at breakfast time. Suitably armed with bacon and egg sandwiches, we all sat in anticipation. There were no subs in those days, and not more than a dozen lads wanted to play for the Works on a Saturday afternoon anyway, not with St. Andrews just up Kingston Hill, so the team virtually picked itself.

Bro. Hall was coming to the end of his motivational speech. "I know you'll all do your best. Just remember, it's been well over 10 years since the Works won a cup or the league."

"That was when we had a proper team" said Pricey. "What yer say, Billy?"

We looked round to see Pricey playfully slap Billy Little on the back. The big wire drawer smiled ruefully.

"Them was the days, young John," replied Billy. "Six till two on the morning shift, a couple of quick pints, a game of football in the afternoon and Saturday night on the piss."

Bro. Hall quickly interrupted. "I want you all to be at the ground at two o'clock, and NO DRINKING before the game." He looked at Mickey Madden, Jim and me, as we'd all been known to have a quick pint before a match. As we stood up to go back to work, the famous Wire Mill chorus, led by Billy, started up.

"We shall not, we shall not be moved, we shall not, we shall not be moved. Just like a team that's going to win the FA Cup, we shall not be moved."

"Fucking gorra win now, ain't we," said Mickey as we went to swill our

307

mugs out. Bro. Hall must have heard, because he stopped and turned round before climbing the stairs up to his office. "Yes, you have got to win. That's why I called you all together this morning and made sure a lot of the old players who won the last trophy would be there as well."

We all exchanged glances. We'd been motivated.

Putting my right sock on before my left and my shin pads and boots in the same order, I looked around the changing room. The facilities were excellent. There were clothes hooks, clean walls and spotless showers. Bro. Hall was fussing about like an old hen as Mickey and I enjoyed a cigarette.

Johnny Pearce was in his first year as an apprentice and wasn't 17 years old yet. He was exceptionally fast and skilful and extremely fit. He was the highest scorer of goals in the Works League that season, but as yet no professional club had signed him up. He had had trials for the Villa and Walsall, but his big test would be next week at Manchester United.

'Kin 'ell I thought as we ran out. Half the bloody factory's here. From the shouting and good-natured banter coming from the touch line I guessed they had all been in the bar upstairs before being chucked out at ten to three.

"I've got me boots if yow ain't up to it" Pricey roared. He took a quick sip from a hip flask. "Yer can't stand up yer prat, let alone play football," countered Graham.

I hoped I wouldn't let in any silly goals. I dreaded that, especially in front of this lot. I'd never live it down.

At half time it was 1:1 and I had let in a bit of a soft goal, but no one was taking the piss, not at this stage of the match anyway. All the blokes from the factory were standing with us on the pitch as we sucked our oranges, geeing us up by slapping us on the back and telling us we could beat 'em. Bro. Hall didn't mind that the team had suddenly acquired another 20 managers. He was doing his bit as well.

Halfway through the second half, they scored. Afterwards in the bar everybody said it was unstoppable, even Pricey. With 20 minutes to go we were 2:1 down. All through the game young Pearce had been heavily marked and badly knocked about by their defence – in fact our only goal had been from a penalty when he had been chopped down. He had rubbed his shin, shrugged his young shoulders and smiled at the bloke who had whacked him before placing the ball on the penalty spot. A subtle body swerve sent their goalie totally the wrong way.

The next 15 minutes was a lesson to everyone playing and watching, including the Manchester scouts scribbling in their notebooks. Johnny Pearce scored two goals, one an outstanding solo effort in which he dribbled round three defenders before blasting it past their keeper, the other slotted in from a ball headed down into his path from Mickey Madden.

We were winning 3:2 with less than five minutes to go when Jim Richmond pulled down their centre-forward in the penalty area. Oh shit, we didn't deserve this. Standing on my line and wondering which way to dive, I concentrated on the bloke's eyes as he placed the ball on the spot. Then I focused on the ball. You could have heard a pin drop. Everyone was holding their breath, including me.

He struck the ball. I went to my right, my strongest side. I just managed to push the ball round the post. Everybody went barmy, slapping me on the back and getting into position to defend against the corner. Our penalty area was packed solid with 22 players, even their goalie was pushing me about until I stamped on his foot.

Mickey headed away their corner, and a minute later he nodded one into the net at the other end from a Pearce cross. We'd won 4:2, and young Johnny had scored a hat trick.

It might not have been the FA Cup, but you'd have thought it was, in the bar after the game. I think Pauline's going to be driving home, I thought, as the second pint quickly followed the first.

I felt really chuffed looking at the blokes from the factory who had turned up to support us, especially the half a dozen or so who had won a similar cup back in 1954. Big Billy Little and Pricey were slapping all the players on the back, congratulating them but also telling them that their team would have knocked spots off us.

Billy stopped and slowly shook his head. "We didn't have a kid like young Pearce in them days."

"He'll play as a professional, he's that good" Pricey nodded in reply. Within three months however, Pricey would sadly be proved wrong.

Johnny Pearce enjoyed an orange juice and lemonade, modestly accepting the pats on the back and praise from everyone in the bar before leaving with his dad. He'd got a big week in front of him.

I was well impressed with my Austin 1100. It was much more comfortable than my Mini and a lot quieter on the road. I hadn't realised how much drumming noise the van made.

Driving to work on the Sunday morning following our cup success, I was looking forward to the craic in the factory. Gordon Banks was bound to get a mention. The cup was on show in the Security Office.

"Bro. Hall is that chuffed he brought it in early this morning" said Mr Cadwallander, the Security Officer, as I walked past down the stairs to clock in. Apart from a few 'well dones', the old 'uns in the Fitting Shop didn't seem that much concerned. They were much more interested in the two old-fashioned cast-iron lamp posts leaning against the wall next to Caggy's office. I hadn't noticed them, because after clocking in I had gone into the Wire Mill to have a chat with a couple of the lads in the team and walked into the shop from another door.

"They were delivered just after you lot buggered off to play football," said Scotty. He wasn't a football fan. He also wasn't a Ted Smart fan. "Atlas and Penis carried 'em in one at a time and then went home" he said. Everyone looked puzzled.

"Come on shower, time to start work" Joe shouted. "Even the cup winners."

Raking out the swarf from the Dean Smith, I started to set up the four-jaw chuck. "What's with the lamp posts, Joe?" I asked.

"One's Caggy's and the others is that prat Smarty's" he replied contemptuously. "We've got to do 'em up so that they can put 'em in their back gardens."

310

The lamp posts were old, obviously obtained from the City Council. They were manufactured in cast iron with a cross member at the top to support a ladder for a man to clean the four glass panels at the top which originally used to house a gas light, but had been converted to electricity, probably about 1920.

Bob Crockett the electrician was first on the job, ripping out the old wiring and fittings and replacing them with new. I was on the lathe watching what was going on. It didn't take long for the factory tom-toms to work.

"I bet yer they cost a fucking fortune," Black Bat said. He had joined us for breakfast. "I'll tell yer another thing an all. Caggy ain't paid a sodding penny." Everybody nodded in agreement. "Yer right, Alf" said Pat. He was a great stirrer.

"Free lamp posts as well as free beer on a Friday night then" Scotty chuckled. "To be sure, I'll be the next foreman in the shop." We all chuckled. The younger apprentices looked at me. "I'll tell yer later" I said quietly. Once I'd told them what I knew, I would need their help.

When Caggy turned up at about 10 o'clock, Smarty rushed to meet him before he had even had chance to light up. I was working just outside the office.

"Need both of them out of the factory today" Caggy said. "Don't want the gaffers to see 'em in the morning."

"Yes Tom" Ted replied.

"You OK driving the small three-ton lorry?" Caggy asked. Smarty nodded. "Put the keys back in my office." He was away home to wait the arrival of his lamp-post.

"How are you going to get it out of the factory?" asked Doug. Ray, Ken and Mickey Madden looked expectantly at me for an answer. I'd told the young apprentices about Ted Smart, Mickey already knew the history and I had just told them about my plan to steal his lamp-post.

"We'll hide it somewhere in the factory" I said. Mickey agreed.

"What if someone sees us?" asked Ray.

"They'll look the other way. Nobody likes the bloke," said Mickey.

"And we'll wait till everyone's clocked out" I added, in hope rather than confidence.

It was just after 12 when Bert and Ted carried Caggy's lamp-post out of the Fitting Shop, down the corridor and carefully up the stairs past the Security Office. The big silver cup was still on display. Bro. Hall didn't take it away for a week.

Because I was interested in future plans, I was watching as they loaded it on to the small drop sided vehicle. There was a sharp crack, followed by the sound of breaking glass and a curse. "Bollocks" said a voice. I disappeared back into the shop.

Five minutes later, Bert and Ted returned. One of the ornate panes of glass had broken. It didn't take long to replace, and with the top of the lamp-post suitably protected with sacking they carried it out again. It was a quarter to one, and everybody was washing their hands before clocking out.

As we queued up to clock out I estimated that it would take Ted and Bert about an hour to drive to Caggy's house in Sheldon and back again to pick up Smarty's lamp-post.

After we had clocked out, the four of us split up and agreed to meet up back in the Blacksmith Shop in 10 minutes' time. That would be plenty of time for the factory to clear.

I'd decided the best place to hide the lamp-post was in the cellar under the Casting Shop. It was a huge area. The roof was only about four feet high and it had no lighting. I'd been down there many times with a torch. Mickey Madden agreed. The only snag was that we couldn't carry the bloody thing along Adderley Street in broad daylight. We would have to go through the factory, and that was a right bloody trek - across the Wire Mill and then across the canal bridge, down a flight of stairs into the Britannia Mill and up another flight of stairs into the Casting Shop. Still, there were four of us.

"What the fuck are you lot up to?" We had just arrived in the Casting Shop and were 10 yards away from the entrance to the cellar when Johnny Price looked out of his office window. He listened to the tale, his smile growing wider and wider. "I done my National Service for two years in the late 50s and I don't mind admitting I was fucking glad I'd missed the war" he said. He picked up the phone, which had an outside line. "But that bloke Smarty is a right bastard. I can't believe he can hold his head up."

He offered everybody a cigarette and we all lit up. "Can you keep yer traps shut?" he said. "Yes John" we all replied. He replaced the phone and took a long drag. "That lamp-post will look a treat in my back garden."

"Yes John" we all replied.

Ten minutes later a flatbed lorry arrived at the gate in Glover Street. "Come to collect a lamp-post for Mr. Smart" The driver announced to the security guard. Pricey gave his nod of approval. Job done.

I'd have loved to have seen the expression on Ted's face when he walked into the Fitting Shop to collect his lamp-post, but I was having a pint with Arthur in the bar of the Waggon. I'd just made it before last orders. After that the gaffer locked you in the pub, but I'd be away before then.

"Working a bit of extra overtime today then, Steve," said Arthur with a twinkle in his eye, nudging his mate John the Blacksmith gently in the ribs.

I quickly looked at both of them. "I was having a chat with some of the football team about the game yesterday" I replied.

"You boyos did well," said the old Blacksmith. "I'm surprised you all had the energy to come to work this Sunday morning, let alone carry a big heavy cast iron weight half the length of the factory." I laughed and got to my feet. "My wife's got the dinner on," I said, draining my pint. "See you Tuesday morning." I was at College the following day.

While I was having a quick pee in the outside gents before driving home to Yardley Wood, I could hear raucous laughter coming from the lounge next door. Carefully opening the door, I stood just outside listening. A large group of blokes, some from the factory, and some tough-looking geezers were standing at the bar.

Pricey was in his element. "I'll tell yer another thing." He downed his whiskey in one. "All the goalposts at the Delta Sports Ground are being

313

replaced by fucking lamp posts so the Dago bastards can practise in the dark." The room erupted.

I quietly closed the door and drove home to my roast beef.

The City & Guilds Production Engineering Technician's course was not easy. While I was enjoying it, it meant a lot more home studying. I'd guess the other apprentices were on the staff, so they didn't have to work overtime to make up their wages. Weekends could be devoted to revision and study. Most of my weekends were taken up with earning. That was my choice, and I wasn't complaining.

"Exams next week then, Steve" said Ron Smith from Wards as we sat down to our evening meal in the canteen at South Birmingham Polytechnic. I'd been there since nine o'clock that morning, and after eating our tea we would continue with our studies until nine that night. Ron was the same as me. We took our studies seriously and helped each other along when and where we could.

"Bloody hell!" he exclaimed. "You've had a busy weekend." He paused. "And had a good laugh as well."

"You're right mate" I replied. "But now I've got seven nights of revision before the exam, and I'll do it."

We put our plates back on the counter, collected our briefcases and proceeded to the next lesson. Yes — I had finally chucked my rucksack away. I was moving up in the world.

The following morning I arrived at the factory early. The sun was shining as I walked across Adderley Street from the car park and headed towards the Security Office and the main entrance to the works. I stopped to light up a cigarette. Loud voices were coming from Mr Cadwallander's office.

"I'm telling yer, some bastard has stolen my property from the factory and I'm reporting this matter to you as Senior Security Officer!" Ted Smart was ranting. I had plenty of time before clocking in, so I leaned against the wall outside, thinking I would enjoy my fag in the sunshine.

Sergeant Cadwallander was ex-Army, and proudly wore the three stripes he had earned the hard way during the war. The row of coloured ribbons above his left breast pocket quietly spoke volumes. He was also a pal of Billy Little, and they occasionally had a drink together.

"Well, what are yer going to do about it?" Smarty angrily demanded.

"If you'll calm down I'll fill in the form reporting a theft" said Cadwallander quietly. "Now then, first can you tell me what's missing?"

As I stood there in the sunshine, the penny dropped. The old sergeant was slowly and very deliberately taking the piss. I wondered how long it would take Smarty to suss it.

Asking Smarty his full name, clock number and the department he worked in, Cadwallander finally recorded the fact that a lamp post belonging to Mr Edward Smart, clock number 315, had been purloined from the factory some time between 1 pm and 2 pm on Sunday. "I'll just get you to countersign this report Ted, and I'll make sure it gets to the appropriate authority as soon as possible" he said.

Smarty was getting mad. "You were here on duty yesterday. You must have seen the bastards, unless you were asleep." I winced.

Cadwallander calmly continued. "The log on Saturday shows two lamp posts delivered at 1.25 pm. The log for yesterday shows two lamp posts left the factory, one at 12.30 pm and the other 15 minutes later at 12.45 pm." He paused. "Both items in question were carried by…" a small pause. "Ah yes – a Mr Edward Smart and a Mr Albert Thompson."

"Yes – no - that was the same lamp post. Mine was still down in the shop," Smarty spluttered.

"I'm sorry Mr Smart, but I have work to do," said the old sergeant. I rushed down the stairs and clocked in.

Sitting in the dining room, supping my tea and cadging a look at Bob Brown's Daily Mirror, I glanced at the other apprentices who had helped me. They were all grinning. The large double wooden doors that opened into the Wire Mill from the Fitting Shop were rolled back. Casey, the big Irish fitter from the Britannia Mill, strode into the shop, followed by the sound of the Wire Mill in full song.

"I'm leaning on a lamp post at the corner of the street in case a certain little lady goes by, oh me, oh my, I hope that certain little lady goes by..." George Formby would have been right proud. Everybody was pissing themselves.

"How did you do it?" Pat Dowling asked me. I was working on the Dean Smith outside Joe and Caggy's Office. "Do what?" I asked him. He studied my face for a second. "You'd mek a fucking good Paddy you would, to be sure," he said. We both smiled. "It weren't a bad craic, was it?" I asked.

Before he could answer me, we both looked over our shoulders towards Caggy's office. He was going ballistic at Ted Smart. Even with the door shut, all the shop could hear Caggy shouting.

"Yer stupid bastard! Don't yer realize everybody in the factory knows about my fucking lamp post now! The gaffers upstairs, every fucker! Yow was supposed to keep it quiet and get 'em out on Sunday." Caggy stopped for breath and shook his head. "Yer've even started an official enquiry. Jesus Christ, man!"

Pat and I looked at each other as Scotty joined us. "Tommy Rushton and one of the directors wanted one of them fucking lamp posts. You've cost me my fucking job, yer prat." Caggy was still ranting when Smarty walked out.

"I reckon Caggy will have to buy his own beer now on Friday nights. What d'yer think Pat?" I said.

"I think yer might be right, Steve" he replied.

"Smarty's promotion has probably been put on hold an' all" Scotty said. "And his garden will be a bit dark."

Everywhere in the factory that Smarty went after that, George Formby was there waiting for him, leaning on a lamp post. The craic lasted a week. The World Cup started then.

"Gwen and Mick have invited us around to see the new house they've bought in Kingsbury on Saturday night" said Pauline. "She rang me at work today." We were sitting in our flat in Chilton Road watching TV. "What do you think, Steve?"

"Sounds like a good idea" I replied. "I've spent a lot of time on Kingsbury Ranges. I'll show you where I used to shoot."

Mickey Plant was a first-class turner who had left Delta Wire about two years before to join a contract toolroom on much more money. He was five years older than me, not tall but good looking, with thinning blonde hair and blue eyes. He looked like Ilya Kuryakin from The Man from Uncle. We had been out many times as a foursome, even sharing a week's holiday on a caravan park in Ilfracombe. They were good friends.

As I drove over the small narrow stone bridge that spanned the river I was surprised to see a new housing estate directly in front of me, along with two or three shops. It hadn't been there when I was shooting.

"Before we go to see Mick and Gwen, can I have a look at the Ranges?" I asked. A trip down memory lane, I thought to myself. Turning right, away from the village of Kingsbury, I drove half a mile and turned left into the narrow single-track lane.

I parked up and got out. It was seven o'clock on a summer evening and the sun was low but still warm. In my imagination I stood there just behind the 500-yard firing point, looking down the range at the targets. Crack – crack - crack... I felt the smooth, oily movement of the bolt ejecting the spent brass cartridge case and watched it tumble on to the grass. I imagined a new round being slotted into the breech and the shooter peering into the short telescope set up on a tripod to check his shot being marked. I could see Billy, Frank, me and Pete Cassidy lying there getting soaking wet. I could even hear Lt Croyer asking us if we wanted to be second AGAIN. Only five years had passed, but it seemed a lot longer. Now it seems a lifetime ago.

"You all right, Steve?" Pauline asked. "Yeah" I replied. "Lets go and see Mick and Gwen."

Turning into Mill Crescent and passing the shops on our left, we drove up the slight hill and saw the row of six brand new town houses, one with a red Mini Cooper on the drive. The up-and-over garage door was open, and Mick was just putting the car polish away.

"How's the old place going then, Steve?" We were sitting on a comfortable sofa in the lounge enjoying a cup of tea.

"It don't change mate. Old Joe sends his regards." I knew Mick had worked on the chargehand's pride and joy. "He even lets me on the Dean Smith now." We both smiled.

"Let me show you round," said Gwen, putting her cup on the coffee table and leading us out into the hall. "Kitchen's here." I saw Pauline's face light up as her eyes swept the large kitchen with brand new units along the one wall, the fridge, the sink underneath the window looking out on to the front garden and drive. A twin-tub washing machine completed the picture.

"Gwen, it's really lovely," said Pauline, looking over her shoulder. I think her feet were glued to the tiles on the floor, but Gwen was already halfway up the stairs.

"Bathroom here, with airing cupboard" Gwen continued as we strolled around upstairs inspecting each of the three bedrooms. Pauline's expression was a picture as we all descended the stairs.

"It's a lovely house mate, you've done well." I was sitting with Mick in the lounge, the girls in the kitchen nattering. "Do you mind if I ask..." Mick interrupted. "No need to ask. I'll tell yer." He chucked a cigarette across to me and we both lit up.

"Three thousand three hundred quid for the house, but that don't include kitchen units or carpets," Mick said, looking down at the bare floorboards. "Gwen wanted the kitchen sorted first." We both smiled and nodded. "The mortgage people wanted a 10% deposit and the rest over 25 years, and they took a proportion of Gwen's wages into consideration."

"25 years, 'kin 'ell Mick!" I said. He shrugged and smiled. "That's the usual mortgage term." I was learning.

We were approaching the Tyburn House before a word was spoken. Fifteen minutes of silent driving and thinking as the fields and countryside of the Kingsbury Road past by.

"Gwen told me that the sale of the house next door but one had fallen

318

through and the builder was putting it up for sale again" Pauline said, giving me a quick side glance before reverting her eyes to the approaching traffic island on the Chester Road.

"Better make an appointment with the building society then" I said as I changed down and drove around the island. 25 years seemed a hell of a long time. I'd be 45, an old man, before I'd paid it back.

Monday I was at South Birmingham Poly and we'd just finished the first three-hour exam. "How did you get on?" I asked, putting my cup of tea down. I was sitting with Paul and Ken, two apprentices from Cadburys, and Ron from Wards, having a sandwich lunch in the Canteen. Our next exam was in half an hour's time. The general consensus was that we'd done OK. Another two exams today and three more tomorrow. But on a brighter note, England had reached the quarter finals of the World Cup.

Driving home from the Poly after three long and difficult exams, I thought to myself that it was a bloody good job I'd swotted up every night last week. I pulled into the car park of the Haven feeling I had deserved a pint. Pop was sitting in his usual chair in the corner of the bar. Carrying two pints of M&B Mild from the bar, I put one in front of him and took a welcome sup from the other.

He applied a flaming Swan Vesta to his pipe, lovingly puffed it and blew the smoke up towards the dark-stained ceiling. He shook the match out and slowly placed it into the painted M&B ashtray.

"Yer look as if yer've had a hard day Steve."

"Three exams, each three hours long" I replied. "I'm flipping tired." Not the other F-word – I had never sworn in front of my grandparents.

Pop continued contentedly puffing. "Yer know, I've never passed an exam." He took a sup, smiled and nudged his old pal sat next to him.

"That's cos yow've never sat an exam Jack, same as me" his mate replied with a toothless smile.

"Yer right, but I tell you what though Horace" said Pop, taking his pipe from his mouth. "The young lads today have a better chance than we did."

Horace slowly nodded, his face saddening. "They'll never see anything like the Somme, Jack."

My grandfather drained his glass. "I hope they never do Horace. Yer know my missus says I still have nightmares, but I can't remember."

"Another pint, Pop?" I said jumping up. I thought I had seen my grandfather have a funny turn once. Nan said it was because he had been wounded in the First World War and never regained consciousness until he woke up in a hospital in England two weeks later, with his mother and sister standing alongside his bed. Pop told Nan that he'd thought he had woken up in heaven, but changed his mind when he couldn't find his local.

"We'll have one more and then toddle off home" said Pop.

"I've booked an appointment for 12 noon Friday at the Nationwide Building Society" Pauline said as I sat down. "The lady said we both need to bring evidence of our earnings for the last three months and references from our employers."

We were sitting on our grey settee, drinking a mug of coffee in our lounge upstairs. We were of course extremely grateful for the start my grandparents had given us, but we were both wondering if we could buy that three-bedroom house with a bathroom upstairs, a beautiful kitchen and a garage. Would it still be for sale?

I had nine hours of exams to look forward the following day and £3300 to find. I still owed Nan £250 on the car. We had just over £300 savings in the building society...

"Steve, are you awake? Are you all right?"

Pauline led me back to bed. I'd been sleepwalking.

"Looking at both your current earnings and the fact that Mr Phillips will be receiving the skilled rate of pay in February, I'm fairly confident the Nationwide could advance you up to £2800." Mr Hawthorne, the mortgage consultant, paused and stroked his chin. Pauline and I glanced at each other.

"What would the repayments be?" I asked him nervously. He consulted his papers and looked up.

"Over a 25-year term that would be nineteen pounds fifteen shillings per calendar month. But the problem we have is that you can't legally purchase a house until you are 21 years of age." He glanced at our application form. "That's in eight months' time."

"But I'm 21" said Pauline

"Unfortunately building societies are not inclined to grant mortgages to a young woman as the leading name on the loan" Mr Hawthorne replied.

Our disappointment must have been obvious. "Listen" he said. "The best advice I can give you is for you both to come back in October and we'll make out a proper application. It usually takes about a month or so to process, so the funds would be available by the end of January next year. Continue your £25 per month savings in our Society, it will help your application. Good day to you."

We both sat in the car for a couple of minutes. "I can't see that house still being for sale in four or five months' time" Pauline said with a grimace. I agreed.

"Where yer watching the final then, Steve?" Doug asked. We were all enjoying our breakfast and reading our papers. Even I had bought one that morning. It wasn't every day England reached the World Cup Final.

It was Black Bat's 65th birthday and he and his mate Andy had joined us in the dining room. He even tipped a small drop of whisky into everybody's mug. "Happy birthday Alf!" We all chorused.

"Do you remember Mickey Plant, or had he left before you started?" I asked Doug.

"I remember him, he worked on your lathe" Doug replied.

"Well he's just bought a brand new 21-inch telly. He's invited a crowd of us round to watch the final. Bring yer own beer, but sandwiches laid on."

Doug's eyes opened in amazement. "A 21-inch telly? Bloody hell!"

"He must be doing all right then," Pat said. "I wonder how much they pay in them Contract Toolrooms?"

"Fifteen bob an hour basic," I said.

321

Black Bat spluttered into his mug. "Bit too much whisky in yer tea Alf?" Scotty enquired with a grin. "Fifteen shillings a fucking hour!" Alf went on, looking round at the other old craftsmen. "I've said it before, us old 'uns were all born 40 years too early." All the elderly blokes nodded in agreement.

With my seven-pint bumper can of Ansells' Bitter carefully wedged into the rear seat of the 1100, we drove over the narrow stone bridge and pulled up outside the showhouse in Kingsbury.

"Phase 1 is virtually completed," said the smartly dressed saleswoman, consulting a big wallchart. "There are four houses still unsold. Phase 2 will begin to be delivered in the spring of 1967." She introduced herself as June. We were sitting in the garage of the showhome, which had been furnished and was acting as a temporary Sales Office.

"We are interested in number 62 Mill Crescent," I said. She flicked through the papers on her desk. "I think that may be sold," she said. She studied her paperwork. "Anyway, let me take your details and I can ring you next week."

June patiently and carefully listened to our situation regarding the problem of us not being able to buy a house until I reached 21 years of age.

"We have the £500 deposit" I lied. "The Nationwide have tentatively agreed to our mortgage application, but it's been put on hold until the end of the year."

June made a note of Pauline's office telephone number. "I'll speak to my manager next week" she said. "I'm confident we can sort it out."

The other good news of the day was of course that England won the World Cup on Mickey Plant's super-duper 21-inch black-and-white television set. Germany played in white shirts, England in a sort of medium grey.

As Pauline drove us home to Yardley Wood, an idea began to germinate in my mind. Robbing a bank was out of the question - I didn't have a gun. Fitting a loose plate on a racehorse wasn't an option either, as I wasn't a blacksmith at the curragh and this wasn't the 1930s. Yet somehow we had to raise five hundred quid within the next six months. Pauline woke me up as we turned into Chilton Road.

"Can yer give Pat a hand this morning Steve, the Demag hoist above the pickling vats has packed up?" said Joe. Variety is the spice of life, I thought to myself. It was double time on a Sunday morning, and I'd clocked in at 7.15 am. I'd even bought a paper. The papers were full of England's win, and while the old 'uns and the Paddys didn't seem all that interested, all the apprentices were jumping up and down.

"What a brilliant game" someone said. "Ace" agreed Doug.

I looked up from my News of the World. "Nearly as good as our Cup Final" I said with a smile. "Yerrr." The young 'uns agreed.

"Come on shower, we've all got work to do." Joe strode out of his office.

The pickling vats were run by Herbert Danks and his son Oliver and the plant was in its own shop, just outside the Fitting Shop in the corner of the Wire Mill. During the process of cold drawing to reduce the diameter of the wire, the brass would work-harden and would have to be annealed (softened) before re-drawing, otherwise it would crack or break. After annealing, the coil of brass wire needed pickling in acid to open the pores prior to the next drawing process.

The plant consisted of four huge plastic tanks 20 feet long, five feet wide and four feet deep, running for 100 feet down the shop. An overhead Demag crane ran the length of the shop. The first tank held cold water, the second and third contained a mixture of 20% nitric acid and 80% sulphuric acid, and the final tank held hot water as a swill. The phosphor bronze jigs each held 10 coils of wire, which were lowered into each tank, immersed for three minutes, withdrawn and moved to the next tank.

The smell of chemicals hit you the minute you walked into the shop. It was just like sucking a very strong acid drop, the flavour of a metal tooth filling.

Herbert Danks was a small thin bloke in his late fifties with sharp, pinched features and thinning grey hair that looked as though it needed a bloody good anti-dandruff shampoo. His moustache and the front of his dark waistcoat were covered in brown snuff. His shoulders had a dusting of white flakes, as though he had just come in out of the snow.

He was sitting on a battered old car seat, bent over a gas ring with a frying-pan full of bacon in one hand and a pinch of snuff in the other.

"Might as well have an early breakfast," he said, sniffing up first one nostril then the other. He didn't notice the residue of fine brown powder which was gently settling on to the sizzling bacon along with the dandruff which was already cooking.

"Yow blokes fancy a sandwich?" he asked.

"No thanks Herbert" Pat and I quickly replied in unison. "Got to get on with the job, it's a breakdown," Pat added.

Manhandling long wooden planks across the tanks provided a working platform for Pat to gain access to the Demag hoist and rails. With me assisting, we managed to get the wheel off the shaft and remove the shear pin.

All conveyors and moving machinery have a shear pin. They are designed to break first if there's a problem, stopping the conveyor. Otherwise the machinery would continue running and literally smash itself to bits.

Not a comfortable working environment, I thought to myself, with the stink of chemicals and the fact that only a plank of wood was stopping me from falling into a bath of acid.

"Nearly as dangerous as Herbert's frying pan" I chuckled to Pat. "I'd sooner fall into the tank below" he replied.

"OK Herbert, it's sorted" said Pat as we sat down in the Danks' kitchen. Herbert and Oliver donned their long rubber aprons, wellington boots and rubber gloves that reached the elbow, and Pat and I lit up. I glanced into the frying pan. It was horrendous. There was congealed fat and the remains of who knows what. It should have been incinerated.

"Do yer know Bert Carrington wants us to work on a bit today, Dad?" said Oliver as he grabbed hold of the hanging control panel that operated the Demag hoist. Herbert nodded and sneezed into the frying pan.

"What shall we do about summat to eat?" Oliver asked.

"Got a few old sausages left over from last week?" said Herbert. "We could have a bit of a fry-up here son, and get paid double time an' all." Father and son nodded in agreement and went to work.

"Where are you going for your holidays, Steve?" Doug Smith asked. We were sitting round the dining table in the Fitting Shop. It was breakfast time on Saturday morning, and the factory had shut down the previous day for the annual two-week holiday (last week in July, first in August – the traditional Brummie fortnight). Maintenance departments had to work during the shutdown so that Production Machinery could have their annual service and repairs. It certainly suited me, because not only could I choose when I wanted to take my holiday, I earned a load extra on overtime. I always favoured a late holiday anyway.

"Not sure yet" I replied. "It'll be a cheap one anyway, because we're going to buy a house next year." I doubt if Doug heard my reply, because he was itching to get his own news out.

"A gang of us are going to Spain, last week in August," he said. All the apprentices looked up. "I'm going an' all" young Ray said. He was now 18. Doug was 19. I was beginning to feel like an old man.

"It's only thirty-nine quid and the place is full of dolly birds" Doug said, rubbing his hands together in gleeful anticipation.

"You'll have the shits for a week and come back with the pox, the fucking lot of yer" said Black Bat, a true romantic. All the old 'uns smiled and nodded.

"And yer hotel won't be finished" Greeny said with a laugh.

Pat and Scotty looked at Doug. "Yer'd do better coming to sunny Ireland" Pat said.

"Nah, it's hotter in Benidorm and there's more crumpet" Doug replied. I thought Ray's head would fall off his shoulders, he was so keen to agree with Doug.

"I know one old married man who won't be going to Spain with the lads chasing the colleens" Scotty said, digging me in the ribs. The stupendous news that I was buying a house didn't even register.

★ ★ ★ ★ ★ ★ ★ ★ ★

"I tell you where we could go for a week's holiday," I said. We were sitting in our lounge in Chilton Road watching the telly. Pauline looked up. "Auntie Mary's in Bournemouth." Auntie Mary was really my Great Uncle Norman's daughter and my Mom's cousin, but I'd been brought up to call older relations aunties or uncles as a term of respect. "It wouldn't cost much either."

Pauline nodded in agreement. Bournemouth also happened to be where the huge, new Loewy 2500-ton extrusion press was manufactured. I'll see if I can arrange a factory visit, I thought to myself.

So the last week in August we sunbathed in sunny Bournemouth, courtesy of Auntie Mary. Strolling along the cliff gardens and looking out to sea on a bright morning, we noticed a huge billboard outside the Winter Gardens: THE KINKS HERE TONIGHT. While the Kinks were no way a Mod group like the Small Faces or The Who, we both liked their music. After exchanging glances we bought tickets there and then.

"You both look a real pair of Mods" Auntie Mary said as we came down the stairs and walked into the lounge. "And stop calling me auntie, it makes me feel ancient." Mary was 35, a bit younger than my Mom. She had met and married her husband Peter 10 years before when working a summer season in one of the hotels.

Pauline had her hair cut in the short Mary Quant style and was wearing a mini dress that was just about decent. I was in my Mod burgundy suit, complete with stiff detachable cardboard collar and Slim Jim tie. We looked the business.

"Oh to be 20 again" Mary sighed, as her two young sons clambered up on to her lap. "Have a good time, and I hope they play Dedicated Follower of Fashion."

"Do you know where Mr Johnson is?" said a voice. Glancing sideways, I saw a middle-aged bloke looking directly at me. Pauline had gone to hang up her coat and I was standing in the foyer of the Winter Gardens, having a quick cigarette.

"No" I replied, thinking no mate, I don't know you or Mr Johnson.

"He won't like you smoking" the stranger said, and dashed off.

"He probably thought he knew you, or you've got a double," Pauline said after I'd told her about the stranger. I nodded, thinking to myself that whoever he was I liked his suit.

The Kinks arrived on stage over half an hour late, but within minutes the audience had forgiven them. We were treated to a fabulous show and yes, they did play Dedicated Follower of Fashion.

"I'll just pop to the loo," Pauline said as we joined the throng of fans leaving the auditorium. "I'll wait here" I replied, lighting up and leaning against the wall outside the Ladies.

"You shouldn't be hanging about here smoking, you should be in the main foyer." The same bloke had appeared again, He rushed past, leaving me shaking my head in disbelief.

We approached the foyer – and then both of us stopped dead and stared. Then Pauline grabbed hold of my arm and started chuckling. I don't know what the people around us thought, but within seconds we were both laughing our heads off.

On each side of the big glass-panelled main doors stood a commissionaire, dressed impeccably in an extremely smart burgundy suit. As he saw me, a brief look of puzzlement appeared on the face of the bloke who had spoken to me. Then I could see a smile of understanding as he slowly nodded his head.

"I'm sorry about the mix up, I thought you were one of the temporary blokes we got in for tonight's show," he said.

"No problems" I replied. "We've had a good laugh. Who's Mr Johnson, anyway?"

He dropped his voice. "See that prat over there with the carnation in his buttonhole?" I nodded. "He's the manager." We shook hands. "Nice suit" he said with a smile. We walked out into the night air.

I had an interesting morning's visit to the Loewy factory, where the new extrusion press was manufactured. I was well looked after by David Thompson, the engineer responsible for the installation and commissioning of the press in our Works. When the press was experiencing problems, David used to drive up to Birmingham in his Triumph Stag and stay for a couple of days while he sorted them out. He was a good-looking bloke in his late twenties, and the image he projected, the car and the job, impressed all the apprentices.

When we arrived home on the Sunday afternoon, our week's post was carefully laid out on my grandparents' table in the bay window. Exam results, I thought, as I recognised the buff A5 envelope sitting on the top of my pile. The previous four years I had passed every exam and completed the City & Guilds Craft Practice, but these were the first exam results from my new Production Engineering Technicians Course. My employer, now Delta Wire, had agreed to sponsor me for the next three years to attain this higher qualification. It would enable me, if I wished, to have letters after my name, provided I kept passing the exams.

"I'm going to the loo," I said, walking out of the kitchen door. "I'll put the kettle on," said Nan. Pop struck a Swan Vesta and proceeded to stoke up his pipe.

During the past year I felt I had grown up a bit. I was married, had a decent car and was saving up for a deposit to buy a house. The guys I met at PERA and the apprentices who were on the Technicians' Course had made me realise I needed higher qualifications if I wanted to achieve the goal I'd set myself – Works Manager.

Standing outside the kitchen door and looking down the garden towards the shed where I'd parked my motor bikes only two years before, I took a long drag and stubbed the nub end out in the coal bucket. 'Kin 'ell I thought. I walked back into the kitchen.

Three pairs of eyes were on me as I opened the envelope. I looked up and gave a sheepish grin.

First Class Pass.

CHAPTER 21

It was September 1966. I was five months away from completing my apprenticeship, with the holy grail of ten bob an hour getting closer and one month away from re-applying for a mortgage. I'd passed my recent exam and would be starting the next year's course in a week's time. I was first-choice goalkeeper for the Works now that Pricey had retired due to old age and injury. It was 7.15 in the morning and the sun was shining. I clocked in and jumped down the stairs two at a time.

The Benidorm brigade had returned all as pink as shrimps, and were showing their holiday snaps around the dining table.

"There were birds on the beach topless, showing their tits and everything." Young Ray and Doug couldn't get their news out fast enough. "And we pulled, an' all" Ray added. Some of the old 'uns looked up from their newspapers.

"The only thing you pulled was yer plonker," Greeny said. We all chuckled.

"Hope yer scrubbed yer cock after" Scotty said. "Them Spanish birds are full of the pox." Ray looked a bit worried. "Naw, these girls were all right, they came from West Bromwich." Everybody pissed themselves.

"Before you start work Steve, can you nip up to Jack Insall's office? He wants to see yer."

"Yes Joe" I replied, knocking the Dean Smith off. Jack's in early, I thought to myself as I climbed the stairs up to the main offices.

I knocked on the door. "Come in." Bro. Hall and Peter Williams, the apprentice supervisor, were sitting there. 'Kin 'ell, I thought. What's up?

Jack stubbed out his Senior Service in the glass ashtray on his desk and looked up. "Young Johnny Pearce is seriously ill. He's been in Selly Oak Hospital for nearly two weeks and is not yet out of danger." He looked at Bro. Hall and Peter.

"We're asking you as senior apprentice to inform the rest of the young lads in the factory and the other football players."

"He's only just 17" I said. "How can he be ill? Was it an accident?"

"Unfortunately he has contracted meningitis" said Peter. "It can be fatal."

I was stunned. As I walked back down the stairs to the factory I thought, there was I thinking to myself how life was all hunky dory. What a fucking shitter. Young Johnny had left full-time college in July and had worked in the factory for just four weeks, apart from his three-day trial at Manchester United.

Breakfast and lunch were a bit subdued. Johnny's friend and fellow apprentice from the same year, John Cashmore, was very quiet.

In the end Johnny Pearce survived, but it was two long months before he could return to work. His illness left him deaf in one ear, and while he was still the best player on the field at works football level and went on to manage the team, he had been cruelly robbed of the extraordinary speed and brilliant talent that should have taken him to the highest level in the game.

"What about a day's outing to see the lights at Blackpool?" I suggested. Everybody looked up from their newspapers, their tea mugs frozen in mid air.

"That sounds a good idea," Bob Brown said. "Yer know, I've never seen the lights, in fact I've never been to Blackpool."

"I tell yer what, it's a great place for a piss up," said Pat. I noticed even the old 'uns as well as the young lads were looking up in interest. "The biggest fairground in the country, and some of the best fish and chips an' all" said Doug. Dave and Les Green nodded in agreement.

"I'll sort out a price for a coach and see how much it'll cost us each" I said. "Men only?"

"Yerrrr!" was the unanimous reply.

"What's this about a coach trip to Blackpool then?" Pricey asked as I walked past his office in the Casting Shop. "I'm trying to sort out the price for a coach" I replied, leaning on the open door.

Pricey chucked me a cigarette. "I've heard its men only." I nodded. "Sure your new missus will let yer go?" Pricey winked at big Jim Cooper, the Casting Shop Superintendent.

"I'll be there" I replied, not realising the barney I was going to have with Pauline when the date of the trip was finalized.

"Put me down for at least four seats, it'll be good to have a day on the piss" Pricey called as I walked down the three steel steps from his office.

Tommy Carter, or Caggy as we all called him, had retired the previous week and he left extremely suddenly. He was over 65. He might have said his goodbyes to Joe Healy, but he didn't speak to any of the blokes in the Fitting Shop. He just hung up his brown cowgown and walked out of his office.

Caggy was always surly and dour and was not a popular foreman. Even at my tender age I could appreciate that a supervisor or manager could not be too familiar with his blokes, otherwise some of them would take the piss, but Caggy was a miserable bugger. I don't think too many were sad to see him go.

Walking into the shop from the Wire Mill, I could see Peter Williams, the Apprentice Supervisor, standing in what was now the office of Frank Nunn, Maintenance Superintendent. Through the window he was beckoning me in.

Frank Nunn had been transferred from one of the other Delta factories and had taken over from Caggy. This was Frank's first week, and we had only had a very brief chat when he introduced himself. He was tall, over 6 feet, 40-odd and slim with Brylcreemed dark hair parted to one side. My first impression was that he was not to be trusted. He seemed a bit too smarmy for me.

"Sit down Steve" Frank said, offering me a Senior Service. That's an improvement, I thought. Caggy only smoked Woodbines.

"Peter's been bringing me up to date with all the apprentices and their training schedules. As you're the senior apprentice I thought I would start with you." He looked down at something on his desk, presumably my training record.

"You've done well. I'll have to watch out for my job," he said smiling, or was it smirking?

Peter coughed slightly, as if clearing his throat. "I've got the date of the second Senior Apprentice Course at PERA" he said, looking at his notes.

"It's a week's residential as before, commencing next Monday. The last one is at the end of February next year."

I might be away for my birthday, I thought to myself. The brown stuff would hit the fan when the coach was booked for the Blackpool Trip, but I didn't know that yet.

"Before you go Steve, you'll be working in the Britannia Bar Mill starting the week after next. You haven't worked in there yet, have you?"

"No Frank" I replied. "Thanks for the dates of the course, Peter." I walked out of the office and closed the door.

"Yes Frank, No Frank, three bags full Frank!" A low-volume chant greeted me as I approached the dining table. I poured myself a mug of tea from the communal pot and sat down.

"Frank's cigarette" I said, putting on a Groucho Marx act as I lit up.

"Don't take some people long to get up the new superintendent's arse, does it" Scotty said, looking at the other blokes.

"Me old mate Frank, he's a great bloke he is," I said. "We're like that, we are." I crossed the first two fingers of my right hand and gave them a little shake. "He's even booked me on another free week's holiday in a posh hotel. I won't have a word said against him."

The young apprentices looked up. "Free beer again, Steve?" Ray asked. I nodded. "I'm taking my missus this time an' all."

Everybody smiled. It was only the craic. Pat and Scotty shook their heads in admiration.

"Yer should a bin a Paddy" Pat said with a grin. "I've had some fucking good teachers," I whispered in reply.

★ ★ ★ ★ ★ ★ ★ ★ ★ ★

"What d'yer think of the nun, then?" Arthur Twamley asked. He was operating the vertical Milling Machine that Billy Wiggins used to work. I was performing a difficult task of machining a half-inch keyway in the bore of a large cast-iron driving gear. Arthur's thumbs were playing up (he'd suffered from gout in his hands for years) and Joe the chargehand had given me the task on Arthur's shaping machine. He was still, in Arthur's words, bringing me on.

"He's all right. He told me I'm in the new Bar Mill next" I replied, carefully watching the small high-speed tool bit remove another 10 thou (0.010 ins) of crumbly cast-iron swarf.

External removal of metal on a shaping machine or planer involved the clapper box being loose and able to lift up as the return stroke travelled back across the cut. The clapper box would then snap back ready for the forward cutting stroke which would remove the metal. If you were internal shaping (usually a keyway) you locked the clapper box, because you were only winding the cut on in the vertical plane. There was no horizontal traverse. It was a bit tricky. I stopped the machine and chucked Arthur an Embassy. He nipped off the filter tip and lit up.

"I play dominoes with a bloke who's a fitter at Delta Rods in Cuckoo Road in Nechells" he said. "Frank Nunn was his foreman till he came here as Superintendent." Arthur took a drag and blew the smoke out of the corner of his mouth. "None of the blokes liked him."

I thought for a minute. "Nobody liked Caggy," I said. Arthur nodded in agreement. "Caggy was a right miserable bastard and a funny fucker an' all, but I tell yer what, yer knew where yer stood with him and he backed us up against the Gaffers upstairs." He shrugged. "This Frank bloke, I ain't sure."

I eased the clutch lever in and watched the tool bit move slowly forward to remove another 10 thousandths of an inch of cast iron.

I could understand Arthur's concern, and I would guess a lot of the old blokes in the Fitting Shop felt the same. Tommy Carter had been their foreman for 20-odd years. They might not have liked him, but in Arthur's words, you knew where you stood with Caggy. Where would they stand with a new superintendent who was keen to make an impression in his new job?

A few of them would be worried about 'gooin' down the road'. At least five men in the Fitting Shop were over retirement age. Billy Law was over 70. Joe Healy, my mentor, was 66, the same age as Arthur. Apart from a regular 43 hours per week, plus up to another 20 hours of overtime (Harry Hanson held the record of 100 hours worked in one week, but he had recently died), all these blokes had to look forward to was the state pension. No houses to sell or inherit and no private or company pensions to look forward to, not in the 1960s. Not for these workers anyway.

Pauline was catching the bus to her Mom's tonight. "Fancy a pint when we knock off?" I asked. Arthur nodded in reply.

I'd be 21 in February. By the time I was 24 all the old craftsmen who had helped me to learn my trade would have been forced to retire, or in their words, go down the road – Arthur Twamley, Joe Healy, Billy Law, Alf George, Bonehead, Leo the Pole. Looking back after 45 years, I suppose it's called progress. In fact that's why we apprentices were taken on in the first place – to replace these guys. It didn't mean a thing to me then because I was young and had the world at my feet, but as I write this story I'm close to tears.

Before the week ended I had the only date available, at such short notice, for a coach trip to Blackpool. Pauline would not be amused.

"I don't mind the week away at PERA, I can understand and accept that," she said. We were sitting in our lounge, and she was having a right old go. "But a men-only trip to Blackpool on the day before our first wedding anniversary? Surely you can change it so we can go out on the Saturday night. And why do you have to go anyway?"

I'd tried frantically to arrange another date, but Saturday October 15 appeared to suit everybody from the football team to Uncle Tom Cobbley. In any case all the coach firms I'd tried were fully booked until the first Saturday in November. I had only found this one because of a cancellation.

"I've got to go because I've organized it" I replied weakly, thinking of the gigantic piss-taking I'd get if I didn't go. I'd have to be hospitalised for an alibi, and if Pauline didn't calm down, I would be. On and on she went, her voice slowly rising in volume. But what could I say? I just kept quiet and waited for the tirade to subside. It didn't end until she had walked out of the room, slamming the door loudly behind her. I think I heard her say, "I'm off to bed", but I couldn't be sure. My ears were ringing too much.

I sat looking at our little rented black-and-white TV and finished my coffee. I know what Harry Fisher would have said.

Before I set off to PERA the following day all was, almost, forgiven. I was booked into a hotel in Grantham this time and I arrived about 5 pm on the Sunday. The new car radio in the 1100 was working great. My Nan had treated me to it. "Can't see yer driving all that way without a wireless for a bit of company."

The second week was similar to the first course, maybe a bit more intense and more strictly marked, but we all did reasonably well. As we had been promised the last time we met, the highlight of the course was to be the last night out on St John Temple-Fry.

"You saved my bacon and my E-Type," he announced, slapping me soundly on the back as he ordered the champagne. "Left the Jag at home this week. Too small for a party, so I've got the Roller. What d'you say Blue?" I smiled and nodded in agreement. He still favoured the outlandish shirts and wide red braces, but he now sported a moustache. "Got to look a bit older, don't yer know, now the old man's made me a Managing Director." He paused as he handed out the cigars. "Don't slack with the shampoo you buggers" he roared. "We've got an empty bottle here."

When I had first met St John I had thought he was a prat. Now I felt he was a great character, a real one-off.

I can't remember much of that night. I vaguely recall being helped out of a huge car that smelt like a posh furniture shop specialising in leather.

I woke up fully dressed on my bed, with the phone ringing.

"Morning call Mr Phillips, it's 7 o'clock."

I left Grantham early on the Friday afternoon and it was just 5.30 when I turned off the Coventry Road at the Swan. As I passed the Speedwell in Stockfield Road I noticed a large sign on the main double front doors - BAR

STAFF REQUIRED. I did a quick U-turn in a break in the dual carriageway and pulled into the car park.

"Ever worked behind the bar before?" Jack Walker was a good six foot, if not more, with a huge barrel chest and shoulders to match. He was in his late forties and his once blonde hair was tinged with grey. "No Jack." I replied.

"Are yer working?"

"I'm serving my apprenticeship in engineering" I replied. He tilted his head in thought.

"Why do yer want to work in a pub then?"

"We want to buy a house and we need to save five hundred quid in the next six months" I blurted out.

Jack relaxed against the bar and folded his arms across his chest. "What yer think, Doris?" Mrs Walker looked me straight in the eyes.

"What does yer missus do?"

"Secretary to the Export Manager at Wilmot Breeden."

"Can she pull a pint?"

"Not yet."

She smiled. "Can yer both call in tomorrow before we shut?" She looked at her husband. Jack nodded. "Before half two" he added.

Following the Saturday afternoon interview at the Speedwell (I'd been to work on the morning to pick up my wages as well as earn time and a half), we'd had a night out at the Reservoir in Earlswood. It wasn't the 'in place' by any stretch of the imagination, but quite a few of our friends went there on a Saturday night because it was a good night out.

"We could probably save an extra forty quid a month if we worked in the pub" I said to Pauline. We were back in our flat sipping a late-night coffee. "What d'yer think?"

Pauline slowly nodded her head. "If we pay your Nan back for the car we'll still have over £100. We've been saving £25 pounds a month and I guess we could increase that if we don't go out." I nodded again and took a deep breath. "I think we could save nearly £100 a month. By February that'll give us over £600."

"I'll book another appointment with the building society, then" she said, putting her empty cup on the table. She stood up. "I wonder if that house in Kingsbury is still for sale?"

Just before I dropped off to sleep I thought of a way of saving another thirty bob a week. But then what would I do with my Ronson gas cigarette lighter?

Still – Sunday in the morning, and that's double time.

As I drove home on the Monday night from South Birmingham Poly I reflected that I would have to catch up on the college work I had missed the previous week due to the PERA course, but I wasn't unduly worried about that. What I was really concerned about was my first night behind the bar of the Speedwell. I'd clocked out at 5.30 pm and we had arrived home just after six. A quick meal and I was on the way to the Speedwell, arriving just before my starting time of 7.30.

I slipped out of my jacket and hung it up on a row of hooks down the far end of the bar, next to the door that led up to Jack and Doris Walker's private living quarters. Jack insisted all the barmen wore collars and ties and short white jackets. The tie was either red or blue and had the M&B emblem on it, and the jacket had the same emblem on the left breast pocket.

Suitably attired, I stood for the first time behind the bar. There were 50 pairs of eyes staring at me, and I felt as nervous as a kitten.

"Whether it's one pint or six, you use a tray to hold the glasses on when you're pouring the beer. I won't have bar staff walking up and down this side of the bar dripping ale all over the floor" Jack said, placing two empty pint glasses on a red metal M&B tray. His beefy fist grabbed hold of the 18-inch long pump and pulled sharply. "The first pull should be full to the stop, and it'll drop half a pint." He expertly demonstrated the technique. "Then you repeat the process on the next glass and the next." He looked up and I nodded. "Then yer top em up by gradually shorter pulls." He produced two perfect pints of mild, with a good foaming head on each. The dark ale slowly dribbled down the glass into the tray.

"Any beer spills in the tray, yer tip in that bucket" he whispered.

He placed the tray on the bar. "That'll be three and six please, Ken."

Turning back towards the till, he spread his huge hands across the typewriter keys and depressed the three shillings key and the sixpence key. The tray of cash sprang out. He placed the two two–bob coins the customer had given him on the small shelf above the tray. "This is important, Steve" he said. "Three and six was the bill." He took out a sixpence. "That's four shillings then, ain't it?"

I nodded. "You count the change back out of the till, then?" I said.

"Right. Now, let's see if you can pour a decent pint." He lifted the tray and carefully poured the spilt beer into a stainless steel bucket tucked under the bar next to the washing–up sink.

I just about coped. It was a Tuesday night, so the pub was not particularly busy and I didn't have any complicated orders. If I'd had anything more difficult than pints of mild or bitter to serve I think I'd have packed it in there and then.

"Yer've done all right," said Jack. "What do yer want for yer staff drink?" I removed my white jacket. "Half of bitter please" I replied.

I turned into Chilton Road just after 11.30 pm. I hadn't had a cigarette all day.

I described the old Bar Mill in chapter 4. It was the place where I'd started getting my hands dirty just over four years before, on the other side of Adderley Street behind the canteen and snooker room. The old 1500-ton extrusion press had been dismantled and the draw benches had fallen into disrepair. The Die Shop had been transferred to the main works two years before. The new Bar/Rod Mill had been purpose-built when the Britannia Extrusion Press had been installed five years before and contained four Schumag draw benches, each capable of cold-drawing brass rod up to two inches in diameter and 30 feet in length.

The 2500-ton extrusion press could produce either twin coils of red-hot brass wire for subsequent cold drawing in the Wire Mill across the canal or one long red-hot bar. This bar of brass would be squeezed through a tungsten

338

carbide die, just like a line of toothpaste. A bloke, usually stripped to the waist, would grab hold of the glowing metal with steel tongs and walk or run the length of the track guiding the extruded rod. The rod would be cut to length and the bloke would walk swiftly back to await the next extrusion. It was bloody hard collar.

Charlie Colley, the old Britannia Mill foreman, had retired six months before at the time when Delta Wire had taken over the factory. The two press drivers, Harry Smith and Harry Harcourt, had been promoted to Superintendent and Foreman respectively of the whole Britannia Mill, encompassing the 2500-ton press, the draw benches and the state-of-the-art automatic rod storing system. Sid Payne was the chargehand.

"Any seats left on the Blackpool trip, Steve?" Sid asked, looking up from his Daily Mirror. We were sitting in the main production office in the Bar Mill finishing our early morning tea. He was a small slender bloke with thinning white hair scraped back, and he was always on the go. In those days there were no formal inspection techniques. It would be another 25 years before the Japanese would teach us about SPC (Statistical Process Control), so the checking of size and quality was generally left to the chargehands. Sid was renowned for measuring the diameter of every bar or rod of brass that came off his beloved Schumag draw benches.

"I think there's about five seats left, but Pricey wants them to store the crates of beer on. I'll let you know later" I replied as we stood up.

"Come on then Steve, let's get cracking." He handed me a two-inch micrometer and rushed out of the office.

The long lengths of brass bar were in strong supporting racks lifted out by small localized Demag hoists. The operator would position one end of the bar into the pointing machine, which acted like a huge rotary pencil sharpener. The tungsten carbide cutters would literally point the end, which in turn would be inserted in the highly-polished tungsten carbide drawing die. Two massive gripping dogs would then be clamped to the bar and the machine would slowly pull the metal through, imparting a bright, shiny finish and size accurate to plus or minus 0.001 inches (one thousandth of an inch). It was a cold process, as opposed to hot extrusion.

The die had been sized and polished in the Die Shop, but Sid always checked. "What d'yer mek it, Steve?" he asked as I carefully eased the micrometer off the finished diameter. "1.750 inches" I replied.

"Can I just double-check?" he asked. It was his responsibility, after all. He nodded. "Bang on. They told us yer knew what yer were doing."

I smiled. "Thanks Sid."

I had just finished helping Bernard, one of the drawers, place a finished rod in the racks when I felt a light tap on my shoulder and heard a familiar voice.

"D'yer want a sandwich for yer breakfast, Steve?" I turned to see Eric Barnfield standing there with a large cardboard box in his hands. Everybody called him Clubby, because he had one leg shorter than the other and had to wear a built-up boot. Eric had been the muffle man working in the cellar under the old press, and when the plant shut down he'd been transferred to the new shop as labourer. He was great old bloke who had helped me when I first started work in the old Bar Mill. I always said hello when we passed, but I hadn't seen him for ages.

"Me old Mom died less than a month ago and it knocked me about a bit," said Eric. He paused and wiped his nose on the sleeve of his overall. "Then the council said I had to move out of the house, cos it had two bedrooms." He sniffed again. "I was born in that house, both me dad and me Mom died there an' all, but they said I'd got to be rehoused to a one-bedroom flat." He shrugged in resignation. "Can't do nothing can I? And I'm 65 soon. I don't how I'll manage."

"How's the cats?" I asked, thinking it might brighten him up. It worked. His old blue eyes lit up.

"Harcourt giz me half an hour every morning to nip across to the old cellar and feed 'em, there must be over a dozen" he chuckled. "But I have to carry me broom and shovel when I cross the road just in case one of the big gaffers sees me."

I smiled to myself, wondering what the new Delta régime would make of that. I bet even Ian Watson, the Managing Director, would agree it was cheaper than bringing in Rentokil to keep the rats down.

"Come on Clubby, it'll be fucking dinner time soon" Harcourt shouted. He wasn't a bad foreman. I'd heard that he and Harry Smith gave Clubby a couple of bob each week to help with the cat food, but it must still be costing the old labourer a pound a week of his own hard-earned cash.

With my order of 'sos and tom' scribbled in his notebook, Clubby set off as fast as his six-inch built-up wooden boot would allow.

* * * * * * * * * *

I'd done three nights in the Speedwell, and was beginning to enjoy it. It wasn't easy to come home from a full-time job in the factory, have a meal and then set off to work again, but by half eight you had the blokes who were on the 10 pm to 6 am shift calling in for a couple of pints before they started work, so the time went by quickly.

I arranged with Jack Walker to work six nights a week (Mondays I was at the Poly until nine). Pauline would work Friday, Saturday and Sunday nights. He was also aware I couldn't work the next night because I was going to Blackpool.

"You nervous?" I asked Pauline as we drew up in the Speedwell car park. "Not really" she replied, getting out of the 1100. "By the way, I forgot to tell you - 62 Mill Crescent is still for sale."

"Better fix up a meeting with that woman at the showhouse in Kingsbury then" I said with a smile.

"I have, Sunday afternoon."

"What about the Building Society?"

"4.30 on Tuesday." She grinned. "Best start work then." We walked into the bar.

The café in Watery Lane was absolutely packed. I had warned Jeff and his missus that a couple of blokes might want a bit of a sandwich earlier than usual on Saturday morning because we'd organized a coach trip to Blackpool. But blokes were queueing up outside – it was heaving.

Pat Dowling worked part-time in the Rainbow on the corner of Adderley Street and Digbeth and he'd arranged on a sale-or-return basis enough crates of beer to sink a ship. So at eight o'clock, with virtually a full coach at two quid a head, we set off for the seaside.

"When are we stopping for a piss then?" Pricey asked. He was standing in the aisle, supporting himself against the gentle swaying of the coach, a bottle of beer firmly grasped in his hand. I was sitting up near the front with Dave Wilmer, enjoying a drink as the pleasant Cheshire countryside slipped by. Looking at the sky, it promised to be a fine day.

"We'll be stopping at Charnock Richard Service Station in about 10 minutes" the driver said over his shoulder. From my seat I had noticed a length of two-by-two timber wedged alongside the driver's right leg, keeping the accelerator pedal pressed hard to the floor. Cruise control hadn't been invented in 1966.

"We have a 20-minute break, ladies and – er – sorry, gentlemen. Goo and have yer piss and I'll see yer in a bit." The coach driver lit up a fag and turned off the microphone. Everybody tumbled off the coach.

Strolling back from the loo I could see Pat Dowling struggling. "Do you want a hand, Pat?" I asked. He was carrying the crates of empty bottles down the steps of the coach.

"There's another three still in the aisle" he replied, disappearing round to the huge boot at the back.

"That's seven crates of empties, and it ain't half ten yet" I said.

"Got some thirsty boyos on board, but they'll slow down a bit on the way back" Pat replied, heaving another full crate out of the boot.

"I can see the Tower!" cried young Ray.

"And the Big Dipper" Doug joined in. "I'm on that first." He leaned over the seat in front of him and slapped the other young apprentices on the shoulders. Even the old 'uns were stretching up from their seats to catch a glimpse of the famous Tower.

The friendly banter and piss-taking had gradually increased in volume as we had turned off the M6 (it only went as far as Preston) and took the main road towards Blackpool. I looked back down the aisle of the coach to see everybody smiling and having a laugh. No wonder, I thought to myself. There were another five empty crates of beer stacked up.

"Had me first shag up here" said Black Bat. The old grinder was sitting next to his pal Andy, enjoying a cup of whisky-laced tea from a flask. Andy looked up, along with about another 10 blokes. I nudged Dave, but he was already listening.

"When was that Alf?" asked Andy. Black Bat took his pipe out of his mouth and with a faraway look on his face stroked his chin.

"Last week, were it Alf?" Les Green shouted. Everybody roared.

"Ill tell yer when it was. I was an apprentice and the gaffer of the factory had laid on a charabanc trip to celebrate the end of the Great War."

Black Bat had been too young for the First World War and too old to be called up for the Second World War, but it didn't stop him as an ARP walking into a blazing house and rescuing a mother and her three kids during the bombing of Birmingham in 1940.

"She worked as a barmaid in her father's pub down one of the back streets off the front, near the North Pier." He slowly shook his head. "Can't think of the name of the pub, but I reckon I can find it." He struck a match and got his pipe going. We were all listening intently. Black Bat might have been a miserable old bastard, but two years before I had worked closely with him for four months, and he had imparted an enormous amount of his craft to me. The sort of stuff you don't find in books. He was all right.

He took a pull on his pipe. "It was about three in the afternoon by the time she'd finished all the washing-up in the pub, and we'd arranged to meet round the corner. We had a lovely stroll down the front and I bought her a bag of chips an' all."

"Always the one for splashing out, Alf" Scotty said. There were chuckles. By this time half the coach was listening to the tale. Andy topped up Alf's mug with a drop more whisky.

"Our charabanc was unlocked and empty and I suggested we had a bit of rest after our stroll."

"Back seat job then, Alf?" Pat suggested.

Alf drained his mug and slightly cocked his head. "Them was the days."

"What was her name, Alf?" Andy asked.

A crafty smile came over Black Bat's face. "If she's still working behind the bar here I'll ask her." The coach shook with laughter.

"Gentlemen, we leave bang on midnight," said the driver. "One minute past and you're walking home. Mr Alf George has booked the back seat for an hour later this afternoon for a bit of a rest."

The driver turned off the microphone as we all tumbled down the steps into the massive coach park. There had to be over 100 coaches all lined up there. Dave voiced the same opinion. "Hope we can find it again" he said.

All the bars in the Tower Lounge shut at eleven o'clock, and as we all staggered out into the cool air the full impact of the lights made us stand and gaze in admiration. Trams were trundling past lit up as brightly rocket ships, sailing galleons and steam trains. It was a fabulous sight, with overhead Chinese lanterns swinging in the light breeze and every lamp-post adorned with an array of flashing bears and animals. Truly amazing.

* * * * * * * * * *

"Come on you lot, we've got half an hour to get back to the coach" I said, trying to organize the swaying gang. I felt like a sheepdog. The first chip shop slowed us down as we ordered 10 cod and chips. We were still moving in the right direction when we all noticed a big crowd hanging over the rails on the sea wall, hooting and hollering. Crossing the road and dodging the rattling trams, we joined the throng.

Ten feet below us on the sand, I could see a pair of shapely white knees pointing to the dark sky. One outstretched hand was clutching a white plastic handbag. The other held what looked like a bag of chips and a pair of knickers.

A fish-and-chip supper and a live show, what a day out, I thought. The crowd upped the tempo to match the action below.

"You all right, love?" a concerned voice shouted above the din. The lady on the sand looked up.

"Course I am yer prat, just tell him to hurry up, me chips are cold and if I miss the coach me husband'll kill me."

"It's ten past twelve. I've got to get cracking" the driver said, looking at his watch. Two blokes were still missing. I'd counted 50 on that morning and the driver had double-checked with me. I was a bit puddled now, but the driver had assured me that only 48 were so far on board. I looked out of the door.

Pricey stood swaying on the bottom step of the coach, trying to help 22-stone big Jim Cooper up the rest. "Did yer see the shag on the beach?" He took a step back and then lunged forward to push Jim up.

"Took short, had to have a shit" Pricey said as he slumped into his seat.

"Fifty on board then, Steve" I nodded to the driver.

I tiptoed up the stairs to our bedroom and crept into bed, glancing at my watch. I'd have to be up again in a couple of hours. Sunday morning was double time.

"62 Mill Crescent is still available" June said as Pauline and I sat down in the sales office in Kingsbury. It was Sunday afternoon, and I was feeling a bit tired.

"I've spoken to my manager, and we can put a reserve on the property for two weeks. We shall then require a holding deposit of £100 prior to your mortgage acceptance by the Nationwide. Would you like to view the property?"

Pauline was already halfway up Mill Crescent.

We left the Speedwell and pulled up in Chilton Road just before midnight.

I can have a bit of a lie-in tomorrow, I thought. It's Monday and I don't have to be at the Poly until nine o'clock. I was asleep before my head hit the pillow.

* * * * * * * * * *

The Britannia Mill ran almost the full length of Glover Street, with one large sloped entrance for access by articulated lorries halfway down and another entrance at the bottom near the very modern automatic racking system. A large modern toilet block ran the length of the back wall.

"The schedules come down from the Production Control office upstairs supposedly on a weekly basis. It's me and Harcourt's job to load each individual draw bench." Sid took a sup from his mug.

"But it's always being changed from one day to the next. Rush job this, rush job that. The blokes don't like it, cos it affects their piecework."

I nodded. "What does Harry Smith do?" I asked.

"Norra fucking lot. Na, Smithy's all right really. He can be a right bastard, but I tell yer summat, he looks after his blokes." He paused. "Look at old Clubby, worked for Smithy and Harcourt for donkey's years. There's no real need for him to work overtime, but Harcourt lets him so he's got a bit of extra money to feed his cats. I'll tell yer another tale an all." Sid liked a chat. "Yer know Dasher Murphy who works the Wagging Machine?"

I nodded, remembering I'd seen him washing his socks and underpants in the sink the other morning. Sean Murphy was a large red-haired man, 30-odd, who wore an old-fashioned bib-and-brace type overall. He was the hardest worker I'd ever seen. He didn't walk anywhere - he ran. Once the coil of extruded wire had cooled, and before it was transferred by overhead crane across the canal into the Wire Mill, it had to be tested for porosity. Sean would dash down the long lines of coils, jumping over some of them in his haste to get the job done. Using a pair of bolt cutters, he would cut off a length of wire about a foot long and clamp one end into the fixed vice on the wagging machine, with the other end clamped in the moving vice. When he pressed the start button the moving vice would wag backwards and forwards until the wire broke. Sean would then run down to the Production Office to show one of the supervisors the sheared ends. Any porosity in the wire would show like miniature bubbles in an Aero chocolate bar. Suspect coils were subjected to further investigation in the laboratory upstairs. I'd spent a couple of days working in there the previous year, operating the tensile testing machines and other bits of kit.

Sid offered me a cigarette. "Packed them up" I said proudly.

"Dasher got chucked out of his lodgings three days ago" Sid continued. "Smithy told him he could sleep in the factory till he was sorted." He glanced around.

"Don't spread it about, for fuck's sake."

"I won't" I replied.

I had realised some years before the power the shop-floor foreman and superintendents wielded, and no way could they be a soft touch. With the exception of Percy Hollingshead in the Die Shop, all these supervisors ruled their departments with rods of iron, swearing and bollocking their men up hill and down dale.

I was beginning to understand that most of the blokes on the factory floor respected authority. They wanted to know where they stood, and from what I could see these hard disciplinarians also looked after their men at the same time. Don't forget, this was the 1960s. If a foreman gave a bloke a bollocking it wouldn't bring the factory out on strike as it would today.

It wouldn't be too long though before the employment laws, disciplinary procedures, verbal and written warnings and a whole host of legislation would be on the Statute Book and in factory written rules. This had already started since the Delta Group had taken over, but in the meantime it was still a bit like the Wild West.

★ ★ ★ ★ ★ ★ ★ ★ ★ ★

"Please sit down," said Mr Hawthorne, the Mortgage Manager. "Would you like a cup of coffee?"

"Yes please" we both replied. We were sweating.

"Shan't be a moment" he said. He picked up the phone and asked his secretary to sort out three coffees. Then he opened a buff-coloured file and took out a mortgage application form.

"You've recently increased your savings with the Society" he said, looking at the papers on his desk and nodding approvingly. "Considerably so, well done." He studied the papers for another minute. It felt like an hour. The coffee arrived, but I was too nervous to pick my cup up.

"I've already had a chat with my superiors. Based on your current earnings Mrs Phillips, and yours Mr Phillips – especially in your case, you will receive a good rise in wages as a skilled man very shortly –"

The bloody telephone started to ring. "Excuse me a moment," he said. Two hours later (it was probably more like a minute) he replaced the phone.

"Ah yes" He smiled. "Let's get the application form filled in."

I glanced at Pauline. "Does that mean…?"

He nodded. "I don't see a problem." He paused to sip his coffee. "We won't rush this application because we have a month or so, but in due course you will receive an offer of the sum to be borrowed and you will need to return it on or immediately after your 21st birthday, with the acceptance form duly signed." I felt like shouting Hurrah.

"Have you got the £500 deposit yet?" he asked.

"We will have by February," I blurted out.

"I believe you will young man, I believe you will."

We danced out of the office, out of the building and all the way down New Street to where we'd parked the car. I didn't know when we'd be able to celebrate our good news because I was working seven days a week in the factory and six nights in the pub and doing one evening at night school, but it didn't matter - we were going to buy a house.

I was in the Bar Mill, helping Sid and the despatch chargehand where the new automatic bar storing rack was located. The racks went from floor to ceiling, stretching up 60 odd feet, and when you pressed the correct button in the control panel a complete rack of brass rod of a particular diameter, size, length and material specification would automatically be delivered to floor level. Then rods ready for loading on a lorry would be removed, or new rods and bars just manufactured would be loaded on to the rack and stored. It was a fancy bit of kit.

I'd got into the routine of getting home from work, having a quick meal and setting off to the Speedwell for another three or four hours pulling pints behind the bar. Once I was there I really enjoyed it, and at weekends Pauline would be with me.

I had found out why the spilt beer in the trays was saved in a bucket under the sink. "I only put it in the mild, it would upset the bitter too much" Jack told me. I never drank mild ale again.

I noticed how James, the full-time head barman and cellarman, would serve beer from the pumps in the bar but ring the price up in the till for the lounge or gents-only room. Those rooms charged an extra tuppence and threepence a pint. It was in Jack's interests to tell the brewery he had sold five barrels in the gents only and 10 in the bar, when in fact he had sold three barrels in the gents only and 12 in the bar. Each barrel was 45 gallons, so Jack would make an extra three quid a barrel. Again, it's not possible today.

Another thing that surprised me was that Jack put Pauline to work in the bar and not as I had expected in the posh lounge at the rear of the pub, which was only open on Friday, Saturday and Sunday nights anyway. His reasoning soon became obvious. Pauline would not stand for any rudeness or bad language. I couldn't believe it. Any effing and blinding and she wouldn't serve them. Great big blokes would apologise and even hold their hands out across the bar to be smacked. Within two weeks she'd introduced a swear box for one of the local children's charities. Again, times are different now, but in the 1960s most men respected a woman's presence. If a young barmaid tried that today in certain pubs, she'd probably get a glass in the face.

"I've watched you both now for a couple of weeks and I've regularly checked your tills." Jack gave a nervous cough. "I always do that with new staff." He sat down on his high seat behind the bar. Nobody dared sit on that seat apart from Doris his wife. "

"Did you notice that smartly-dressed bloke I was talking to tonight?" he said.

"I served him a half of bitter," replied Pauline.

"That's him" Jack replied. "He's my Area Manager. He's asked me to see if you're interested in joining M&B as trainee managers. You could be running your own pub in 12 months' time."

All the washing-up was done and we were having our staff drink. The rest of the staff were sitting in the lounge. It was somebody's birthday, and Jack had allowed a couple of people to be locked in.

"Think about it" said Jack. "Me and Doris think yer naturals. If yer know the wrinkles there's good money to be made." He winked.

It was after midnight by the time we both arrived home. It was tempting, but I knew what the answer was going to be.

"Hell of a bloody stink down there." I'd arrived in the Bar Mill Production office after a quick visit to the toilet and washing block down at the far end of the shop. Sid and Harry Harcourt looked up. "Yow ain't blocked the bog up have yer?" Harcourt said with a smile, nudging Sid. "These kids can't wipe their own arses today."

After nearly five years I was an experienced factory worker, fully qualified in taking the piss and just as importantly in receiving it.

"Turds ankle deep all over the floor and they're still coming out of the bogs like a volcano" I said with a straight and serious face.

Harcourt jumped out of his chair as though he'd been shot. "Fuck me, not again" he shouted, rushing out. "Clubby, get yer shovel!" Eric skipped behind him as fast as he could as they both charged down the shop. Harcourt gave me a wry smile when he returned.

"I s'pose I asked for that, yer young bugger."

"Yes Harry" I replied.

He turned to Sid. "It ain't too bad, but if it gets any worse we'll have to get it sorted" he said. He looked round the office. "Come on you fuckers, get cracking, we've all got work to do."

"Yes Harry!" we all shouted, rushing out of the office.

"And what the fuck are you doing Clubby, leaning on yer shovel and gorking? It ain't fucking Butlins Holiday Camp yer know." Eric skipped off as fast as he could, dragging his broom and shovel behind him. Foreman's authority and order restored, everybody knowing exactly where they stood.

The following Sunday afternoon we took my grandparents to see our new house in Kingsbury. I stopped off at the showhouse to pick up a key and parked outside number 62. I opened up our front door for the first time and we walked into the house. Pop nodded and puffed his pipe. Nan was almost in tears.

"You've both done so well! Haven't they Jack?" She dabbed her eyes. "Me and yer Nan always wanted to see yer get started. Yer've both done a treat."

He looked at the back garden, full of builder's rubbish and brick ends. "Got me another part-time job, by the looks of it."

Reluctantly we left the house and I locked the front door.

"Can we have a quick visit to Coleshill on the way back home?" my Nan asked. I knew she'd been born there. "Of course we can" I replied, helping them into the rear seats. I'd seen the house, but not for about 10 years. My Nan's mother, Granny Andrews, had died in the front bedroom in Chilton road which was currently our lounge. That was seven years after I was born in the same room - probably in the same bed.

As a young woman, Granny Andrews had fallen in love with the leader of a little Palm Court orchestra which had played tea dances in a hotel owned by her parents opposite the Accident Hospital. Returning many years later with two children in tow, she found her mother (my great-great-grandmother) had died in mysterious circumstances. She had fallen down the stairs and broken her neck. Her drunkard of a father had married again, to the woman who had been his housekeeper, so Granny was turned away destitute. This was 1889.

She was very lucky in her circumstances to find a position in service, and in 1895 she married Henry Andrews, a coachman in the service of a rich up-and-coming industrialist. My grandmother was born in 1903 in a small terraced tied cottage in Coleshill, not far from the river.

We found the house and I parked up and helped Nan and Pop out of the car. She stood still, not moving a single muscle. After looking at the front door and the upstairs window for a couple of minutes, she uttered a long sigh.

"63 years is a long time," she said. We all nodded in agreement.

"Come on Gladys, let's go home" said Pop.

After a late Sunday lunch Pauline and I set off to the Speedwell, hoping Jack would not be unduly bothered about us not wishing to consider a possible full-time career in pub management.

* * * * * * * * * *

I crossed the bridge over the canal from the Wire Mill and skipped down the stairs into the Britannia Mill. The huge 2500-ton extrusion press was working full pelt and the long cooling track full of coils of wire was creeping slowly down the shop. All the draw benches were busy.

The smell hit you in the face. It was bloody awful.

"Bogs are all blocked, I shouldn't go down there if I was you" Sid said as I walked into his office. "And shut the bloody door."

With all the office windows shut the smell was just about bearable, but every time someone opened the door the overpowering odour of foul sewage wafted in. I didn't even fancy a cup of tea. "What's happened?" I asked.

"When the new Casting Shop and the Britannia Mill were built about six years ago the old sewers in Adderley Street couldn't handle the increased load, so a new pipe was laid down the length of Glover Street" said Sid. He shook out a Woodbine and tapped the end on his desk. "Still off em?" I nodded.

"Have yer noticed that Glover Street runs downhill from Adderley Street?" Sid asked. He took a sup of his tea. "The dispatch area near the new racking system is the lowest part of the whole factory, and they built a huge holding tank or cesspit to collect all the sewage. When the level reaches a certain height a pump kicks in and literally pumps all the shit into another main sewer round the corner." He looked up as Clubby poked his head round the door.

"What yer having for breakfast Sid, the usual?" Sid nodded.

Clubby looked at me. "Nothing for me" I said quickly. I felt sick.

Clubby hurried out. "Shut the bloody door!" shouted Sid. Clubby returned and gently closed the door.

"Did yer see the state of old Clubby's wellington boots?" Harry Smith had walked into the office, followed by Harry Harcourt.

"He's been trying to clean the floor in the toilets. It's all backing up from the bogs," said Harcourt.

Smithy chuckled. "It looks as though he's bin paddling in it. Gerrim to clean up before he fetches the breakfast, otherwise they'll never let him in the café."

"The pump's packed up again then?" Sid said. It was more of a statement that a question.

The two supervisors nodded in agreement. "I rang him an hour ago, he'll be here in a bit" said Harcourt. Smithy stood up. As he opened the door he turned back to us. "And make sure the blokes don't waste too much time walking to the bogs in the Casting Shop, we've got a fucking shop to run here."

Sid looked at Harcourt and very slightly lifted his shoulders. Harcourt scratched the back of his neck and rose out of his chair.

"Can yer give Snotter a bit of a hand this morning Steve, I daren't spare anybody else the way Smithy's gooin' on" he said. I nodded, wondering who the hell Snotter was and what I'd let myself in for. I asked Sid.

"It's Harcourt's brother in law, comes from Darlaston" Sid explained. He started to laugh and shake his head. "His full title is Snotter the Shithole Diver."

I chuckled. "You serious Sid, or what?"

He coughed and laughed at the same time, wiping his nose with the back of his hand. "You'll find out in a bit," he said. Stretching up from his chair and looking out of the window. "He's stood outside talking to Smithy and Harcourt."

"This is my assistant, young Lenny" Snotter said as we walked down the Bar Mill towards the underground tank. "Me sister's eldest lad."

Snotter was a small wiry bloke with a crafty face, not much over 40. He looked as fit as a fiddle as he strode purposefully down the factory, his eyes flicking left to right as though he thought somebody was watching him. His jet-black hair and long sideburns suggested he was a big fan of Elvis. Young Lenny appeared to be about 17 and about the same height and build as his uncle. He wore a Beatle haircut like mine. While Snotter was dressed in an old dark blue boiler suit, his assistant was smartly turned out in a light blue roll-necked sweater and what looked like a brand new pair of jeans.

"Back the lorry in Lenny, and let's see what we've got" Snotter said as he fished two small T hooks out of his pockets. Inserting the hooks into the cast-iron manhole cover, he nodded to me to grab hold of one. We slowly lifted the cover up and slid it to one side.

The stench rose up and hit you in the face. It was full to the brim. The top looked like the crust of a nicely baked and browned apple crumble. The top rung of a steel access ladder fixed to the wall of the pit was just visible.

"Over 1000 gallons in there" said Snotter proudly. "I reckon four trips."

"How the bloody hell do you get that lot out?" I asked in amazement.

"The big firms roll up with a tanker and pump it out before they goo down and clean it all out." He paused to pop a Fisherman's Friend throat sweet into his mouth. "Trick of the trade, takes the taste away, yer want one?" I gratefully accepted.

"They charge a bloody fortune, and they don't do as good a job as I do neither."

"What about the pump?" I asked.

"Once it's all spotless and disinfected, I inspect the pump. Nine times out of 10 it's blocked with summat or other. I clear it out and away we goo. It's surprising what some folk shove down the lav." He grinned. "Most of our work is in the Black Country. There's hundreds of old factories there with sewer problems and it ain't everybody that'll do my job."

I nodded in agreement. "Can I have another sweet please?"

Parking up the tattered old flatbed lorry, Lenny dropped the tailgate and the two sides and proceeded to unload what appeared to be rubber suits. He carefully laid them on the floor.

"We'll have a spot of breakfast afore we start. It'll save a bit of time if yer can nip to the caff while me an Lenny get kitted up" Snotter said, handing me a couple of half-crowns. "Two bacon, egg and beans for us, and get yerself what yer want." I was grateful for a bit of fresh air.

When I walked back into the factory I couldn't help but laugh. Snotter and Lenny looked like a couple of frogmen who had lost their flippers. They were encased in black rubber from their feet to their waist, the top halves of the suits hanging down at the back, no doubt to be pulled on when they started work. They sat on a couple boxes looking into the pit.

I handed out the sandwiches and gave Snotter his change.

"Yer don't fancy yer breakfast then?" I shook my head. "Bought a packet of Fisherman's Friends instead" I replied.

Helping each other to pull up the top halves of their suits and lowering their face masks and goggles, they set to work. Snotter plunged the end of a two-inch rubber pipe into the cesspit and Lenny put the other end into a 45 gallon oil drum on the back of the lorry. On a nod from Snotter I pressed the start button on the pump and stood back. As instructed, I watched Lenny closely. After a minute or two he shouted "Knock it off Steve" and I switched off. One drum full. Lenny lifted the dripping pipe out of the full drum and put it into an empty one. At his nod I started the pump again. Within 30 minutes all six drums on the lorry were full and the lids had been tightly sealed by tapping the curved lips into place with a small hammer.

"You can hose us down now, Steve" Snotter said as he and Lenny stood on the footpath. I duly obliged. "Where are you taking it?" I asked.

"Big effluent plant down the road" he replied. "Shan't be too long."

The three-ton lorry swung out of the factory, the small block and tackle fixed to the bed swinging to and fro as it turned into Glover Street. Within half an hour they were back, and the process of putting on all the gear, filling up the six drums and hosing them down was repeated. The effluent plant can't be far away I thought, as I aimed the jet of water at Lenny's grinning face, protected behind his goggles and face mask. I was beginning to enjoy this.

"Perfect job, smells like me rose garden now, well done." Tommy Rushton, the Works Manager, was dressed immaculately as usual in a three-piece suit. He stood looking down into the spotlessly clean and disinfected pit. He strode off with Harry Smith the Superintendent.

Snotter had done a brilliant job. The pump had been unblocked, all the walls had been hosed down, the floats that controlled the pump, had been set for the correct levels and the toilet block had been hosed and disinfected. The bogs could now be reopened.

After a final hosing down and stripping off the rubber suits, Snotter and Lenny had walked up to the showers in the Casting Shop. They returned smartly dressed. Snotter's overalls were in the cab.

"What's the damage, mate?" Harcourt asked. "The gaffer'll want to know."

"I'll put me bill in at the end of the month, but it's 10 quid for me day's wages and three quid for our Lenny" said Snotter. He looked at his reflection in the office window and pulled a comb out of his top pocket, sweeping it through his damp, long jet-black hair. Elvis had not yet left the building.

"The big bill, as usual, will be from them robbing bastards at the effluent plant, but they've got yer by the bollocks, yer gotta pay it." Harcourt nodded understandingly.

"Five quid a drum if it's solids, and there were 24 drums" said Snotter.

As they walked out of the office Snotter and Harcourt seemed to bump into each other and I noticed a quick, almost invisible hand movement between them. Ah well, somebody's been given a drink, I thought.

Snotter joined me as I walked down the shop. "Yer've done well today, have a drink," he said, slipping a pound note into my hand. "Not every bloke's got the stomach for this job, specially a young lad. If yer ever want a job let me know. There's good money if yer know the ropes."

As I entered the dispatch area I could see the lorry loaded up with the final six drums. It had been hosed down and Lenny was stood on the back, his feet on the side gate, his hands gripping the rail at the back of the cab.

"This one lid won't fit right," he said. "I've tried everything."

"I'll fetch a pair of pliers," I said, thinking the gripping lips needed opening up.

"Naw, I'll sort it" he replied, placing both his feet on top of the offending lid. Supporting his weight with his hands, he gently jumped up, landing softly on the lid. It appeared to do the trick.

"One more go," said Lenny. He jumped high, his knees bent almost up to his chest, and came down heavily on the top of the drum.

Time stood still. As if in slow motion, the lid twisted through 90 degrees and flipped up into the air, skidding over the low upright side gates of the lorry and gradually rattling to a rest on the factory floor like an enormous spun coin. Lenny was in the shit big time. Or to be more precise, up to his armpits.

"Wahhhhh! Get me out, get me out!" he roared. His arms were hanging over the oil drum, and the brown stuff was dripping off his shoulders. Lenny was stuck.

While the overhead hoist was being fitted with webbing slings, Snotter jumped up on to the lorry with a bucket of water and clean rags to sponge off Lenny's face and hair. "You're not hurt are yer?"

"Naw, don't think so. Me new jeans'll need a bit of a wash" Lenny replied as the slings were tucked under his arms and he was lifted out of the drum.

Without the rubber suit, he was freezing by the time I'd finished hosing him down.

"Got nothing to wear" he moaned between chattering teeth, slapping his arms around his body to try and warm up. Snotter looked concerned. "There's a bag of old clothes and rags in the cab, tek em up to the showers again," he said. "It'll see yer home. Unless yer want to sit in the cab naked."

By now everybody in the shop had had a good laugh and Smithy had bollocked the blokes back to work. Lenny clutched his change of clothes and began the long walk through the Britannia Mill, up the steps, across the canal, through the new Casting Shop and into the toilet and shower block. When he came back he was wearing an old lady's frock in a pretty floral print.

It stopped the Casting Shop and the Britannia Mill. It wasn't young Lenny's day, but at least he had earned three quid.

* * * * * * * * * *

A couple of days after the incident with the brown stuff, I was about to stroll down to the Britannia Mill when Joe Healy called me into his office. "Black Bat's got a load of work on and there's two rush jobs," he said. He picked up his phone.

"Yes, I know." He lifted his eyes to the ceiling and held the handset away from his ear. "I'm trying to sort it NOW." Joe was usually a gentle sort of bloke, but someone was getting up his pip. Putting the phone down, he took a deep breath.

"Our new superintendent don't arrive for another half hour and I've got this lot to sort out" he sighed.

Joe had been my chargehand for over four years, and he had carefully nurtured me and slowly passed on some of his great skill and experience to me. I truly respected him.

"Young Doug and Bryn are at college, so I want you in the toolroom today" he said.

"I'm on my way, Joe."

It was just after eight o'clock when I walked into the toolroom. Sandpaper Arse had returned from his morning ablutions across the road in the old Bar Mill (he preferred the bogs there because they had wooden seats) and was polishing an extrusion die while doing the Daily Mirror crossword. Alfie Rodgers, the oiler and greaser, were peering over his shoulder. "Two fs in effusion" Alfie advised, pushing his wire-frame spectacles back up his nose. Percy the foreman didn't start till half eight.

"Need yer on the universal grinder Steve" Black Bat said. "I'm setting up the surface grinder and Smithy and Harcourt want both jobs done yesterday." For all his moaning about the gaffers, deep down he didn't want his ability to get the job done questioned, especially now he was over 65.

Within 15 minutes both machines were removing metal, albeit only a few thousandths of an inch per cut. I was grinding up a set of tungsten carbide segmented dies, held in a special grinding jig, using a diamond-impregnated grinding wheel. When the segments were mounted in their holder for production they would form a perfect hexagon. This would enable the extruded brass hexagon bar to be drawn through, to impart an accurate finished size and a highly-polished surface. The finished hexagon bars would then sold on to other factories countrywide to produce brass nuts for the nut and bolt industry.

Black Bat was grinding a long support blade, again tipped with tungsten carbide to give extended use during production. Even fully hardened steel did not have the wearing properties of carbide. It was a slow process.

"We're not cutting wind this morning then Alf?" I asked over my shoulder. Alf smiled, his pipe gripped tight between his teeth in concentration. Many years before when I had first worked with this old craftsman, he had told me to slow down and 'cut a bit of wind'. In my exuberance I was working too fast. Cutting wind meant having the machine and grinding wheel running with a good supply of cooling suds but not actually removing any metal. There wouldn't be much cutting wind today.

By lunchtime we were about half way through our respective jobs. We had both worked hard and had only been visited once by Harcourt and a couple of times by Percy the toolroom foreman. Percy was a nice old bloke, much gentler in his approach, but in a rush job he would slow you down by his chat.

Although it was chilly outside, the sun was shining and Andy the toolroom turner opened the small half-door that acted as a fire escape out on to the towpath of the canal. In the summer months a lot of blokes would sit on the canal side to eat their sandwiches and watch the brightly-painted barges and houseboats glide by.

"What's it like?" Black Bat asked.

"Mostly all cleared up Alf, but you'll need yer coat" Andy replied, carefully taking two large mugs of tea from his old mate as he handed them through the low door.

"Gorra have a bit of fresh air," Black Bat said as he put his cap on and buttoned up his new car coat. He noticed my appreciative look.

"Tain't only you young buggers that can look trendy, yer know," he said as he ducked low through the door.

"No Alf" I replied, following him through with my mug and sandwiches. No more canteen lunches for me, I was saving to buy a house.

Sandpaper Arse always walked up to the main Die Shop to eat his sandwiches, because he had worked in there for years before the Britannia Mill and toolroom were built. Alfie Rodgers normally had his sandwiches in the toolroom. Alfie was about 40 was one of the factory oilers and greasers, with full reign over the whole of the site. He carried a huge grease gun, four inches in diameter and two feet long, and a large metal railway-style oil can with a plunger. Carrying all this equipment was not easy for a small, thin bloke, especially as he had a withered arm. But he was always bright and smiling. Alfie had threatened to kill me once. He chased me all over the factory because I'd put the little pieces of cardboard clock card clippings into his half-empty grease gun. It took him hours to clean it out. He forgave me after I bought him a pint.

There was a bit of warmth in the sun as we all sat on old boxes leaning against the factory wall, Black Bat puffing contently on his pipe, Alfie reading his Mirror and Andy smoking his Capstan Full Strength.

"Yer know, the lads today have got the world at their feet." Black Bat took his pipe out of his mouth. "We had two wars, the bloody depression in the thirties when hardly any bugger had a job and if yer did yer wuz frightened of losing it. The gaffers had yer by the bollocks, I tell yer."

He stoked up his pipe. "I'm 65 and the furthest I've bin is the Isle of Wight."

Andy glanced up. "And Blackpool, Alf." We all smiled.

Black Bat continued. "Them young buggers have just come back from fucking Spain and I tell yer another thing, the young 'uns today can walk out of one job, goo round the corner and gerranother one with an extra five bob an hour." I joined in the nodding.

"That's sewage," I said, looking into the water. They all looked up.

"Yow ain't gooin' for a swim, are yer Steve?" Alfie asked with his usual grin.

"No, but where's all that lot come from?"

"That's nothing," Andy said. "You should have seen it yesterday and the day before." Black Bat took up the tale. "In all me years I'd never seen fuck all like it. There were hundreds of turds floating and bobbing about, it were like Cowes Regatta."

We all were all chuckling and laughing about it. And then the penny dropped. I must have gone silent.

"You all right, Steve?" Andy asked. "Yer look as if yer've seen a ghost."

I scratched my head. "Er... no, I'm just thinking about something. I was just thinking about the poor fish in the canal." Surely not, I was thinking.

"Ain't bin any fish in the cut for over 20 years, not round here anyway" said Black Bat. "All the factories chuck all sorts of shit and chemicals into it." He struck a match and re-lit his pipe. "The old acid Herbert Danks chucks in is nobody's business. If there were any fish swimming about they'd glow in the dark." The others all smiled.

"Our kid works in the chrome plating place round the corner, and he reckons it's even worse there" Alfie Rodgers said. "For over 100 yards the water's gone a silver colour." He folded up his Daily Mirror and winked at me. "A young lad in the street chucked a rusty old bicycle wheel in last week. When he pulled it out after a couple of days it was better than a brand new un." Even I was laughing now.

"I tell yer what though," Black Bat said with a groan as he struggled to his feet. "All them turds, I ain't got a clue where they came from."

I have, I thought to myself. A couple of them are probably yours.

I was laughing to myself and shaking my head as I ducked under the door back into the toolroom. Snotter had worked hard for his day's wages of ten quid. Knowing the ropes had earned him an extra £120.

CHAPTER 22

Christmas Eve and New Year's Eve 1966 were working parties for Pauline and me. We had two great nights in the lounge at the Speedwell serving a large crowd of revelers, friends and family members of Jack and Doris Walker, along with the Old Bill.

"You're both on free drinks all night" Jack said as he locked up the pub and ushered everyone into the lounge at the back. "And wages of course" he added.

It was almost three in the morning on January 1 1967 when Pauline turned into Chilton Road. "I'll be on ten bob an hour soon" I mumbled as I tried to get undressed. My last thought before I dropped off to sleep was, its Sunday today, I don't have to go to work this morning.

But I did. New Year's Day was not a public holiday, and Sunday morning was still double time.

"You'll be 21 years old next month Steve, and officially your apprenticeship will be completed." I was sitting in Jack Insall's office with Tom Rushton, the Works Manager, and Peter Williams, the Delta Apprentice Supervisor.

"You're doing well on the Production Engineering Technician's Course, so the company is quite happy for you to continue on a day-release basis until it's completed." Jack looked at Peter. "That's another two and a half years. What's your long term plan, Steve? Where do you see yourself in five years' time?"

Tom gave Jack a Senior Service, then offered one to me.

"No thanks Mr Rushton, I've packed them in," I said. "When I've completed the Technician's course I'll be awarded the Full Technological Certificate (Production) CGLI. It's equivalent to the HNC in Engineering. Then I intend to enroll for the Institute of Works Managers. It's a two-year course and I can do it attending college two nights a week."

I paused to take a breath. Tom gave a wry smile. "I think you'll do it as well, young man."

Peter gave Jack a quick questioning glance. Jack Insall very slightly raised his eyebrows and lifted his shoulders.

"I'd like to show you the Apprentice Training School in the main Delta Metals factory in Dartmouth Street, Steve," said Peter.

"When?" I asked.

"Now's as good a time as any" said Peter, putting his cup and saucer on Jack's desk and standing up. We said our goodbyes to Jack and Tom and walked across the road to the car park behind the snooker room. What was all this about?

I opened the door to Peter's car and got in. I'd soon find out.

"The main Delta Metals Board have approved an expansion and development of the Apprentice Training School and Workshop and it will be completed in the next 12 months," said Peter. "Last year we took on 18 craft apprentices. This year that will be increased to 25." He opened the door and we walked across to his office.

There were centre lathes, millers, grinders, drillers, everything a young apprentice would require, including a heat-treatment section for the hardening and tempering of tools. Three long workbenches fitted out with cupboards and vices were neatly positioned down the far wall. I was well impressed.

"Within the greater Birmingham area we have almost 10 factories, and we're actively increasing our training facilities to be able to supply the skilled craftsmen required for the future," said Peter. "I'll organize a coffee."

He left me in his office and I stood up and looked out of the window. Lads of 16 were busy marking out small sheets of steel with engineer's blue, using rules, scribers and centre punches. Some were carefully setting up the drilling machines to produce the holes they had marked out. A small group of four lads were standing around an elderly grey-haired bloke who was introducing them to the centre lathe.

"Takes you back Steve" said Peter, pushing the door open with his elbow and placing two mugs on his desk. "What do you think?"

"I'm impressed" I replied.

"Within the next 12 months I'll be looking to recruit an Assistant Supervisor responsible for Workshop Training. Would you be interested?"

I sat down with a bump. No doubt he could see the surprise on my face.

"It's too early at this stage to know what the salary level would be, but it's a staff job. Don't hold me to it, but I would guess it would be about £1100 a year." He smiled. "Drink your coffee before it gets cold."

"It's a staff job, Steve," said Pauline. "That means you get paid if you're off sick or if you're injured playing football."

It was late Saturday afternoon and we were sitting in our lounge. After I'd finished work at one o'clock Pauline and I had found a secondhand shop selling gas cookers and kitchen furniture, on Constitution Hill just down from the Church Tavern.

"It's not definite, and even if it does come off it could be a year away" I replied. "And I'm not sure it's what I want to do. Plus the fact that when I'm on the top rate in a month's time, with overtime I'll be earning 34 quid a week. That's £1700 a year."

I walked across to the alcove in the corner and switched the kettle on. "Anyway, how do you like our new cooker and kitchen table and chairs?" smiled Pauline. "Hope they fit in the shed down the garden before we move in."

Two hours later we were pulling pints in the Speedwell.

The week before my 21st birthday I had attended the third and final week's residential Senior Apprentice Course at PERA. I had returned home on the Friday afternoon proudly clutching my certificate. Pauline had stayed at her Mom and Dad's for the five nights I had been away, and her Dad had taken her to and from the Speedwell every night so Jack would not be short of staff while I was away.

On Monday February 27 1967 I attended South Birmingham Polytechnic as an apprentice for the last time. I turned right into Adderley Street, passing the Rainbow on the left and the Waggon and Horses on the right before parking behind the snooker room and canteen. I'd waited five and a half years for this day, I thought.

As I took my clock card out of the rack I noticed that someone, presumably from the Wages Office, had written in small print 'Change of Rate'. I almost shouted out loud "Fucking Yes!" but I didn't. I smiled, inserted the light brown 8 inch x 3 inch card into the slot under the clock face and pulled the brass handle down.

I was on ten bob an hour.

A small family dinner to celebrate my 21st was arranged the following Saturday at the Barn in Hockley Heath. As I looked round the table at my Nan, Pop, Mom, Pauline, her parents Ivy and Albert and her younger brother Bobby, I couldn't help but think what Harry Fisher, the lecturer who had started me on the right road five years before, would say.

EPILOGUE

We gave Jack and Doris at the Speedwell a month's notice and continued to work in the pub until the end of March 1967. We moved into 62 Mill Crescent on April 1. On the day of the move I had just £7 left in the bank.

Black Bat retired three months later, and I took over his job as Toolmaker and Universal Grinder in the Toolroom.

In 1970 I was awarded The Full Technological Certificate (Production) CGLI. The same year I was promoted to Toolroom Foreman. I successfully completed the Institute of Works Manager's Course and was made an Associate of the Institution in 1972.

I left Delta Wire late in 1973 to take up an appointment as Factory Superintendent in an aerospace company. By then our son Daniel was a year old; his brother Matthew was born in 1974. I achieved my goal of Works Manager in 1978, at the age of 32. Delta Wire closed down in 1980.

On separate occasions during the 1980s, when I was rocking and rolling as a mobile DJ, I bumped into Bert Carrington, Pat Dowling, Doug Smith and Les Green. My fellow apprentices of the time would now all be in their sixties, and Dave Wilmer and Johnny Waller would be approaching 70. I'd heard young Ray Tysall had emigrated to South Africa. Otherwise I haven't seen or heard of any of those guys, but I'd guess they are all still alive and kicking - Bryn, Doug, Kevin, Ken, Jim, Frank, Johnny Pearce, John Cashmore.

During my working life I was sacked once and made redundant once. I had job titles of General Manager, Sales Manager and Sales and Marketing Director. I worked for some nice gaffers, some nasty gaffers and one raving madman, but it was all within the wonderful world of engineering.

In 2006 I took an early retirement package and moved to Cyprus with Janet, my second wife. We live in the village of Kapparis in South East Cyprus, 10 kilometers from the famous resort of Aiya Napa.

In 1967 I had a piece of paper in my hand that said I was a skilled man. I didn't know it at the time, but of course I was still just a learner. The real skilled men were Harry Fisher, Joe Healy, Billy Wiggins, Arthur Twamley, Old Bonehead, Black Bat, Andy Uprichard, Leo the Pole, Billy Law, Harry and Ronnie Hanson, Bill Casey, John the Blacksmith, Pat Dowling, Mac the Welder, Scotty, Bob Brown, Big Harry, Norman, Les Green and Ted the Draughtsman. These were the men who taught me my trade. Sadly they must all have passed away by now. Even characters like Johnny Price and Graham Morris, if they're still alive, would be in their late seventies.

As I write, I'm actually crying.

★ ★ ★ ★ ★ ★ ★ ★ ★ ★ ★

"Yow've gorra meet my brother-in-law, he's a Bluenose" Andy said as he rang up the 15 euros for a tray of beer. "He lives in the same road as you, just down from the Dangerous Bend."

Andy was the manager of the local off-licence. He was a staunch Villa man, but he couldn't help that. Janet and I walked out of the offy into the brilliant blue sky and 35-degree heat of Cyprus.

"And we'll stuff yer the weekend!" Andy shouted after us. They did – Villa got lucky.

About a month later we were in the offy again when a big guy walked in. "Here's the bloke I've been telling yer about," said Andy. "Another bloody Blues supporter."

The stranger was as tall as me, but broader in the shoulder and more heavily built. He had strong features and a full shock of dark hair, with just a few greying streaks. He looked about my age, maybe a year or two younger.

"So I'm not the only Bluenose in the village then?" I said, holding my hand out. The stranger stopped, his hand half-stretched towards mine. A puzzled frown crossed his face. He looked at me long and hard.

"I know you," he said. I stared in puzzlement, racing back through the years – factories, pubs, apprentices, technical college, school, Army cadets – but I couldn't think quickly enough.

"Where did yer work?" the stranger asked. I mentioned a couple of firms before I got to Delta Wire.

"You're Steve Phillips, we used to play football…"

Recognition dawned. "And you're Mickey Madden" I replied.

'Kin'ell.

THE END

Printed in Great Britain
by Amazon.co.uk, Ltd.,
Marston Gate.